Berlin: offene Stadt

The City on Exhibition

With the kind support of

Thanks are due to Cornelius Hertling, Ingrid Kuldschun (Berlin Association of Architects), Barbara Hoidn and Katrin Grünert (Senate Department of Construction, Housing and Transport, architecture workshop), Dietrich Flicke (Senate Department of Urban Development, Environmental Protection and Technology), the many architects and investors for information which they kindly provided as well as to the S-Bahn GmbH and the BVG.

Berlin: *open city* – City on Exhibition will be supplemented in the summer months of 1999 and 2000 by an extensive programme of thematic tours on foot, by bicycle, by bus and also by air. "Spielräume" are selected locations in the "New Berlin" where films, theatre, dance and music will be staged. Separate books on these events have been published.

Berlin: *open city*

The City on Exhibition

The Tours

Edited by the Berliner Festspiele and the Architektenkammer Berlin

NICOLAI

A project of Berliner Festspiele GmbH commissioned by the Senate of Berlin in association with Partner für Berlin,
Architektenkammer Berlin (Berlin Association of Architects),
Federal Ministry of Transport, Construction and Housing,
Senate Department of Construction, Housing and Transport,
Senate Department of Urban Development, Environmental Protection and Technology as well as Land Office for the Preservation of Historical Monuments and Buildings and further partners.

Overall responsibility: Ulrich Eckhardt
Concept, editor-in-chief: Reinhard Alings, assisted by Roland Enke

Berlin: *open city*
Vol. 1 The City on Exhibition
Vol. 2 Die Erneuerung seit 1989 (Renewal since 1989, with English abstracts)
Edited by: Berliner Festspiele GmbH and Architektenkammer Berlin
Authors vol. 1: Roland Enke, assisted by Reinhard Alings, Bernhard Schneider, Gerwin Zohlen
Project editor, vols. 1 and 2: Gerwin Zohlen
Special adviser: Andreas Rochholl (Architektenkammer Berlin)
Research: Elke Dorner
Editor: Antje Heer (Nicolai Verlag)
Photo acquisition: Petra Klinger (Architektenkammer Berlin)
Photographer: Erik-Jan Ouwerkerk
Graphic design and maps: GrafikBüro Adler & Schmidt
English translation: Robin Benson, Andrew Boreahm, Michael Dills (signposts), Felicity Gloth, Francesca Rogier

"Stadt-Zeichen" (signposts)
Concept: Jan Fiebelkorn-Drasen
Graphic design: GrafikBüro Adler & Schmidt
Production: mediapool

The production of "Stadt-Zeichen" was made possible by the Senator of Construction, Housing and Transport.

"Spiel-Räume" ("Places to Play"): Reinhard Alings, Roland Enke, Dieter Hansen, Nele Hertling, Torsten Maß, Siegfried Paul, Barbara Seegert

Press officer and public relations: Nana Poll (Berliner Festspiele Office 1999/2001)
Bärbel Petersen (Partner für Berlin)
Co-ordination: Nikki Schmidt (Berliner Festspiele Office 1999/2001)
Winfrid Schwank (Partner für Berlin)

Printed in Germany
ISBN 3-87584-773-3

Index

"Berlin: *open city* – The City on Exhibition" – is a reflective self-portrayal of a city which has always been in flux and is at present undergoing radical change. "Open" means: ready for change, receptive, forward-looking, open to what is strange, different, new. Open doors and buildings – so to speak a metaphor for the processes of transformation intended to create a redesigned European metropolis of mediation, communication and exchange. The special achievements of the city – both those which have already taken place and those anticipated – are presented in order to illustrate these prospects. Following the catastrophe of the Second World War, the two parts of Berlin were the antithesis of an open city for decades. The western half resembled an island and the eastern part was a controversial capital city, only accessible by detours, whose inhabitants felt walled in. Gates and bridges which were sealed off, interrupted underground cables and pipes, truncated traffic routes, marginal areas and wasteland in the centre of the city, checkpoints, walls, border patrols, anti-tank obstacles and even the use of firearms in the case of illegal attempts to cross the Berlin Wall were all reality. It is only ten years since a not entirely unambiguous East German press release and the courage of the city's population made the unthinkable possible by peaceful means.

Today *open city* not only stands for the end of the political division of the city and the urban integration of both parts, given concrete expression in the form of developments on the former wasteland in the centre of the city – Potsdamer Platz, Pariser Platz, Ministers' Gardens, Band des Bundes to name just the most prominent areas. The title is also to be understood as what the city claims to be: Berlin as a cosmopolitan city, "open to the world". A claim which was once vital for its survival, still is and will become all the more so in the future. The city has always thrived on the foreign influences it attracted – sometimes from far away – both intentionally and accidentally. And Berlin always suffered when this influx threatened to peter out. It is also for this reason that the New Berlin will be, want to be and have to be an open city. The foundation stone has, to use the language of architects, been laid.

This publication is intended as a guide through the labyrinth of the city. "Berlin: *open city*" sets the stage for a nascent "New Berlin" by presenting ten suggested routes. These routes were deliberately selected for their wealth of themes; it is the aim of each route and of all of them collectively to show the diversity of the city and the people who live in it and with it. The variety of architectural styles, squares and city districts, ranging from the realisation of an entirely new urban centre from scratch to the restoration of neglected historical buildings. Planning was based on the latest technology in the field of ecological building and the buildings which have been constructed are intended to satisfy the requirements of sustainable urban planning for the 21st century. But visible scars also remain for the time being. Far from being complete, the development of Berlin will continue to progress towards a future which can only be seen in outline at present. Certainly not a task to be completed in ten years, rather one which will take a number of generations.

The "New Berlin" also remains a city of contradictions: sophisticated innovative architecture of the 21st century interspersed with buildings of no significance, socially deprived areas bordering luxury shopping streets, ugly roadways in close proximity to inviting parks, seemingly derelict areas suddenly giving way to districts full of vital, urban life – a fascinating juxtaposition concealing nothing and, instead, revealing the specific character of the metropolis of Berlin. A juxtaposition which makes the city what it is, gives it a distinctive character. And it is this intricate jumble itself which can provide the breeding-ground for creativity, innovation and unconventional ways of life.

The ten routes through the "New Berlin" presented here attempt to capture these contradictions. The focus is not only on the present and the future, but also on the past, in both east and west, north and south. The theme is not only the "capital city" but also everyday life in a housing estate of prefabricated buildings, not only new business districts and shopping centres but also local infrastructure which is part of day to day to life. Museums and office centres are featured as are pumping stations and substations, streets and bridges as well as parks and squares, modern design proposals are seen in contrast to buildings and structures dating from very different past epochs. Efforts have been made to include examples of the typical functions of the city in the routes in order to provide an idea of the widely varied role of a city and a capital.

It is not a coincidence that six of the ten routes take in both east and west. Two are entirely confined to what was once West Berlin and a further two to former East Berlin. While the focus is on the buildings in the government and parliament district of the new capital of Germany and on new service centres, projects in the areas of trade, business, culture, the media, science, leisure, technical infrastructure, transport and housing are also described.

The routes, each of which take around four hours on foot, are not typical tourist tours of the sights. Ugly roadways and bad architecture are as much a part of reality as are idyll and harmony, chaos and disgraces exist alongside highlights and high-tech. The routes lead from the sites of the projects of the future to the relicts of the past, taking in examples of urban design and architecture dating from the time of Prussian supremacy, the German empire, the Weimar Republic, the "Third Reich", East and West Berlin up to the buildings constructed in the last ten years. Different historical layers making up the varied development of Berlin are reflected along each of the routes and, in some cases, by a single building or structure. It is this aspect which makes this more than just a guide to architecture in Berlin. The aim of this book is not only to describe individual places but also their urban context or contradiction, their integration or, in some cases, implantation in the historical city landscape.

Needless to say, it was not possible to include everything. There are other examples which would have been more apt, but were not on the way, some places on the way are trivial. Despite this, the routes collectively provide a varied picture of the "New Berlin" which is not confined to the obvious attractions such as Potsdamer Platz and the new Lehrter Bahnhof railway station complex. The routes take in streets as diverse as Kurfürstendamm and Karl-Marx-Allee, the Federal Chancellery and the "Tacheles" centre of alternative culture, the contrasting districts of Charlottenburg and Prenzlauer Berg, Wedding and Friedrichshain.

During 1999 and 2000 the projects dating from the last ten years to restore or convert buildings and construct new ones will be marked and briefly explained by means of special signs along the routes. A route map is posted at the starting point of each route – close to an underground or S-Bahn (city railway) station. Signs relating to the individual building ensembles have been installed along the way and provide explanatory information in the form of ground plans and brief descriptions. In addition, there are signs on individual buildings and structures. However, this guide does much more than marking points of interest in the city. It not only provides further information on the individual buildings included in the routes, but also draws attention to places of historical significance which lie along these routes. In this way, the routes through the "New Berlin" are also a brief outline of the history of the city.

The routes are to be understood as suggestions and a street café, beer garden, restaurant or just a park bench in the sun as an invitation to take a break and digress. There is plenty to discover to the right and left of the routes and, indeed, this is one of their purposes. As is so often the case: The journey is in itself the purpose, and lingering is allowed. Anyone wishing to find out more about the modernisation of Berlin and the changes in its urban structures in the last ten years is referred to the book "Berlin: *offene Stadt* – Die Erneuerung seit 1989" ("Renewal since 1989", with English abstracts), which was conceived as a complement to this guide. It is also published by Nicolai Verlag.

"Berlin: *open city*", individual discovery of the city – supplemented by events held at "Places to Play" chosen for their architectural or urban interest – is based on an idea of Nele Hertling. Special thanks are due to her and to Dr. Volker Hassemer (Partner für Berlin) for their active and committed to support in planning and realising this project.

Das Band des Bundes

The government and parliament district

Route 1 follows the transformation of Berlin into the capital of the Federal Republic of Germany. It takes us through the new government and parliament district and through the three very different districts of Moabit, Tiergarten and Mitte. As we follow the tour, we pass through approximately 400 years of city history.

Moabit, on the northern side of the Spreebogen (a deep curve traced by the River Spree), is among the oldest districts outside the historical city. For a long time, the character of the district was shaped by the presence of the armed forces and industry. Thus, for example, up to the early 19th century, powder magazines and a hospital for plague victims were located here on the outskirts. The urban development of the adjacent residential area with its population of small and medium-sized craft enterprises made it "respectable". It went into decline in the decades when Berlin was divided by the Wall. The prison used to be the most striking feature of Moabit. Since the mid '80s, however, it has undergone carefully planned redevelopment, with vacant and underutilised industrial and trading sites being transformed into service and trading enterprises. Owing to the changes that have taken place, its proximity to the River Spree, the Tiergarten Park and the new Government district within the Spreebogen Moabit has been upgraded to an unforeseen extent.

The route passes the apartments for Federal Government employees in Moabit Werder and continues to nearby Bellevue Palace, the main residence of the Federal President, and the newly constructed Federal President's Office. The route then continues along the Spree to the former Congress Hall and traverses the Tiergarten to the government and parliament district within the Spreebogen. With the "Band des Bundes" a large scale urban-development project is being completed to establish a home for both parliament and the government in Berlin. Connecting the Chancellor's Park in the west with the Federal Chancellery and the deputies' offices in the Alsen and Luise Blocks (Paul Löbe and Marie Elisabeth Lüders House) in the east, it symbolises the unity of East and West Berlin after they were divided for forty years.

With the construction of the government and administration buildings, the century-long history of planning and construction within the Spreebogen – from a prestigious residential quarter and forum during the Wilhelminian Empire and the Weimar Republic – has come to a happy end. For the first time in the history of German democracy, both the parliament and the government will have direct contact with one another at one place. With the conversion of the Reichstag into the new German Bundestag (the Federal Parliament), the Platz der Republik (Square of the Republic) will regain its former significance. As a result the Spreebogen has thus become the country's political centre, whilst the Soviet Monument in the centre of the capital city stands as a reminder of the history of Berlin, Germany, Europe and the world.
The newly constructed Kronprinzen Bridge reestablishes the link between the Tiergarten and Berlin Mitte districts. The Bundes-Presseamt (Federal Press Office) and the German public television company (the ARD's capital studio) have chosen to locate themselves between parliament and Friedrichstrasse S-Bahn station. Route 1 crosses the renovated Marschall Bridge and traverses an old district with heterogeneously designed buildings dating from the early 19th century as well as streets lined by "slab buildings" from the 1970s. It continues past the Charité University Clinic, whose surrounding grounds are idyllic in places, and the renowned Deutsches Theater. At the newly designed square before the Neues Tor (New Gate), our route encounters the old northern border of Berlin's historical city centre. There it takes us into Invalidenstrasse and past the ministries of economics, building and transport which are located in old buildings and new extensions. After crossing the reconstructed Sandkrug Bridge, which served as Invalidenstrasse Checkpoint for many years, the route passes the Museum for Contemporary Art at Hamburger Bahnhof station and ends at the construction site of Lehrter Bahnhof railway station. Europe's largest interchange station for Inter-City Express routes in all directions is under construction here. The station will link the European railway network with the city railway and underground lines. In the year 2004, Berlin will have a central station for the very first time.

1 2.1

S-Bahnhof Bellevue

Bellevue S-Bahn station

Johann Eduard Jacobsthal;
Dörr, Ludolf, Wimmer, Berlin
1878–80;
1995–97
Bartningallee

Bellevue S-Bahn station, still housed in the original buildings, was called after the Palace of that name in Tiergarten park. It is located on the stretch of raised viaduct carrying S-Bahn trains and inner city rail services between Charlottenburg Station and Ostbahnhof Station. The S-Bahn (city railway) was opened in 1882 as an extension of the suburban railway network around Berlin. The whole construction, classified as a historical monument, is considered a masterpiece of 19th century architecture and engineering. In 1995-98 the raised line was modernised at a cost of more than one billion deutschmarks. The technical improvements, which included a low-noise solid track, were necessary to cope with the increased volume of railway traffic.

Bundesministerium des Innern

Federal Ministry of the Interior

Ensemble

Kühn-Bergander-Bley, Berlin
1992–94
Alt-Moabit 98-101

The area between Kirchstrasse, Alt-Moabit and Stromstrasse consists of three architectural complexes: Focus Teleport, the Bolle Dairy and the German Federal Ministry of the Interior. It is an excellent example of the transformation of erstwhile production locations from the industrial age into modern service-industry sites.
In 1996, the German Federal Ministry of the Interior leased the new building for 30 years. The U-shaped office block, completed in 1994, opens towards the River Spree, its location making it

2.3

the westernmost ministry in Berlin. Furthermore, there is direct access to the parliamentary and government offices via the River Spree. In Kirchstrasse the area is bordered by the new Moabit district court. Apartments are located in the curving head of the building facing the River Spree.

2.2 *Ensemble*

Wolf-Rüdiger Borchardt, Berlin
1993–95
Alt Moabit 98-104

Alte Bolle Meierei mit Hotel

The old Bolle Dairy and the Hotel Sorat

The old Bolle Dairy building has largely survived intact. From the late 19th century on, this dairy supplied the greater part of Berlin with milk. The original brick building was erected in 1890 and traverses the entire depth of the plot. The building has now been converted into retail outlets and the Hotel Sorat.

2.3 *Ensemble*

Ganz & Rolfes, Berlin
1988–92
Alt-Moabit 91-96

Focus Teleport

The grain mills belonging to the Kampffmeyer company once stood on the western side of the area. However, after the company closed down at the end of the 1980s, the buildings were almost totally demolished and the premises, which were in a state of progressive dilapidation, were then used for storage only. In 1988, the Focus Teleport was re-zoned as a "new enterprise-founders' centre" and a location for technology companies. The building complexes for office and commercial use stylistically follow the tradition of Berlin's industrial architecture.

Untersuchungshaftanstalt Moabit
Moabit Prison
Heinrich Hermann, August Busse
1877–82
Alt-Moabit 12a-13/ Rathenower Strasse

The eastern part of Moabit was already dominated by the presence of military buildings when the large criminal court was constructed in 1877. The court has not survived (the new building on Turmstrasse dates from 1905), the prison, however, is still in use today. It is built on a star-shaped ground plan and has a central domed hall, thus adopting the same building style as the prison in Lehrter Strasse built in 1849.

Carl-von-Ossietzky-Park
Alt-Moabit/Paulstraße

The park was created from what had been the private garden of the entrepreneur Pflug, who, in 1850, had moved his production facilities to the River Spree. After the land had been purchased

by the Prussian military authorities it became known as the "General's Garden". In 1950 the park was redesigned. It was renamed in 1965 in memory of Carl von Ossietzky, the pacifist writer and Nobel Peace Prize winner.

Wohnungen für Bundesbedienstete

Residential area for government employees

3
Ensemble

Georg Bumiller, Berlin,
Müller, Rhode & Wandert, Berlin
1997–99
Paulstrasse

This complex comprises 718 apartments for government employees and deputies. It is the largest government-run residential building project in Berlin. The area was originally used as a powder magazine in the 18th century prior to its subsequent use as a rail goods yard and storage. Although it was situated in a prime location alongside the River Spree with a view of the Tiergarten, the site was reserved for commercial use until the Berlin Wall fell. In 1995, after a number of competitions, Bumiller's plan was finally chosen for the site. Standing close to the "Band des Bundes", the 320-metre-long building winds along Südallee. To the north of the promenade, four residential apartment blocks designed by Müller, Rhode & Wandert have been constructed at right angles to one another. The clinker-faced school is a listed building. It was originally constructed in 1934 as administrative offices for the German Imperial Railways. Power is supplied by a unit-type heating and power station. A footbridge across the River Spree provides the shortest link between the residential areas and the government district.

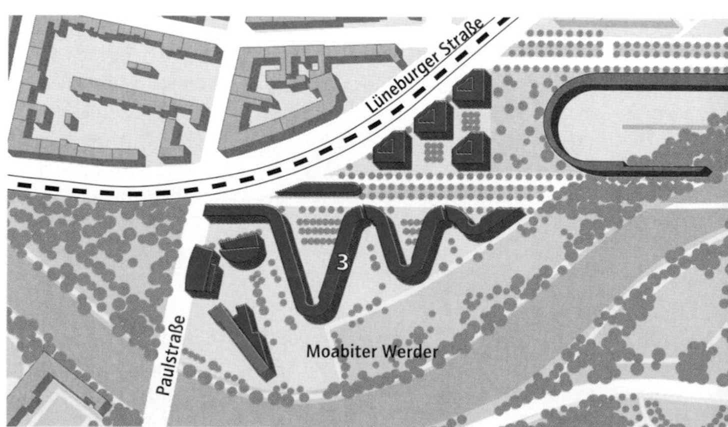

4.1

4.1 *Ensemble*

Philipp Daniel Boumann
1785–90;
1955–59
Spreeweg 1

Schloß Bellevue
Bellevue Palace

The triple-winged Bellevue Palace forms a key architectural boundary ("point de vue") in the baroque line of vision from Potsdamer Platz. In 1927, the palace, formerly belonging to the German Kaiser, passed into the hands of the Prussian state. In 1938 it became a guesthouse for the German Reich Government. It was damaged during the war. In 1955-59, it was reconstructed as the second official Berlin residence of the German Federal President, the main residence being in Bonn. In 1993, the then German Federal President Richard von Weizsäcker officially declared Bellevue Palace the main residence of the President of the German Federal Republic. Originally, it had been intended to close the Spree embankment for security reasons; following public protest, a new wall was built, making the closure unnecessary.

4.2 *Ensemble*

Architekten
Gruber + Kleine-Kraneburg,
Frankfort on the Main/Berlin
1996–98
Spreeweg 1

Bundespräsidialamt
Office of the German Federal President

Approximately 150 people are employed in the administration department of the Office of the German Federal President. In 1994, architects Martin Gruber and Helmut Kleine-Kraneburg won an Europe-wide competition, in which 240 participated, with a design for a four-storey building constructed on an elliptical ground plan. Natural ventilation and an ecological thermal-façade have been chosen in place of an air-

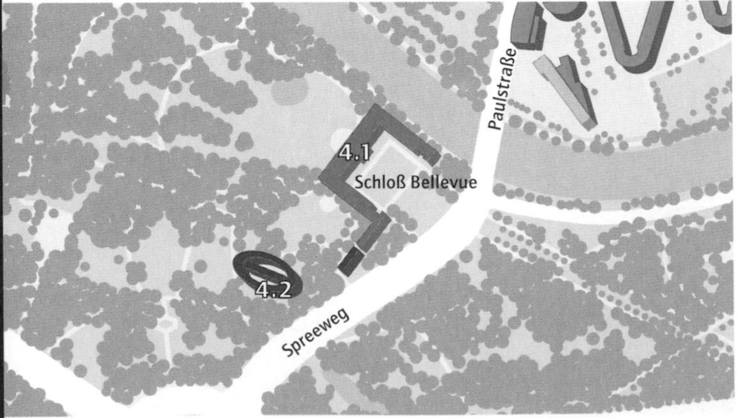

4.2

conditioning system. On the roof, solar cells supply approximately 50 per cent of the office energy requirement. With a length of 82 metres and a width of 41 metres, the dimensions of the building correspond to those of the Bellevue courtyard. The eaves height of 15 metres also corresponds to the proportions of the palace. Its structural form and the black-and-green "Nero Impala" from South Africa reflect the existing trees in the Tiergarten. The Office of the Federal President is the only new building to be constructed in the Tiergarten.

Tiergarten/ In den Zelten

Peter Joseph Lenné
John-Foster-Dulles-Allee

From the 16th century on, the "Grosse Tiergarten" grounds were used for hunting. The Great Elector, Frederick William, had the park redesigned in 1671 and provided with linear perspectives. In 1740 Frederick the Great opened the gardens to the public. In the first half of the 19th century, the Berlin landscape architect, Peter Joseph Lenné, redesigned the park as an English landscaped garden. The park was bordered on the north-east by the road called "In den Zelten" (In the tents), which was flanked by grandiose buildings, all destroyed during World War II. The road was named after the tents of two Huguenots, who, in the mid 18th century, sold refreshments here. Nowadays, the only reminder of this once popular place is the radial Kurfürstenplatz square near the Congress Hall.

Haus der Kulturen der Welt

House of World Cultures

Hugh A. Stubbins,
Werner Düttmann,
Franz Mocken
1956–57
John-Foster-Dulles-Allee 10

The former Congress Hall was constructed in 1957 as the independent American contribution to the "Interbau" international building exhibition in Berlin. The site in the Tiergarten was carefully chosen for its proximity to the Russian-sector border and its direct line of vision to the Reichstag. The daring roof-construction, which was supported on only two points, collapsed in 1980. When it was rebuilt, a flaw in the construction was rectified. Since then, the building has been used by the "Haus der Kulturen der Welt" to stage events presenting non-European cultures. Its programme is financially supported by the Department for Foreign Affairs and the institution by the Land Berlin. Henry Moore's sculpture "Butterfly" was presented by the German government to Berlin on the occasion of the 750th anniversary of the founding of the city in 1987.

5.1

Carillon

Bangert, Jansen, Scholz, Schultes
1988

Daimler Benz presented the carillon to Berlin on the 750th anniversary of the founding of the city. It was positioned in the middle of the Tiergarten. Now that the Berlin Wall has fallen the carillon unexpectedly lies between the capital's new government buildings. Its 68 bells make it the largest of its kind in Europe.

5.1 *Ensemble*

Bundeskanzleramt

Federal Chancellery

Axel Schultes Architekten, Frank, Schultes, Witt (Axel Schultes with Charlotte Frank), Berlin
1997–2000
Willy-Brandt-Strasse

On the 20th June, 1991 the German Parliament decided to make Berlin the capital city of a united Germany and the seat of government and parliament. The "Spreebogen", the area partially circumscribed by the River Spree next to the Reichstag, was chosen as the central location for the new government buildings. In 1993, the architects Schultes and Frank won the urban-development competition with their design for the "Band des Bundes". In a competition involving 835 participants (a competition unprecedented anywhere in the world), their design triumphed over rival concepts planning to distribute solitary buildings across the riverside landscape. The "Band des Bundes" spans the river at two points, forming a bridge between what were once East and West Berlin. In 1995, the same architects won the competition to design the new Federal Chancellery. The building establishes an architectural, political and institutional dialogue with the Reichstag, the Paul Löbe House and the Marie Elisabeth Lüders House. The distinct cubic main building rises

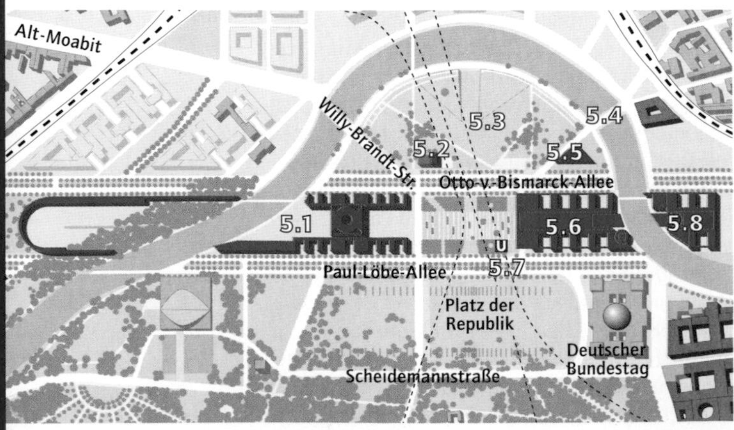

5.2

high above the side blocks housing the administrative offices, whilst nonetheless demonstrates respect for the higher Reichstag building. The soft lines of the columns along the east and west facades lend articulation to the symmetrical building. On the north and south side, the facade is broken up by cycloid windows. The comb-like wings of the office blocks enclose a ceremonial courtyard on the front side, where the main entrance is located. To the west, a bridge connects the complex with the Chancellor's Garden.

Schweizerische Botschaft

Swiss Embassy

5.2 *Ensemble*

Since 1919, the Swiss Embassy has been located in this magnificent palatial building, in the once exclusive district known as the Alsenviertel. The building was erected by Hitzig in 1870, and extended by Paul Baumgarten (the elder) in 1910. It survived Albert Speer's megalomaniac plans for Berlin, for the new "Germania Metropolis" as the city was to be called from 1950 on; it was here that Speer wanted to erect the "Grosse Halle" (Great Hall) for 180,000. In order to realise his plans, he initiated the large-scale demolition of many buildings in the heavily built up area. All of the plans envisaged tearing down this building. At first, the Swiss were supposed to find a different location for their embassy, however, they decided in favour of the Spreebogen. An extension was added to the eastern side of the building. It was designed by the Swiss architects Diener & Diener, using exposed concrete to emphasise the strict, harmonic, simple use of form.

Friedrich Hitzig;
Diener & Diener Architekten, Basel
1870;
1999–2000
Otto-von-Bismarck-Allee 4

Gestaltung Spreebogen

Spreebogen design

5.3 *Ensemble*

Following a competition in 1997, the landscape architects Müller & Wehberg and Weber & Saurer were assigned the task of landscaping the green areas in the government district. The semi-circular area to the north of the "Band des Bundes" is to be landscaped as a public park. In the vertex of the arc, Weber & Saurer plan to create a pit of limited length bordered by polished steel walls and diagonal lawns, looking towards Humboldthafen (Humboldt harbour). Müller & Wehberg

Cornelia Müller, Jan Wehberg, Berlin,
Toni Weber, Lucius Saurer, Solothurn
1999–2001

will be landscaping the square, the Platz der Republik, in front of the Reichstag. Their design foresees a paved area, with lawns and groups of trees. They are also landscaping Ebertplatz, a small square to the east of the Reichstag. As definite plans for the Bürgerforum (the area between the Chancellery and the Paul Löbe House) do not yet exist, the architects are provisionally including it in their park design.

5.4 *Ensemble*

Kronprinzenbrücke
Kronprinzen Bridge

Santiago Calatrava, Zurich
1992–97
Kronprinzenufer/
Schiffbauerdamm

The elegant new Kronprinzen Bridge, funded by European Union grants, is a symbol of how the city of Berlin is growing together again. The bridge crosses the Spree and links two districts that had been separated for quite some time. The previous bridge, the old "Unterbaumbrücke", dating from the 18th century, was demolished in 1972 because it lay in the border area between West and East Berlin. The old bridge once served as a customs post. It is the symmetrical counterpart to the Moltkebrücke.
The design by the Spanish architectural engineer Calatrava uses a modern, filigree steel construction, taking up the traditional three-arch structure of bridges over the River Spree.

5.5 *Ensemble*

Kindertagesstätte
Child day-care centre

Gustav Peichl & Partner,
Vienna
1998–99
Otto-von-Bismarck-Allee 2

The child day-care centre right alongside the River Spree, to the north of the Paul Löbe House, has been built for children of parliamentary deputies and employees. The single-storey building has been constructed on a triangular-shaped ground plan. The variable group-rooms overlook a large green play area on the south side. There are rest areas in the spherical and tent-shaped structures. The ecologically friendly measures taken here include the use of rain water, natural ventilation and the provision of passive solar energy through large window surfaces. The Austrian architect Gustav Peichl was chosen in an EU-wide competition. The centre's exclusiveness provoked angry reactions in Berlin.

Paul-Löbe-Haus

Paul Löbe House

Stephan Braunfels, Munich/Berlin
1997–2000
Paul-Löbe-Allee

Architect Stephan Braunfels won the first prize in a competition, held in 1994, with his design of the offices for the parliamentary deputies. His design fitted harmoniously into the "Band des Bundes", which provided the basis for this urban development. The Paul Löbe House and the Marie Elisabeth Lüders House (previously known as the Alsenblock and the Luisenblock, see p. 25) constitute a formal and functional unity. They link the areas of East and West Berlin via a bridge over the River Spree. The Paul Löbe House is named after the politician who, until 1933, was the last parliamentary president. The main feature of the building is its comb-like structure, taking up the form of the Federal Chancellery in the western part of the complex. It contains about 1,000 offices for the parliamentary deputies. The offices face north and south, looking out on smal inner courtyards. Set back in these courtyards, running along the east-west axis, there are rotundas with conference and committee rooms. The parliament buildings are linked by a system of subterranean tunnels.

Sowjetisches Ehrenmal

Soviet War Memorial

Lew Kerbel, Vladimir Zigal, Nikolai Sergijewski
1945–46
Strasse des 17. Juni

The Soviet War Memorial was erected a few days after the end of the Second World War using marble and granite taken from Hitler's Neue Reichskanzlei (New Imperial Chancellery). It was built at the intersection of the main "east-west axis" route and the former Siegesallee (Victory Boulevard). From 1873 on, the latter led to the Victory Column then standing in front of the Reichstag on the square then known as Königsplatz. From 1901 on, Königsplatz was adorned with numerous memorials to the Brandenburg-Prussian rulers. The Soviet War Memorial was erected to commemorate the Soviet soldiers who fell in the war. Until the Russian troops left Berlin in 1993, there was a permanent Russian guard of honour on duty here. There are three Berlin memorials to the Soviet Army (in the Tiergarten, in Pankow and in Treptow); they will be duly conserved and maintained in accordance with the terms of the treaty on reunification.

6

5.7 *Ensemble*

U-Bahnhöfe U5
U 5 underground stations

1997-2004

The development of the public transport system includes an improved connection between the Spreebogen and the historical centre. This will involve extending the U 5 underground line to Lehrter Bahnhof central station by 2004. Work has been in progress on the first section since 1997. The stations along this section will be Lehrter Bahnhof, the Reichstag and Brandenburger Tor. Thus, no further work will be necessary in this area after the German government has moved from Bonn to Berlin. In the second phase of development early next century, work will be undertaken to complete the new stations of Unter den Linden, Spreeinsel and Rathaus.

6

Deutscher Bundestag
German Federal Parliament

Paul Wallot;
Sir Norman Foster & Partners, London/Berlin
1884–94;
1994–99
Scheidemannstrasse/
Ebertstrasse

On 29 October, 1991, after the decision had been taken to make Berlin the capital city, the German Parliament voted to use the Reichstag again as the seat of the German Parliament.

The Reichstag was built in 1884-94. This impressive building, situated in front of the gates of Berlin's historical centre, was designed to house Imperial Germany's parliament. The inscription "Dem Deutschen Volke" ("To the German people") was designed by Peter Behrens, but was only added to the building, much against the will of Emperor William II, in 1915, after the outbreak of the First World War. The original plenary hall was completely destroyed during the Reichstag fire in 1933. The original dome was demolished in 1954. In 1961, Paul Baumgarten refurbished the building as the Berlin department of the Bundestag and as a conference and exhibition centre.

In June 1993, English architect Sir Norman Foster was commissioned to carry out the conversion work. He was one of the three prize-winners tying for first place (alongside Pi de Bruijn, whose design envisaged a plenary hall outside the Reichstag building, and Santiago Calatrava, who designed a dominant dome). Work began, in 1994, stripping the building of all later fixtures. In 1995, following a controversial debate, the Parliament rejected Foster's original plan to erect a baldachin-style roof over the whole building

7.1

and surrounding site. Instead, they voted in favour of reconstructing the original Reichstag dome of more modest proportions in a modern design. The glass structure (right above the parliamentary chamber) providing natural ventilation is open to the public. The dome's sophisticated lighting system directs light into the chamber during the day using mirrors and an awning; at night, artificial light is directed out of the chamber. During the conversion, great value was attached to installing an ecologically friendly air-conditioning system. This system consists of an underground, unit-type co-generation station, fuelled by rape seed oil; the refrigeration and heating storage units extend to a depth of up to 300 metres below the ground.

Parlamentarische Gesellschaft

Parliamentary Society

Ensemble 7.1

Directly opposite what was formerly the main entrance to the Reichstag, Wallot built a spacious city villa as the official residence for the Reichstag President. After the Reichstag fire in 1933, the parliamentary library moved into the building, and also provided storage space for a collection of literature denounced by the Nazis as "un-German". In the German Democratic Republic, the building was used by the Institute for Marxist-Leninist Studies. Since 1994 the house has been part of the complex of buildings constituting the Jakob Kaiser House. It has been converted for official use by both the German Parliament and the Parliamentary Society.

Paul Wallot;
Thomas van den Valentyn
with Johannes van Linn,
Cologne
1897–1904;
1998–99
Ebertstrasse 30-31/
Reichstagufer

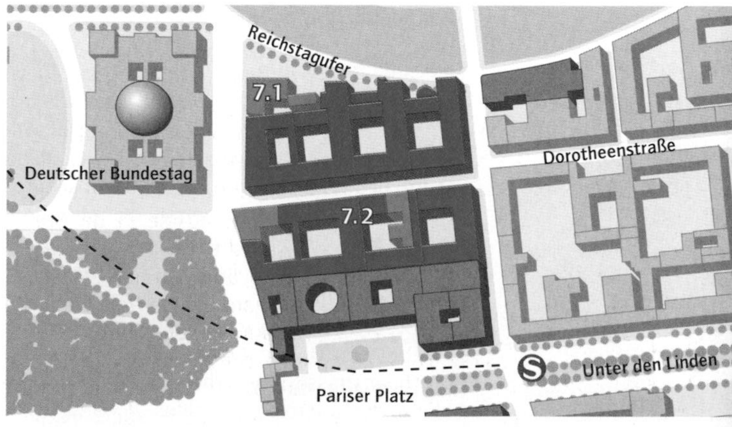

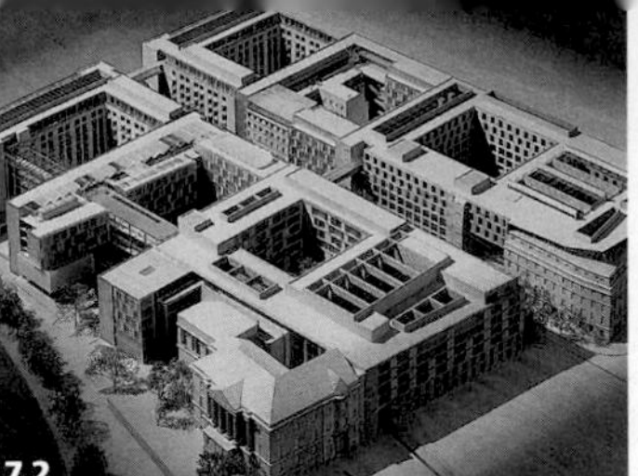
7.2

7.2 *Ensemble*

Jakob-Kaiser-Haus
Jakob Kaiser House

Planungsgesellschaft Dorotheenblöcke PGD, Berlin
1996–2000
Dorotheenstrasse/ Wilhelmstrasse/ Ebertstrasse

The buildings on either side of Dorotheenstrasse are to house parliamentary administrative offices as well as offices for the parliamentary parties and deputies. The buildings will include some listed as being of historic interest, such as the "House Sommer" (at Dorotheenstrasse 105, built in 1854-57 by Friedrich Adler), the Vereinshaus der Deutschen Ingenieure (the association of German engineers at Ebertstrasse 27, built in 1912-14 by Reimer & Körte) and the most prominent old building, the former official residence of the Reichstag President. A planning team, established in 1995 and consisting of the architectural offices of Busmann & Haberer in Cologne, De Architekten Cie in Amsterdam, gmp von Gerkan, Marg & Partner in Hamburg and Thomas van den Valentyn in Cologne, is working on the overall design of the Jakob Kaiser House. Proceeding from the notions underlying "Critical Reconstruction", the historical block building and the existing divisions are being used in a way that permits each of the total of eight buildings to retain its individual character whilst, at the same time, forming part of a functional whole. All of the buildings are linked with each other and with the Reichstag via a tunnel, thus fulfilling the requirement of creating the shortest route to parliament. Initially, the Dorotheenstrasse was to be closed to traffic, but the Senate was against such a closure. It will now remain open to trafic.

8

Landesvertretung Berlin
Land Representation of Berlin

Paul Spieker; Senatsbauverwaltung, Berlin
1873–83;
1998–99
Wilhelmstrasse 67/ Dorotheenstrasse

The Federal Land of Berlin is opening its official representation at a central location – at the former principal's residence on the corner of Wilhelmstrasse and Dorotheenstrasse. The building used to belong to the natural science institutes at the university. The university complex, constructed from 1873 in a number of stages, originally occupied the whole block, but during the war the buildings along the Reichstagufer were destroyed. There is a memorial to the German bacteriologist Robert Koch in the Institute on Dorotheenstrasse. It was there, in 1882, that he isolated the tuberculosis bacillus.

Bundestagsverwaltung 9

Bundestag Administration

In 1994, the German Parliament decided to make greater use of existing old buildings to house federal ministries. The building in Dorotheenstrasse was constructed in 1937 as an extension to what was then the Ministry of the Interior, whose main office had been on Unter den Linden since 1837. It was the only part of the whole complex to survive the war intact. When conversion work is completed, it will house some of the administrative offices of the German Parliament.

Konrad Nonn;
Mark, Schlenkhoff & Wähning, Berlin
1936–37;
1998–99
Dorotheenstrasse 93

Schadowhaus

The Schadow House

Johann Gottfried Schadow (co-designer)
1805;
1851
Schadowstrasse 10 11

Here lived and worked the famous Berlin sculptor Johann Gottfried Schadow until his death in 1850. He not only designed the reliefs on the facade, but also contributed to the design of the house itself, which is considered to be the most important surviving private residential building from the period around 1800. It contains the first example of what became known as a "Berliner Zimmer"; a room running between the front of the house and the wing, with a window in the furthest corner looking onto the back courtyard.

Botschaft der Vereinigten Staaten von Amerika

The United States Embassy

Hermann von der Hude, Julius Hennicke
1886–87
Neustädtische Kirchstrasse 4-5/ Dorotheenstrasse

Although the building is reminiscent of a town house, it was originally designed as an Army and Navy general store. From 1906 on, it was used as a club house. From 1977 until 1990, it housed the American Embassy in East Germany before becoming first the American Consulate and then, as of 1998, the embassy again. It will continue to serve this function until a decision has been taken on the new Pariser Platz building.

Presse- und Informationsamt der Bundesregierung 10

Federal Press Office

The Federal Press Office is the most important information office of the German government. The main entrance is on the Reichstagufer, and the offices are spread through a complex of several pre-war buildings, some dating from Imperial Germany and others built in the German Democratic Republic. The administration and

KSP Engel and Zimmermann, Berlin
1996–2000
Dorotheenstrasse/
Reichstagufer/
Neustädtische Kirchstrasse

offices are housed in a 1980s' building on Dorotheenstrasse and in the former Postal Giro and Savings Office. The latter was designed by Alfred Lempp and constructed from 1913-17. It stretches from Dorotheenstrasse down to the Reichstagufer, where its richly decorated facade faces the River Spree. In front of the eastern gable wall there now stands a narrow, newly constructed office block .

11

ARD Hauptstadtstudio

The ARD studio in the capital

Ortner & Ortner,
Vienna/Berlin
1996–98
Wilhelmstrasse 67a/
Reichstagufer 7-8

The German public TV and radio station, ARD, opened its studio in the new German capital on the 22nd May, 1999, on the eve of the election of new German Federal President, with the first broadcast of a political news and commentary programme "Report from Berlin" (previously called Report from Bonn). While the editorial offices are partly grouped around the covered central patio and partly look onto the River Spree, the facade facing Wilhelmstrasse is dominated by one single large window, providing a view of the seat of parliament and government. The building also contains restaurants and shops open to the public.

12

Marschallbrücke

Marschall Bridge

Benedict Tonon,
Gerhard Pichler, Berlin
1881;
1997–98
Wilhelmstrasse/
Luisenstrasse

The Marschall Bridge is a listed work of architecture. Consequently, any conversion work had to preserve the characteristic three-arch structure. The team of Tonon and Pichler received the commission for the project. They divided the bridge into a central road flanked by footbridges. The northern arches under the walkways have been preserved, as have the iron pillars in the water, remainders of the original iron bridge (1881). The modern steel construction joining onto this gives the whole structure a new emphasis.

13

Bundestagsverwaltung

Bundestag Administration

The administrative offices of the Imperial Patent Office were designed to meet the highest de-

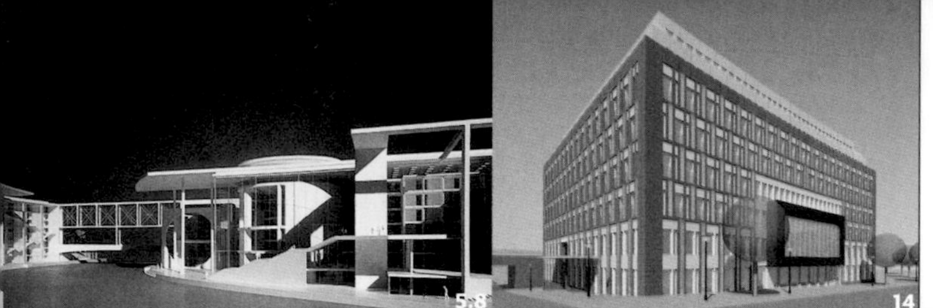

mands that could be placed on a prestigious building. With its lavish facade decoration, the building is a typical example of Wilhelminian architecture around 1890. It survived the style-purging of the post-war period. After accommodating the Imperial Insurance Office, it housed the East German Director of Public Prosecutions. Once it has been renovated, it will be used as offices for parliamentary deputies.

August Busse;
Bernhard Bietmann,
Berlin
1887–91;
1998–99
Luisenstrasse 32-34

Marie-Elisabeth-Lüders-Haus

Marie Elisabeth Lüders House

Ensemble 5.8

The Marie Elisabeth Lüders House (named after the Reichstag parliamentary deputy and champion of women's rights) on the eastern bank of the River Spree creates a functional and formal unity with the Paul Löbe House on the western bank. The two buildings are connected via a public footbridge. Access to the rooms in the Marie Elisabeth Lüders House is via a glass-covered central hall. Next to the river stands the rotunda housing the parliamentary library. The library collection here is among the largest in the world. In addition to the parliamentary archives and other academic and scientific services, the building also houses offices and a main hall for parliamentary hearings. The surrounding parliament buildings form a decorative public square by the river.

Stephan Braunfels,
Munich/Berlin
1998–2001
Schiffbauerdamm

Bundes-Pressekonferenz

Federal Press Conference

14

The Bundes-Pressekonferenz is composed of an independent team of journalists who are involved in reporting on political events in Germany. Like the major broadcasting companies and editorial boards, they have also chosen to base themselves close to the centre of government and parliament by the River Spree. In addition to the "Bundespresseclub" (federal press club), the building will house agencies, television companies and correspondents. The main conference room, where press conferences take place, faces the Reichstag and can be seen from the outside by its large slanted window. The large covered atrium provides space to meet and discuss as does the restaurant, which is open to the public.

Nalbach + Nalbach, Berlin
1998–2000
Schiffbauerdamm 35-39/
Reinhardtstrasse

15

Landesvertretung Sachsen-Anhalt

Land Representation of Saxony-Anhalt

gmp von Gerkan, Marg & Partner, Hamburg
1827;
1998–2000
Luisenstrasse 18

The German Land of Saxony-Anhalt has chosen this attractive pre-war building to house the offices of its permanent representation. The building is one of the oldest town houses in the former Friedrich-Wilhelm-Stadt. In 1874, it was converted into a grand palatial building. In the early years of the 20th century, a Freemasons' Lodge had its seat here. From 1946 on, "Die Möwe",an artists' club, was located here.

16.1 *Ensemble*

Wohn- und Geschäftshäuser

Residential and commercial buildings

Eller + Eller Architekten, Berlin/Düsseldorf;
Walter A. Noebel, Berlin
1994–95;
1998–99
Reinhardtstrasse/
Luisenstrasse

The eight-storey two new corner buildings on Luisenstrasse offer a contrast to the lower, historical buildings around them. They place the intersection with Reinhardtstrasse in a new context. To the south is the glass office block (1994/95), designed by the Düsseldorf architects Eller + Eller. The steel construction projecting over the street serves as a sun-shield. In contrast, the apartment and office building to the north (1998-99) is clad with light-coloured sandstone blocks. It was designed by Berlin architect Walter A. Noebel, who employed the high tower to accentuate the angle at the corner. On Karlplatz opposite, there stands a memorial to Rudolf Virchow, the German pathologist and liberal politician. Designed in 1906 by Fritz Klimsch, it shows a Titan fighting the Sphinx, a metaphor for the struggle of medical knowledge against illness.

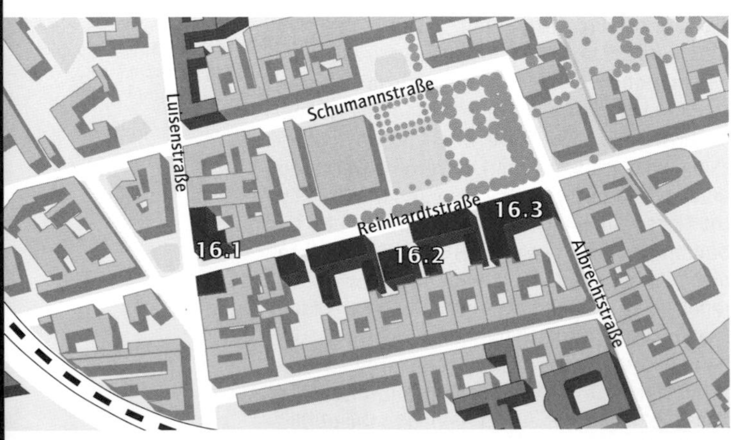

16.1

Wohnanlage Reinhardtstraße

16.2 *Ensemble*

Residential complex in Reinhardtstrasse

The ground floor of this extensive residential complex is given over to restaurants and shops. Set into the building are the remains of the portal to the Exerzierhaus, constructed by the military builder Carl Hampel in 1828 after a design by Schinkel. The Deutsches Theater has its rehearsal rooms in the basement levels. They used to be located in the old Exerzierhaus.

Bellmann & Böhm
with Krüger, Schuberth, Vandreike,
Berlin
1996–98
Reinhardtstrasse 29
Bellmann & Böhm,
Berlin
1996–97
Reinhardtstrasse 31

Medienhaus

16.3 *Ensemble*

Media House

The residential and commercial building continues the new block along Reinhardtstrasse, forming a transition to the historical buildings in Albrechtstrasse. Its name is indicative of its partial use by communication companies.

Kny & Weber,
Berlin
1998–99
Reinhardtstrasse 23-27/
Albrechtstrasse

Hochbunker

Overground air-raid shelter

1943
Reinhardtstrasse/
Albrechtstrasse 24-25

During the Second World War, numerous new shelters were constructed in Berlin as part of an air-raid-shelter programme. From 1941 on, due to the cost of constructing underground shelters, there was an increasing tendency to build them overground. The striking feature is the shelter's ornamental facade, designed to make it as inconspicuous as possible. The concrete building, which would have been extremely expensive to demolish, found temporary use as a way-out discotheque in the mid 1990s.

Deutsches Theater und Kammerspiele

The Deutsches Theater and the Kammerspiele

Eduard Titz
1850
Schumannstrasse 12-13a

The "Deutsches Theater", which is steeped in tradition, goes back to the "Friedrich-Wilhelmstädtisches Theater". The "Deutsche Theater" was founded in 1883 and became the first theatre for the well-to-do middle-classes in Berlin. In 1905, Max Reinhardt, the theatre director, purchased it, together with the ballroom next door, which he then set about converting into a smaller theatre called the "Kammerspiele". Both theatres enjoy an excellent reputation. Over the last few years, the "Baracke", a former rehearsal stage, has become well known for its production of sensational contemporary pieces.
The various cultural and scientific facilities as well as restaurants and cafes located alongside

buildings serving a political function demonstrate the urban-planning strategy of ensuring that the new Government district was not isolated.

17.1 *Ensemble*

Georg Diestel
1897–1917
Schumannstrasse 20-21

Krankenhaus Charité

Charité hospital

When the Charité was founded in 1710 as a military hospital and hospital for plague victims, it lay outside the city boundaries. The lack of space as well as scientific and medical developments meant that, by the late 19th century, there was a need for new and comprehensive restructuring. The architect Georg Diestel designed the new hospital buildings, and construction work started in 1897. A major alteration was made to the historically established structure of this "city within a city" when, in 1977-81, a new 20-storey hospital block, with extensions, was erected on the site. The Charité, together with the related research institutes, now forms the Humboldt University Clinic. The Charité also houses a medical museum, established by Rudolf Virchow, the founder of modern immunology, while he was working at the hospital. Although the original comprehensive collection of 25,000 preparations was badly damaged during the Second World War, the museum is still of enormous medical interest. The collection has been systematically enlarged since 1994 and, on the centenary

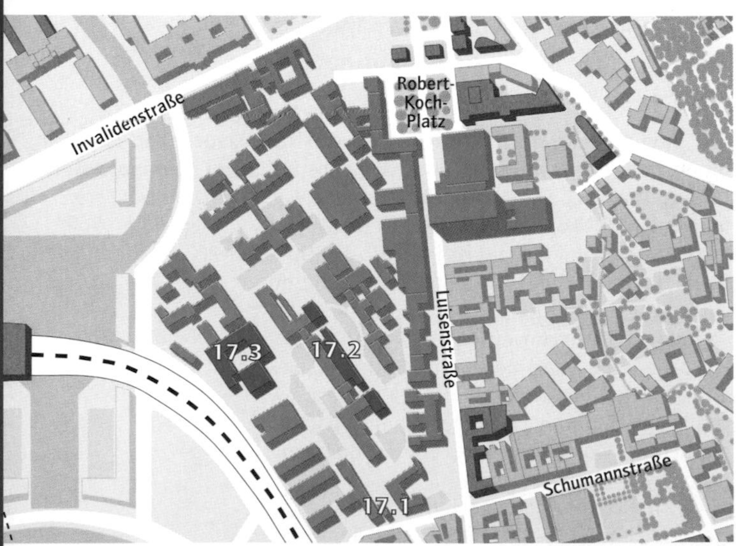

17.3

of its founding, in 1999, it will be reopened in the original restored historical setting. At the corner of Luisenstrasse and Schumannstrasse there is a memorial to the founder of modern ophthalmic medicine, Albrecht von Graefe.

Klinik für Innere Medizin

New building for Internal Medicine

Ensemble 17.2

Since 1990, the Charité has been going through the process of restructuring. The main building for Internal Medicine is being refurbished and an extension added. The new construction along Sauerbruchweg will be placed symmetrically in front of the main building, which is listed as being of historical interest.

G.S. Dybe + Partner,
B. Halbach,
Berlin
1995–99
Schumannstrasse 20-21

Max-Planck-Institut für Infektionsbiologie

Max Planck Institute for the Biology of Infections

Ensemble 17.3

For the area west of the main thoroughfare, the architects Deubzer and König have designed a symmetrical complex consisting of two compact U-shaped institute buildings. In the first stage of construction, the northern building will be completed, housing the Max Planck Institute and the Rheumatism Research Centre. Its counterpart to the south is still in the planning stage. The small inner courtyard will be bordered off by a multi-storey building containing special laboratory facilities. Thus, the Charité will include important major research establishments.

H. Deubzer,
J. König, Berlin
1997–99
Schumannstrasse 20-21

Anatomisches Theater

Anatomy Lecture Theatre

Carl Gotthard Langhans
1790
Luisenstrasse 56

A large, three-winged complex opens out onto Luisenstrasse. It was erected in 1840 by Ludwig Ferdinand Hesse for the Royal Veterinary College, founded in 1790. The Anatomy Lecture Theatre was the first building completed. It now stands unobtrusively in the courtyard area. This circular lecture hall with steeply-ascending rows of seats for the students to observe the animal dissections is an outstanding monument to the history of science and architecture. It was designed by Carl Gotthard Langhans one year after he had completed his plans for Brandenburg Gate. The ornamentation in the dome was produced by Bernhard Rode.

18.1
Ensemble

Robert-Koch-Platz/ Platz vor dem Neuen Tor

The two squares: Robert Koch Platz/ Platz vor dem Neuen Tor

Karl Friedrich Schinkel, Peter Joseph Lenné
1830–40;
1993

The Neues Tor, like the Brandenburg Gate, Oranienburger Tor and Hallesches Tor is one of the access points to the old Berlin city centre. This area, with its twin squares, was based on designs by Schinkel. The green area was landscaped by Peter Joseph Lenné. From 1830-40, Schinkel constructed two customs' buildings at the city excise-wall. These two gate-houses were damaged in the Second World War and later demolished. The two new gate-houses gave the square back its original form. A marble statue (made in 1916 by Louis Tuaillon) of Robert Koch, the bacteriologist and Nobel Prize Winner, stands where Luisenstrasse meets the square. In 1906, Ernst von Ihne built the "Kaiserin-Friedrich-Haus für das ärztliche Fortbildungswesen" (Empress Friedrich House for Advanced Medical Training) at Robert-Koch-Platz 7. The Soviet military headquarters occupied the building from 1945-49. In 1992, the building was handed back over to the Kaiserin-Friedrich-Stiftung.

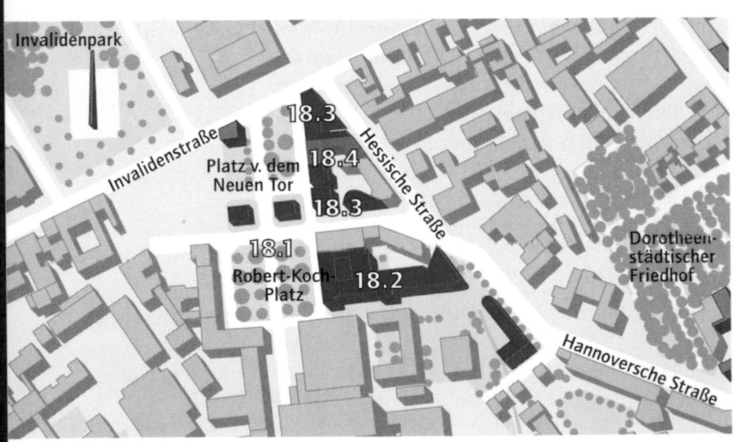

18.2
Ensemble

Luisen Carree

Stefan Ludes, Berlin
1996–98
Robert-Koch-Platz 4/
Hannoversche Strasse 19-22/
Philippstrasse 14

The "Luisen Carree" consists of an office and business block extending from Robert-Koch-Platz to Hannoversche Strasse. It includes a separate residential building at the corner of Hannoversche Strasse and Philippstrasse. The office block

18.2

closes the front of the square. The courtyards and garden area can be reached via a small passageway. A stretch of the small River Panke, previously hidden in subterranean "piping", is now being uncovered and returned to its natural condition. It will thus become a part of a planned green strip running from Invaliden Park through the University campus down to the River Spree.

Wohn- und Geschäftshäuser

18.3 *Ensemble*

Residential and commercial buildings

Josef Paul Kleihues, Berlin
1994–98
Platz vor dem Neuen Tor

The new buildings to the east of the Platz vor dem Neuen Tor restore the square to its original historical form. The "Prismahaus", designed by Kleihues, stands on the triangular plot fronting Invalidenstrasse. On Hannoversche Strasse, which runs south, he also designed two apartment blocks and a block of studio apartments whose fan-shaped facade faces the courtyard. The remains of the old excise wall have been integrated into the base of the buildings.

Bundeszentrale Bündnis 90/ Die Grünen

18.4 *Ensemble*

The federal headquarters of the Bündnis 90/ Die Grünen political party

Wolfgang Poggemann, Georgsmarienhütte
1998–99
Platz vor dem Neuen Tor 1

The main headquarters of the Bündnis 90/Die Grünen party are also located at the Platz vor dem Neuen Tor. They occupy a former residential house, built in 1880, consisting of a front building, side wings and one wing facing Hessische Strasse. The building is currently being totally renovated. The attics have been converted and the facade given a new colour scheme.

Museum für Naturkunde

The Natural History Museum

August Tiede
1883–89
Invalidenstrasse 42-43

Building work was started on the Natural Science Institute in 1875, on the site of the old Royal Iron Foundry. The Museum für Naturkunde built between 1883-89 forms the present centre of the symmetrical complex. The museum is flanked to the east and west by the former College of Agriculture, built between 1876-80, and the State Geological Institute, built between 1875-78. These prestigious buildings all have a covered quadrangle that can also serve as an exhibition hall. With around 50 million specimens and

the biggest known dinosaur skeleton, the museum is one of the largest of its kind anywhere in the world.

19.1 *Ensemble*

Bundesministerium für Verkehr, Bau- und Wohnungswesen

Federal Ministry of Transport, Building, and Housing

Max Dudler, Zurich/Berlin (new building),
Gerber & Partner, Dortmund (converted building)
1997–99
Invalidenstrasse 44/
Invalidenpark

The German Ministry of Transport, since 1998 Ministry of Transport, Building, and Housing, occupies the former State Geological Institute and the adjoining new building. The old building was designed in 1875 by August Tiede as a part of the complex accommodating the natural science institutes. During renovation and refurbishment, the large covered quadrangle and its arcades were also restored. The new structure was consciously designed to contrast with the existing section, which also serves representational purposes, whilst the new six-storey extension housing administrative offices is of a purely functional nature. By taking up the cubic form and outline of the older structure the new building echoes the old, to which it is linked by a foyer and a staircase tower. The four-winged building, designed by Max Dudler, encloses a courtyard containing three conference rooms. The wall between the windows of the inner courtyard is equipped with solar power panels. The main exterior facade of the building is clad with natural stone. The entrance to the new building is located on the Schwarzer Weg, along which the small River Panke has been uncovered again.

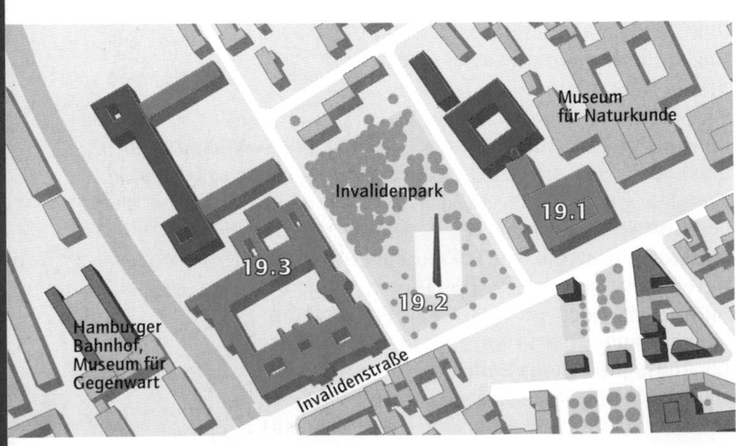

Invalidenpark

19.2
Ensemble

Christophe Girot, Paris
1993–97
Invalidenstrasse/
Scharnhorststrasse

"Invaliden Park" was designed by Peter Joseph Lenné in the middle of the 19th century. It was intended as a place of rest and recreation for those living in the nearby residential "Invalidenhaus".
In 1852, a column, the "Invalidensäule", was erected to commemorate the soldiers who fell during the 1848 revolution. The Gnadenkirche (the Church of Mercy) designed by Max Spitta, was built in 1895. The whole complex was destroyed during the Second World War, and until 1990, the site was classified as a restricted area owing to its proximity to the border. Over the past few years, Christophe Girot has redesigned it as a green space serving the catchment area around the new Lehrter Bahnhof central station and nearby the government ministries. The square was officially opened on 3rd October, 1997 – on the public holiday commemorating German reunification.

Bundesministerium für Wirtschaft und Technologie

Federal Ministry of Economics and Technology

19.3
Ensemble

Isaak Jacob Petri;
Cremer & Wolffenstein;
Baumann & Schnittger, Berlin
1746–48;
1905–10;
1997–99
Invalidenstrasse 48-49/
Scharnhorststrasse 36-37

The Ministry of Economics is housed in what was formerly the Kaiser-Wilhelm-Akademie and the old Invalidenhaus. It provides an example of a costly yet worthwhile reconstruction of existing old buildings for the government. The Kaiser-Wilhelm-Akademie was built between 1905-10 and designed by the prominent architects Cremer & Wolffenstein as an impressive four-winged building. From 1951 until 1972 it housed the East German supreme court before it was turned into the East German government hospital. The "Invalidenhaus", on the north side, was built in 1746 by Isaak Jacob Petri and is the oldest building in this area. It was a foundation sponsored by Frederick the Great to accommodate war veterans. The two wings enclosing the ceremonial courtyard have been completed with the addition of the newly built middle wing, designed by Baumann & Schnittger, where the orientation is clearly taken from the form of the older buildings. On the west side, facing the canal, there are two further new buildings. One of the largest solar

21

power installations in Germany can be found on the glass-covered western roof area.
Lying further to the north, and of historical interest, is the Invalidenfriedhof cemetery. The tombs here include, for example, that of the Prussian general and military reformer Gerhard von Scharnhorst.

20

Sandkrugbrücke

Sandkrug Bridge

Ingenieurbüro Grassl GmbH, Berlin,
Thomas Baumann,
Birgitt Welter, Berlin
(advising)
1994–96
Invalidenstrasse

The newly completed Sandkrug Bridge was opened in 1996. It has been widened to better accommodate vehicles and to allow river traffic to pass through. The low steel construction links Berlin's new central station, Lehrter Zentralbahnhof, and the government ministry buildings. There has been a bridge here since 1704, when a wooden bridge was erected, near the "Sandkrug" inn, across the newly constructed Schönhauser Graben, which led to the River Panke and continued to the palace of Schloss Schönhausen. In 1857, the Schönhauser Graben was developed into the Berlin-Spandau shipping canal across which a new bridge was built, linking the nearby district of Friedrich-Wilhelm-Stadt with Hamburger Bahnhof railway station. This bridge was destroyed during the Second World War. The provisional bridge constructed afterwards survived until 1994.

21

Hamburger Bahnhof

Hamburger Bahnhof railway station

Friedrich Neuhaus;
Josef Paul Kleihues, Berlin
1846–47;
1993–96
Invalidenstrasse 50-51

The terminus, built in 1847, was one of the oldest in Germany and served as the model for many other stations. Within a few decades, however, it proved inadequate to cope with the rapidly expanding rail traffic and was closed in 1884. The central hall was constructed to house the transport and building museum, which was opened in 1906. The wings of the ceremonial courtyard were added in 1911-16. The building came under the East German Reich Railway administration and, although it was located in West Berlin, it was only accessible to the responsible British Allies. It was only when the S-Bahn (city railway) was placed under the control of the west in the nineteen-eighties that it became pos-

sible to reconsider the station's future. A greater part of the pieces on exhibition there were placed in the Deutsches Technikmuseum in Berlin and in the Verkehrsmuseum in Dresden. Since 1996, Hamburger Bahnhof station building has been the home of the Museum für Gegenwart der Staatlichen Museen (the Museum of Contemporary Art), bringing together works from both the Neue Nationalgalerie and the Marx' private collection. To accommodate the museum exhibits, a long gallery has been added to the east of the central hall.

Landessozialgericht
The Higher Social Court
Friedrich Neuhaus
1874
Invalidenstrasse 52/
Heidestrasse

The Higher Social Court building was initially constructed to house the administrative offices of the railway company whose trains ran from the neighbouring Hamburger Bahnhof station to the northwest of Germany. When the station was closed, the Prussian Building Commission moved into the building.

Tiergartentunnel
Tiergarten tunnel

Ensemble 22.1

1995–2004
Heidestrasse

"The plan for traffic in central areas" project provides for the construction of new stations and tunnels for Berlin's underground and city railway system as well as for regional and inter-city rail traffic. It also includes the development of the major road tunnel in Tiergarten for Bundesstrasse 96. Until 1961, this road ran via Friedrichstrasse to the north of Germany, but after the Berlin Wall was built in August, 1961 it had to be

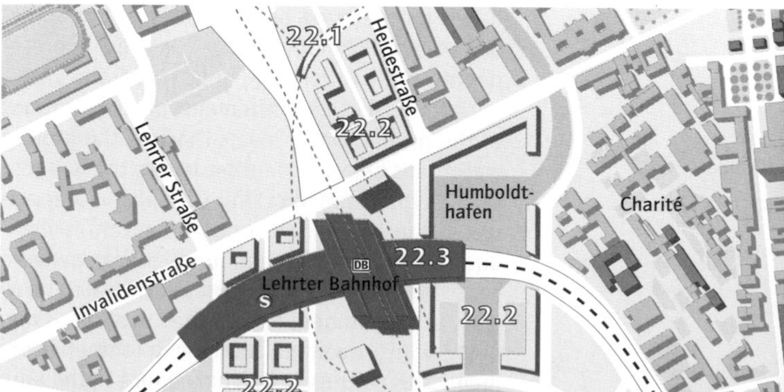

re-routed west of the border and ran through the Tiergarten on the relief road known as the Entlastungsstrasse. The construction of the present traffic tunnel provided the optimal solution both from the point of view of urban planning and traffic organisation to relieve the parliament and government quarter of the otherwise heavy through-traffic. It also has the advantage of restoring the original lanes through the Tiergarten. The tunnel begins at the Landwehrkanal and runs underground for 2.4 kilometres, with connections for Potsdamer Platz and the Sony and Daimler complexes. There are further access roads and exits at Kemperplatz and Lehrter Bahnhof station. The tunnel emerges north of the station and joins the overground section of the main road at Heidestrasse. Where the road, subway and inter-city rail links pass under the River Spree, the tunnel is 110 metres wide. As it was not possible to perform underground construction work on this section, the course of the River Spree had to be diverted temporarily so that the open-pit work could be carried out.
Furthermore, a sophisticated system of ground water management was necessary during the operation (primarily carried out by underground shield driving) to ensure that the trees in the Tiergarten were not cut off from their water supply: In Berlin, the ground water level lies only a few metres below the ground. Hence, waterproof troughs are needed for buildings constructed deep into the ground. It was initially feared that the flow of water into such troughs might lower the ground water level and thus endanger the Tiergarten and the buildings in the area. For this reason, ground water management was established for the large building sites at the Spreebogen and Potsdamer Platz – a step unprecedented in the Federal Republic – with the aim of performing daily measurements and evaluations of the ground water levels there. If the ground water falls below certain set levels, the water in the troughs flows back into the subsoil seepage wells. Constant monitoring and carefully managed seepage have made it possible to perform construction work on an unheard-of scale and to carry out a number of such measures simultaneously, whilst avoiding damage to the environment. This method is still in evidence in the area round Lehrter Bahnhof.

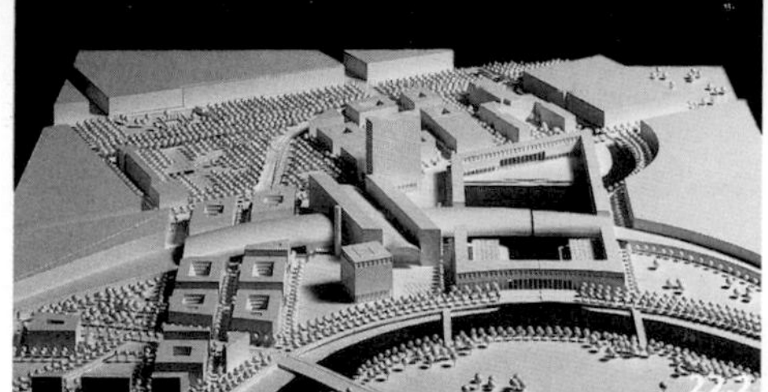

The symmetrically laid-out harbour area was used for the transshipment of goods between Hamburg and Warsaw. All the building materials necessary for the development of Berlin in the 19th century were unloaded here, and it remained the largest harbour in Berlin until the completion of the Westhafen harbour in 1923. From 1857 on, the Schönhauser Graben was developed into the new Berlin-Spandau canal. The stretch of canal running to Nordhafen was carefully restored as a historical structure (1997-98). The canal serves as an important artery for building materials during the construction work in the Spreebogen area and on the Lehrter Bahnhof station complex.

Humboldthafen
Humboldt Harbour
Peter Joseph Lenné
1842–48
Friedrich-List-Ufer/
Alexanderufer

Umfeld Lehrter Bahnhof 22.2

The area around Lehrter Bahnhof railway station

In the area around the new Lehrter Bahnhof railway station complex a whole new quarter is being built. To the east lies Humboldthafen, bordered by a colonnade. To the west, a block-like structure of office buildings will straddle the railway lines. For quite some time, this area was used to isolate activities considered dangerous or disturbing in a city environment, thus, for example a munitions factory and a plague hospital were located here. From the early 18th century on a powder-mill occupied a large site here. It was not until 1830 that Lenné and Schinkel drew up development plans to integrate numerous military buildings into the prevailing urban and block structure. Railway facilities and the 1879 trade fair left their mark on this area well into the mid-20th century.
The Swiss-German architect Max Dudler has designed apartment blocks in and around Heidestrasse, using a combination of compact block and individual structures. The area to the south of Invalidenstrasse is to be developed by the Cologne architect Ungers, who plans to integrate the station, as an independent structure, into the cityscape by creating other dominant points in the form of an office tower block to the north, and a cubic hotel building to the south.

Oswald Mathias Ungers,
Cologne/Berlin,
Max Dudler, Zurich/Berlin
1999–2002
Invalidenstrasse/
Heidestrasse

22.3 *Ensemble*

Lehrter Bahnhof

Lehrter Bahnhof railway station

gmp von Gerkan, Marg & Partner, Hamburg
1996– ca. 2004
Invalidenstrasse

Lehrter Bahnhof station was named after the town of the same name near Hanover. The conversion of Lehrter Bahnhof will turn the station into a centrally located railway interchange integrated into the Europe-wide high-speed railway network. The station will also be linked to the Berlin underground and city railway system as well as to tram and regional rail services. A subterranean line will also be provided on the north-south route for the planned Transrapid rail link to Hamburg. Altogether 250,000 passengers are expected to use this station every day.

Before the First World War, there already existed plans to transform the former terminus, opened in 1871, into a throughstation. However, the two World Wars stopped the implementation of this project. In 1992, a decision was taken to redirect long-distance and regional rail traffic through the middle of the city and to convert Lehrter Bahnhof station into Berlin's central interchange. The north-south rail link will pass through the tunnel beneath the Tiergarten and the River Spree. The east-west long-distance routes, regional trains and city rail links will cross overground on the raised city railway line. The project development is the most costly and extensive ever undertaken in Berlin by the Deutsche Bahn AG (the German rail company).

Selected from a number of variations on this theme, the "mushroom concept" is designed to combine all of the east-west and north-south inter-city and regional rail links, directing them through the city centre and bringing them together at Lehrter Bahnhof. The term "mushroom concept" reflects the shape formed by the rail links. The curved northern section of the city railway passing through Gesundbrunnen station forms the "cap" of the mushroom, whilst the "brim" is formed by the city railway links on either side passing through Zoologischer Garten and Ostbahnhof. Finally, the "stem" of the mushroom can be seen in the north-south link between Papestrasse station and Lehrter Bahnhof itself. Lehrter Bahnhof's glass upper hall will be equipped with 3,500 square metres of solar panels.

Berliner Höfe und „Steinerne Stadt"

Berlin courtyards and the "city of stone"

Route 2 begins at Hackescher Markt, Berlin's bustling new pleasure centre, taking us through the oldest surviving residential area and centre of craft enterprises and into the heart of the densely built-up 19th century "city of stone".
Spandauer Vorstadt in the north of the vast S-Bahn (city railway) network is bordered by Friedrichstrasse in the west, Torstrasse in the north and Prenzlauer Allee in the east. Its name is a geographical reference to the town of Spandau to the west of Berlin. Most of the old street network has been preserved in its original form, as one of the surviving testimonies to the historical city centre of Berlin dating from the 17th century. Consequently, in 1993, Spandauer Vorstadt was officially declared a development area worthy of preservation.
In contrast to the once splendid area in the south between the S-Bahn and Alexanderplatz, Spandauer Vorstadt and the Sophienviertel, in particular, were always conspicuously poor areas. This was the home of small craftsmen and workers employed in the wool and silk industries as well as, from 1671 on, the so-called Schutzjuden (Jews granted protection by the Prussian ruler). Auguststrasse was popularly known as the "Armengasse" (Poor Lane), whilst Grosse Hamburger Strasse was called "Toleranzstrasse" (Tolerance Street) because of the diverse religions which coexisted peacefully there. The former Jewish Cemetery, the Protestant Church of Sophia and the Catholic hospital of St. Hedwig as well as the former "Volkskaffeehaus" (People's Coffee House) and the older residential houses still suggest something of the atmosphere once prevailing in this district. The former Wertheim Department Store and the mail transport office building in Oranienburger Strasse, in contrast, testify to Berlin's evolution into a 20th-century city.
Route 2 takes us through countless inner-courtyards containing many new buildings and conversions. Trade, culture and dwellings form an urbane unity here. Many of the courtyards are extremely well executed instances of the revival of what is now frequently regarded as a prime example of urban mixed-use of the past. The noisy small and large machines of old have

meanwhile given way to environmentally compatible handicraft and cultural enterprises. Galleries have been set up in the floors that used to accommodate warehouses and production halls. The Hackesche Höfe and Sophie Gips Höfe are merely the best-known and most splendid among the numerous courtyards that will be traversed on route 2. A glance at the stairwells and court facades is certainly worthwhile, since it gives one an opportunity to see the exemplary results achieved through the cooperation between Berlin preservationists and investors.

The urban character of this district has also been shaped by the recent alternative culture, which was beginning to create its own scene even before the Wall was opened up: in empty and derelict old houses such as the Kunsthaus Tacheles in Oranienburger Strasse and the Hackesche Höfe. Furthermore, Jewish life, which has traditionally been an essential part of the district, has also undergone a mild renaissance around the New Synagogue and the Centrum Judaicum with cafés, restaurants, shops and museums. However, the continuing trend towards ever more pubs and restaurants is a challenge to urban planners to ensure that the district is not paralysed by monoculture. Now in the process of a social transformation, Spandauer Vorstadt as a whole provides an example of gentrification. The ennoblement of both properties and their use is putting pressure on indigenous social classes and tending to force them out of the area.

Route 2 leaves Spandauer Vorstadt at Oranienburger Tor and traverses an old quarter that played a significant role in the industrial history of the city. Chausseestrasse was the cradle of the mechanical-engineering industry (Egells and Borsig) in Berlin. The route takes us on to the Berlin Wall Memorial Site at Bernauer Strasse and continues along Anklamer Strasse, Brunnenstrasse and Ackerstrasse, which are among the longest and oldest streets in Berlin. These streets once went beyond the city limits. The route comes to an end in the middle of the 19th century "city of stone" at Rosenthaler Platz.

1

S-Bahnhof Hackescher Markt

Hackescher Market S-Bahn station

Johannes Vollmer; ArchitektenSocietät Figallo, Rottwinkel, Rottwinkel-Tuncel, Birkel, Berlin
1875–82; 1995–97

Hackescher Market S-Bahn station is a part of the city railway viaduct that was opened in 1882. It was named after Commander Graf von Hacke, who had the market square laid out in 1751. For reasons of cost, the Prussian state had the line constructed as an overhead railway with two lines each for local and long-distance traffic. Altogether the line extends twelve kilometres and passes over 757 brick arches. As far as Jannowitzbrücke station, the overhead railway runs over filled-in trenches that once surrounded the city. Hackescher Markt was the first station to be restored when the S-Bahn network was restructured and converted. For a time, there was talk of calling it the "Museum Island" station. The roof of the original hall (which has been preserved as a listed building), with its richly ornamented facade, is modelled on the former shed roofs as well as a continuous glass strip which allowed a greater amount of light onto the platform. The lighting, furnishings and locator system were designed in present-day style.

Hackescher Markt, Umfeld

The area around Hackescher Market

2.1 *Ensemble*

The area around the S-Bahn station, which forms part of Spandauer Vorstadt, is full of small buildings and corners. The area as a whole is now protected as a historical site to prevent any new developments of a magnitude that might disturb

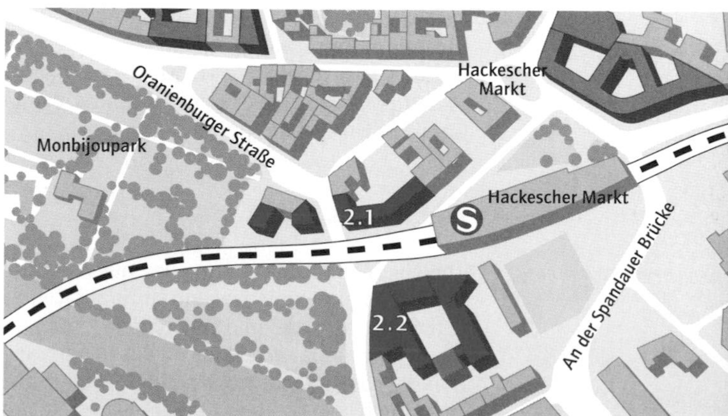

2.2

existing proportions. The old buildings are being conserved and integrated into the overall planning concept. The residential building at the Neue Promenade, erected by Reymer & Partner, Berlin, in 1997-98, is exemplary in the way it closes the gap between the buildings. A large number of restaurants and cafés have been established beneath in the S-Bahn viaduct arches at Monbijou Park. Originally, arches were left open so that the viaduct would not appear to cut the city in two. Later, most of them were walled in and some used as storage space. In the eighties, people once again discovered that the arches, once converted, would provide charming locations for retailers and cafés. Berlin architect Steffen Lehmann has converted the viaduct arches at Monbijou Park for use by restaurants and cafés. These arches will serve as archetypes of the many still to be developed.

2.2 *Ensemble*

Quartier an der Museumsinsel

Building complex at the Museum Island

Steffen Lehmann
Architekten, Berlin
Karl-Heinz Cammann, Berlin
1997–99
Burgstrasse 28-30

A complex of four residential and commercial buildings has been erected to the south of the railway lines. Together with the factory building of 1888 situated inside the block they enclose a rectangular courtyard. The building at the western end of Burgstrasse is occupied by the Federal Banks Association. The adjacent parts, parallel to the railway, are used by the Versorgungsanstalt Deutscher Bühnen, which represents all those employed at German theatres. The building, constructed on a triangular plan with undulating facades, forms the transition to the residential building that constitutes the boundary to the east. The southern and western sides are taken up by older buildings of which the building at Burgstrasse 21, the former vicarage of the Garnisonskirche dates from 1722.

3

Hackesche Höfe

Kurt Berndt, August Endell;
Weiß & Partner, Berlin
1906–07;
1995–96
Rosenthaler Strasse 40-41

The Hackesche Höfe are an exemplary mixture of residential, commercial and cultural facilities in the centre of old Berlin. The complex, comprising eight courtyards, follows an old Berlin tradition, by combining a front building, wings and cross buildings. Its unique features include the

Art Nouveau design of the facade and of the interior of the first courtyard based on a plan by Endell. In 1990, young people occupied the vacated rooms. Soon afterwards, artists and the Cabaret Chamäleon moved in. A concept was elaborated with the users that aimed at reviving the complex in a modern style whilst preserving the small scale of the component parts. After the structure of the building had been thoroughly restored, it was again put to mixed use with residential, commercial and cultural facilities. The Hackesche Höfe have meanwhile become a cultural focal point in Spandauer Vorstadt and became the model for similar redevelopment schemes in this area.

Neuer Hackescher Markt

Götz Bellmann & Walter Böhm, Berlin, with GBK, Berlin, Marc Kocher, Zurich, Neuer Jasinski, Berlin
1996–98
Hackescher Markt 1/ Dircksenstrasse/ Rosenthaler Strasse

The architecture of the New Hackescher Markt echoes that of the old Hackesche Höfe next door and restores to the place Hackescher Markt its original urban structure. With a total of twelve buildings serving both residential and commercial purposes, the new complex also reiterates the concentrated building style and small plots and structures typical of Spandauer Vorstadt. It was constructed after designs by various architects, who have taken their orientation from the district's former architectural diversity and wealth of detail. Shops and restaurants will face the street.

Ehemaliges Kaufhaus Wertheim

The former Wertheim Department Store

Alfred Messel
1903
Rosenthaler Strasse 28-31/ Sophienstrasse

The old department store is of great significance economically, socially and with respect to architectural history. It is the only surviving historical building of the Wertheim department-store chain. It was "Aryanised" in 1937, i.e. its Jewish owners were robbed and dispossessed. Alfred Messel, the architect who designed so many Wertheim buildings, not only gave the store a "rational" contemporary style, but also made the transition to the modern architecture of the 20th century.

6

Wohn- und Geschäftshaus
Residential and commercial building
1886–87;
1929
Rosenthaler Strasse 46-47/
Neue Schönhauser Strasse 10

This mighty residential and commercial building is located in the midst of the low developments constructed in the early 19th century. In 1929, coloured, horizontal stucco banding was used to lend the facade a "rational" quality. When the building was restored in 1996, parts of the old facade dating from the Gründerzeit (the years of rapid industrial expansion in Germany after 1871) were made visible. One of the two stairwells reveals neo-Renaissance frescoes executed when the building was constructed.

Ehemaliges Volkskaffeehaus
People's Coffee House
Alfred Messel
1891
Neue Schönhauser Strasse 13

In 1891 "Volks-Kaffee- und Speisehallen-Gesellschaft" commissioned Alfred Messel to design a building in which the poor would be supplied with coffee and side dishes at a low price. This charity organisation is mentioned here as a representative example of the countless social amenities provided by the Jewish and Christian communities in Spandauer Vorstadt. The building now accommodates an elegant restaurant and provides an example of gentrification.

5 Kurt-Berndt-Höfe

Kurt Berndt;
Annette Axthelm, Potsdam
1912;
1998–99
Neue Schönhauser Strasse 20

The complex, named after the Berlin architect Kurt Berndt, is one of the countless buildings he designed based on the typical Berlin pattern of linking residential dwellings in the front building with commercial premises in the wings facing the courtyards. A conspicuous feature is the economic but effective use of ornamentation and façade materials. The complex was restored as a listed structure in 1998-99.

6 Sophie-Gips-Höfe

Becker Gewers Kühn & Kühn, Berlin
1996–97
Sophienstrasse 21/
Gipsstrasse 12

The Sophie Gips Höfe comprise three courtyards. The new design not only sought to enliven the complex, but also to offer artists an opportunity to create art works in keeping with the locality. The Hoffmann private collection exhibits outstanding works by contemporary artists. It is located in the upper floors of a former sewing machine factory in the first courtyard building, to which two additional floors have been added. Visitors can view the collection on Saturdays on prior appointment.

Sophienstraße

Sophienstrasse passes the rear end of Sophienkirche (the Church of Sophia). There one can see small-scale buildings that were erected in Spandauer Vorstadt in the 18th and 19th centuries. The new building contained within the block at Sophienstrasse 29-33 was designed by the architects Hilmer & Sattler in 1991-94.

Sankt-Hedwigs-Krankenhaus

Saint Hedwig's Hospital

Vincenz Statz, Albert Kinel
1851–55
Grosse Hamburger Strasse 5-11

Saint Hedwig's Hospital) was the first Catholic hospital in Berlin. It was realised by Berlin architect Albert Kinel after plans by Vincenz Statz, the Cologne Cathedral master builder who erected the hospital for the Order of the Sisters of Mercy. Their patron saints still survive in the form of sculptures on the facade of the core building facing the courtyard. Various extensions were added right up until 1928.

Sophienkirche

Church of Sophia

Johann Friedrich Grael; Kurt Berndt
1712,
1732–34;
1903–05
Grosse Hamburger Strasse 29

The Sophienkirche was donated to the parish of Spandauer Vorstadt by the Prussian queen Sophie Luise. The tower, which can be seen from afar, was not added until 1734. The neo-Baroque building flanking the entrance side was designed by Kurt Berndt, who was also commissioned to convert the interior in 1892. Funerals took place in the cemetery until 1830. Among those buried here are Leopold von Ranke, the historian, and Carl Friedrich Zelter, the director of the Singakademie.

Ehemaliger Jüdischer Friedhof und Jüdische Knabenschule

The former Jewish Cemetery and the Jewish Boys School

1672;
1906
Grosse Hamburger Strasse 25-26, 27

The small Jewish community was expelled from Berlin in the 15th century. It was not until 1671 that another Jewish community came into existence here outside Spandauer Gate and established the cemetery by Grosse Hamburger Strasse. By 1827, the cemetery contained almost 3,000 tombs. Among those buried here were Moses Mendelssohn and Veitel Heine Ephraim, Frederick II's banker. The Gestapo ordered the complete destruction of the cemetery in 1943.
From 1942 on, some 50,000 Jews were rounded up in the Jewish Old People's Home which has not survived and the Jewish Boys School of 1906, before being deported to an extermination camp. Now a group of figures, designed by Will Lammert in 1957, and a memorial plaque commemorate this chapter of German history.

7

7

Bank für Sozialwirtschaft

Dissing & Weitling
AIS Arkitektfirma, Copenhagen
1996–97
Oranienburger Strasse 13-14

The Bank für Sozialwirtschaft (Bank of German Charity Organisations) erected its new building at the site that was once the centre of its activities. The bank was founded in the Weimar Republic during the period of high inflation in 1923. With the "assistance fund" at their disposal, the Caritas, the Red Cross, the Zentralwohlfahrtsstätte der deutschen Juden (the main charity organisation of German Jews) and other charity organisations established their own financial basis. In 1927, the bank acquired a building in Oranienburger Strasse. In 1933 it was forced into line politically, in 1943 the building was destroyed. In 1992, the Treuhand retransferred the property to the bank. The new building, with its round gable and irregular courtyard, follows the proportions of its predecessor.

Monbijoupark

Eosander von Göthe;
Walter Hinkefuß;
Agence TER, Paris
1706;
1960;
2005
Oranienburger Strasse/
Monbijouplatz

The park was named after the Lustschloss Monbijou (a pleasure-house) erected by Eosander von Göthe in 1703. It served as the summer residence of Queen Sophie Dorothea until 1757. In 1877, the newly founded Hohenzollern Museum moved into the building. It was completely destroyed during the Second World War, the collection moved elsewhere and part of it carried off as booty. A green with a children's pool was laid out on the site and opened to the general public in 1960.

The Parisian office Agence TER won combined landscape-gardening and urban-planning competition held in August 1993. Their concept aimed to implement the basic idea of creating a Spree landscape setting with terraced grounds, attractive lookouts and a continuous embankment.

8.1

Ensemble

Haupttelegraphenamt

Main Telegraph Office

1900–13
Oranienburger Strasse 73-76/
Monbijoustrasse 1/
Ziegelstrasse 20-21

In the late 19th century, the block between Monbijou-, Oranienburger-, Tucholsky- and Ziegelstrasse belonged to the German Reich Post Office. Alongside the telephone exchange (designed by Felix Gentzen) of 1926 at Tucholskystrasse 6-14 and the "Grosse Landesloge Deutschlands" (German Grand Freemason's Lodge) of 1791, the former central telegraph

office is the biggest and historically most important building here. The monumental façade of the latter building faces Monbijou Park.

Jewish Communication Center

Ensemble 8.2

The new building, which is now occupied by Jewish facilities and amenities, fills a gap left by Second World War. It is the home of restaurants and cafés, the Jewish Cultural Association and the Anne Frank Centre, and provides a meeting place for people interested in culture, the function it served until 1933.

Braun & Voigt & Partner,
Berlin
1997–98
Oranienburger Strasse 26/
Krausnickstrasse

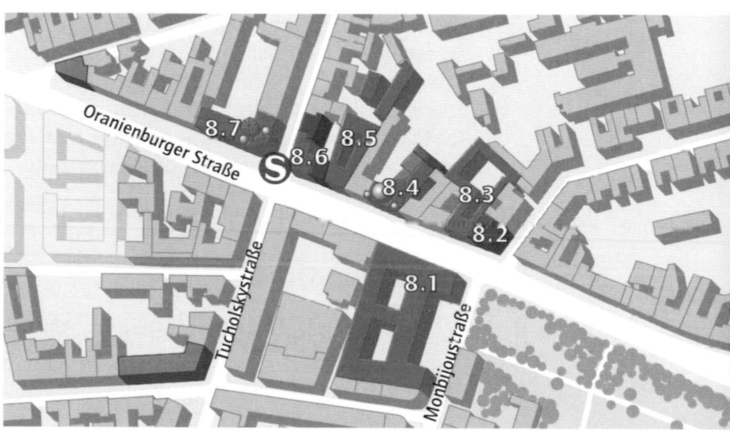

Kunsthof

Ensemble 8.3

The late-classical complex was completed between 1840 and 1866. It has been completely preserved and provides a typical example of the Berlin combination of a residential building with commercial premises located in the courtyard. After 1989, the Kunsthof Gesellschaft developed new concepts to use it as offices for those involved in artistic and creative work. Faced with dilapidation, considerable financial backing was provided by preservation society and private investors to conserve and thoroughly modernise the complex.
Café Silberstein takes up the tradition of a restaurant of 1910 bearing the same name. There are galleries and other restaurants in the courtyard buildings.

architekturbüro civitas,
Regina Bolck,
Rüdiger Reißig,
Berlin
1840–66;
1997–98
Oranienburger Strasse 27

8.4 *Ensemble*

Eduard Knoblauch,
Friedrich August Stüler;
Bernhard Leisering
1859–66;
1988
Oranienburger Strasse 30

Neue Synagoge/Centrum Judaicum

New Synagogue/Centrum Judaicum

The New Synagogue was opened in 1866. Seating approximately 3,000, it was the biggest and most splendid place of worship for Jews throughout Germany. Built in Moorish style, it was the conscious cultural expression of the established Jewish-German middle-classes. With its organ music, mixed choir and prayers in German, the synagogue was the focal point of the liberal section of the Jewish community. Its total destruction during the November pogrom in 1938 could be prevented.
The building was seriously damaged during the bombing raids of 1943. What was left of the main room had to be demolished in 1958. The golden dome – a striking feature of the cityscape – was restored in 1988; the synagogue was opened as the Centrum Judaicum in 1995. Together with Jewish institutions in the area, the Neue Synagoge is a cultural centre for exhibitions and events.

8.5 *Ensemble*

1890;
1998–99
Oranienburger Strasse 32

Heckmann-Höfe

This complex comprises a number of courtyards and extends as far back as Auguststrasse. It takes its name from the Heckmann engineering company, which had its main administration offices here. Now that it has been converted and restored, the courtyards offer plenty of space for commercial enterprises, restaurants, cafés and pubs.

8.6 *Ensemble*

Braun & Voigt & Partner,
Berlin
1997–98
Oranienburger
Strasse 33-34/
Tucholskystrasse 18-20

Wohn- und Geschäftshäuser

Residential and commercial buildings

This old building – completed in 1792 – at the corner of Oranienburger Strasse and Tucholskystrasse is one of the oldest residential buildings in Spandauer Vorstadt. It has been restored as a historical building and extended by a new building on each side. Taking their orientation from the eaves height of the existing buildings, the new structures harmonise with their surroundings. The interplay of wall surfaces and diversified window apertures structures the facades and lends the group a "rational", modernist quality.

9

Postfuhramt
Mail transport office

Carl Schwatlo, Wilhelm Tuckermann
1875–81
Oranienburger Strasse 35-36/ Tucholskystrasse

The brick building of the former Postfuhramt now dominates the intersection. Its size and prestigious character reveal just how much the postal services had gained in importance after the founding of the German Reich. In this building, the first pneumatic post system linked the most important authorities and companies in Berlin to one another. The imposing octagonal tower above the entrance corresponded with the parcel post office that once stood opposite and was built in a similar design. The facades of the two-winged Postfuhramt were adorned with terracotta designs. Allegorising the tasks of the postal and telegraph services, they also show portraits of people who had rendered outstanding services to postal, transport and technological developments. Over the years, the building has been converted a number of times. Owing to the restructuring of the postal services, it has stood empty since 1989. It is occasionally used for staging art exhibitions. No decision has been made concerning its final use.

9

Synagoge Adass Jisroel
Adass Jisroel Synagogue

Christian Dierkes, Berlin
1999–2000
Tucholskystrasse 40

On its inherited property, the Adass Jisroel community, founded in 1869, is erecting the first new synagogue to be constructed in Berlin since the Second World War. The existing front building, which was constructed in 1904 after plans by Johann Hoeniger, once incorporated the community facilities. The synagogue, which was demolished in 1967, stood in the courtyard. The synagogue community, which is committed to strictly observing tradition and the law, was forcibly dissolved by the Gestapo in 1939. The community established a new centre on its traditional site in 1989.
Christian Dierkes, the architect, has planned an octagonal structure – slightly sunken – with indirect lighting to house the synagogue with room for 300 people. It will also contain classrooms. The ritual bath Mikwe will be located in front of the synagogue and a playground in the first courtyard.

10

Feuerwache Stettin
Stettin Feuerwache fire station
1859
Linienstrasse 128-129

The Feuerwache of 1859 is the oldest surviving fire station of the regular fire brigade, which was founded in 1851. It remained in use until 1955 and now serves the voluntary fire brigade. With this station a new type of building was created that remained the obligatory model for many years to come. In an expanding city with a growing population density, fire protection could no longer be ensured by enlarging the fire brigade alone, and increasingly became the subject of building regulations aimed at fire prevention.

10

Tacheles und Johannisviertel
Tacheles and the Johannisviertel district

Franz Ahrens
1909
Oranienburger Strasse 54-56a/
Friedrichstrasse 110-112

In 1990, young artists occupied the ruin of the old department store, then facing demolition, and founded the Kunsthaus Tacheles (a cultural centre). The former "Friedrichstrasse Passage", built in 1909, linked Friedrichstrasse with Oranienburger Strasse and was one of the most important shopping arcades in Berlin, along with the Kaisergallery. New plans, due for implementation since 1996, conflicted with the desire to preserve Tacheles as a cultural centre of the so-called "off scene". A provisional agreement was reached with the investor in 1998. By the year 2003, some forty buildings are to be around Tacheles in known as the Johannisviertel district. Tacheles is to be preserved as a historical building and made available for autonomous art events for ten years for a symbolic rent of one deutschmark a month. The construction work at the Johannisviertel will see the development of the last big urban wasteland in Berlin.

11

Wohn- und Geschäftshäuser
Residential and commercial buildings

Hans Kollhoff,
Helga Timmermann, Berlin
1997–99
Friedrichstrasse 119/
Hannoversche Strasse
und Friedrichstrasse 116/
Torstrasse

Two residential and commercial buildings will border the northern entrance of Friedrichstrasse at Oranienburger Tor.
The buildings will be erected by two property developers. However, their uniform design will create visual cohesion. The individual structural elements of the western building already erected differ in both the processing of materials and the design. The residential building in Friedrichstrasse has a horizontal articulation, whilst the

11

commercial building combines vertical and horizontal articulation elements. Luxury apartments are located in the three-storey tower block. Friedrichstrasse is continued in the north as Chausseestrasse (Chaussee being the German word for country road).

Bundesministerium für Bildung und Forschung 12

Federal Ministry of Education and Research

Hans Scharoun;
Jochem Jourdan & Müller, Frankfort on the Main
1949;
1999–2000
Hannoversche Strasse 30

The attic of a residential building dating from the 19th century was converted by Scharoun into the Institute for Building in 1949. After the two separate German states were founded, the institute was incorporated into the German Academy of Building. The projects planned here included the development of Stalinallee, now Karl-Marx-Allee. Between 1971 and 1990, the Permanent Representation of the Federal Republic in the German Democratic Republic had its residence here. Since then, it has been the official seat in Berlin of the Federal Ministry of Education and Research, whose head office remains in Bonn.
The attic is to be reconstructed in accordance with Scharoun's plans. An extension, designed by the architects Jourdan and Müller, is to be completed in April 2000. The "last time the first sod was turned" for the construction work necessitated by the move of the government from Bonn to Berlin was on 12 January 1999.

Katholische Akademie, Deutsche Bischofskonferenz 13

Catholic Academy, German Bishop's Conference

Höger Hare Architekten, Berlin,
RKW Rhode, Kellermann Wawrowsky & Partner, Berlin
1998–99
Hannoversche Strasse 5/ Chausseestrasse 128-129

The Katholische Akademie is building a "cloister in the city" on the site of the first Catholic cemetery in Berlin. It was laid out in 1750, at the same time as the adjacent graveyard of the Protestant Dorotheenstädtische and Friedrichwerdersche parish. It was abandoned in 1900 and partially developed.
The Akademie, founded in 1990, aims to establish a Catholic forum in a predominantly Protestant region. The site is bordered by other old buildings along Chausseestrasse.
The striking new building for the German Bishops' Conference creates the transition to the

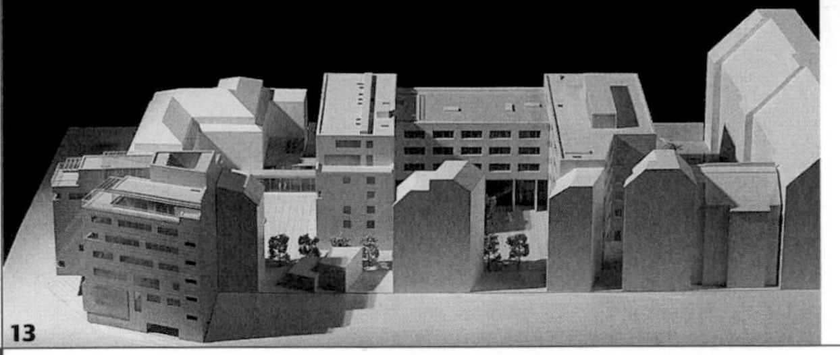
13

interior courtyard around which an administration building and a guesthouse as well as an auditorium are grouped. A small church and a garden with a cloister walk accentuate the sacred atmosphere which the complex is intended to convey.

Dorotheen-städtischer Friedhof
Dorotheenstadt Cemetery
1762;
1780
Chausseestrasse 126-127

The cemetery was laid out in 1762 outside the city walls for the parishes of the new suburbs of "Dorotheenstadt" and "Friedrichwerder". Here, artists and scholars of great importance, such as Schinkel, Rauch, Schadow, Fichte, Hegel, Brecht, Weigel, Becher, Eisler and Heartfield lie buried. The Dorotheenstädtisch-Französischer Friedhof (French Cemetery) of 1780 testifies to the great significance of the French parish. It was founded by the Protestant Huguenots, who – expelled from France – settled in Berlin in 1685 following the Edict of Potsdam. The house in which Brecht and Weigel lived after 1953 borders on the northern edge of the cemetery.

Borsighaus
The Borsig House
Reimer & Körte
1899
Chausseestrasse 13

The Borsig House of 1899 was the administrative headquarters of the mechanical-engineering company of August Borsig. It is a surviving reminder of the iron and mechanical-engineering industry that was once located here, settling outside the old city limits from 1822 on. This industry became a decisive motor of the industrialisation of the Prussian state. Along with the Royal Foundry in Invalidenstrasse, Egells, Borsig and many other industrialists established their production centres outside Oranienburg Gate. The area consequently became known as the "Birmingham of the Mark" (the Mark being a region around Berlin).

Postamt
Post office
Georg Werner
1934–36
Am Nordbahnhof 3-5/
Invalidenstrasse 29-30

The main post office serving the north of Berlin was located opposite Stettiner Bahnhof railway station. The technical equipment required for sorting and distributing the mail called for a flexible ground plan, which was made possible by the skeleton mode of construction. The mail was dispatched directly to the station through a tunnel. The travertine lining of the facade, the strict alignment of the windows and the roof cornice lend the building a monumental impact.

15

Nordbahnhof

Nordbahnhof railway station

Lüttich
1934–36
Invalidenstrasse 20-27/
Am Nordbahnhof

The urban wasteland around Nordbahnhof station used to be a lively quarter. Its character was moulded by Stettiner Bahnhof station, which was built in 1876. It was from this terminus, which was demolished in the sixties, that trains travelled to the Baltic and Scandinavia and, from 1903 on, to the northern suburbs as well. In 1934 a tunnel was built to Anhalter Bahnhof, thus linking the northern and southern lines. The Nordbahnhof railway station was built in a "rational" style.
Like the large-scale buildings for the Anhalter, Potsdamer, Görlitzer, Spandauer and Ostbahnhof stations, the Nordbahnhof also imposes itself on the city like a mighty ramp.
In 1995, an urban and landscape planning competition was held to determine the park and development conception for the former rail and track system. The winning design by Romuald Loegler (Krakow) and Martin Janotta (Berlin) provides for a landscaped park containing residential and commercial buildings as well as a sports complex. No decision has been taken as to when this project will be implemented.

14

Gedenkstätte Berliner Mauer und „Kapelle der Versöhnung"

Ensemble

15

One of the few original sections of the Berlin Wall has been left standing at Bernauer Strasse, in addition to that by the East-Side-Gallery

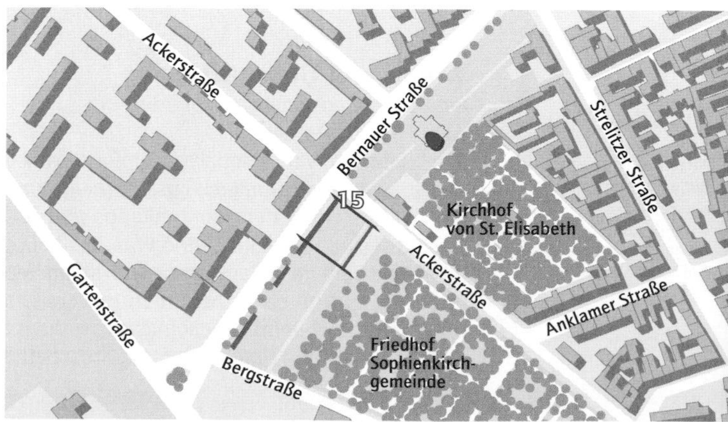

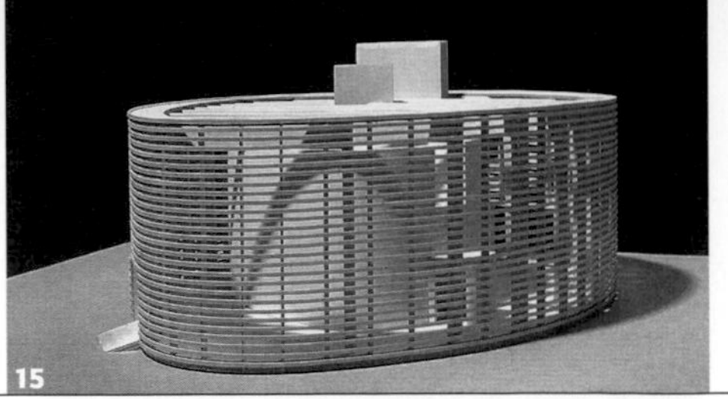
15

Kohlhoff & Kohlhoff Architekten, Stuttgart, reitermann/sassenroth architekten, Berlin
1997–98;
1999–2000
Bernauer Strasse/
Ackerstrasse/
Am Sophienfriedhof

(p. 250) and the fragment near the Martin Gropius Building (p. 77). The Berlin Wall stood along the northern border of the Sophienfriedhof cemetery and replaced the original cemetery wall in 1972. Neighbouring houses, from which many East Berliners had made spectacular escape attempts, were torn down. In 1985, the Church of Reconciliation of 1894 was demolished because it was standing in the firing line in the middle of no-man's land. The memorial centre erected here was inaugurated in 1998. The parallel walls running either side of no-man's land (referred to in West Germany as the "Todesstreifen", or "death strip") were enclosed in 7-metres-high steel walls after award-winning designs from 1993. The reflections of the polished inside surfaces seem to extend the border fortifications. The visitor can look into the inside through a small slit. In 1999, a documentation centre, whose roof provides a view of the fortifications and steel walls, is opened at Bernauer Strasse 111. The construction of a small "Chapel of Reconciliation" on parts of the ground plan – which has been uncovered again – of the destroyed Versöhnungskirche (Church of Reconciliation) will complete the ensemble. It will stand as a sacred building in the middle of what was once no-man's land. The oval chapel, which is situated in the middle of Hussitenstrasse, combines two building elements. The interior also contains an oval, non-supporting, solid core building made of compressed clay. The core structure is visible from the outside through a light, transparent, wooden slat facade. The inner structure will hold about 100 people and contain the wooden altar screen from the Versöhnungskirche.

16

Wohn- und Geschäftshaus

Residential and commercial building

Architektengemeinschaft Birgit Hansen, Barbara Kellig, Berlin
1995–96
Brunnenstrasse 31/
Anklamer Strasse

The seven-storey residential corner house, which also provides for commercial use in the ground floor, closes a gap between buildings that has existed since the Second World War. The house has a light-coloured, plain facade with staggered upper floors. The eaves height corresponds to that of the neighbouring buildings. A penthouse with a cantilevered sloping roof accentuates the corner.

„WeiberWirtschaft" 17

Inken Baller, Berlin
1993–96
Anklamer Strasse 38-40

"WeiberWirtschaft" ("Women's Business") is a centre for women wanting to found enterprises. It comprises renovated old buildings as well as a new residential and commercial building. The German-wide cooperative, founded in 1987, aims to promote the economic, social and cultural interests of women; only women can become members and tenants. After it had been acquired from the Treuhand in 1992, the residential building, which was erected in 1860, and the courtyard building, which used to house a pharmaceuticals factory constructed around 1910, were sensitively renovated and refurbished to accommodate traders, service companies, a restaurant, flats, studios and a child day-care centre. The architect, Ms. Inken Baller, designed a new residential and commercial building facing onto the street.

Zionskirche
Church of Zion
August Orth
1866–73
Zionskirchplatz

The Zionskirche was built as an ex voto church following the assassination attempt on King Wilhelm I in Baden-Baden in 1861. It marks a rise in Rosenthaler Vorstadt and can be seen from each of the five streets converging here. The lavishly adorned brick building takes up the tradition of Schinkel. The high tower dominates the urban setting. In the former German Democratic Republic this church, like so many others, served as a melting pot for opposition groups. Its "Environmental Library" became an important source of unofficial information in East Germany.

„Stadtresidenz am Weinbergpark" 18

Urban residential complex at Weinbergpark

Maier–Voigt–Wehrhahn, Berlin
1997–99
Veteranenstrasse 10-13

This complex consists of a group of new houses and three old buildings, which enclose a triangular inner courtyard. The new group, which comprises five houses, extends well into the Volkspark (people's park). Most of the flats, which vary in size, look onto the park. There is a small child day-care centre at the south-east corner. The old buildings, which are under a preservation order, were constructed in 1875 and have recently been modernised. An apartment at Veteranenstrasse 11 has been preserved in the lavish state in which it was furnished by the sons of the founder of a major furniture store in 1934.

19

Neue Brunnenhöfe

Richard Bloos;
Abelmann & Vielain Architekten, Berlin
1908–09;
1991–96
Brunnenstrasse 181

The Brunnenhöfe courtyards are an exemplary instance of the conversion of former commercial enterprises – in this case a furniture factory – into service-industry centres. The structure of the complex, whose four courtyards are faced with white scumbled brick facades, has been preserved in its original form. The complex is listed as a historical building. Its principle user is the library of the Berlin Mitte district in the historical centre. The new buildings blend into the old. A foyer designed in a modern filigree steel-and-glass structure in the third courtyard provides access to the library complex. The old silo for wood shavings in the second courtyard has been converted into a staircase tower.

Ehemaliges Warenhaus Jandorf
The former Jandorf Department Store
Lachmann & Zauber
1903–04
Brunnenstrasse 19-21

The corner house with the vertically articulated natural-stone facade represents the typical turn-of-the-century department store. Adolf Jandorf, the pioneer of the department store in Germany, also founded the KaDeWe department store in 1907. The Art Nouveau building accommodated the central fashion institute of the GDR.

St. Elisabethkirche
Church of St. Elisabeth
Karl Friedrich Schinkel
1832–35
Invalidenstrasse 3/
Elisabethkirchstrasse

Schinkel designed a large number of churches for the growing suburbs in Berlin. They served as architectural models for other churches. The Church of St. Elisabeth owed its singular appearance to its clear, simple forms. After the Second World War, it remained a ruin. There are endeavours to have the church reconstructed.

„Ackerhalle"
"Ackerhalle" market hall
Hermann Blankenstein
1886–88
Invalidenstrasse 158/
Ackerstrasse 23-26

The architect Blankenstein held the post of municipal building surveyor from 1872-96. Hardly anyone had such an impact on contemporary building in Berlin as Blankenstein with his simple, "rationally" designed buildings. Apart from numerous schools, churches and hospitals, he was also responsible for constructing a grand total of 14 market halls. The "Ackerhalle" standing in the inner courtyard of a block of houses was restored in 1990-91.

Route 2 ends at Rosenthaler Platz S-Bahn station.

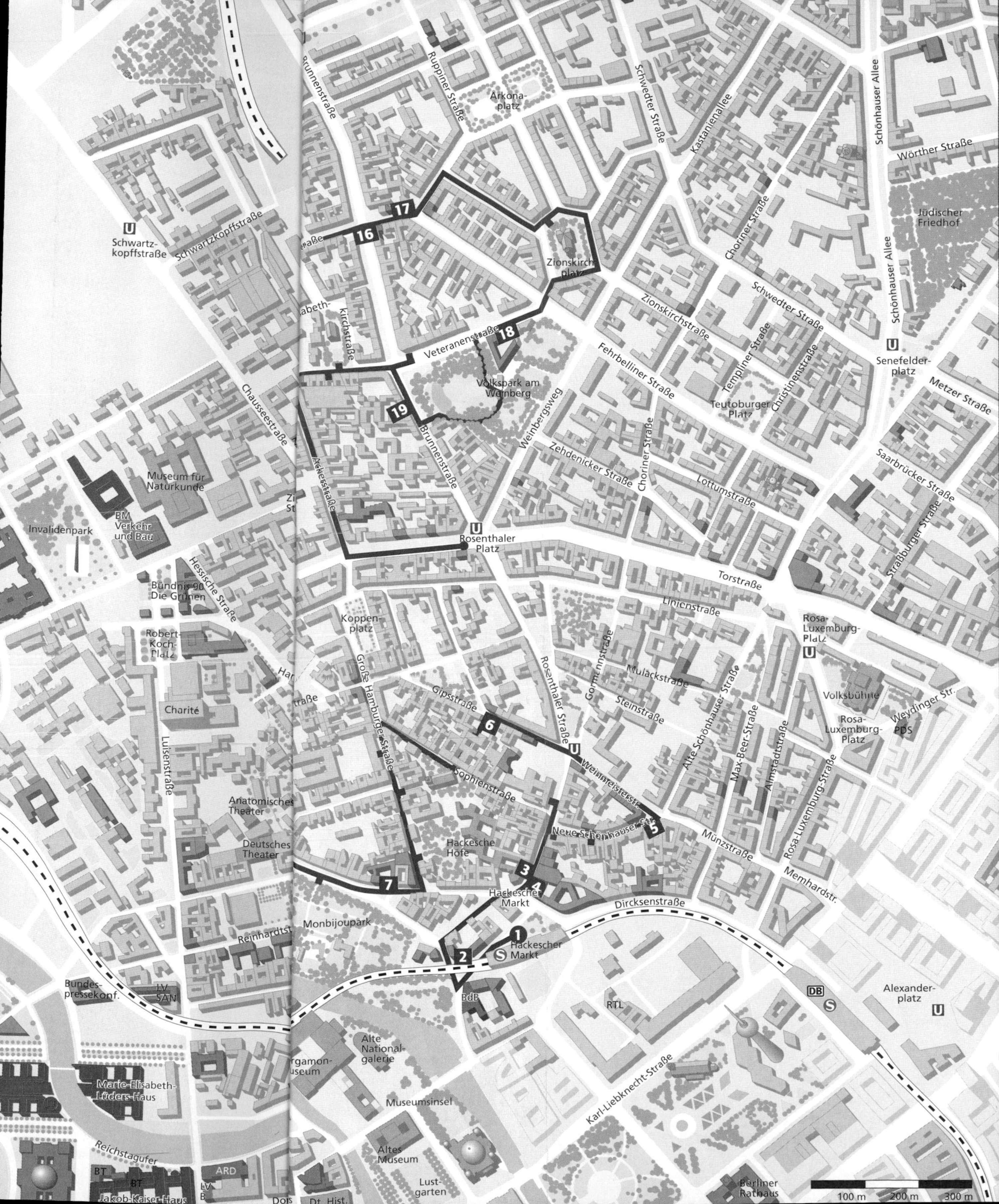

Route 2
Brunnenstraße
Ruppiner Straße
Arkonaplatz
Schwedter Straße
Kastanienallee
Schönhauser Allee
Wörther Straße
Schwartzkopffstraße
Schwartzkopffstraße
Jüdischer Friedhof
Zionskirchplatz
Choriner Straße
Zionskirchstraße
Schwedter Straße
Templiner Straße
Christinenstraße
Senefelderplatz
Veteranenstraße
Volkspark am Weinberg
Fehrbelliner Straße
Weinbergsweg
Teutoburger Platz
Metzer Straße
Chausseestraße
Ackerstraße
Brunnenstraße
Zehdenicker Straße
Choriner Straße
Lottumstraße
Saarbrücker Straße
Museum für Naturkunde
Invalidenpark
BM Verkehr und Bau
Rosenthaler Platz
Straßburger Straße
Torstraße
Hessische Straße
Bündnis 90 Die Grünen
Koppenplatz
Linienstraße
Rosa-Luxemburg-Platz
Robert-Koch-Platz
Gormannstraße
Mulackstraße
Große Hamburger Straße
Gipsstraße
Rosenthaler Straße
Steinstraße
Volksbühne
Charité
Alte Schönhauser Straße
Max-Beer-Straße
Almstadtstraße
Rosa-Luxemburg-Straße
Rosa-Luxemburg-Platz
Weydinger Str.
PDS
Luisenstraße
Sophienstraße
Weinmeisterstr.
Anatomisches Theater
Neue Schönhauser Str.
Münzstraße
Memhardstr.
Deutsches Theater
Hackesche Höfe
Hackescher Markt
Dircksenstraße
Monbijoupark
Reinhardtstr.
Hackescher Markt
Bundespressekonf.
LV SAN
BdB
RTL
Alexanderplatz
Pergamonmuseum
Alte Nationalgalerie
Marie-Elisabeth-Lüders-Haus
Museumsinsel
Karl-Liebknecht-Straße
Reichstagufer
Altes Museum
ARD
Lustgarten
Dt. Hist. Museum
Berliner Rathaus
Jakob-Kaiser-Haus
100 m
200 m
300 m

Straße des 17. Juni
Behrenstraße
LV BY
Französische Straße
Glinkastraße
Ausstellung Bundeshauptstadt Berlin
Auswärtiges Amt
Kurstraße
EKD
Konzert-haus
IRL
SAT 1
pro 7
tv.Berlin
Jägerstraße
BM Familie
Gendarmen-markt
Hausvogtei-platz
MA
Taubenstraße
BM Gesundheit*
Reuters
BM Justiz
Mohrenstraße
Stadt-mitte
ZDH
Kronenstraße
Musikinstr.-museum
Kunstgewerbe-museum
Tiergartenstraße
ZA
IND
LV BW
A
TR
ET
Diplomatenviertel
Philharmonie
Museum für Post und Kommunikation
BG
Mauerstraße
Krausenstraße
Kammer-musiksaal
Gemälde-galerie
Kunstbibliothek Kupferstichkab.
4
Kulturforum
Staats-bibliothek
Schützenstraße
Sigismundstraße
Stauffenbergstraße
Neue National-galerie
Musical-Theater
Zimmerstraße
BM Verteidigung*
Haus am Checkpoint Charlie
Wissenschafts-zentrum
Kochstraße
Charlottenstraße
Markgrafenstraße
Axel-Springer-Straße
Reichpietschufer
Landwehrkanal
Schöneberger Ufer
Feilnerstraße
Puttkamerstraße
GdW
Besselstraße
Lindenstraße
Magdeburger Platz
Lützowstraße
Wilhelmstraße
HdV
Friedrichstraße
Berlin Museum
Franz-Künstler-Straße
Klückstraße
Potsdamer Straße
Alte Jakobstraße
19
Jüdisches Museum
Pohlstraße
Flottwellstraße
Neuenburger Straße
SPD
Kurfürstenstraße
Hebbel-Theater
18
Mehring-platz
Theater am Halleschen Ufer
Gitschiner Straße
Bülowstraße
Hallesches Tor
Waterlooufer
Mehringdamm
Blücher-platz
Zossener Straße
Johanniterstraße
Amerika-Gedenkbibliothek
100 m
200 m
300 m

Zwischen Mythos und Zukunft

Between myth and future

Route 3 takes in three phases of the more recent history of urban design and development in Berlin. It begins at the principal event of the nineties in Berlin, the development of Potsdamer Platz following the opening of the Berlin Wall. From there, it goes back in time to the Cultural Forum, which documents the urban design ideals of the '50s and '60s, namely the idea of an open-plan city, the "urban landscape". Following this excursion into the past, it once again touches on the '90s in the vicinity of Potsdamer Platz and then moves on to the attempts of the IBA 87, the International Building Exhibition held in Berlin in 1987, to reintroduce architecture to the principles of planning adopted in block developments. The route ends at Mehringplatz in the municipal district of Kreuzberg; this square is an excellent example of the way in which inspired Baroque architecture was replaced by crude and massive structures.

The controversy in 1991 surrounding the development of Potsdamer Platz marked the beginning of the reconstruction of the centre of Berlin. Under discussion were all fundamental parameters of significance in the urban development project of the century with which Berlin has been faced over the last ten years. One of the most controversial issues was the question as to whether the city of Berlin would succeed in asserting public interests against the interests of the investors. Consideration had to be given to matters of road planning such as a north-south tunnel under the Tiergarten park as well as to reducing the ratio of private cars to local public transport to 20:80 per cent in the entire city centre for ecological reasons. Potsdamer Platz was also to be made easily accessible by rail. Another point of dispute was whether Berlin was to have a new high-rise district here, which would be a counterpart to Alexanderplatz, which is the eastern boundary of the city centre, or whether it might be possible to set history aside and make a new start with radically avant-garde visions. The development at Potsdamer Platz is a compromise between these differing proposals. The homogenous development of buildings with glass facades at the Sony site is reminiscent of an "American" plaza. In contrast, the streets and buildings around the public square named after Marlene Dietrich are in keeping with the traditional conception of a "European" city. The Potsdamer Platz Arcades are a compromise between a public street and a shopping mall. And Potsdamer Platz itself is to become the focal point of the new high-rises.

The Cultural Forum is in sharp contrast. Its design reflects the efforts of the post-war generation in the '50s and '60s to replace the historical city of the 19th century, where very different forms of use were in close proximity to each other, by spatially separate "function bands" for living, working, shopping, politics and culture and to create function centres to form a new "urban landscape". The Cultural Forum in Berlin documents this approach to modern urban design, which was echoed nationally and internationally, and includes such outstanding examples of architecture as the Philharmonie, the New National Gallery and the new Picture Gallery, which was completed in 1998.

The route includes cultural and historical monuments located to the east of Stresemannstraße. The Foundation Topography of Terror and the German Museum of Technology are, in addition to the German Museum of History and the Museum of Post and Kommunications, the most important new museum buildings in the city. This is where the route encounters the architecture and urban designs of the IBA Berlin 87, which were intended to start a process of urban revitalisation in an area which had suffered neglect and decline due to its proximity to the Wall. Mehringplatz is a prime example of architecture and urban design which is largely discredited today. 30 years ago the circular, Baroque plaza was built up in order to cut the residential buildings and the square off from a motorway which was planned parallel to the Landwehr Canal.

Potsdamer Platz

Hilmer & Sattler, Munich/Berlin

The publicly sponsored "Potsdamer/Leipziger Platz competition for urban design ideas" in 1991 marked the beginning of the process of urban renewal in Berlin following the opening of the Berlin Wall. The competition provided a forum for discussion on the fundamental principles of city design at the end of the 20th century. It attracted international attention as none of the densely built-up capitals and large cities of Europe and America offered this unique opportunity of completely redeveloping such large and vacant areas which were also centrally located. Added to this, was the legend of Potsdamer Platz, which was renowned as Europe's busiest city square in the '20s. With the exception of two buildings (Weinhaus Huth and Grandhotel Esplanade), no building structure from that time had survived.

The competition area covered 480,000 square metres from the triangular Lenné site in the north to the Landwehr Canal in the south. It included Leipziger Platz and Potsdamer Platz and was bounded on the west by the Cultural Forum, thereby defining a new urban district between Berlin-Mitte and the City West. Some of the investors, among them the Daimler-Benz automobile group, had already decided to locate at this central site in 1989 before the opening of the Berlin Wall.

16 architecture offices from all over the world were invited to submit entries for the competition. The principal challenge they faced was to develop a "use mixture" of shopping and leisure, culture and business, residential accommodation and office space in order to allow the site to develop into a "metropolitan centre" with "round-the-clock" vitality and to avoid monostructures. The Cultural Forum, an example of modernist urban design of the '50s and '60s and a gateway to the City West was to be linked to the new district.

In 1991 the competition was decided in favour of the office Hilmer & Sattler. The architects had proposed dense, medium-height development in keeping with the style of the "European city", i.e. buildings approximately 35 metres high, streets, alleys and squares. Only directly at Potsdamer Platz itself did they propose setting architectural accents with high-rise buildings of up to 90 metres high. A conscious decision was taken

1

against an Americanising city of high-rises or a radically avant-garde new type of city in favour of homogenous master planning which essentially reflected the historical layout of Potsdamer Platz and Leipziger Platz. After heated public debate, the design of Hilmer & Sattler prevailed over a design by the English architect Sir Richard Rogers, which was financed by Sony and Daimler-Benz.

1

Regionalbahnhof Potsdamer Platz

Potsdamer Platz regional railway station

Hilmer & Sattler,
Munich/Berlin,
Hermann + Öttl,
Modersohn & Freiesleben
Architektengemeinschaft,
Berlin
1997–2000
Potsdamer Platz

The new subterranean Potsdamer Platz station which is on three levels will link the regional railway service with the underground and city rail networks. In contrast to the old Potsdamer Platz station, which characterised the entire area until World War II, today only two cubic steel and glass structures indicate the existence of the subterranean railway station. The regional railway services run on the lowest level in a north-south direction through the new Tiergarten tunnel between Gleisdreieck and Lehrter Bahnhof station. It is served by the inner platforms, while main-line services pass through on the outer tracks. The passerelle which lies at a higher level serves as a concord and access to the shopping arcades located on the Daimler Benz site. The glazed platforms of the planned new underground line 3 (Wittenbergplatz-Weißensee), located at a higher level and diagonal to the lines of the main-line and regional services, provide a view of the structure of the station as a whole.

2.1 *Ensemble*

Delbrück-Haus

Delbrück Building

Kollhoff & Timmermann,
Berlin
1998–2000
Potsdamer Platz/
Ebertstrasse

The high-rise building of Delbrück, a private Berlin bank, dominates the triangular Lenné site on the north side of Potsdamer Platz; the staggered height of the building provides a transition from Ebertstrasse and the other tower buildings. It also provides a counterpart to the tower building of similar design on the Daimler Benz site, designed by the same architect. The building seems – although its entire facade is of light-grey natural stone – to consist of a number of sections. It is structured by a variety of facade grids and

window sizes. Doors and windows are faced with bronze. The first nine stories will be office space, the next nine will be apartments. The uppermost storey, which has a vertical profile, contains the technical installations of the building.

Lenné-Dreieck

Lenné-Dreieck site

2.2 Ensemble

Ebertstrasse/
Lennéstrasse

The Lenné-Dreieck, the triangular site between Ebertstrasse, Bellevuestrasse and Lehrter Strasse, has only been part of the municipal district of Tiergarten since 1988 and was a piece of wasteland until the opening of the Berlin Wall. Although not enclosed by the Wall, it was officially part of East Berlin. The urban master plan by Hilmer & Sattler envisages mixed development for this site. Two main buildings are planned in the south part; of these the Delbrück Building is already under construction. The long strip on the west is to be developed by the department store group Karstadt AG. Five freestanding buildings are planned on Lennéstrasse.

Bundesverband Öffentlicher Banken Deutschlands, Deutscher Landkreistag

Federal Association of Public Bank, German County Councils Association

2.3 Ensemble

Lennéstrasse will be the site of the westernmost of five buildings planned to house the national headquarters of two German institutions. The

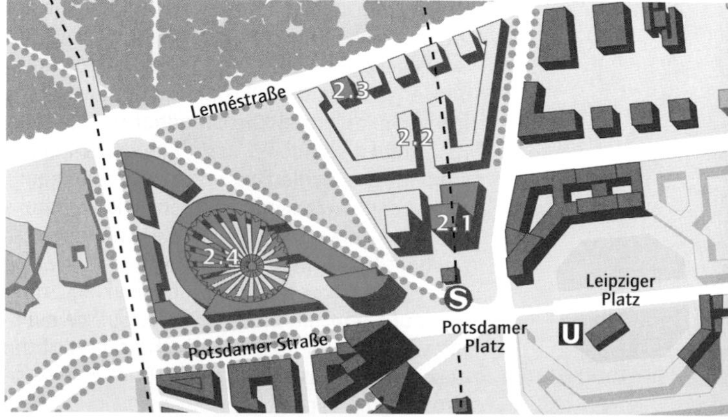

2.4

Edwin Effinger,
WEP Effinger Partner,
Berlin/Munich
1998–2000
Lennéstrasse 1

two institutions which were founded in Berlin in 1916, the Federal Association of Public Banks and the German County Councils Association, will return to Berlin. The lower five stories will house the offices behind light facades with large window areas.

2.4 *Ensemble*

Sony-Areal

Sony site

Helmut Jahn,
Murphy/Jahn Architects,
Chicago
1996–2000
Potsdamer Strasse/
Bellevuestrasse

The Sony Center by the German-American architect Helmut Jahn is located on a triangular site. Its homogenous design in steel and glass provides an antithesis to the variety of the Daimler development. The Sony urban design has provoked sustained debate on its merits. The ensemble, which is made up of a number of building structures with glass facades, is grouped around an oval public forum (Sony Plaza). The oval roof structure of steel cables and rods, which requires no supporting mast and appears to float above the Forum, is a feat of construction engineering. The tent-like roof, under which lengths of fabric are stretched, is supported by steel cables radiating from a ring beam attached to the buildings surrounding the Forum. The Forum has been conceived as an urban entertainment center with cinemas, restaurants, shops and cafés. It is dominated by the 25-metre high IMAX 3D-screen. The Forum is surrounded by seven buildings containing offices, apartments, the Berlin Filmhaus which houses the German Mediatheque, and the European headquarters of the Japanese electronics group Sony. Three Berlin institutions of significance, the Film and Television academy, the Cinematheque and the Arsenal Cinema are located in the Filmhaus. The building located on Bellevuestrasse housing the Esplanade Residence Apartments will span the remains of the former luxury hotel, the Grandhotel Esplanade. Its "Breakfast Room" and "Emperor's Salon", which are classified as historical monuments, have been extensively restored. The Emperor's Salon, which weighs 1,300 tonnes, was moved as a whole by 75 metres in 1996 by means of a spectacular translocation undertaking using hydraulic principles. The 26-storey office building which is 103 metres high, the tallest of the ensemble, stands on Potsdamer Platz on a semicircular ground plan.

Henriette-Herz-Park

Henriette Herz Park, located to the north of Bellevuestrasse, leads to what was once Kemperplatz, the starting point of the imperial Siegesallee, which also no longer exists; this boulevard was once lined by magnificent residential buildings and adorned by a Roland fountain. The new park is named after Henriette Herz, who had a famous salon in Berlin in the early 19th century. The park forms part of the stretch of green which links the Tiergarten park with the Tilla Durieux Park (see p. 74) and the park located to the south at Gleisdreieck. Following a landscape architecture competition, it will be designed by a Dutch architecture office, which was also commissioned to create the Tilla Durieux Park. In the '80s this was the terminus of the test route of a magnetic railway which began at Gleisdreieck.

DS Landshapsarchitekten
Bruno Doedens,
Maike van Stiphout,
and S. Koren, Ouderkerk
1999–2002
Lennéstrasse/
Bellevuestrasse

Kulturforum
Cultural Forum

4.1 *Ensemble*

The Cultural Forum is one of the most important designs for new urban development in Berlin since World War II. The planning idea is based on the urban design proposals by Hans Scharoun dating from 1946 and 1957. These envisaged specific areas of the city for specific functions. The area was conceived as an urban landscape, an antithesis to the regularity of the city of the 19th century, which was seen to be uniform. Building of the Philharmonie in 1963 may be

Potsdamer Strasse

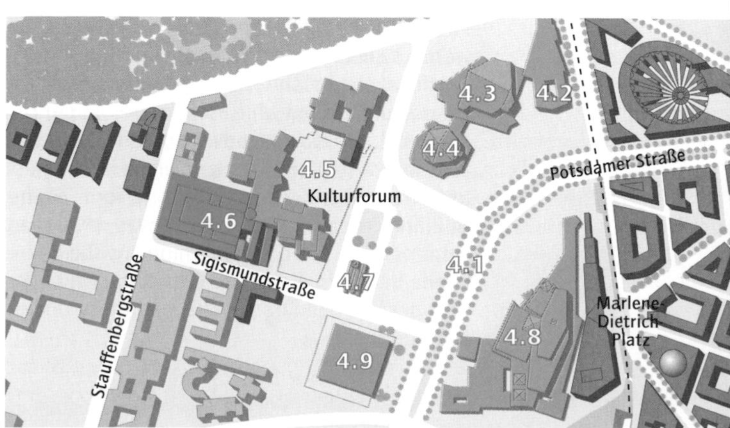

seen as the foundation stone of the Cultural Forum. The Philharmonie and the Chamber Music Concert Hall, which was completed in 1987, offered those living in West Berlin a replacement for the concert halls no longer available to them after the Berlin Wall was built. The development which was included in Scharoun's plan and realised was supplemented after 1968 by further new buildings designed by Rolf Gutbrod. The Munich architects Hilmer & Sattler assumed responsibility for master planning in 1988.
Following the redevelopment of Potsdamer Platz and Leipziger Platz, the Cultural Forum has been given a new urban context. The two districts are to complement each other through their differences.

4.2 *Ensemble*

Musikinstrumenten-Museum

Museum of Musical Instruments

Edgar Wisniewski,
Hans Scharoun
1978–84
Tiergartenstrasse 1

Wisniewski, who was an assistant of Scharoun for many years, designed the building from a freehand sketch by Scharoun. The Institute of Music Research forms an annexe to the museum.

4.3 *Ensemble*

Philharmonie

Philharmonic Hall

Hans Scharoun
1960–63
Herbert-von-Karajan-Strasse 1

It was originally planned to build the Philharmonie in Schaperstrasse in the municipal district of Wilmersdorf. The decision to build it at Kemperplatz was taken in 1959. Scharoun, the leading protagonist of organic architecture, designed a building which has attracted much acclaim; its sweeping silhouette and gold-anodised facade were a symbol of West Berlin for many years.
The focal point of the Philharmonie is the orchestra podium around which seating for audiences of up to 2,200 is arranged in ascending tiers. The tent-like ceiling, the shape of which is recognisable from outside, and the entire form of the building reveal that its exterior was developed from its interior. The Philharmonie is the home of the Berlin Philharmonic Orchestra, which for decades has been one of the best of its kind in the world.

4.6

Kammermusiksaal
Chamber Music Concert Hall

4.4 *Ensemble*

The Chamber Music Concert Hall designed by Edgar Wisniewski complements the Philharmonie. In keeping with the underlying idea for the Philharmonie, namely that music should form the focal point, seating for audiences of up to 1,200 is grouped around the stage where the musicians perform. The Philharmonie and the Chamber Music Concert Hall are linked with each other by a foyer.

Edgar Wisniewski
1984–88
Matthäikirchplatz/
Herbert-von-Karajan-Strasse

Kunstgewerbemuseum, Kunstbibliothek, Kupferstichkabinett
Arts and Crafts Museum, Art Library, Collection of Drawings and Prints

4.5 *Ensemble*

The architect Rolf Gutbrod was commissioned in 1968 to complete the Cultural Forum. He designed the Arts and Crafts Museum and a diagonally ascending piazzetta to link it to the new Art Library and the Collection of Drawings and Prints. The design also included an exhibition hall. However, of his designs only the Arts and Crafts Museum, the shell of the Art Library and the piazzetta were realised.

Rolf Gutbrod
1978–85
Matthäikirchplatz

Gemäldegalerie
Picture Gallery

4.6 *Ensemble*

Following general widespread criticism of the Gutbrod planning, Hilmer & Sattler assumed responsibility for completing the Art Library, the Collection of Drawings and Prints and the exhibition hall which can be reached from the inclined piazzetta. The Picture Gallery, which was opened in 1998, completed the western side of the Cultural Forum. This architecturally interesting building is an appropriate setting for one of the most precious collections of paintings in the world. In contrast to the architectural "individualists" of the Cultural Forum, the Philharmonie and the New National Gallery – free-standing buildings which are impressive when seen from a distance –, the interesting feature of the Picture Gallery lies in its interior – a hall made up of three branches. The hinge between the Picture Gallery

Hilmer and Sattler
with Partner T. Albrecht,
Berlin/Munich
1992–98
Matthäikirchplatz 8

4.9

and the central main entrance on the piazzetta is a rotunda with a glass cupola which is expressionist in style. An area between Tiergartenstrasse and Stauffenbergstrasse, behind the other museums, has been set aside for the sculpture collection of the state museums. The project has been postponed indefinitely for the time being.

4.7 *Ensemble*

St.-Matthäus-Kirche
St. Matthew's Church

Friedrich August Stüler
1844–46
Matthäikirchplatz

St. Matthew's Church was the only building at this site to survive demolition work carried out by the National Socialists in 1939 to make way for the monumental buildings for Germania (see p. 17). The church suffered extensive damage during the Second World War.

4.8 *Ensemble*

Staatsbibliothek
National Library

Hans Scharoun,
Assistant:
Edgar Wisniewski
1967–76
Potsdamer Strasse33

The tall, gold-anodised book stockroom of the National Library forms the eastern boundary of the Cultural Forum. The reading rooms of the building are much lower and have an extensive window front. Following Scharoun's death in 1972, the project was completed by his pupil and assistant to many years, Edgar Wisniewski. The building was constructed across the original route of the old Reichsstrasse 1, Potsdamer Strasse. Creating access via the National Library to the buildings on Potsdamer Platz has been rejected for the time being.

4.9 *Ensemble*

Neue Nationalgalerie
New National Gallery

Ludwig Mies van der Rohe
1965–68
Potsdamer Strasse50

The New National Gallery, the only museum building in the world designed by Mies van der Rohe, was added to the Cultural Forum in 1968. This commission gave him a reason to return from exile to Berlin, the place of his early work. He created a modern temple of art in steel and glass on a massive base. Its underlying form is a contemporary adaptation of the architecture of the Old National Gallery on the Museum Island. The monumental steel roof is supported by eight slender steel supports and appears to float over

the base of the building. The separation of inside and outside space has been reduced to a glass membrane.

Wissenschafts-zentrum Berlin
Berlin Centre of Sciences
August Busse;
James Stirling,
Michael Wilford
1891–94;
1984–87
Reichpietschufer 48-58

James Stirling, at the time the leading British architect of post-modernism, designed the Science Centre for the International Building Exhibition in Berlin in 1987. With a collage of different historical types of building such as a columned hall, a fortified tower, a church and an amphitheatre it extends the old building which was once the Reich Insurance Office. The original building, which was built by August Busse in 1894, once housed the administration of the compulsory sickness, accident, invalidity and pension insurance schemes which date from the social security legislation enacted by Bismarck in the 1880s.

Daimler-Benz-Areal
Daimler-Benz site

5
Ensemble

1993–98
Potsdamer Strasse/
Linkstrasse

In 1992 Daimler-Benz AG invited proposals for designs to be realised on its site. The basis of planning was the urban design for "Potsdamer/Leipziger Platz" by Hilmer & Sattler. 14 architecture offices were invited to submit designs for the 75,000 square-metre site bounded by Linkstrasse to the east, Schelling-

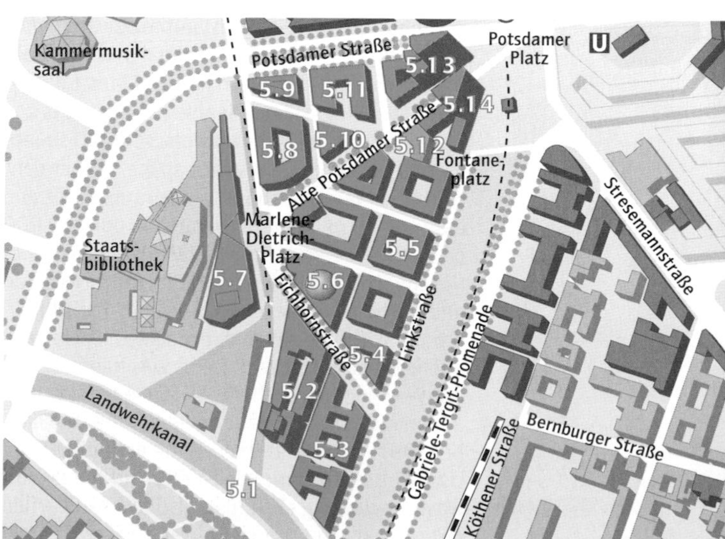

strasse to the west, Potsdamer Platz to the north and the Landwehr Canal to the south. The competition brief required a design which would develop the Daimler-Benz site into a link between the Cultural Forum and the new business district being built at Leipziger Platz. There was heated debate between the municipal authorities and the investors on the issue of converting public roads into private enclosed space (a mall) and ultimately this was only done in the area of the Arcades.

The competition was won by the architects Piano/Kohlbecker; their entry succeeded in creating a link between the free-standing buildings of the Cultural Forum and the disciplined block development envisaged by the plan of Hilmer & Sattler. The focal point of the design was what is now Marlene-Dietrich-Platz and the element water, which provides a reference to the nearby Landwehr Canal in the form of a large expanse of water in an artificial basin planted with reeds. By giving the Platz public and cultural functions, they provided the old Potsdamer Strasse, which had become a cul-de-sac when the National Library was built in 1968, with a new function.

On the central areas of the site they made use of the historical road system and a number of new streets and small squares to develop an intricate complex consisting of a total of 19 blocks designed by different architects. The architectural ensemble is given height by the debis high-rise (90 metres) in the southern part of the site by the Landwehr Canal and two high-rises designed by the architects Hans Kollhoff and Renzo Piano. The useable floor space of the Daimler Benz site, which totals 340,000 square metres, is 50 per cent office space, 30 per cent cultural amenities, shops, restaurants, cafés and bars and 20 per cent residential. Around 10,000 people will eventually live or work in this part of the city. The Potsdamer Platz city railway station and the new Mendelssohn Bartholdy Park underground station provide direct access to the local public transport system. Debis was the first company to move here when it opened its new administrative offices at its head office in October 1997. In order to reduce the volume of road traffic above ground, deliveries and removal of waste including all refuse disposal are carried out centrally via the Tiergarten tunnel. The call

5.2

for buildings which use ecological principles has largely been met by the utilisation of rainwater, combined co-generation for the Potsdamer Platz air-conditioning control unit in Stresemannstrasse (see p. 75), heat insulation and optimal use of daylight.
Daimler-Benz chose leading international artists to enhance the sculptural landscape of Berlin. The open spaces contain "Boxer" by Keith Haring, "Ballon Flower" by Jeff Koons, "Riding Bikes" by Robert Rauschenberg and "Galileo" by Mark di Suvero.

George-C.-Marshall-Brücke

George C. Marshall Bridge

Ensemble 5.1

gmp von Gerkan, Marg & Partner, Hamburg
1996–98
Reichpietschufer

The new bridge over the Landwehr Canal is named after George C. Marshall, the American Secretary of State who instituted financial help for Europe (Marshall Plan) after the Second World War. The steel structure serves as a feeder and intersection between the north-south traffic and east-west traffic. As in the case of the other bridges crossing the canal, the adjacent roads have been elevated to achieve the headroom necessary for shipping to pass underneath.

debis-Hauptverwaltung

debis head office

Ensemble 5.2

Renzo Piano, Paris,
Christoph Kohlbecker, Gaggenau
1994–97
Reichpietschufer/
Schellingstrasse/
Eichhornstrasse

The slender, tall headquarters of the debis head office is topped by a green cube, which is the company's trade-mark. It has been placed on the funnel which serves as the ventilation shaft of the Tiergarten tunnel. The two elongated wings of the administrative building encompass the public, glass-covered cathedral-like atrium, which is 90 metres long, 14 metres wide and 33 metres high. It also serves as an exhibition area. "Méta-Maxi" by Jean Tinguely, "Light Blue" by François Morellet and "Nam Sat" by Nam June Paik are on exhibit. A remarkable feature of this ensemble is the design of the facade: shimmering transparency by the Landwehr Canal, gradually giving way to ochre-coloured, terracotta tiles of ever decreasing size on the long sides, uniformly stone at the centre. The facade makes use of upward warm air currents to provide the building with natural ventilation, thereby reducing energy costs.

5.3 *Ensemble*

Büro- und Geschäftshaus
Office and commercial building

Steffen Lehmann, Berlin, and Arata Isozaki, Tokyo
1994–98
Linkstrasse

The head office of the Berliner Volksbank consists of two parallel rectangular blocks which are not exactly opposite each other; they are intersected by Schellingstrasse. The two blocks are linked by five three-storey bridges. The central conference room arches outwards high above the Landwehr Canal. The completely flat facade is structured by slanting window reveals and coloured ceramic sections. A part of the narrow strip between the blocks is to be planted with greenery and laid out as a garden. Originally, this building was considered as the seat of the Federal Ministry of the Interior. The Berliner Volksbank who now uses the Building, abandoned its plans for a new building in Charlottenburg.

5.4 *Ensemble*

Wohngebäude „Grimm-Haus"
"Grimm-Haus" residential building

Ulrike Lauber, Wolfram Wöhr, Munich
1995–98
Eichhornstrasse/
Linkstrasse

The "Grimm-Haus" building consists of two rectangular blocks, which – like the office building to the south – have a north-south alignment. They are joined by a flat tract on the south side and a higher one on the north side. The building, which is faced with reddish terracotta tiles, accommodates apartments, shops and a children's day centre.

5.5 *Ensemble*

Bürohaus
Office building

Sir Richard Rogers, London
1995–98
Linkstrasse

The three office, commercial and residential buildings designed by the British architect Sir Richard Rogers face the new park on Linkstrasse to the south of the small square named Fontaneplatz. The unusual design of the facade – staggering in the inner courtyards and round towers inserted into the building's corners which have been cut open – was chosen to provide the rooms at the front with good lighting and to accommodate large shops and businesses on the lower floors. All office and residential areas have daylight and windows which can be opened. The green inner courtyards are intended to improve the residential quality of the building and the quality of the air.

Kino Big Screen, IMAX 5.6

Big Screen Cinema

Ensemble

The cinema building at Marlene-Dietrich-Platz is characterised by the cupola of the projection room. It was created in a spectacular engineering feat by applying layers of cement to an inflated balloon. The cinema has a number of different screening techniques at its disposal. The auditorium has a screen of over 550 square metres. Projection onto the interior of the cupola – an area of 950 square metres – creates three-dimensional effects.

Renzo Piano, Paris,
Christoph Kohlbecker,
Gaggenau
1995–98
Marlene-Dietrich-Platz/
Eichhornstrasse

Musicaltheater, Spielbank 5.7

Musical Theatre, Casino

Ensemble

The Musical Theatre and the Casino form the western boundary of the Daimler site. And, at the same time, their elongated form and gleaming silver-grey facade provide a reference to the gold-anodised facade of the National Library and to the Cultural Forum beyond. Both buildings have glazed foyers facing Marlene-Dietrich-Platz. Their jutting porches cover a small square, which can also be used as a place for performances. The walls of the National Library are visible as a background through a narrow slit between the two buildings.

A proposal to create access from here to the Cultural Forum via the National Library has so far been rejected.

Renzo Piano, Paris,
Christoph Kohlbecker,
Gaggenau
1996–98
Marlene-Dietrich-Platz

Hotel Grand Hyatt 5.8

Ensemble

The first hotel to be opened in Germany by the American luxury hotel chain follows in the tradition of the once flourishing hotel district around Potsdamer Platz. The facade of red sandstone stands out against the light colours of its surroundings. In addition to 340 rooms and suites, conference facilities and a ballroom with a capacity of 800, the hotel has a fitness centre and a swimming pool on the roof terrace.

José Rafael Moneo, Madrid
1995–98
Marlene-Dietrich-Platz 2

5.9 *Ensemble*

José Rafael Moneo, Madrid
1995–98
Potsdamer Strasse

Mercedes-Benz Zentrale

Mercedes-Benz AG head office

Following completion of the building in August 1998, parts of the headquarters of the automobile group Mercedes-Benz moved from Stuttgart to Berlin. The building has a covered atrium, which can be seen from outside through a incision in the facade on Potsdamer Strasse.

5.10 *Ensemble*

Ulrike Lauber,
Wolfram Wöhr,
Munich
1995–98
Alte Potsdamer Strasse/
Voxstrasse

Wohngebäude

Residential building

The eleven-storey residential building lies to the south of the cinema complex on a triangular site. Like most of the buildings on the Daimler site it has small shops on the ground floor. The top two stories are set back, thereby creating space for an extensive roof terrace on the tenth floor.

5.11 *Ensemble*

Ulrike Lauber,
Wolfram Wöhr,
Munich
1995–98
Potsdamer Strasse/
Voxstrasse

Kino Cinemaxx

Cinemaxx Cinema

The complex has 19 cinemas and a total capacity of 3,500. The entrance on Voxstrasse has been designed as a foyer, the cinemas for audiences of between 50 and 600 are in the basement and on the first floor. The International Berlin Film Festival will be held here and at the neighbouring Musical Theatre from 2000 on. The name of the street is reminiscent of the Voxhaus; it was from this building that the first radio broadcast was made in Germany in 1923.

5.12 *Ensemble*

Heidenreich & Michel;
Renzo Piano, Paris,
Christoph Kohlbecker,
Gaggenau
1910–11;
1996–98
Alte Potsdamer Strasse

Weinhaus Huth

The former premises of the wine merchants Huth, which is characterised by its cupola, is the only building to have completely survived the Second World War and the subsequent demolition of buildings at its original site in the once so densely settled area. Today this building documents the original route of the old Potsdamer Strasse. Extensive structural alterations were necessary to convert and enlarge the cellars to create underground access to the regional railway station and the shopping mall. The building houses again a wine shop and also a restaurant.

Büro- und Geschäftshaus

Office and commercial building

5.13 *Ensemble*

Renzo Piano, Paris,
Christoph Kohlbecker,
Gaggenau
1995–99
Potsdamer Platz

The 18-storey office building defines Potsdamer Platz on the triangular plot between a new park and Alte Potsdamer Strasse, forming the gateway to the Daimler-Benz site. As in the case of the debis building the facade is faced with ochre-coloured terracotta tiles in order to give the buildings a uniform appearance. The angular glass corner of the building underlines its transparent appearance, which is in contrast to the dark clinker of the building opposite. The two wings of the building, which line the street in descending steps, provide a transition to the adjacent buildings.

Büro- und Geschäftshaus

Office and commercial building

5.14 *Ensemble*

Hans Kollhoff, Berlin,
with Jasper Jochimsen
1995–99
Potsdamer Platz 1

Together with the neighbouring Sony high-rise the northern head building of the Daimler-Benz site forms the gateway to Potsdamer Strasse. The pointed corner of Hans Kollhoff's building, which has a triangular ground plan, has an observation platform on the top storey (88 metres) overlooking Potsdamer Platz and Leipziger Platz. The wings, which have a west alignment, descend like a flight of stairs in two steps to 38 metres. The facade of dark-blue clinker and granite is structured by sections – the upper section soars upwards vertically, the middle section is like a lattice, the lower section gives the appearance of breadth.

Verkehrsturm Potsdamer Platz

Potsdamer Platz rostrum

5.15 *Ensemble*

1924–25;
1997
Potsdamer Platz

The traffic-lights rostrum erected on Potsdamer Platz in 1925 was the first set of traffic lights in Europe. The model originated from New York and had been adapted for conditions in Berlin. Each of its five sides faced one of the roads which led to Potsdamer Platz. The light signals were aligned horizontally and were operated by a traffic policeman positioned in the "look-out". A vertical alignment of signal lights became compulsory in Germany only one year later in 1926. While this made the rostrum essentially redun-

7

dant, it rapidly became a symbol of the fast-moving pace of life in Berlin. In 1997 financing was made available for a reconstruction, which was built as a joint work by trainees from a number of companies. It was originally located on Leipziger Platz and will be moved to its ultimate location on Potsdamer Platz in 1999.

6

Tilla-Durieux-Park

DS Landshapsarchitekten,
Bruno Doedens,
Maike van Stiphout,
Ouderkerk
1998–2000

The park, named after the famous actress Tilla Durieux, is located on the tracks of the former Potsdamer Bahnhof station, which was demolished in 1958. The park links Tiergarten with the green areas to be laid out at Gleisdreieck. Plans were drawn up in the 1980s to convert the open piece of wasteland where Potsdamer Bahnhof station once stood into a park. This planning was incorporated into the 1991 Potsdamer/Leipziger-Platz competition to find urban design ideas. An international landscape design competition held in 1995 was won by the Dutch landscape architects Bruno Doedens and Maike van Stiphout. They designed the entire length of the narrow strip as an earth sculpture with various angles of inclination. The park provides the new city district with an important fresh air corridor, which extends from Tiergarten in the north to the park to be laid out on the present location of the building site logistics company and other corridors further south in the city.

7
Ensemble

Park Kolonnaden am Potsdamer Platz

Giorgio Grassi, Milan,
Diener & Diener Architekten, Basel,
Architekten Schweger & Partner, Hamburg/Berlin,
Jürgen Sawade, Berlin
1996–2001
Potsdamer Platz/
Gabriele-Tergit-Promenade/
Köthener Strasse

The site of the Park Kolonnaden to the east of the new Tilla-Durieux-Park was also covered by the 1991 "Potsdamer/Leipziger Platz" competition to find urban design ideas. Its development is in keeping with the criteria set by Hilmer & Sattler. The Italian architect Giorgio Grassi was commissioned to create master planning. He proposed a strictly disciplined and symmetrical sequence of five buildings; only the northern head building and the southern residential building deviate from the rational H-shaped ground plans. The head building on Potsdamer Platz (Schweger & Partner) reflects the rounded form of "Haus Vaterland", a famous place of enter-

tainment in its day (designed by Paul Schwechten in 1912), and has direct access to the underground station from its foyer. The adjacent three office buildings (Grassi, Sawade) are linked with the head building by a passage. All three buildings including the entirely residential building designed by Diener & Diener are faced with redbrick.

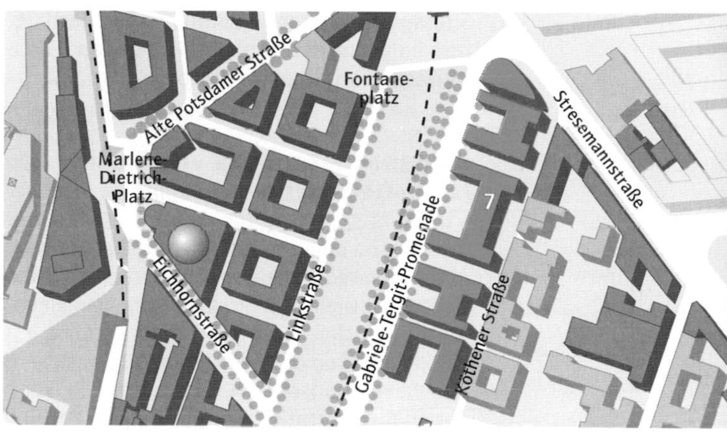

Umspannwerk und Kältezentrale Potsdamer Platz

Potsdamer Platz substation and cooling centre

Hilmer and Sattler
with Partner T. Albrecht,
Berlin/Munich
1995–96
Stresemannstrasse 126

The central energy plant which serves Potsdamer Platz consists of a substation and a cooling center. Environment-compatible electricity is generated at the central combined heating and power plant of the municipal district of Mitte (see p. 191) and fed to Stresemannstrasse via the electricity grid. The innovative central production of cooling for the air conditioning of the office complexes, which uses absorption cooling units to transform heat generated at the Mitte combined heating and power plant into air conditioning supplied from a central point, means on balance lower energy consumption in the form of centrally operated air conditioning systems. The design of the facade in red-brown and dark-blue – red for heat and blue for cooling – underlines the differing functions. Modern technology and noise insulation have made it possible to integrate the utility building into the urban development.

9

Bürohaus „Stresemann 111"

"Stresemann 111" office building

Alsop & Störmer Architekten,
Hamburg/London
1996–98
Stresemannstrasse 111

The office building closes a gap which existed for many years in the proximity of the Berlin Wall. The facade and its integrated fluorescent tubes are reminiscent of the city architecture of the '20s and provide a contrasting night view of the building. The adjacent old building in Dessauer Strasse 1-2, designed by Bruno Schmitz in 1906, is slightly reminiscent of Art Nouveau and, since its restoration, is also an office building.

10

Abgeordnetenhaus von Berlin

House of Representatives of Berlin

Friedrich Schulze;
Jan and Rolf Rave,
Marina Stankovic,
Walter Krüger, Berlin
1892–1899;
1991–93
Niederkirchnerstrasse 5

In 1993 the deputies elected to the parliament of the reunited Federal state of Berlin met in the building of the former Prussian state parliament for the first time. Hardly any other building is a better reflection of German history.

The Revolution of 1848 led to the Prussian national constitution, which envisaged parliament in the form of an upper chamber and a house of representatives. Both chambers were, in view of the fact that the Prussian monarchy protracted construction of new buildings, forced to hold their sittings in provisional buildings in Leipziger Strasse for many years. Despite numerous plans, no decision to erect new buildings was taken until 1889. Once building work was completed, each chamber had its own prestigious seat in adjacent buildings. The first sitting of the Prussian state parliament was held in the central assembly room in January 1899. The facades of the free-standing cube were designed in the style of the Renaissance with columns and gables.

State elections held in 1932 saw the NSDAP emerge as the strongest parliamentary party. Following Hitler's appointment as Chancellor, the last sitting of the house of representatives was held in May 1933.

The parliament which was elected in free elections in 1947 was, despite the fact that the war damage to the building had been removed, unable to use it as the city was facing imminent division. Government of the city was split into the (West) Berlin house of representatives at Rathaus Schöneberg (Schöneberg Town Hall) and the (East) Berlin city council at the Stadt-

11.1

haus (City Hall). No permanent way of using the seat of the former Prussian state parliament, which was next to the Wall, could be found. It was only after the Berlin Wall was opened that this prestigious building was completely restored and modernised. The design of the forecourt by Regina Poly, a Berlin landscape architect, is strictly modern in form.

Mauerreste, Mauerstreifen
Remains of the Wall, strip marking the course of the Wall
Niederkirchnerstrasse

The Berlin Wall was built in August 1961 and improved upon and made more secure in the years that followed. Following the opening of the Wall on 9 November 1989 and German unification on 3 October 1990, it was removed virtually in its entirety, parts of it being recycled for use as road-metal. A number of sections which bore paintings or graffiti were acquired as historical documents by museums and galleries around the world. For months souvenir hunters ("Wall woodpeckers") chiselled out pieces and splinters.
As a reminder of the division of the city, the course of the Wall, which followed the historical boundaries of the city's municipal districts, is marked by a red asphalt line at certain points in the city. Artistic works to mark the course of the Wall were tried out in Niederkirchnerstrasse in 1994 as an extension of the section of the Wall still standing adjacent to the site of the "Topography of Terror". "Inlaid work in concrete" lies next to the "copper strip". A double row of cobblestones at the intersection of Niederkirchnerstrasse and Wilhelmstrasse marks the position of the Wall.

Martin-Gropius-Bau
Martin Gropius Building

Ensemble 11.1

Martin Gropius,
Heino Schmieden;
Hilmer & Sattler & Albrecht, Berlin/Munich,
with Volkhausen & Lubkoll
1877–81;
1998–99
Niederkirchnerstrasse 7

The Martin Gropius Building, which today is named after its architect, was built as an arts and crafts museum. The design of the interior and of the reliefs and mosaics on the facade made the building a place of interest for the craft industry in Berlin. The building suffered serious damage during the Second World War and was only saved in 1966 due to the intervention of the grandnephew of its architect, the founder of the Bauhaus Walter Gropius. The building was threatened by demolition to make way for an urban motorway until the '70s. Since its restoration

11.2

between 1977 and 1981 by Kampmann and Weström and the first exhibitions held there – the Schinkel Exhibition in 1980 and the Prussia Exhibition in 1981 –, the Martin Gropius Building has been one of the city's most renowned exhibition venues. The course of the Berlin Wall made it necessary to move the main entrance from the north to the south side of the building. Alterations to the building have been carried out by Hilmer & Sattler & Albrecht since 1998. The main entrance will once again be on the north side from May 1999 on.

11.2 *Ensemble*

Peter Zumthor, Haldenstein
1997–2001
Niederkirchnerstrasse 8

„Topographie des Terrors"

Foundation Topography of Terror

Between 1933 and 1945 the National Socialist command centres which spread terror across Europe were located on the site of the "Topography of Terror". The headquarters of the secret police (Gestapo) and the security service of the SS, which were merged in 1939 to form the central security organisation of the Reich, were located at the Prinz Albrecht Palais, the Prinz Albrecht Hotel (1888) and the former school of arts and crafts (1905) on Niederkirchnerstrasse. The buildings, which were bombed out in the Second World War, were levelled after 1950. The first proposals to build a memorial which would draw attention to the historical significance of the site were made in 1980. A citizens' action group uncovered the remains of the cellars of the former Gestapo prison in 1986. As part of the events to mark the 750th anniversary of

Berlin in 1987, the Berliner Festspiele arranged a temporary exhibition at this authentic site, which provided graphic documentation on the way that people throughout Europe were kept under surveillance, persecuted and murdered. Following a competition held in 1996, the Foundation Topography of Terror is to have a new administrative, documentation and exhibition centre designed by the Swiss architect Peter Zumthor. The long building of rows of concrete supports joined by sections of glass stands on the remains of the cellars of the former headquarters of the Gestapo in the Prinz-Albrecht-Hotel. The building is to be opened in 2001.

Wohnhaus

Residential building

Zaha Hadid, London
1993–94
Stresemannstrasse 109/
Dessauer Strasse

The residential building was designed by Zaha Hadid, an Anglo-Iranian architect. With its angled wall and window areas and its metal facade it is an expression of the radically avant-garde architectural movement of deconstructivism which was the subject of international debate in the '80s and '90s as the successor to Modernism in architecture in the 20th century. Zaha Hadid was commissioned to design this building as part of the 1987 International Building Exhibition in Berlin (IBA 87). The southern part of Friedrichstadt, which had degenerated into an urban and social marginal area following the building of the Wall in 1961, was, in addition to the Tiergarten district, the most important development area. The prime aim of the IBA 87 was to revive the urban mix of residential, work, leisure and cultural aspects.

Deutschlandhaus, Europa-Haus

Ensemble 11.3

Bielenberg & Moser;
Otto Firle
1926;
1928–35
Stresemannstrasse 90-92

Following a competition held in 1924, the architects Bielenberg & Moser were commissioned to develop the west side of the Prinz Albrecht site. The Deutschlandhaus was the first building to be realised (1926). Otto Firle has built the Europa-Haus complex in 1928 as one of the first office high-rises in Berlin. The functional building opposite what was once a busy station (Anhalter Bahnhof) served as a gateway to the city of Berlin. The building was damaged during the Second World War and rebuilt in 1960; it has been the second official seat of the Federal Ministry of Economic Cooperation since 1996.

12

12

Büro- und Wohnhaus am Askanischen Platz

Office and residential building at Askanischer Platz

HPP Hentrich-Petschnigg & Partner KG, Berlin
1996–97
Askanischer Platz 4/ Schöneberger Strasse

The new office and residential building stands on a corner site at Askanischer Platz, which was once the forecourt of the old Anhalter Bahnhof station. The clear, cubic building has differing facades: the facade facing Schöneberger Strasse has french windows, while the one facing Askanischer Platz is structured horizontally by large office windows.

Anhalter Bahnhof
Anhalter Bahnhof station
Franz Schwechten, Heinrich Seidel
1875–80
Askanischer Platz 6–7

Anhalter Bahnhof station was once one of the largest railway terminuses in Europe. The only evidence of its former magnificence which still remains is the entrance gateway. The building containing the platforms, which suffered bomb damage during the Second World War, remained operational and could have been restored. Its demolition 1959-61 was a loss for the cityscape of Berlin. The facade of the building, which was designed by Franz Schwechten and completed in 1880, was lavishly decorated in brick and terracotta. The platforms were covered by a large hall, which was designed by the engineer and writer Heinrich Seidel. Together with Potsdamer Bahnhof station, Anhalter Bahnhof station was the main form of access to the city centre of Berlin and the starting point of routes which led to southern and western Germany and Europe.

13

Tempodrom

SL Sonderkonstruktionen and Leichtbau, Leinfelden-Oberaichen, with Frei Otto, Munich
2001

The site of what was once Anhalter Bahnhof station and was unused for many years is the new location of "Tempodrom", a venue for alternative music and theatre. "Tempodrom" was established in 1980 and quickly earned itself an excellent reputation. Originally located at Potsdamer Platz in what was once a circus tent, Tempodrom moved to a location next to the Kongresshalle in Tiergarten in 1984 and was forced to move again in 1999 to make way for the new Federal Chancellery building. The envisaged new structure was planned by Frei Otto of Munich, a pioneer in the design and building of marquees and

13

lightweight buildings (designer of buildings for the 1972 Olympic Games in Munich). The design envisages two arenas for audiences of 3,000 and 500 persons respectively. An open-air arena able to accommodate up to 800 persons will be let into the ground. The boundaries between inside and outside areas will be flexible. The "Liquidrom", a salt-water pool as a place for events and the "Eurodrom" as a multi-media arena will make entirely new cultural events possible. The structures fully fulfil the criteria of ecological building.

Hochbunker

Overground air-raid shelter

1943

Schöneberger Strasse

Numerous air-raid shelters were built both below and above ground in Berlin from 1941 on. This building programme was intensified following Joseph Goebbels' call for "total war" in 1943. Despite this the air-raid shelters would only have been able to accommodate six per cent of the population. Following the Blockade of Berlin (1948-49) food ("government stocks") was stored here until 1989 for any future emergencies.

Internationale Bauausstellung Südliche Friedrichstadt

International Building Exhibition southern Friedrichstadt

Josef Paul Kleihues, Nalbach + Nalbach, Haus Rucker & Co., Kohlmaier/Sartori

1987–90

Schöneberger Strasse

The purpose of the IBA 87 (International Building Exhibition) was to save the southern part of Friedrichstadt from further decline by building more housing and enabling a variety of commercial and business uses. In order to accomplish this aim, approximately 80 per cent of the property in the area was bought by the city. This made it possible to construct modern buildings in a variety of sizes as part of a publicly subsidised housing programme. An almost entirely new district came into being between Schöneberger Strasse and Köthener Strasse. Proposals for solutions to urban design and architectural problems were worked out by a group of eminent German and international architects headed by the Berlin architect Josef Paul Kleihues. The adjacent Mendelssohn-Bartholdy-Park is located on the site of Schöneberg docks which were built in 1850 and filled in in 1960.

Ehemalige Pumpstation, „Lapidarium"

Former pumping station, "Lapidarium"

What is now known as the "Lapidarium" was the first pumping station in Berlin's sewer system to go into operation in 1876 following its complete modernisation. James Hobrecht, a pioneer in urban development, had devised a new radial system of sewers which revolutionised hygiene

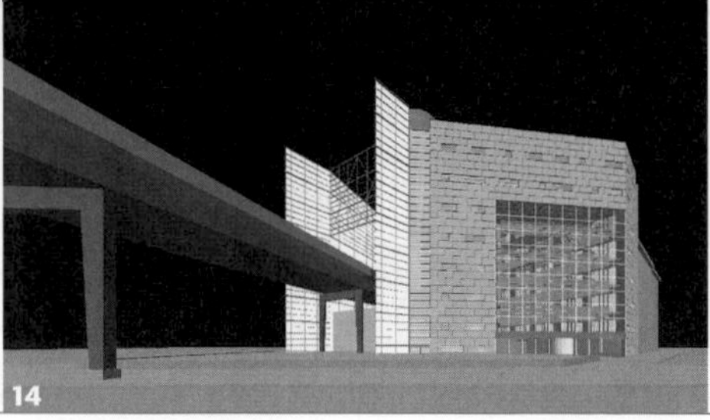
14

James Hobrecht
1873
Hallesches Ufer 78/
Schöneberger Strasse

and sanitation in the city. With the assistance of the physician Rudolf Virchow, he had developed a mixed system which made it possible to separate the supply of drinking water from the disposal of waste water. He divided the city into twelve segments from which the waste water flowed to the pumping stations along sewers which followed the natural slope of the land. The pumping stations pumped the water to the sewage farms located outside the city. The water was cleaned thanks to the filter effect of the ground and then fed back into the ground water. The technical installations of the pumping station are still intact. The building is classified as a monument to technology. Its functions were taken over by a modern pumping system in the adjacent building in 1972. Since 1978 the pumping station has served as a storage place for the stone sculptures which once stood on Siegesallee and, hence, has been given the name "Lapidarium".

Ehemalige Königliche Reichsbahn-Direktion

Former Royal Railway Administration

Armin Wegener;
Richard Brademann
1892–95; 1929–38
Schöneberger Ufer 1-3/
Schöneberger Strasse 14-15

The building became the headquarters of the Royal Railway Administration in 1895. A modern extension was added to the redbrick building in German Renaissance style by the chief architect of the State Railways, Richard Brademann, in 1929. After 1945 the complex was used as a hospital of the state-owned railways. Today it houses the administrative offices of the DB-Immobilien GmbH, a property company of the German Railways.

14

BVG Bürogebäude

BVG Office building

Joachim Ganz, Berlin
1997–99
Tempelhofer Ufer 30

Until the Second World War Gleisdreieck was a symbol of Berlin's modern transport network. Today it is still an underground and overground intersection of water, road and rail traffic and the trains of the elevated railway once again pass through the sea of houses.
The new building designed by the Berlin architect Joachim Ganz for the BVG, Berlin's public transport company, is intended to give Gleisdreieck its earlier symbolic significance; the building flanks the route of the railway with two tall, illuminated pylons, which effectively emphasise the railway. The main facade of the office building has a glass atrium facing the Landwehr Canal.

Deutsches Technikmuseum Berlin 15

German Museum of Technology, Berlin

Ulrich Wolff, Helge Pitz, Berlin
1995–2000
Trebbiner Strasse 10-15/
Tempelhofer Ufer

The German Museum of Technology has, after Deutsches Museum in Munich, the most important collection documenting the history of the technology of the industrialised era in Germany. It began as a society in 1960.
Since 1984 the Museum has been located on the site of the former Anhalter Bahnhof goods station and houses objects which were once scattered over approximately 100 different collections. Innovative technologies mean that it has been possible to make the extension building itself part of the museum's exhibits. The building was conceived as a low-energy building. It serves as a research and demonstration object for a number of institutes. Natural light is not only used as a source of energy but, with the help of mirrors and glass cables, also provides lighting for the exhibits. The entire load-bearing structure and the technical installations are visible for didactic reasons. A "Candy Bomber" from the Berlin Blockade in 1948/1949 is to be mounted on the roof of the glass section of the building by the Landwehr Canal as an eye-catcher. Two exhibition floors of different heights house the shipping and a further two the aviation collections. The southern tract contains the archives, the libraries and administrative offices. One section has been inserted into the load-bearing structure at the point where the railway lines pass underneath.

Baulogistikzentrum Potsdamer Platz 16.1

Ensemble

Building logistics centre for Potsdamer Platz

The vast concentration of building projects between Potsdamer Platz and Lehrter Bahnhof station made precise co-ordination of building work and transportation vital. For this reason, the state of Berlin and the investors formed a building logistics company – Baulogistik GmbH – in 1993. The northern logistics centre at Lehrter Bahnhof railway station is responsible for organising supplies by rail and private roads as well as via the Landwehr Canal and the Spree for the Spreebogen and government district in the northern part of Friedrichstadt; the southern

16.1

logistics centre is responsible for Potsdamer Platz. The result is that supplies can be brought in and waste materials removed without placing excessive strain on the environment and the city. Transporting 17 million tonnes of excavated earth and 16 million tonnes of cement and building materials by lorry would have led to completely chaotic traffic conditions. All materials which are transported by rail to or from a central point are put into interim storage at terminals and processed further. Each logistics centre has its own cement making facilities. A train unloading station was built for part-loads, sections of cranes, machinery, facades, equipment and fittings. Materials are supplied to their ultimate destination or removed by lorries. Traffic is navigated by satellite from a central control centre. The sites of the logistics centres will be put to another use or developed after the building work has finished. The Technical University of Berlin has compiled a scientific study of the work of the logistics centres. The experience and insights gained are to be made available internationally to building projects on a similar scale.

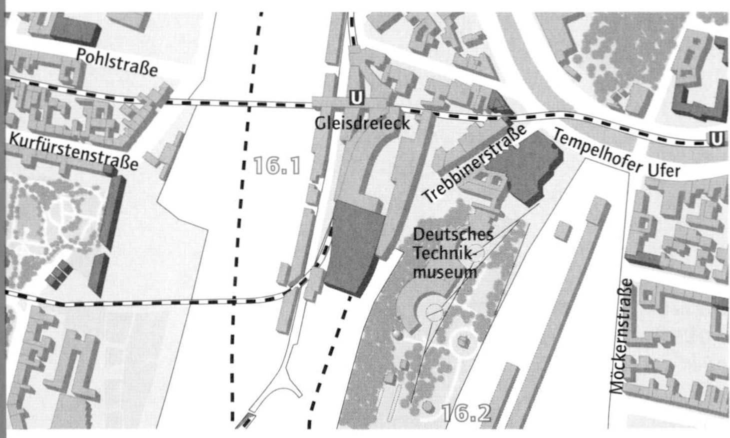

16.2

Parkgelände Gleisdreieck
"Gleisdreieck" park

Möckernstrasse/
Yorckstrasse/
Dennewitzstrasse

The 60-hectare site between the Landwehr Canal and Yorckstrasse to the south is to become a large municipal park. It will derive its character from the historical transport structures at Gleisdreieck with the elevated railway track as well as the routes of the city and main-line railways. This

was once the place where the lines from the Anhalter Bahnhof and Potsdamer Bahnhof yards and goods stations came together. After demolition of the stations and the building of the Wall, an inner-city biotope developed on this site. In 1990 it was considered as a potential site for the Federal Horticultural Show.

Familiengericht

Family court

17

The building of the family court encompasses and extends an old building in Möckernstrasse dating from 1921. The new building was designed by the Cologne architect Oswald Mathias Ungers. It consists both structurally and in terms of design of geometrical variations of the square. The facades are characterised by square windows, the strict grid of the main facade is interrupted by a cube projection. In keeping with its function as a family court, there is a small kindergarten on the forecourt. The sculpture in front of the court building by the American artist Sol Le Witt reflects the geometrical structure of its architecture.

Oswald Mathias Ungers & Partner GmbH, Berlin
1993–95
Hallesches Ufer 62-64/
Möckernstrasse 124-127

Postamt Kreuzberg

Post office building in Kreuzberg

Kurt Kuhlow, Georg Werner
1933–36
Möckernstrasse 135-141/
Hallesche Strasse

The state postal service had numerous buildings erected for different sections of the postal service in the first third of the 20th century to enable it to perform its wide-ranging letter, parcel and money services.
The two-wing sorting office, built on a steel frame and with a facade of travertine is stylistically a mixture of the modern-functional and monumental forms of the '30s. The central sorting office by Kurt Kuhlow and Georg Werner was designed to deal with three million letters per day and equipped to sort them manually. Letters were dispatched via a tunnel link to Anhalter Bahnhof station.

Kindertagesstätte

Children's day-care centre

Hochbauamt Kreuzberg
1986–88
Hallesche Strasse 20-22

The clinker building on an L-shaped ground plan can accommodate 113 children. It was planned in close consultation with residents. This children's day-care centre fulfilled one of the aims of the IBA 87, namely to provide the southern part of Friedrichstadt with social facilities.

18

Grundschule Clara Grunwald
Clara Grunwald primary school
Hermann Blankenstein
1874
Hallesche Strasse 24-28

Hermann Blankenstein, the town councillor who was responsible for all public building work in the city between 1872 and 1896, built a total of 15 schools. The former Askanische Grammar School was built according to his plans. This building, which has a magnificent front section, an assembly hall and classroom tracts, defined a type of school building which remained standard for many years. Today the building serves as a primary school.

Wohnbebauung am Stadtplatz Stresemannstraße
Residential development at a square on Stresemannstrasse
Großbeerenstrasse 95/
Stresemannstrasse 35-37

The development at the square on Stresemannstrasse dates from the time of the IBA 87. The building exhibition provided a concept for the southern part of Friedrichstadt which, in contrast to the urban development of the '50s and '60s, envisaged restoration of the historical layout. Streets and squares were once again defined by perimeter block architecture and could be experienced as living space. It was not possible to realise this and some of the numerous plans dating from the IBA 87 until the '90s.

Hebbel-Theater
Oskar Kaufmann
1907–08
Stresemannstrasse 29

With his Art Nouveau design for the Hebbel Theater dating from 1908 the architect Oskar Kaufmann was able to establish his reputation as an architect of theatre buildings. Numerous prominent buildings followed; these included the Volksbühne in Mitte, the Renaissance Theater, the Komödie and the Theater am Kurfürstendamm in Charlottenburg. The Hebbel Theater suffered only slight damage during the Second World War. The building was forgotten during the '70s and was not revived until the '80s as a theatre without a regular ensemble. Since Nele Hertling became theatre manager in 1989 it has earned itself an international reputation.

18

Willy-Brandt-Haus (SPD Bundeszentrale)
Willy Brandt House (Headquarters of the Social Democratic Party of Germany)

Helge Bofinger & Partner, Wiesbaden/Berlin
1993–96
Wilhelmstrasse 140-141/
Stresemannstrasse 28

The SPD, the Social Democratic Party of Germany, was the first party to move to new headquarters following the opening of the Berlin Wall in 1989 and the decision in 1991 to move the German government and parliament to Berlin.

Its party headquarters, which were inaugurated in 1996, are named after the party's chairman of many years Willy Brandt, who was Governing Mayor of Berlin (1957-66) and Chancellor of Germany (1969-74). The party had had its headquarters in the same area until it was banned in 1933. In terms of architecture and urban development this new building is the counterpart of the building of the metalworkers' union IG Metall, which is located to the east of Mehringplatz in Lindenstrasse (by Erich Mendelsohn, 1929). The plans of the architect Helge Bofinger for the new building date from 1983 and were intended for the IBA 87, which envisaged locating national cultural and political institutions and foundations here. The characteristic feature of the triangular building is a glass-covered atrium.

Tommy-Weißbecker-Haus

Abram Mott,
Harald Schönig
1982–87
Wilhelmstrasse 9

Some of the IBA 87 projects were concerned with restoring old buildings structurally (IBA old). The Tommy Weißbecker House is named after an alleged member of the Baader Meinhof group, who was shot and killed by a police officer. During the '80s it was a prominent building in the squatting movement, which aimed to draw attention to the large number of unoccupied and dilapidated buildings in the city. It was "legalised" in 1982 and public funds were made available to the squatters to enable them to restore and repair the building. Workshops, cafés and communal facilities were included, the individual apartments merged to form larger shared apartments. The house provides homeless young people with a home and the opportunity of learning a trade.

Theodor-Wolff-Park und Umfeld

Theodor Wolff Park and surrounding area

Regina Poly, Berlin
1989–90
Franz-Klühs-Strasse/
Friedrichstrasse

The Theodor Wolff Park is named after Theodor Wolff, a journalist and politician who was persecuted by the Nazis. The park is based on plans dating from the IBA 87. When the southern part of Friedrichstadt was redeveloped, parts of the vacant areas were envisaged as public parks. The landscape architect Regina Poly has used walls lining paths, areas of lawn, playgrounds and the entrance colonnade both to indicate the daily networks of routes and also to make reference to the earlier block development.

Mehringplatz

Werner Düttmann
1966–75

Mehringplatz, formerly called Belle-Alliance-Platz, with its perfectly circular "Rondell" once represented the Baroque urban architecture of the 18th century. Together with Pariser Platz and Leipziger Platz it was one of the central prestigious squares at the gates to Berlin. It marked the southern end of Friedrichstadt and was the point at which Lindenstrasse, Friedrichstrasse and Wilhelmstrasse converged. The only evidence of this which remains is the Peace Column designed by Christian Cantian, which was erected in 1843 and topped by a figure of Victoria by Christian Daniel Rauch. The square suffered war damage and subsequently its original circular form was reduced in diameter and traced by low buildings. Behind these, residential tower blocks of up to 17 stories provide a square boundary and form the southern boundary of Friedrichstrasse. The present-day development at Mehringplatz is evidence of the architecture and town planning of the '60s. It is based on designs by Hans Scharoun, which were realised by Werner Düttmann and relates to planning for a motorway system along the Landwehr Canal which was not abandoned until the '70s and envisaged a motorway intersection with on and off ramps at Hallesches Tor.

In contrast to Pariser and Leipziger Platz – they today again form a connection between the centre and the adjacent area – Mehringplatz lost its old function as a connecting square. Traffic was shifted to Wilhelm- and Lindenstrasse as a result of the conversion.

Vom „Oktogon" zum „Rondel"

From the "Octagon" to the "Rondelle"

Route 4 covers the part of Berlin that used to be the old town of Friedrichstadt, which was created during a period of Baroque-style urban expansion during the 17th century under the Elector Friedrich III, who gave his name to the town. The area is bounded by the ingenious application of three ideas of the time on spatial division – the square, in the shape of Pariser Platz, the octagon, formed by Leipziger Platz, and the circle, at Mehringplatz (formerly Belle-Alliance-Platz) – which arose when the city was extended in 1732. Leipziger Platz is being recreated in its old form as a junction interface in the New Berlin where the octogon will once again be an elegant and distinguished gate and city square, complete with commercial buildings and the Canadian Embassy. The development at Mehringplatz, on the other hand, from the 1960s and 70s reflects the suspension of urban through traffic. The city traffic flow within Friedrichstadt towards the southern city districts of Schöneberg and Kreuzberg is now interrupted by contemporary urban development.

Route 4 begins by following Leipziger Strasse, which, prior to the Second World War, formed the industrious, well-to-do middle class backbone of Berlin's inner city area. It was a main artery for inner city life, pulsating with the flow of people from the railway station at Potsdamer Platz, in its day the busiest station in Berlin. Here could be found both the first and largest departments stores of their time as well as innumerable small shops and stores. In contrast to Unter den Linden – the prestigious boulevard running parallel to the north, divided between royal residences and civic buildings – the line of Leipziger Strasse between the octagon and Spittelmarkt was a centre for middle-class business life.

At Mauerstrasse, route 4 passes traces of the old Baroque city boundary from 1688. Mauerstrasse runs diagonally across the geometrical pattern of Friedrichstadt. In recent history – here, on the Baroque city boundary – was what used to be Checkpoint Charlie, the Allied border control point, the political frontier between the two major powers in the Cold War period. It has now been reborn as the "Checkpoint Charlie Business Centre" with offices and business premises. This is directly next to the old newspaper publishing centre of Berlin, which has regained part of its former glory through being the location of such well-known German publishers' offices as the Springer Publishing House, the Mosse Centre and the German Government Printing Office. Once you reach the eastern edge of Friedrichstadt, route 4 then follows the efforts made during the 1980s for Berlin's International Building Exhibition in 1987 (IBA 87) to reconstruct this partially destroyed historical city area. The sites had not been systematically developed after the war, and newer architectural styles were employed without attempting to recreate the shapes of the original buildings; there are examples ranging from the old streets of Alte Jakobstrasse and Feilnerstrasse, to the blooks of houses bordering the streets around the Berlin Museum, to the spectacular architecture of the new Jewish Museum, with its avant-garde style reacting to the traditional city plan.

While on route 4, you will come across two particular locations reflecting political problems characteristic of the reunified Germany. At the very start of the route, you will cross the former "Ministergärten" (the Ministers' Gardens) and Wilhelmstrasse – both of which, up until the Second World War, were the main centres of power in the German Empire. Now, the centre of government has moved to the Spreebogen and a suitable use has been found for the "Ministergärten", thanks to the majority of Germany's Laender representations taking offices in this part of the city; in addition, there are roads and paths allowing public access to it. A little further on is the second place worth mentioning in this context: the vast complex of buildings which today houses the Bundesministerium für Finanzen (the Federal Ministry of Finance), a complex burdened by its historical associations, since the Nazis used it to house their Reich Ministry of Aviation (Reichsluftfahrtsministerium). After reunification, Germany had to meet the challenge, through the confrontation with such buildings, of coming to terms with its own past and the role National Socialism played in it.

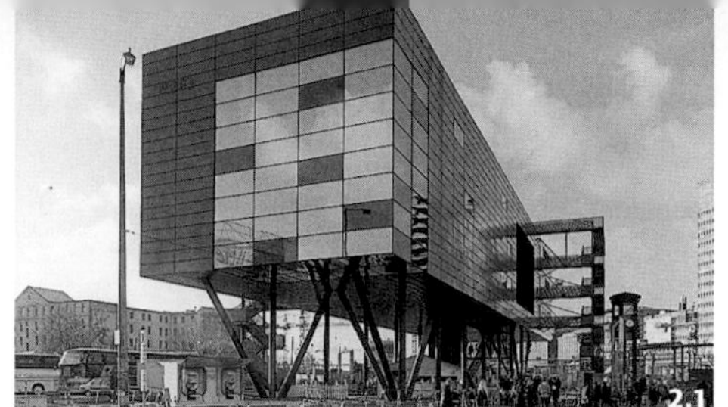
2.1

U-Bahnhof Potsdamer Platz/ Leipziger Platz

Underground Station Potsdamer Platz/ Leipziger Platz

Even in the 18th century, three squares stood out as among the most attractive in Berlin: Leipziger Platz (also known as the "Octagon"), Pariser Platz (the "Quarrée" or square) and the former Belle-Alliance-Platz (the "Rondelle"). Unlike Potsdamer Platz, which was a major intersection, Leipziger Platz was architecturally designed as a "town" square. In 1823, Schinkel built two customs houses on the city excise boundary wall, which simultaneously functioned as gatehouses separating Leipziger Platz from Potsdamer Platz. None of the buildings around Leipziger Platz escaped serious damage during the war and after 1945, when Berlin was divided, they were all completely demolished. Buildings lost in this way include those designed by Alfred Messel for the Wertheim department store.
In 1991, the architects Hilmer & Sattler won the urban-planning competition "Potsdamer/Leipziger Platz". Their design entails recreating the original shape and style of Leipziger Platz, with its octagonal form and surrounding blocks of buildings bordering the street, thereby re-establishing the narrower historical shape of Leipziger Strasse. Although Leipziger Platz, in contrast to Pariser Platz, was not planned in accordance with public planning regulations, a large degree of unity in design could be achieved through architectural competitions by invitation. In 1999, a competition is to be held to find designs to be realised on three of the sites on the south side of the square.

Info Box Leipziger Platz

Ensemble 2.1

Schneider & Schuhmacher, Frankfort on the Main
1995
Leipziger Platz 21

The red Info Box, with its viewing terrace, is a temporary structure. Inside, it contains information presented by the building authorities and investors on the rebuilding and restructuring taking place in the city, in the course of which Berlin has come to resemble a large building site. With nearly two million visitors to the Info Box each year, it is one of Berlin's most popular attractions. The Info Box design has won a number of architectural prizes and counts as one of the EXPO

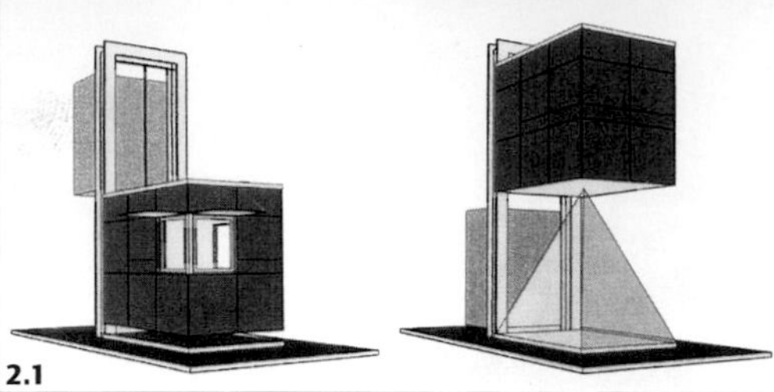
2.1

2000 projects in Berlin. Once building work starts on the south side of Leipziger Platz, (planned for 2001), the Info Box will need to be dismantled. However, it is so designed that it can be reconstructed on another site.
The multimedia "Grüne Floh" (Green Flea), created by the group "Berlin Design-Büro 213", is located underneath the Info Box. The "Grüne Floh", Berlin's answer to London's "Millennium Dome", is a main information centre on events during the period up to and around the millennium.

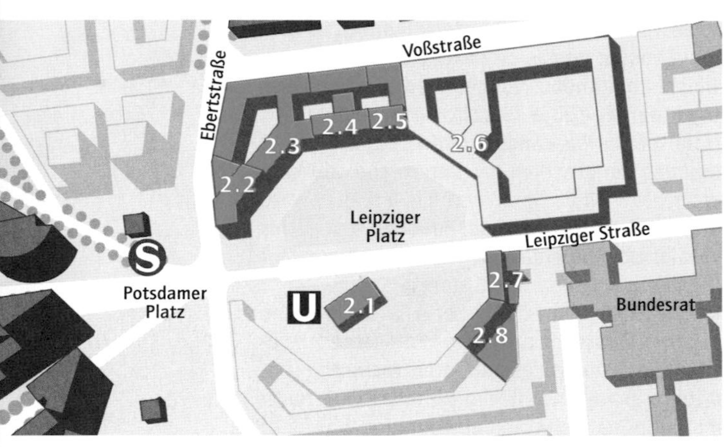

2.2 *Ensemble*

Deutsches Reisebüro

German Travel Agency Headquarters

Rave & Partner, Berlin
Building date undecided
Leipziger Platz

Designs have already been developed for the headquarters of the German Travel Agency on the north-west side of Leipziger Platz, which foresee a building following the octagonal shape.

2.3 *Ensemble*

Kanadische Botschaft

Canadian Embassy

Kuwabara Payne McKenna
Blumberg Architects,
Architectes
Gagnon, Letellier, Cyr,
Smith Carter Architects
and Engineers Incorp.,
with Vogel Architect, Toronto
1999–2001
Leipziger Platz 16-17

In March, 1999 a Canadian team of architects won the architectural competition for the Canadian Embassy.
The site is 6,000 square metres with the Mosse Palais bordering the western edge. The building is not expected to be completed before the year 2001.

Mosse Palais

2.4
Ensemble

The "Mosse Palais" takes its name from the Jewish publisher Rudolf Mosse, who used to live here. The building houses both residential and commercial premises. It fits in with the octagonal form of Leipziger Platz and is connected, via a narrow wing, to the building behind it on Voßstrasse. The building was commissioned directly from HDS & Gallagher in Boston and is now home to the American Jewish Committee.
While the building was under construction, a public debate began on how best to design Leipziger Platz as a whole. The step between the seventh and eighth floors marks what used to be the permitted building height in the square.

Hans D. Strauch,
HDS & Gallagher, Boston, USA
Dieter W. Schneider and Partner, Berlin
1995–97
Leipziger Platz 15

Geschäfts- und Wohnhaus
Residential and Commercial Building

2.5
Ensemble

There will be a further residential and commercial building adjacent to the Mosse Palais. The design by Berlin architect Jan Kleihues won the competition by invitation held in 1998.

Jan Kleihues, Berlin
1999–2000
Leipziger Platz 14

Ehemaliges Wertheim-Grundstück
Former Wertheim department store site

2.6
Ensemble

On the north-eastern corner of Leipziger Platz once stood the magnificent and imposing Wertheim department store complex, which set a new standard in large city department store architecture. It was built from 1896 on in several construction phases after a design by Alfred Messel. The building was demolished in 1958, having been badly damaged during the Second World War.
From 1996 on, Italian architect Aldo Rossi developed a typology of multiformed colourful facades, including one for the Canadian "Cirque du Soleil". However, technical and financial difficulties led to the plans being shelved in 1998, not least because the underground line U2 runs under the site and is in need of renovation. Instead of being built as part of a large scale project, the site is to be divided up into smaller sections and then developed as a new contract.

Building date undecided
Leipziger Platz/
Leipziger Strasse/
Vosstrasse

3

2.7 *Ensemble*

Walter A. Noebel, Berlin
1999–2000
Leipziger Platz 11

Palais am Bundesrat

The building under construction on the south-eastern side of Leipziger Platz will consist of offices to eaves height, and above this of apartments. The two-storey base facing Leipziger Strasse will be a colonnade.

2.8 *Ensemble*

Axel Schultes, Berlin
Building date undecided
Leipziger Platz 8-10

Bürohaus

Office block

The "Anwaltshaus" (Lawyers' House) by Axel Schultes is primarily intended to house lawyers' and notaries' offices. The design for this irregularly shaped site was chosen from those submitted in a competition by invitation. The facade is characterised by the reserved modernity evident in the large-scale use of glass and slanting windows. Vertical light vents at either end of the facade serve to separate it from the adjacent buildings. The circular conference room, complete with library, will be reached via a semi-circular foyer accessible from the courtyard.

3

Friedrich Schulze;
Architekten
Schweger + Partner,
Hamburg/Berlin
1899–1904;
1998–2000
Leipziger Strasse 3-4

Bundesrat

Upper House of the German Parliament

In 1996, the Bundesrat, the parliamentary upper chamber, decided to move, along with the Bundestag, from Bonn to Berlin. A new building, directly opposite the Reichstag parliamentary building and within the Spreebogen complex was originally planned. However, in the wake of the policy of making greater use of existing buildings, the Bundesrat voted to occupy the former Prussian parliament's upper chamber, the "Herrenhaus", and set the date for moving into building as summer, 2000.
The Prussian parliament, which had been founded in 1848 following the revolutions in the same year, consisted of an upper and lower chamber. From 1855 on, they were officially designated the Upper House and the House of Representatives. Whereas the deputies in the lower chamber were elected according to the three-class voting system, the members of the upper chamber were appointed by the monarch on the basis of aristocratic lineage. The upper house met at Leipziger Strasse 3.

The Reichstag provisionally met in a neighbouring building from 1871-94 while the present Reichstag, designed by Paul Wallot, was under construction. The Prussian parliamentary upper chamber was given a new home in 1904. The building was designed in conjunction with the adjacent Landtag, now used to house the Berlin parliament (see p. 76).
When the German Empire and the Prussian monarchy collapsed in 1918, the Prussian upper chamber ceased to have any political relevance. From 1935 on, the building was home to the "Stiftung Preußenhaus", which sought to forge a bond between the myth of Prussia and National Socialism. After being badly damaged in the war, the building was reconstructed in 1949-53 and used by the East German government to house a variety of institutions. The complex stands as a memorial to German parliamentary history and has once again found a suitable use.

Ehemaliges Ministerium der öffentlichen Arbeiten

Former Ministry of Public Works

Paul Kieschke
1892–94
Leipziger Strasse 125

Once ornately decorated, the monumental government building between Wilhelmstrasse and Vosstrasse was originally constructed as an extension to the former Ministry of Labour. As of 1921, it housed the Ministry of Transport and the main headquarters of the German railways, and after the division of Germany in 1947, it continued as the seat of the East German equivalents of these organisations. As yet, no decision has been taken on the future development of the large area between Leipziger Strasse, Wilhelmstrasse und Vosstrasse.

Bundesministerium der Finanzen

Federal Ministry of Finance

Ernst Sagebiel;
HPP International Planungsgesellschaft mbH, Berlin
1934–36;
1997–2000
Leipziger Strasse 5-7/
Wilhelmstrasse/
Niederkirchnerstrasse

In June 1994, the German Federal Ministry of Finance decided to move into what had once been the "Third Reich" Ministry of Aviation – one of Berlin's largest administrative buildings. Discussions over whether to demolish the present listed building and rebuild continued well into 1992. However, not only did the decision to utilise the existing building mean reducing costs, it was also a courageous step since it involved the Federal Republic of Germany making use of a characteristic National Socialist style building.

The architect was Ernst Sagebiel. He was office supervisor under Erich Mendelsohn, whose business he took over after Mendelsohn's emigration in 1933. On the site of the demolished Prussian War Ministry, he built the Aviation Ministry. It was finished in less than two years. A few months later he was commissioned to design the new airport complex at Tempelhof. Both of Sagebiel's designs belong to the four major examples of National Socialist monumental architecture in Berlin; the other two are the Reichsbank (central bank) and the Neue Reichskanzlei (New Reich Chancellery).

The modern steel and concrete building is extremely stable and enclosed under a regularly formed stone facade. Even while under construction, measures were taken to ensure it was sufficiently strong to withstand bombing and therefore it survived the Second World War with relatively little damage. On 7 October 1949, the official founding of East Germany took place in the banqueting hall. The building was used for various East German ministries until reunification. In the reception area, there is a Meissen tile mural designed in 1950 by Max Lingner showing the socialist construction of East Germany and replacing the original martial relief. A picture by artist Wolfgang Rüppel is set into the ground commemorating the demonstrators who marched on the building during the people's uprising of 17 June 1953. After unification, the Treuhand was housed here for its work of administering and privatising the former East German state-owned companies. The building was named the "Detlev-Rohwedder-Haus" in memory of the murdered president of the Treuhand.

Prior to the Finance Ministry move, the facade and the grounds are to be renovated; the interior with its representative large halls and more than 2,000 offices will be refurbished, leaving the valuable original interior decorations in place.

Wilhelmstraße

Viewed historically, Wilhelmstrasse forms what used to be the western border of Friedrichstadt. During the 18th century, various palatial aristocratic residences were built along the street. From 1815 on, these were increasingly taken over first by Prussian ministries and authorities, and then, after its founding in 1871, by the German Empire. The concentration of political power in this quarter led to Wilhelmstrasse becoming a synonym for the Prussian, and later, the German government. Under the Nazis, the already existing ministries and authorities were expanded – thus, the idea of world domination was given architectural expression in the new Propaganda Ministry and Ministry of Aviation as well as in Hitler's Reichskanzlei. The Gestapo was housed in a complex to the south of Niederkirchnerstrasse. After the war the East German government made use of existing historical buildings and sites for its own ministries and the part of Wilhelmstrasse lying in East Berlin was renamed Otto-Grotewohl-Strasse after East Germany's first prime minister. However, following German reunification, the name was changed back, exemplifying how the East German legacy of renamed streets has been dealt with through a return to the historical names. With the construction of the chancellery opposite the Reichstag parliamentary building, a new centre has been established for the government quarter.

Geschäftshaus WMF

WMF Building

Eisenlohr & Weigle;
Manfred Semmer,
Hilmar Deutsch, Berlin
1904–05;
1997–99
Leipziger Strasse 112/
Mauerstrasse 12

The corner building with the imposing facade was erected in 1905 for the Württembergische Metallwaren Fabrik, the WMF (Württemberg metal-ware factory). As a listed building, the restoration work has been carefully monitored to ensure that all the requirements have been fulfilled. It is a typical example of late 19th/early 20th century architecture for department-store buildings. The shape of the oval domed tower was originally echoed by other corner towers at this intersection. Above the entrance, one can still see a mosaic with the firm's monogram, logo and the emblem of the WMF, the emu. The building survived the East German government's 1969 plan for the general redevelopment of the area, which led to Leipziger Strasse being widened considerably, and it thus still follows the original line of the street. As it was decided in the mid-'90s that development was once again to follow the historical layout, part of the ground floor is to be replaced by an arcade, which will serve as a throughfare for pedestrians. The building is again a commercial building; on the roof there is a café open to the public.

7

6

Kronenkarree

Mann & Partner M+P, Munich/Berlin
1996–98
Mauerstrasse 14/ Kronenstrasse 1-7

The "Kronenkarree" consists of one pre-war building and five new ones, closing a gap left by the war and completing the block structure around the angled corner. As can clearly be seen, the old eaves height has been a point of orientation for all the new buildings; greater use has also been made of available space in the roof area through having two or three floors set back. One can see two glass-fronted floors above the sandstone covered facade, crowned by a round conference room on the roof garden.
The "Kronenkarree" contains offices and commercial premises. There are apartments on the top floors facing Mauerstrasse.

7

Museum für Post und Kommunikation

Museum for Post and Communications

Carl Schwatlo; Ernst Hake, H. Techow, Franz Ahrens; Klaus Niebergall; Henze + Vahjen, Brunswick/Berlin
1872–74; 1893–98; 1984–90; 1996–99
Leipziger Strasse 16/ Mauerstrasse 69-75

The German Post Office Museum is the oldest of its kind world-wide. It was founded in 1871-74 and was initiated by Heinrich von Stephan, the then postmaster general of the German Empire. It was initially housed in the Imperial Post Office at Leipziger Strasse 15, built by Schwatlo in 1872-74. Major extensions were carried out by Hake, Techow und Ahrens from 1893-98. Neither the building nor the collection housed within escaped World War II unscathed. From 1958 on, the GDR used the building for the East German Post Office Museum. Restoration work was not started until 1983, and was finally completed in 1999. This involved reconstructing the lavish decorations on the facade, gables, and in the central atrium. During reconstruction work, new technical communications equipment has been added to the collection, and a new section on the history of communications technology.

Abspannwerk Buchhändlerhof

Transformer Station Buchhändlerhof

Hans Heinrich Müller
1926–28
Mauerstrasse 78-80

In the courtyard areas of Mauerstrasse 78-80 stands the huge transformer station, built in 1926-28 as an extension to the second oldest power station in Berlin and now a listed building. The most characteristic feature of the brick structure is the prominent round maintenance building. After the Berlin Wall fell in 1989, the building was used as a disco.

Markierung der ehemaligen Böhmischen Kirche

8.1 Ensemble

Outline of the former Bohemian community Church

Friedrich Wilhelm Diterichs
1735–37
Bethlehemkirchplatz

Since Friedrichstadt has a network of streets which is laid out geometrically, the irregular course of Mauerstrasse, which follows the original course of the historical city wall is even more apparent. At the corner of Mauerstrasse and Krausenstrasse there once stood the church of the Bohemian community. The circular building suffered severe damage in the war and was demolished. In 1994 the remaining foundations were secured and their position was marked on the pavement by coloured cobble-stones. The sculpture by Claes Oldenbourg and Coosje van Bruggen is called "Houseball" and symbolises the meagre possessions owned by exiles.

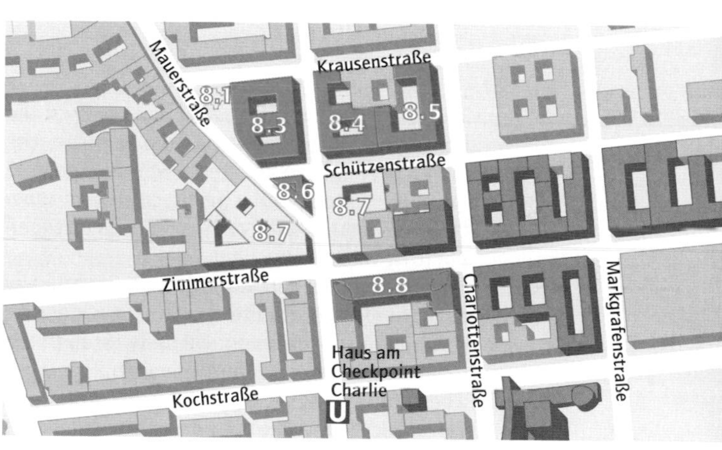

Checkpoint Charlie

8.2 Ensemble

Checkpoint Charlie is famous all over the world as a symbol of the Cold War in Berlin. After Helmstedt ("Alpha") and Dreilinden ("Bravo") it was the third checkpoint and could only be used by foreign nationals and military personnel during the time of the Berlin Wall. At the height of the Cold War in October 1961, Soviet and American tanks stood facing each other here, after the Soviets had issued a number of ultimatums challenging the Allies to leave West Berlin and to grant it status as a politically independent entity. Today, the portraits, by Frank Thiel,

8.3

of an American and a Soviet soldier are a reminder of this confrontation. They were put up in October 1998 as a part of the process of artistically restructuring the former inner-city checkpoints.
A complex of six buildings, the "Business Centre" with offices and commercial premises, was erected on the largely cleared site either side of Friedrichstrasse, those to the west being designed by American architects and those to the east by German ones. Five of these buildings form a group, built by the same developer.
The original division into small plots has been given up in favour of larger blocks of buildings, which, following the principles of "critical reconstruction", take their point of orientation from the historical street route and the Berlin eaves height.

8.3 *Ensemble*

Philip-Johnson-Haus

Philip Johnson House

Philip Johnson, New York
1994–97
Friedrichstrasse 200/
Mauerstrasse/
Krausenstrasse

The Quartier 200 office block is a result of the homage paid in Berlin to Philip Johnson, the doyen of American architects, who studied here in 1929. He took Berlin architecture, and especially the work of Mies van der Rohe, as an example to be followed.
The huge glass and stone facade is vertically structured with granite facing and windowed columns, and is given optical unity through the stone band running across it at sixth floor level. The large glassed areas inside this frame are given additional weight by being drawn forward in places in front of the building line. The building fills the whole block. The foyer lies in the centre of the structure and is accessible from any one of the four sides.
The Quartier 200 is a particularly clear example of the changes taking place in urban architectural form: Whereas there used to be numerous single buildings forming the street edge around a block and leaving the centre free as courtyards, there is now one single structure covering the total block area.

Bürohaus 8.4
Office building

Ensemble

Block 201 a, east of Friedrichstrasse, includes an office building designed by Lauber & Wöhr. The main optical feature of the building is the strong horizontal line of the steel and glass facade.

Ulrike Lauber &
Wolfram Wöhr, Munich
1996–98
Friedrichstrasse 50/
Schützenstrasse

Wohn- und Geschäftshaus „Checkpoint Plaza" 8.5
Commercial and residential building "Checkpoint Plaza"

Ensemble

The eastern part of the block at 201 b is supplemented by a residential section with shops on the ground floor.

1995–98
Krausenstrasse/
Schützenstrasse

Büro- und Hotelgebäude
Office and hotel complex

This complex dates from 1907 and consists of what used to be two parts: the former "Roter Adler" (Red Eagle) hotel on Charlottenstrasse and the office building on Schützenstasse. Both buildings are characterised by richly decorated facades in the German Renaissance style. The corner tower, embellished window surrounds and high gables have largely survived intact.

Otto Michaelsen
1907;
1999
Schützenstrasse 6-6a/
Charlottenstrasse

Büro- und Wohnhaus Triangel 8.6
Office and residential building "Triangle"

Ensemble

The "Triangle" office and residential building at the junction of Mauerstrasse and Friedrichstrasse is not part of the Business Centre complex.
It has been built along the historical route of the street and within the Berlin eaves height of 22 meters. Running across the whole of the granite-faced facade along Mauerstrasse is a glass-fronted loggia. The ground plan of the building consists of two slightly offset right-angles. Inside the relatively compact building are 94 offices and 6 roof-level apartments, each with a terrace.

Josef Paul Kleihues, Berlin
1994–96
Friedrichstrasse 204/
Mauerstrasse

9

8.7 *Ensemble*

Bürohäuser
Office buildings

David Childs, New York (design),
Skidmore, Owings & Merrill SOM, New York
Jürgen Engel (design),
Kraemer, Sieverts & Partner, Frankfort on the Main
1999–2001
Friedrichstrasse/
Zimmerstrasse

Work on the two remaining new office buildings at Checkpoint Charlie will begin in 1999. David Childs, working for SOM, has designed the building on the western corner of Friedrichstrasse and Zimmerstrasse with a round tower to emphasise the line of the corner. This is echoed by the circular courtyard of the building opposite, to the east, designed by Jürgen Engel. This will be the future site of the "Schauplatz Checkpoint", a museum tracing the history of the area.

8.8 *Ensemble*

„Checkpoint Arkaden"

Josef Paul Kleihues, Berlin
1994–96
Friedrichstrasse 45-46/
Zimmerstrasse 20-25/
Charlottenstrasse 31

The "Checkpoint Arcades" runs parallel to the former course of the Berlin Wall. Both corners have raised towers in the form of a ship's bows, a motif which has become a characteristic feature of Kleihues' architectural designs. The facade is dominated by a large-scale rectangular pattern and faced with green-glazed terracotta tiles reminiscent of those in Berlin's underground stations. There were plans to turn the site into a green recreational area at the time of the Berlin International Building Exhibition in 1987.

Wohn- und Geschäftshaus
Residential and commercial building

Christian Koch,
Dress & Wucherpfennig, Berlin
1738;
1987
Friedrichstrasse 206

This building stood directly next to the Berlin Wall in the western part of Checkpoint Charlie. During restoration work carried out as part of Berlin's International Building Exhibition in 1987, it was discovered that the original two-storey building dated from 1738 and was one of the last remaining Baroque buildings of Friedrichstadt. New floors were added at the end of the 19th century. The café "Zum weißen Adler" (At the White Eagle) derives its name from the pharmacy which once occupied the same rooms.

9

Wohnhaus, ehemalige Kontrollstation
Residential building, formerly a checkpoint

While Berlin was still a divided city, this building was designed to incorporate one of the checkpoints for Checkpoint Charlie on the lower floors. However, before construction work was finished

the Berlin Wall fell and the ground floor was converted into commercial space for shops and only the projecting pavilion remains as a reminder of the originally intended use.
The building was designed by the "Office for Metropolitan Architecture" (OMA), whose avant-garde approach to architecture is evident in the multiform facade style with parts both set back and projecting, the tower-like annex clearly separating the building from its neighbour, and the perforated roof surround.
The checkpoint structure in the middle of the street reserved for Allied military personnel, diplomats and foreign nationals was removed and is now on exhibit at the Allies Museum in Dahlem, in the south of Berlin.

OMA, Rem Koolhaas,
Matthias Sauerbruch,
Elia Zenghelis, Rotterdam
1988–90; 1994
Friedrichstrasse 207-208

Haus am Checkpoint Charlie
House at Checkpoint Charlie
Peter Eisenman,
Jaquelin Robertson
1985–86
Friedrichstrasse/
Kochstrasse

The corner building completing the historical structure of the block was rebuilt for the IBA 87. In his design Peter Eisenman, chose to follow the original street route while orientating the building exactly according to the points of the compass, with the result that the slightly shifted line of the building responds to the historical structure of Friedrichstadt with a rational geometric shape. There are state-subsidised apartments in the building as well as, on the ground floor, the museum "Haus am Checkpoint Charlie" devoted to the history of the divided city.

Redaktionsgebäude „tageszeitung"
Editorial building for the "taz" newspaper

Carl Kühn;
Gerhard Spangenberg,
Berlin,
with Brigitte Steinkilberg
1909;
1990–91
Kochstrasse 18-19

The area around Kochstrasse is the traditional Berlin newspaper and publishing centre. In 1989, the editorial offices of the "taz" newspaper moved into the pre-First World War building here. Designed by Kühn in 1909, it typifies the kind of office buildings found in Berlin at the turn of the century. Such buildings, which in the meantime have largely disappeared, were characterised by the flowing line of the facade and the extensive incorporation of windows. In contrast, the work carried out in 1990-91 on an extension and modernisation emphasises the transparency of design and leaves both construction and material open to view. In 1992, the building received the "Bund Deutscher Architekten" (German Architects Association) commendation.

11

GSW Hauptverwaltung
The GSW administrative headquarters

Paul Schwebes,
Hans Schoszberger;
Matthias Sauerbruch,
Louisa Hutton Architekten,
Berlin/London
1960–61;
1995–98
Kochstrasse 22a

The administrative headquarters of the GSW, "Gesellschaft für Sozialen Wohnungsbau", (Association for the building of state-subsidised apartments) was located in a typical 1960s tower block with a shallow projecting pavilion and an adjacent three-storey business centre. The complex was considered to be a confident expression of the reconstruction of Berlin after the damage caused in the Second World War. However, the square-shaped complex was not in alignment with the edge of the street, thus negating the original urban ground plan.

When it became clear that the administrative headquarters needed to be expanded, the question arose of whether to demolish the existing building or to renovate it. In 1990, the GSW held an architectural competition by invitation. The winning design by the German/British architects Matthias Sauerbruch and Louisa Hutton was chosen for two reasons: firstly, because it recreated the historical line of the street and secondly, it offered a "low-energy tower block". The energy saving of around forty per cent led the building to be chosen as a decentralised Expo 2000 project.

The newly built 22-storey tower block is connected to the old building on all levels by a lift and staircase tower. The facade on both front and back consists of a double glass skin which both serves as sound-proofing and helps improve the air in the building. In a one-metre deep space on the west side of the building, warm air rises upwards and draws used air out of the offices, while fresh air is naturally drawn in via openings on the side facing east. The west-facing facade is covered by individually controlled coloured light-protection slats, which, as they are moved, form a new abstract picture every day. The line of the slightly curved, three-storey office building with the elliptical tower follows the original, historical urban ground plan of Kochstrasse.

This building marks the geographical boundary of the controversial construction of tower-blocks in the southern area of Friedrichstadt.

Charlotten-Carrée 12

The Charlotten Carrée project by Thomas Spiegel is part of the planning for a larger area around the Springer Publishing House, which suffered severe damage during the Second World War. The block between Kochstrasse, Charlottenstrasse and Markgrafenstrasse is being rebuilt completely. The existing building at the corner of Kochstrasse and Charlottenstrasse, dating from around 1930, is to be included in the new design and two storeys added. The buildings have shops on the ground floor level, with offices above them, and residential apartments at the top.
In Zimmerstrasse there is a memorial to Peter Fechter, who was shot in 1962 by East German border guards while trying to escape from East Berlin. The memorial is integrated into the complex by an inset in the facade running the height of the building.

Thomas Spiegel, Hamburg
1998–2000
Kochstrasse/
Charlottenstrasse/
Markgrafenstrasse

Quartier Schützenstraße 13

For the design of the Quartier Schützenstrasse, the Italian architect Aldo Rossi, who died in 1997, took as his model the historical urban structure of division of land into small plots with a resulting variety in architecture. Thus, he has merged twelve individual buildings to form an architectural collage which stands out against the surrounding environment through the bright use of colour. The "roofscape" created is a reference to Parisian attic roofs. While the buildings do provide for a mixture of residential and commercial use, two of them are reserved exclusively for residential apartments. The most striking feature on Schützenstrasse copies the front of the 16th century Palazzo Farnese in Rome. The facade copies three of the centre line of windows.

Aldo Rossi,
Luca Meda, Mailand,
Götz Bellmann &
Walter Böhm, Berlin
1994–98
Schützenstrasse/
Markgrafenstrasse/
Zimmerstrasse/
Charlottenstrasse

Mosse-Zentrum 14
Mosse Centre

The Mosse Centre complex is a new, extensive project to restore the block between Schützenstrasse, Jerusalemerstrasse, Zimmerstrasse and Markgrafenstrasse in several phases. A number of architects are designing what will be a media

14 15

Jürgen Fissler & Partner, Berlin, Bernd Kemper, Hannover, Dieter W. Schneider and Partner, Berlin, Hans D. Strauch HDS, Boston
1993–2000
Schützenstrasse 15-25

centre for international publishers and editorial offices, a reference to the area being the traditional centre of newspaper publishing in Berlin. The imposing facade of what used to be the headquarters of the Mosse publishing house was given its dynamic character by Erich Mendelsohn in 1921-23. The conversion work and addition of the corner floors made this building on Jerusalemer Stasse into an architectural symbol for the newly emerging zeitgeist in the Berlin of the 1920s. This major feature of Berlin's architectural history was renovated in 1993 in several stages.

15

Axel Springer Verlag

Axel Springer Publishing House

Franz Heinrich Sobotka, Gustav Müller;
Gerhard Stössner, Thomas Fischer, Berlin
1961–66;
1992–94
Kochstrasse 50/ Charlottenstrasse/ Axel-Springer-Strasse

An extension was built for the Springer Publishing House tower block when "Die Welt", one of the group's newspapers, moved its editorial offices from Hamburg to Berlin. The result of the comprehensive extension work was a 19-storey tower block, which forms a T-shape with the already existing 1966 block. The new construction was given a dynamic glass facade and has space inside for all the various departments.

In 1966, when the original gold-coloured tower block was built, Axel Springer was consciously continuing the tradition of newspaper publishing in this area of Berlin where the publishing house of the renowned publisher August Scherl once stood on the same site and, in the neighbourhood, buildings housing other equally well-known publishers such as Rudolf Mosse or, until the damage caused during World War II, the Ullstein headquarters. However, Springer's choice of location also had a political element. The border to East Berlin ran along Zimmerstrasse to the north, and the Springer newspapers and magazines were all committed to the cause of German reunification. The East German reaction was to construct competing tower blocks on Leipziger Strasse to obscure the direct view of the Springer building. The 1966 building is now listed as being of historic interest.

There have been various plans for a media centre here since 1996. The design envisages residential and commercial premises to the south of Kochstrasse, whereby the Springer printing centre is to be partially demolished and rebuilt as business premises.

The Krausenhof was originally constructed as commercial premises. It has two main facades, one facing Schützenstrasse and the other facing Krausenstrasse, where the Krausenhof formed the block edge of what was then Dönhoffplatz. The UFA (Universum Film AG) had been resident here since 1927. It was later taken over by Alfred Hugenberg's Scherl Verlag and from 1937 on, distributed the National Socialist propaganda "Wochenschau", a weekly cinema newsreel. After the war, the building housed the East German Ministry of Agriculture. Since 1996 it has been the headquarters of the Berlin Office for the Preservation of Historical Buildings

Krausenhof, Sitz des Landesdenkmalamtes Berlin

Krausenhof, Landesdenkmalamt, Berlin Office for the Preservation of Historical Buildings

Hermann Dernburg
1910–11
Krausenstrasse 38-39/
Schützenstrasse

16

Geschäftshaus, „Orte der Erinnerung"

Commercial premises, "Orte der Erinnerung"

In 1909 Hans Bernouli, a Swiss architect, designed these commercial premises in the style of Alfred Messel's department store architecture. Bernoulli's first buildings were constructed in Berlin. In 1912 he returned to Switzerland, establishing himself as an architect for new housing estates. After the Second World War, he exercised considerable influence through his position as an advisor on the reconstruction of European cities.

From 1932 on, the building housed the branch office of the health insurance company, the Barmer Ersatzkasse. After the Berlin Wall came down, the site and the building were returned to the company. From 1990-93 Rupert Ahlborn completely converted the existing building and designed the new one next to it, duplicating the use of colour. A semi-circular tower emerges from the slender street-facing building and the curved form used on the ground floor is leading to in the courtyard.

Here one can find the memorial "Orte der Erinnerung" (Places of Remembrance), dedicated to the synagogue which once stood here, consecrated in 1891, desecrated in 1938, and demolished in 1956. Zvi Hecker, Micha Ullmann, and Eyal Weizman, Israeli architects and artists, have since reconstructed parts of the external walls and erected rows of benches as a reminder of the rows of seats in the synagogue.

Hans Bernoulli,
Louis Rinkel;
Rupert Ahlborn & Partner, Berlin
1909;
1990–93,
1994–96
Axel-Springer-Strasse 44-50

17

Erweiterung der Bundesdruckerei

Extension to the Government Printing Office

BHHS & Partner
(Bayerer, Hanson, Heidenreich, Martinez, Schuster),
Berlin
1993–97
Kommandantenstrasse 15

The Government Printing Office can look back on a long and varied history. The present government printing office dating from 1951 was formed from the German Imperial Printing Office founded on the same site in 1897 (and from 1945 the State Government Printing Office). This in turn was the successor to the Berlin "Oberhofbuchdruckerei" of Decker and the Royal Prussian Government Printing Office. The latter was already housed in 1852 at the back of the site at the corner of Oranienstrasse and Alte Jakobstrasse. The original imposing red brick building, no longer existent, dated from 1890 and had a corner tower. The new building from 1993-97 forms the northeastern edge of a small "city within a city", stretching from Kochstrasse to Kommandantenstrasse. The most noticeable characteristic of the extension is the transparent facade, which allows a view of the production processes inside the government printing office, where bank notes, stamps, identity cards, passports and government stocks are all produced. The point at which the facade slightly protrudes is a reminder of the original site of both the old city custom's wall and the Berlin Wall. The most modern safe in Europe, covered with copper panels, lies behind the main building. Here valuables can be secured completely automatically and stored in a racking control system, using the principle of computer-controlled random decoding. The actual printing section is adjacent to the south.

18

Wohnhaus

Residential building

Carmen Geske,
Thomas Wenzel, Berlin
1992–93
Alte Jakobstrasse 45-46/
Kommandantenstrasse

The pre-war building here forms the northernmost edge of the "Otto-Suhr-Siedlung" housing estate, constructed from 1956-63. The residential block was located directly at the Berlin Wall. A new building has been added at right-angles, whereby the existing tower staircase with its closed facade has been optically blended into the new structure with its unadorned white form rising over the dark base. This gives the open street structure of the estate a partial frame which leads the eye to the opposite side of the street where block street-side structures are to be built.

Wohn- und Geschäftshaus

Residential and commercial premises

Maedebach, Redeleit & Partner, Berlin
1994–95
Oranienstrasse 110/
Alte Jakobstrasse

As with the residential building at the corner of Kommandantenstrasse, the design of this corner house is also a reaction to its architectural environment. On the one hand, it incorporates the position of the existing linear development in the Otto-Suhr-Siedlung estate and, on the other hand, its angled facade follows the course of the streets which meet here at an obtuse angle.

Ehemalige Reichsschuldenverwaltung

Former Reichsschuldenverwaltung (German Imperial Debt Management Office).

German Bestelmeyer
1919–24
Oranienstrasse 106-109/
Alte Jakobstrasse

The massive corner building which formerly housed the Reichsschuldenverwaltung was the first public building erected in Berlin by the German government after the First World War. The central government organisation had existed since 1820 but needed a new building as the amount of administration had grown enormously in the wake of the First World War and the German commitment to pay the immense war reparations.
The red-brick structure and the terracotta facade ornamentation draw on the architectural tradition of Karl Friedrich Schinkel as well as the expressionist architecture of the 1920s.

IBA-Bauten

IBA Buildings

1980–86
Alte Jakobstrasse/
Ritterstrasse

The city block between Alte Jakobstrasse, Lindenstrasse and Ritterstrasse was one of the main International Building Exhibition showpieces in 1987. It involved the creation of a complete city area, combining aspects of both architectural and urban development. The design stemmed from Rob Krier, who followed the idea behind "critical reconstruction" to create this prime example of urban planning. Other aims in the design, admirably implemented, were the reduction of through traffic and the differentiation of the road network into traffic access, residential and play streets. Feilnerstrasse lies in the middle of this development, and it is there that one can find a post-modern copy of Schinkel's 1829 Feilner House. The original building became a part of architectural history because of the functional and clear lines of its facade. It was, however, destroyed in the Second World War. The gaps in Alte Jakobstrasse have been closed with red brick buildings. On "Am Berlin Museum" one can see both the linear development (by Kollhoff and

Ovaska) closing the block on the northern side of the street as well as, (opposite), the transition to the Berlin Museum garden through individual town houses.

20

Jüdisches Museum

Jewish Museum

Daniel Libeskind, Berlin
1993–99
Lindenstrasse 14

The Jewish Museum is one of the most spectacular new buildings erected in Berlin since the Second World War. The design by Daniel Libeskind dates from 1989 and takes as its central theme an imaginary network linking the lives and places of residence of prominent people from Berlin, both Jewish and non-Jewish. The zigzag ground plan which emerged from this conception is supposed to draw together "between the lines" the past and the future. It has also been interpreted as an exploded Star of David. Running through the inside of the building are five empty rooms called the "Voids". Only one of these rooms is actually accessible. Together they express the absence of Jewish life in Berlin and thus symbolise the "presence of absence" in the museum.
The exhibition rooms and the staircase meet to create the image of a labyrinthine space which combines the utilisation of a museum with historical commemoration.
There are irregular incisions in the facade to allow for light and view but which disregard both room plan and division into stories, clearly avoiding the accepted image of a building with windows.
Outside the museum lies the E.T.A. Hoffmann Garden, (named after the German Romantic writer). A walk around it belongs to a tour of the museum. In the garden, there are 49 leaning steles, each with plants and a single slanting base. They are intended as a depiction of the experience of exile.
The design competition held in 1989 originally envisaged the new building as an extension of the neighbouring Berlin Museum, which is why it has no entrance of its own but can only be approached through an underground connection located in the museum. After a protracted and heated public debate, the Jewish Museum became an independent institution in 1998. The building has been open to the public since Febru-

ary 1999, prior to the presentation of the actual collection in the year 2000.
The Berlin Museum is housed in the former "Kollegienhaus", which was later home to Berlin's Supreme Court. The Baroque style three-winged building, designed by Philipp Gerlach in 1735, is the last remaining palatial structure of its time in the southern part of Friedrichstadt. It is the first building in Berlin designed solely for offices, since it was originally built to house the legal departments and administration which had been moved out of the Stadtschloss, the city palace. The site chosen had allowed a direct line of vision, now interrupted by Leipziger Strasse, down Markgrafenstrasse to Gendarmenmarkt.

Verwaltungsgebäude der IG Metall

IG Metall Administration Building

Erich Mendelsohn,
Rudolf Reichel
1929–30
Alte Jakobstrasse 148-155/
Lindenstrasse

The German metal workers union, the IG Metall, was founded in 1891 as the German Metal Workers Association. In 1930, it moved into this new administrative building in the wake of its move from Stuttgart to Berlin. The building was the work of the architect Erich Mendelsohn and was instantly recognised and acclaimed as representative of contemporary modernism. Mendelsohn's design emphasised the acute angles of the triangular plot through the concave cylindrical "spine" ending in a higher front section housing the main conference room, marked by the round glass structure with the flagpole. The deliberately modern architectural design was supposed to express the increased importance of unions in the Weimar Republic. The building was extensively restored in 1995 and an extra wing was added on Alte Jakobstrasse.

Kirche zum Heiligen Kreuz 21

Church of the Holy Cross

Johannes Otzen;
Architektengruppe
Wassertorplatz, Berlin
1884–88;
1990–95
Blücherstrasse/
Zossener Strasse 65

The Church of the Holy Cross was consecrated in 1888. It has now been altered to create a new local community centre. Many large churches in Berlin can no longer be maintained because congregations have shrunk so drastically. Since the Protestant churches were built on municipal land, the land and buildings return to the local authorities if a church is de-consecrated. Extending their use is a way to ensure the survival of these buildings which contribute so much to the architecture of Berlin. Glass walls now separate the transepts of the church from the central area. In this way, conference rooms and catering space have been created. The administration is housed on the mezzanine floor and on the floors above. The glass lift tower symbolises the inclusion of secular functions in this sacred building.

Amerika-Gedenkbibliothek

American Memorial Library

Gerhard Jobst,
Willy Kreuer,
Hartmut Wille,
Fritz Bornemann
1952–54
Blücherplatz

The American Memorial Library was donated to west Berlin by the United States. The gently curved main body of the building houses the administration and stockrooms; the reading rooms and library itself are located in the projecting glass-covered single storey, which ensures an unhindered view to the outside.

By 1998 the stock of the American Memorial Library had been combined with that of the former East Berlin Stadtbibliothek (City Library) in Breite Strasse and sorted by topic. The books were then divided between both libraries, as well as the "Marstall" and Ribbeck House, and are administered altogether as the Central Library for the "Land" Berlin. The American architect Karen van Lengen had planned an extension and a reshaping of Blücherplatz. However, in 1990 the funding for these plans was cut.

The American Memorial Library lends nearly 10,000 books per day and thus ranks among the most used public libraries in Germany. For this reason, plans are being considered to relocate the Central Library for the "Land" Berlin in a new building on Schlossplatz.

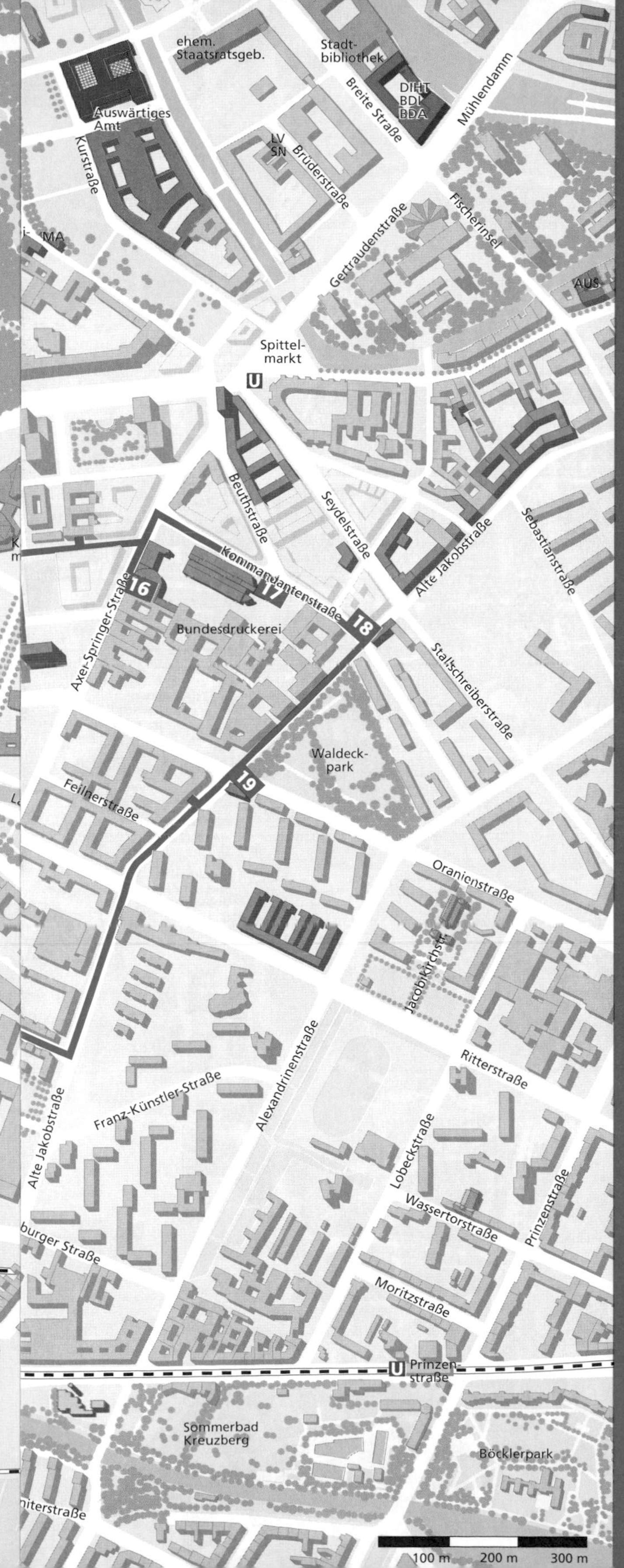

ehem. Staatsratsgeb.
Stadt-bibliothek
DIHT
BDI
BDA
Auswärtiges Amt
Kurstraße
Breite Straße
Mühlendamm
LV SN
Brüderstraße
Fischerinsel
Gertraudenstraße
AUS
Spittel-markt
Beuthstraße
Seydelstraße
Sebastianstraße
Alte Jakobstraße
Kommandantenstraße
16
17
18
Axel-Springer-Straße
Bundesdruckerei
Stallschreiberstraße
Waldeck-park
19
Feilnerstraße
Oranienstraße
Jacobikirchstr.
Ritterstraße
Alexandrinenstraße
Franz-Künstler-Straße
Alte Jakobstraße
Lobeckstraße
Wassertorstraße
Prinzenstraße
burger Straße
Moritzstraße
Prinzen-straße
Sommerbad Kreuzberg
Böcklerpark
niterstraße
100 m
200 m
300 m

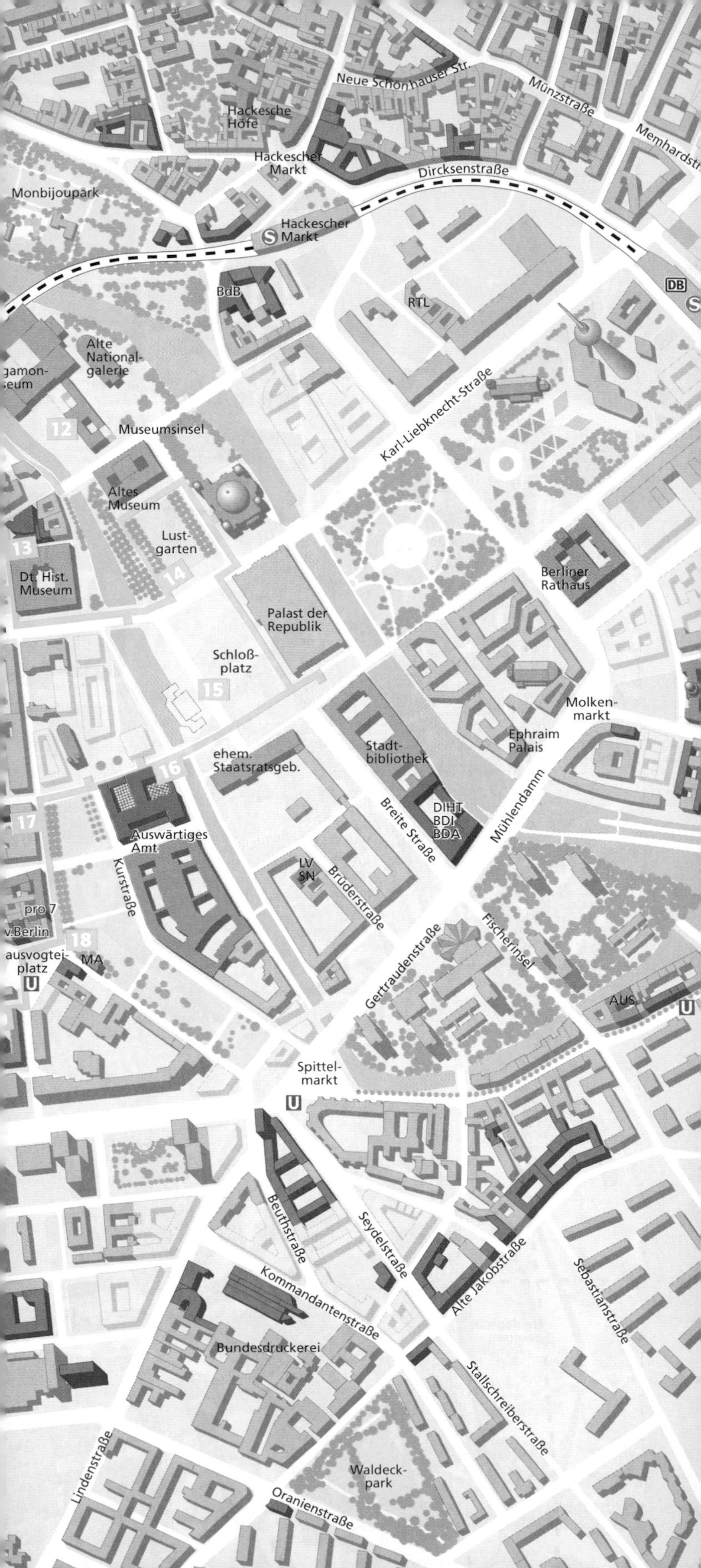

Neue Schönhauser Str.
Münzstraße
Memhardstr.
Hackesche Höfe
Hackescher Markt
Dircksenstraße
Monbijoupark
Hackescher Markt
DB
BdB
RTL
Alte National-galerie
gamon-seum
Karl-Liebknecht-Straße
12
Museumsinsel
Altes Museum
Lust-garten
13
14
Dt. Hist. Museum
Berliner Rathaus
Palast der Republik
Schloß-platz
15
Molken-markt
Ephraim Palais
ehem. Staatsratsgeb.
Stadt-bibliothek
16
17
Auswärtiges Amt
DIHT
BDI
BDA
Breite Straße
Mühlendamm
Kurstraße
LV SN
Brüderstraße
pro 7
v.Berlin
18
ausvogtei-platz
MA
Gertraudenstraße
Fischerinsel
AUS
Spittel-markt
Beuthstraße
Seydelstraße
Alte Jakobstraße
Sebastianstraße
Kommandantenstraße
Bundesdruckerei
Stallschreiberstraße
Lindenstraße
Waldeck-park
Oranienstraße

Die Neue Mitte

Berlin Mitte – the new centre

Route 5 traverses the area where the "New Berlin" is taking shape. From Potsdamer and Leipziger Platz to Pariser Platz, it takes us along that magnificent, wide boulevard Unter den Linden and then up and down Friedrichstrasse as far as Schlossplatz and the Lustgarten. In the process, we shall encounter the new centres of political power and the culture of the past, Berlin's splendid new shopping street as well as centres of science and religion. The route provides an excellent panorama of all that has been planned, excavated and realised in Berlin's inner-city over the past ten years.

Route 5 closely passes behind the former centre of political power in Wilhelmstrasse. This area used to be closed to the city's inhabitants. Today, with its scattered villas housing the diplomatic representations of the German Laender, the area is accessible to the public for the first time thanks to public rights of way. Just before we reach Pariser Platz, route 5 takes us to the site of the planned "Monument for the Murdered European Jews", which has been the subject of impassioned public debate for more than ten years.

At Pariser Platz we encounter a notable feature in the architectural renewal of Berlin. The quadrangular square forms a brilliantly executed Baroque figure and was, for a long time, the bourgeois counterweight to the royal Prussian palace in the centre of the city. Following the war and the construction of the Wall it remained a barren area, where the Brandenburg Gate came to symbolise the fate of Berlin, a city caught between division and unification. There was a heated debate over the redevelopment of Pariser Platz with palatial buildings in modern architectural style. It was supposed to do justice to the image of a fashionable "salon of Berlin".

Route 5 follows Unter den Linden up to the intersection of Friedrichstrasse, providing a glimpse of its growing use again by shops and businesses, cafés and the media. At Friedrichstrasse, our journey takes us north towards Friedrichstrasse railway station, which gained notoriety as a border-crossing between East and West Berlin. It also conjures up memories of the legendary 1920s, when the immediate surroundings were filled with the hustle and bustle of urban life, with bro-

thels and musical theatres, business and entertainment.
From here it is but a stone's throw to the Museum Island, which is listed as one of UNESCO's world cultural heritage sites. With its ensemble of diverse, important museums, the island testifies to the incredible cultural potential of the city. Following a long period of lethargy, it will now be given a new lease of life when the extensive reconstruction work has been completed.
At the Museum Island, and on the rest of the Spree Island, route 5 also traces Berlin's more recent political past. Schlossplatz is not only one of the oldest and politically most important places in the city, but also one of the most controversial anywhere in Germany. The Palast der Republik (Palace of the Republic) was erected here by the East German state in place of the old Stadtschloss (City Palace), which was demolished in 1950 to create the political centre of Socialism that included the State Council Building and the Marx Engels Forum. The current debate indecisively drifts back and forth between demolishing the Palast der Republik and reconstructing the original building, or completely redesigning the area. The old Lustgarten, which is being redesigned in the forms of the late 19th century, has set a signal. And within view, the Foreign Ministry of a united Germany has established its residence at the Werderscher Markt in the extension to the former Reichsbank dating from the Nazi period.
From there, route 5 takes us on to the Gendarmenmarkt, via the former Berlin fashion centre and Hausvogteiplatz, which is now becoming a centre for television stations. Being the site of the Französicher and Deutscher Dom (French and German Cathedrals) and Schinkel's Konzerthaus, it is one of the most beautiful squares in the entire city. Route 5 then takes us to the Forum Fridericianum, just behind the square. The Forum is probably the most important urban development executed under Friedrich II.
Route 5 ends at the section of Friedrichstrasse between Unter den Linden and Leipziger Strasse. Here we arrive at the centre of what was referred to as the "new age of empire builders" in the early 1990s. With its new offices and commercial buildings, whose development has been closely followed and discussed internationally, the legend of the lively, diversified commercial street is being brought back to life.

Potsdamer Platz

Route 5 starts at the railway station Potsdamer Platz (s. p. 59).

Ehemalige Ministergärten

Former Ministers' Gardens

Ensemble

Machleidt & Partner, Berlin
1993
Wilhelmstrasse/
Vosstrasse/
Ebertstrasse

Of the new areas to be developed in Berlin, the Ministers' Gardens between Vosstrasse, Ebertstrasse and Pariser Platz are among the politically most significant. From the early 19th century, the centres of power in Prussia, the German Empire, the Weimar Republic and the "Third Reich" were located here.
The original residences with their extensive gardens were constructed in Wilhelmstrasse during the 18th century. In the early 19th century, work was started on converting them to accommodate the ministries, whilst the Baroque grounds were redesigned as English landscape gardens. The gardens provided direct links, closed to the public, between the ministries. It was there that the ministers and their undersecretaries frequently met for critical and informal talks. Both the first Reich chancellor, Otto von Bismarck, and the very last one, Adolf Hitler, governed from here. In 1938, Albert Speer erected the New Reich Chancellery – with its system of subterranean bunkers – for Hitler in Vosstrasse. The area was badly damaged during the Second World War. Completely cleared as a border area, it remained a scar in the centre of the city for quite some time after the Berlin Wall was erected in 1961. Since the GDR also felt uncomfortable about the view, slab buildings were erected, con-

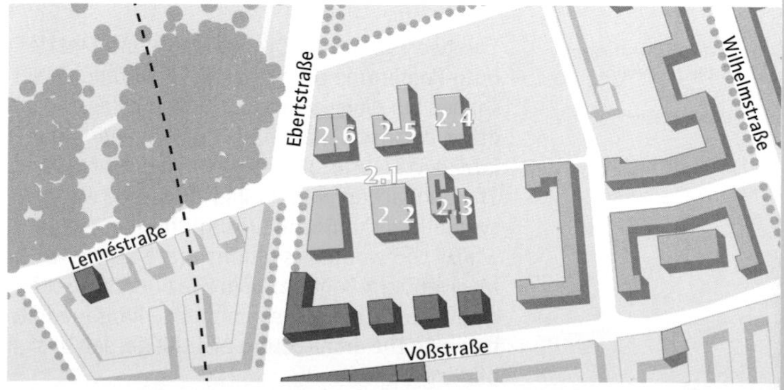

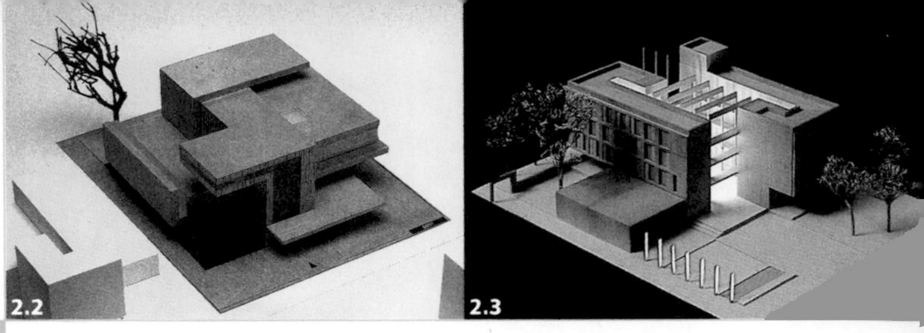

2.2 2.3

taining preference apartments, on the western side of Wilhelmstrasse right up until 1989. After the opening of the Wall, plans were reconsidered to restore the area of the Ministers' Gardens to their former use. In 1993, Hildebrand Machleidt's urban-planning design was accepted, which proposed accommodating the representations of the 16 German Laender in twelve individual buildings in the southern part of the area. Some of the Laender, however, moved into old buildings in Friedrichstadt. A new – and, for the first time, public – network of access routes was created between Ebertstrasse and Wilhelmstrasse. No decision has yet been taken on plans, which were first discussed in 1927, to extend Französische Strasse and thus cut the area in two. Since 1994, the northern part has been set aside for the planned "Memorial to the Murdered European Jews".

2.2 *Ensemble*

Landesvertretung Hessen

Land representation of Hesse

Michael Christl,
Joachim Bruchhäuser,
Frankfort on the Main
1999–2000
Kleine Querallee

The design by the team of Christl & Bruchhäuser of Hesse, for the new building of the Hesse Land representation was chosen in an EU-wide competition in 1998. Standing in a water-pool, the building, with sandstone facing, is composed of a number of cubes inserted into one another accommodating the various functions. The green area, which is designed in the style of a villa garden, can be entered through the high foyer.

2.3 *Ensemble*

Landesvertretungen Brandenburg, Mecklenburg-Vorpommern

Land representations of Brandenburg, Mecklenburg-Pomerania

gmp von Gerkan, Marg
& Partner, Hamburg
1998–2000
Kleine Querallee

The two Laender of Brandenburg and Mecklenburg-Pomerania plan to share a building. Two J-shaped building sections, barely touching one another, enclose a glass hall in the middle, which is intended for official use by both representations. The grid facade, with its shell limestone cladding, symbolises the Brandenburg-Prussian element, whilst the wooden sections are a reference to Mecklenburg-Pomerania in the north. The terraces located before the conference halls mediate between the architecture and the garden design of the grounds.

2.4 2.5

Landesvertretung Saarland

2.4 Ensemble

Land representation of Saarland

Alt & Britz, Saarbrücken
1998–2000
Kleine Querallee

The competition for the Land representation of the Saarland was only open to architects from the Saarland. The team of Alt & Britz designed a divided cube, whose middle section has been cut out, as it were, on the street side and then added to the park on the north side. This has created a house-high glass loggia, which also contains two trees. The strict grid pattern of the building also extends to the more slender building, intended for receptions and functions, as well as the administrative and residential rooms.

Landesvertretung Rheinland-Pfalz

2.5 Ensemble

Land representation of Rhineland-Palatinate

Heinle, Wischer and Partner, Stuttgart
1998–2000
Kleine Querallee

Architects were invited from all over the world to take part in competition, held in 1997, to chose a design for the Land representation of Rhineland-Palatinate. The new building has a three-winged structure. Its interior, opening to the garden, is enclosed by two wings of different lengths. The ground floor contains a foyer, one small and one large hall for receptions and small dining halls with a Palatine wine tavern. The glass rear section encloses open stairs leading to the working area. The separate guesthouse is linked to the main building by glass passages.

Landesvertretungen Niedersachsen, Schleswig-Holstein

2.6 Ensemble

Land representations of Lower Saxony, Schleswig-Holstein

Cornelsen & Seelinger/ Seelinger & Vogels, Amsterdam/Darmstadt
1999–2000
Kleine Querallee

In 1997, the German Laender of Lower Saxony and Schleswig-Holstein decided to erect a joint representation. Following a competition, two parallel six-storey buildings – linked by a one-storey-high glass hall – were constructed after the winning design by Cornelsen & Seelinger/ Seelinger & Vogels. Their design aims to convey the political co-operation of the two neighbouring Laender. The joint multifunctional hall is intended for receptions and functions. Working rooms and apartments are accommodated in the

2.6 3

slender buildings, whose facades are uniformly clad in limestone. The garden will be jointly laid out and used together with the nearby representations of Rhineland-Palatinate and the Saarland.

3

Denkmal für die ermordeten Juden Europas

Memorial to the Murdered European Jews

Peter Eisenman, New York
Ebertstrasse/
Wilhelmstrasse/
Behrenstrasse

Since 1994, there have been plans to erect an official memorial to the Jewish victims of the Holocaust on an area covering 20,000 square metres in the northern part of the Ministers' Gardens. More than 500 proposals were submitted in the first competition, which was held by the "Association for a Memorial to the Murdered European Jews" in conjunction with the Federal Republic of Germany and Land Berlin. A definitive decision has not yet been made on the memorial.

The design by American architect Peter Eisenman and sculptor Richard Serra emerged as favourite from a second competition by invitation. However, Serra withdrew in 1998, following a requested revision of their plan. The winning design, presented by Eisenman in January 1999, now consists of 1,500 rectangular concrete steles up to four metres high, forming a dense, accessible field of steles. Eisenmans plans a 100-metre long building on Behrenstrasse to house a library and a documentation centre.

The debate on the memorial has been going on for more than a decade now. Responses to proposals have ranged from agreement to rejection, reactions which have been independent of affiliation to any particular political or social group. A recent point of contention has been the monumental nature of the designs as well as the selected location. Despite its proximity to political institutions, not being a historical site of the Holocaust it is unable to convey the authentic atmosphere of a memorial centre. Another critical issue is whether there should be a special memorial to the Jewish victims of the Holocaust, or whether all persecuted groups ought to be commemorated in one memorial. Being so well documented, the controversy itself is consequently viewed by many as the true memorial to the Holocaust.

Pariser Platz

Hermann Mächtig
1732–34;
1880; 1992

The quadrangular Pariser Platz behind Brandenburg Gate is a part of the Baroque extension of Berlin from 1732. It was given its name in 1814 when the troops of Prussia and its allies conquered Paris. That same year, the quadriga, which had crowned Brandenburg Gate (1789 by Carl Gotthard Langhans) until being taken to Paris by Napoleon, was brought back to Germany in a triumphal procession and returned to its former site. From 1850, the Baroque developments at Pariser Platz were given a uniform Classical style. The square came to symbolise the pride and cultural ambitions of the emerging middle classes and formed a counterbalance to the royal residence at Schlossplatz.
The buildings at Pariser Platz were badly damaged during the Second World War and subsequently demolished. All that was left standing were parts of the Academy of Arts on the south-eastern corner. The construction of the Wall in 1961 made the Brandenburg Gate, which stood alone in the centre of the "death strip", into a symbol of the division of Berlin and Germany. After the opening of the Wall, the old green area laid out during the Wilhelminian era was restored on the basis of Hermann Mächtig's original design.
In 1993, the Berlin Senate decided to reconstruct Pariser Platz as the "Salon of Berlin" on its previous scale without, however, exactly replicating the historical architecture. To this end, statutes were drawn up stipulating that the design would have to create a palace structure with a natural

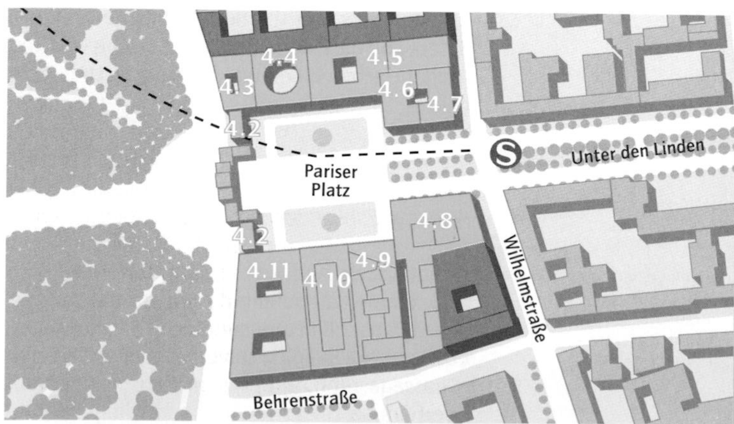

4.2

stone facade, roof parapets and window apertures above a plinth. The basic conception was that the unity of Pariser Platz as a whole should have priority over the individual character of the single buildings. These statutes were the subject of heated controversy among architects and developers and the general public. The buildings constructed here are a compromise solution, because many unite a conservative outward appearance with modern interior designs. The imaginative detail in the facade designs also reflects the response of architects and investors to design statutes.
The location of the United States and French Embassies, the Hotel Adlon and the academy of Arts at Pariser Platz constitutes a return of some of its traditional occupants.

4.2 *Ensemble*

Haus Liebermann, Haus Sommer

Liebermann House, Sommer House

Josef Paul Kleihues, Berlin
1996–98
Pariser Platz 7 and 1

The two new buildings to the north and south of Brandenburg Gate were designed by Berlin architect Kleihues before the ordinance on official design regulations was passed by the Berlin Senate. The twin buildings of the Liebermann House, in the north, and the Sommer House, in the south, take their dimensions, volume, height and facade articulation – even down to the triple windows – from their 19th-century predecessors (1845, by Friedrich August Stüler). Although the buildings are the same height, they contain one storey more than the previous buildings. The small gap left between them and the gatehouses of the Brandenburg Gate is a sign of respect for the position of the columns. Before the destruction wrought by the war, the residential buildings were linked to the gatehouses.

4.3 *Ensemble*

Palais am Pariser Platz

Palace at Pariser Platz

Bernhard Winking, Hamburg, with Martin Froh
1996–98
Pariser Platz 6a/
Ebertstrasse 24

In both scale and articulation, the residential and commercial building on the northwest corner of Pariser Platz follows its 19th-century predecessor. The building combines a courtyard with a passage running between Pariser Platz and Ebertstrasse; the tower on the building accentu-

4.4

ates the corner of the square. The narrow facade of the house overlooks Pariser Platz, its broader facade runs along Ebertstrasse. A two-storey colonnade forms the entrance to the four full-storeys. The two-storey tower contains apartments, fulfilling the Senate's requrement that 20 percent of the building be residential.

Eugen-Gutmann-Haus der Dresdner Bank

4.4 Ensemble

The Eugen Gutmann House of the Dresdner Bank

gmp von Gerkan, Marg & Partner, Hamburg
1996–97
Pariser Platz 5a-6

With its building at Pariser Platz, gmp, a team of architects from Hamburg, has designed variations on the architectural theme of the "palace" by employing stylistic elements derived from the Neue Sachlichkeit of the 1920s. The architects have responded to the challenge presented by the complex area of the property (which is enclosed on three sides and composed of two formerly separate plots) by designing a round atrium in the centre of the structure to illuminate the office rooms and provide space for exhibitions, debates and receptions. The facade to the square does not betray the presence of the atrium. The upper section of the building is clearly defined by the balcony extending the length of the building and the use of pre-patined copper instead of stone for the facade.

Botschaft der Französischen Republik

4.5 Ensemble

Embassy of the Republic of France

Christian de Portzamparc, Paris
1998–2000
Pariser Platz 5

With its new building, the French Embassy is returning to the historical site where it was located from 1860 on. After the opening of the Berlin Wall, the restituted property was extended by purchasing the adjacent plot to the east in Wilhelmstrasse. Parisian architect de Portzamparc won the multi-stage competition in 1997. He is to design the embassy, which will include the residence of the ambassador. The facade overlooking Pariser Platz has a symmetrical articulation. With its "french windows" extending over two storeys, it addresses the style of the palace that preceded it and offers a very individual interpretation of the design criteria of a "perforated facade". The slanted window jambs asym-

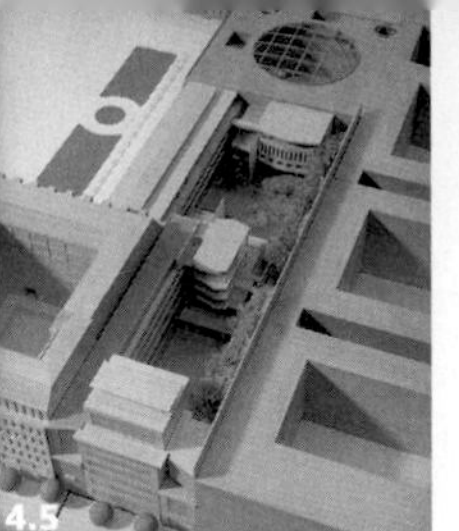
4.5

metrically face Brandenburg Gate. The portico of columns with the car drive takes up the theme of the old embassy building. An eight-storey embassy-administration building is under construction in Wilhelmstrasse. A rich variety of diversely raised and staggered terraces and garden areas have been laid out in the courtyard of the L-shaped complex for official receptions and cultural events.

4.6 *Ensemble*

Geschäfts- und Wohnhaus

Commercial and residential building

Ortner & Ortner,
Vienna/Berlin
1997–2000
Pariser Platz 4a/
Unter den Linden 80

The office and residential building the north-east corner of Pariser Platz adds variety to the square. The dominant motif of an oversized window structures the facade. The building has the same ground area as the adjacent building to the east facing Wilhelmstrasse. Together, they form a U-shape around an inner courtyard. The courtyard of the north-eastern building contains a glass cube that illuminates the basement floors. The mansard roof with dormer windows accentuates the residential use of the top floor.

4.7 *Ensemble*

Wohn- und Geschäftshaus am Pariser Platz

Residential and commercial building

Kollhoff & Timmermann,
Berlin
1997–99
Unter den Linden 78/
Wilhelmstrasse

The residential and commercial building by the Berlin architects Hans Kollhoff and Helga Timmermann forms a transition from Pariser Platz to the intersection at Unter den Linden. Its architectural theme is the typical Berlin commercial building from the turn of the 20th century with a mezzanine on a plinth. The grey sandstone facade clearly reveals the building's structure. The red awning blinds and glazed, green roof tiles provide colour accents. In contrast to many of the new buildings in the inner-city, a special section of the building along Wilhelmstrasse has been set aside for the apartments, so that they are not concentrated on the uppermost stories.

Hotel Adlon

4.8 *Ensemble*

The old Hotel Adlon of 1907 was legendary around the world among the luxury hotels of its day. The then prestigious new building took the place of the Palais Redern, designed by Schinkel in 1829 in Florentine High Renaissance style. In the Second World War, the Adlon was badly damaged during the bombing raids and later demolished.
The present building by the Berlin architects Patzschke and Klotz was the first new building to be completed at Pariser Platz (1997). The facade has been designed in the style of the original Adlon. Two plots have been combined to extend the ground area as far as Wilhelmstrasse. The balustrade-balconies on the upper floors lead to the high roof, which is now used for additional hotel rooms. The roof is visible from afar with its pre-patinaed copper. The Adlon building has triggered a debate about the quality of eclectic architecture in the present day.

Patzschke, Klotz & Partner,
Berlin,
AIC, Munich
1995–97
Unter den Linden 75-77

Akademie der Künste Berlin-Brandenburg

Academy of Arts Berlin-Brandenburg

4.9 *Ensemble*

For the new academy of Arts building, designed by Stuttgart architect Günter Behnisch, exceptions to the design statutes for Pariser Platz were permitted. The academy felt it was particularly important to uphold the results of the competition, held among the members of the department of architecture, where they contradicted official regulations. Following a controversial public debate, it was decided to place a front building with a transparent glass facade (instead of a stone facade punctuated only by windows) before the surviving painting halls of the old academy of Arts. The front section completes the wall to the square and reflects the scale of the original facade. This section, with a foyer, exhibition rooms, a café and a stairwell, will be used for public events and receptions. The old exhibition halls inside the building will be restored and supplemented by administrative areas and further exhibition rooms. The section on Behrenstrasse housing the archives and administration offices will complete the whole.

Günter Behnisch,
Manfred Sabatke
(with Werner Durth),
Stuttgart
1999–2001
Pariser Platz 4

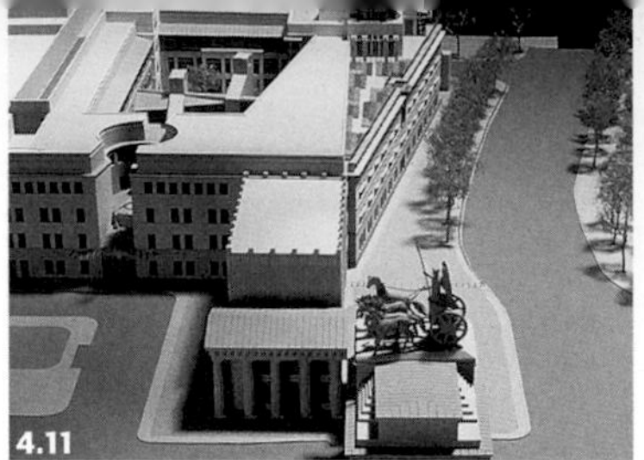
4.11

The academy of Arts originally moved here in 1902. The building itself dates from 1740. After undergoing frequent conversions, it was finally redesigned by Ernst von Ihne for its new use. In 1937, General Building Inspector Albert Speer occupied the building to work on his plans and models to redesign Berlin as "Germania", the capital of the German Reich and the world. (see p. 17). In 1942, he also took over the neighbouring building in his capacity as Minister of Armaments.

4.10 *Ensemble*

DG Bank

Frank O. Gehry,
Santa Monica,
Planungs AG für Bauwesen,
Neufert, Mittmann & Graf,
Cologne
1997–99
Pariser Platz 3

The head office of the Deutsche Genossenschaftsbank in the middle of the southern side of Pariser Platz was designed by Frank O. Gehry, an avantgarde Californian architect. It clearly demonstrates the architectural compromise achieved between the design criteria and the personal objectives of the architect and the bank.
Gehry observed the official requirement for evenly distributed, uniform stone surfaces and open window surfaces by alternating vertical stone pillars and centrelines of windows. He reserved all elements of individual architectural design for the interior of the building. There, in the centre of the atrium, the conference plenary hall is located, covered by an organic, amoeba-like dome. It can be reached via two ramps passing above the glass structure of the basement floor, which contains two more halls for functions. Gehry's architectural language becomes even more apparent at the rear of the building on Behrenstrasse, where the corrugated facade of the residential building is punctuated with oriel windows.

4.11 *Ensemble*

Botschaft der Vereinigten Staaten von Amerika
Embassy of the United States of America

Moore, Ruble & Yudell,
Santa Monica,
Gruen Associates,
Los Angeles
1999–2001
Pariser Platz 2

With its new building, the Embassy of the USA returns to the property it occupied between 1931 and 1941 in the once splendid Blüchersche Palais. The Californian team of Moore, Ruble & Yudell won the 1996 competition to design the embassy building. They have enriched Pariser

Platz with their post-modernist version of a palace by making a house-high incision in the facade to the square. A rotunda is situated behind the facade. It can be seen as an inverse form of the projections that once adorned the Blüchersche Palais at this point. The wings of the building are designed to accommodate the residence, the embassy and the chancellery and enclose the spacious courtyard. New security regulations, following a series of attacks on US embassies, meant that changes had to be made to the plans with ensuing delays in commencing building. They also raised the question of whether to relocate Ebertstrasse and Behrenstrasse or leave the US Embassy where it is now (s. p. 23).

Botschaft des Vereinigten Königreichs Großbritannien und Nordirland

Embassy of the United Kingdom of Great Britain and Northern Ireland

Michael Wilford, London
1998–2000
Wilhelmstrasse 70-71

With its new embassy building, the United Kingdom also returns to the historical site where its ambassadors resided from 1872 to 1939. The former mansion of "railway king" Henry Strousberg, who played a major role in the construction of the German railway network, was designed by August Orth in 1867 and destroyed during the Second World War.
The irregular rectangular site is enclosed on three sides. The English architect Michael Wilford, for many years a partner of James Stirling (1926-1992), designed a five-storey building in Wilhelmstrasse with a traditional regular stone facade and uniform rows of windows on the top three floors. This section mediates between the building and the design criteria for Pariser Platz, whilst the sloping roof of patinaed copper harmonises with Hotel Adlon. The entrance area beneath the bel etage is wide open. At the back of a square courtyard, where an English oak stands, there is a stairwell leading up to a two-storey winter garden. Visitors can view the building up to the second floor. The ambassador's residence is located separately on the upper floors.

6

Seniorenresidenz „Wilhelm Eck"

"Wilhelm Eck" old-people's home

Gustav Peichl & Partner, Vienna
1998–99
Wilhelmstrasse 72/ Behrenstrasse

A high-class old people's home was constructed between the British Embassy and the south front of Hotel Adlon after plans by Austrian architect Peichl. Run rather like a hotel, the home provides individualised services. Shops and a central foyer are located on the glass-fronted ground floor. The main floors are clad with light natural stone. The building is completed with set-back residential and technical storeys situated behind a steel-and-glass structure; slats provide sun-shading.
The corner is accentuated by two vertical grooves, illuminated from within, running the entire height of the facade. Hanging gardens have been laid out in the courtyard.

7

Bürohaus für Parlamentarier

Office building for parliamentary deputies

Manfred Hörner
1961–62;
1993–94
Unter den Linden 69-73/ Wilhelmstrasse

The former East German Ministry of National Education was the first building to be completed for the Bundestag in Berlin in 1994. The prefabricated building by the architect Manfred Hörner, dating from 1962 was completely renovated and given a new facade. In 1995, the adjacent old building (designed in 1903 by Paul Kieschke for the Prussian Ministry of Culture) located in Wilhelmstrasse was also handed over for use by Bundestag deputies.

Botschaft der Russischen Föderation

Embassy of the Russian Federation

A. Stryshewski, Lebedinskij, Sichert, Friedrich Skujin
1950–53
Unter den Linden 63-65
(s. ill. above)

The former Soviet Embassy was the first official building of any of the Allied occupying forces in Berlin after the Second World War. It was constructed on the site where the Imperial Russian Ambassador had resided in the 19th century. The old building was destroyed during the Second World War. The new building was planned in 1948, i.e. before the founding of the German Democratic Republic. The monumental complex – a prime example of Socialist Realism in architecture – occupies almost the entire block and opens out onto a broad court of honour. The high foyer is crowned by a lantern borne by columns. Since the collapse of the Soviet Union in 1991, the building has been used by the Embassy of the Russian Federation.

8 9

Bürohaus für Parlamentarier 8

Office building for parliamentary deputies

This building was erected in 1965 for the former East German Ministry for Foreign and Intra-German Trade. The prefabricated building was completely redesigned for the offices of the Bundestag. When they redesigned the facade, the architects closely adhered to the original articulation. However, they clad the load-bearing skeleton with natural stone and added an attic floor with a pronouncedly cantilevered roof. The completion of the building in 1997 meant that all Bundestag deputies now have an office in Berlin.

Alexander Kolbe Architekten, Berlin
1994–97
Unter den Linden 50/
Neustädtische Kirchstrasse

Haus Pietzsch 9

Pietzsch House

The corner building on the narrow plot is the first commercial building to be erected in the historical street of Unter den Linden since the Wall was opened. It fills a gap that was originally kept free for widening the street Neustädtische Kirchstrasse. The facade – a mere 16 metres in width – facing Unter den Linden, is set off against the neighbouring old building by an L-shaped glass section with a glass-covered atrium behind it. The house-high compartment wall serves as a modern-art gallery for the private collection of the owner.

Jürgen Sawade, Berlin
1992–95
Unter den Linden 42/
Neustädtische
Kirchstrasse 1 2

ZDF Hauptstadtstudio, VEBA Verwaltung Berlin 10

ZDF Capital City Studio,
VEBA Administration Berlin

The capital-city studio of the Zweites Deutsches Fernsehen (ZDF), is moving into a renovated old building in Unter den Linden. Extensive new buildings are to be added for use by Deutschland-Radio, ORF (Austrian Radio and Television) and SRG (Swiss Broadcesting Company) and the energy company VEBA The "Zollernhof" commercial building was designed by architect Kurt Berndt in 1910-11. The facade by Bruno Paul was inspired by American models. In 1938-42, the fashionable commercial building was doubled in size bridging the Kleine Kirchgasse street for the Hugenberg Trust. From 1949-89 it was the seat

Kurt Berndt, Bruno Paul;
Thomas Baumann, Berlin
1910–11;
1997–99
Unter den Linden 36-38

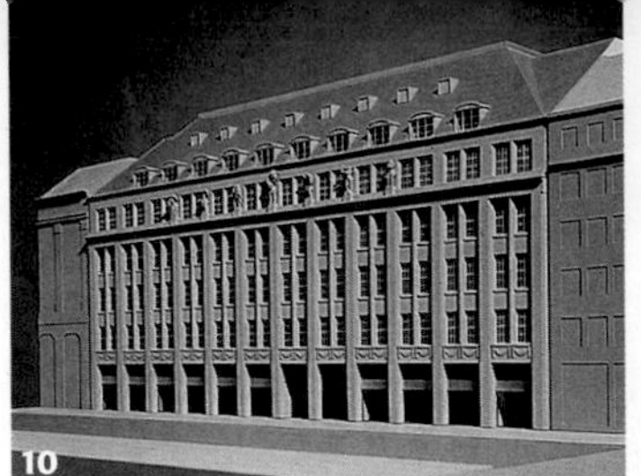
10

of the Central Council of the Free German Youth (FDJ), the youth section of the ruling East German Socialist Unity Party SED. The front building with its historical facade was preserved. The new sections, two side wings and a cross building extending as far as Mittelstrasse, enclose a covered courtyard. These sections accommodate the editorial and technical rooms. The studios themselves will be located on four floors up to 14 metres below street level, thus completely isolating them from outside noise.

11.1 *Ensemble*

Hotel Unter den Linden

H. Scharlipp, G. Boy (Kollektiv);
Steinebach & Weber, Berlin
1964–66
Building date undecided
Unter den Linden/
Friedrichstrasse

The Hotel Unter den Linden is one of the few buildings whose appearance remains unchanged from the days when the Berlin was still a divided city. Located at the famous intersection of Friedrichstrasse and Unter den Linden, the hotel, with its front square, is a testimony to the planning ideas of the '50s and '60s, when there was talk of widening Friedrichstrasse from 22 to 40 metres. Together with the former Lindencorso, (1966) on the opposite side of Unter den Linden, the hotel formed a square that was a popular meeting place in East Berlin. Recent plans envisage demolishing the hotel and erecting a new building on the original alignment of the street. Architects Steinebach & Weber have submitted a design to construct a glass atrium, the height of the building, on Friedrichstrasse, and thus widen the narrow shopping street. No dates have been set for demolition and construction work.

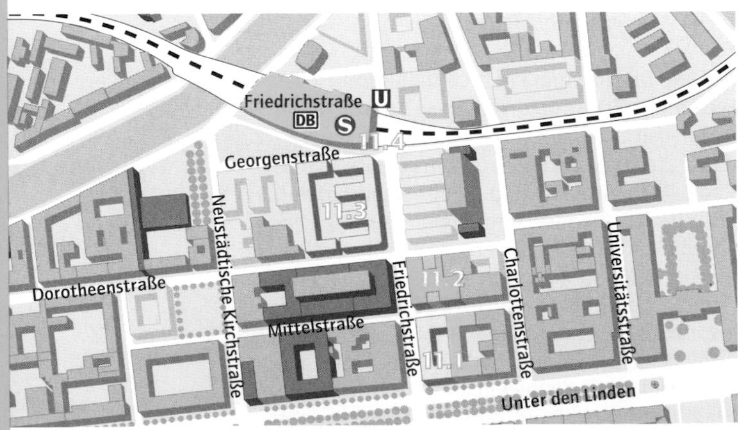

11.2

Topas Arkaden
Topas Arcades

Albert Breslauer
1898;
1996–97
Friedrichstrasse 153/
Mittelstrasse

The "Polish Pharmacy", established at the corner of Friedrichstrasse and Mittelstrasse in 1682, supplied the town of Dorotheenstadt with medicines. The more recent building, constructed in 1898 after a design by Breslauer, also housed a pharmacy. The new building was only ten metres from front to back, and the spaces between the high columns were glazed. It contained separate office rooms extending over two storeys. After it was excavated in 1997, the building was converted into a commercial building.

Haus Dussmann
Dussmann House

11.2 Ensemble

Miroslav Volf, Saarbrücken,
Mario Campi, Franco Pessina, Lugano
1995–97
Friedrichstrasse/
Dorotheenstrasse/
Mittelstrasse

The Dussmann building extends as far as the road in Friedrichstrasse, restoring the original street width of 22 metres. The buildings that formerly stood here were demolished after the Second World War. The colonnades, which also disappeared at the time, have been reconstructed – with the original model in mind – for use by pedestrians. Concerned about the chances of letting his building, Dussmann decided to operate a cultural department store under his own direction. The narrow new building at 39 Dorotheenstrasse is a residential building designed by the Italian architects Campi & Pessina.

Wintergartenquartier
The Wintergarten quarter

11.3 Ensemble

Nalbach + Nalbach, Berlin
Friedrichstrasse 143-149/
Dorotheenstrasse/
Georgenstrasse

The Wintergarten quarter calls to mind the legendary variety theatre »Wintergarten« that once had its home here. The property to the south of Friedrichstrasse railway station, lying between Georgen-, Friedrich- and Dorotheenstrasse is to be redeveloped. To this end, Nalbach + Nalbach submitted a design in 1995. A number of people, however, argue that the site ought to be preserved as a green space in this densely built-up area. The design for the »Wintergarten«, a residential and commercial building, was the product of an international competition (also won by Nalbach + Nalbach) held in 1993 to find an »urban master plan« for the entire area around Friedrichstrasse railway station. The overall plan included developments on the other side of Weidendamm Bridge in order to accentuate the

intersection of the River Spree and Friedrichstrasse. Implementation of these plans has not yet started.

11.4 *Ensemble*

Bahnhof Friedrichstraße

Friedrichstrasse railway station

Johannes Vollmer;
Carl Theodor Brotführer;
Werner Weinkamm, Berlin,
Hans Speicher, Karlsruhe
1880–82;
1919–25;
1995–99
Friedrichstrasse 98-99,
141a-142/
Georgenstrasse

Friedrichstrasse railway station, completed in 1882, was linked with the underground line in 1923 and in 1936 with the (subterranean) city railway running north to south. The construction of the Berlin Wall stopped traffic on the east-west link of the city railway. Friedrichstrasse was converted for use as a checkpoint. The platforms and access points for traffic going to the west or the east were hermetically sealed off from one another. What arose was, for outsiders at least, a confusing labyrinth of passages. Travellers heading west had to pass through the adjacent northern hall, which attained notoriety under the name "Tränenpalast" (Palace of Tears) and is meanwhile used to stage concerts.
Today's Friedrichstrasse is an excellent example of the re-use of old station buildings as commercial centres. Apart from its main function as a junction for local and regional services, it has meanwhile also taken on the character of a shopping arcade. The basements were excavated to accommodate shops. The outside facades again display the brick facing they had in the '20s.

Admiralspalast, Metropol-Theater

Heinrich Schweitzer;
Cremer & Wolffenstein
1910;
1922
Friedrichstrasse 101-102/
Planckstrasse

The Metropol Theater was designed by Cremer & Wolffenstein and built in the courtyard of a spacious complex of buildings in 1922. It replaced an old ice-skating rink and supplemented the Admiralsgartenbad (the Admiral's garden baths), a commercial enterprise that had existed since 1874 and contained restaurants and cafés as well as diverse baths for health and hygiene purposes. In 1890, an indoor swimming pool was built, and in 1910 the prestigious front building, designed by Schweitzer, was constructed with cinemas, pubs, cafés and club rooms. The washing and bathing facilities in the rear section have survived to this day. The very popular and luxuriously equipped establishment, with its diverse amenities, is representative of leisure and recreation centres of the day. The Metropol Theater was closed down in 1997.

12.1

Since the late 17th century, Weidendammer Bridge has linked Dorotheenstadt with the northern part of Spandauer Vorstadt. The present stone bridge was constructed in 1895-97, replacing its wooden – and later cast-iron – predecessor. Along with the Schilling Bridge, it is one of the only two bridges in Berlin not to have been blown up by the SS in 1945. Corrosion damage made complete reconstruction necessary in 1992-94.
In 1985 the original ornamentation of this listed structure was restored and the emperor's crowns, removed in 1918, put back on the "Prussian Icarus" (Wolf Biermann).

Weidendammer Brücke
Weidendammer Bridge
Friedrich Krause
1895–97;
1992–94

The Emperor Alexander Barracks are situated in an excellent location between the banks of the Spree, Friedrichstrasse station and the Museum Island. The large site has been used by the armed forces since the 18th century. The spacious brick buildings, whose facades are designed in German Renaissance style, testify to the size of the garrison that had so many military facilities in the inner city in Imperial Germany. There is talk of converting Barracks for use by the German Historical Museum or the Humboldt University.

Ehemalige Kaiser-Alexander-Kaserne
Former Emperor Alexander Barracks
Wieczorek
1898–1902
Geschwister-Scholl-Strasse 2-6, 5-7/
Am Weidendamm/
Am Kupfergraben

Museumsinsel, Bode-Museum
Museum Island, the Bode Museum

12.1
Ensemble

The Museum Island complex comprises the Altes and Neues Museum the Pergamon Museum and Bode Museum and the Alte Nationalgalerie (s. p. 138). With the museums in Dahlem, the Cultural Forum and the area around Charlottenburg Palace, the Museum Island, the nucleus of a new concept developed by the Staatliche Museen Berlin – Preussischer Kulturbesitz (Berlin State-owned Museums – Prussian Cultural Heritage). With the opening of the Altes Museum in 1830, a construction era began that came to a temporary conclusion with the completion of the Pergamon Museum in 1930. The collections are well endowed and count among the most important in the world, despite the huge losses incurred during the war. The opening of the Berlin Wall made it possible to bring together again collections split up during the Second World War. The Museum Island is to be entered into the UNES-

Ernst von Ihne,
Max Hasak
1897–1904
Am Kupfergraben

12.2

CO's World Cultural Heritage list. Complete restoration is expected to take about 20 years. One day, the Museum Island will house six museums with collections on Egypt, Asia Minor, Islamic art, Byzantine art, Antiquity, Late Antiquity, Pre- and Early History as well as numismatic collections. A number of provisional solutions will be found in the meantime.
The architect Ernst von Ihne designed the old Kaiser Friedrich Museum, which was constructed on the pointed tip of the island. Since 1956, the museum has borne the name of its most famous director Wilhelm von Bode. The building, which can be reached via bridges, seems to rise up out of the water like the bow of a ship, with the rounded point of the island dividing the River Spree from the Kupfergraben. An equestrian statue of Kaiser Friedrich III (smelted down during the war) formerly stood here. A huge dome vaults the foyer and the stairwell. From the year 2001 on, art from the Christian epochs up to the 18th century is to be presented in the Bode Museum. Stocks from the painting collection have been put together with those from Dahlem in the Picture Gallery at the Cultural Forum.

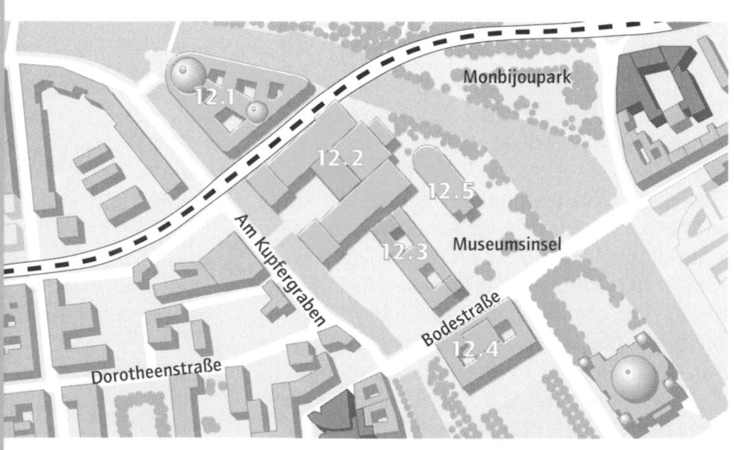

12.2 *Ensemble*

Pergamon-Museum

Alfred Messel;
Ludwig Hoffmann
1909–30
Am Kupfergraben

The opening of the Pergamon Museum in 1930 seemed to signal the conclusion of building work on the Museum Island. After the death of Messel, who designed the complex in 1907, Hoffmann assumed the responsibility for implementing the plans. The construction of the columned hall bet-

ween the side wings had to be abandoned during the First World War and the following period of high inflation. In 1980, a new entrance hall was added to the Pergamon Museum. The central section contains the great hall with the Pergamon altar (from which the Museum takes its name) dating back to the second century BC. The altar was excavated in Turkey by German archaeologists. The wings touching the Kupfergraben house collections of works from Antiquity and Asia Minor and the Museum of Islamic Art. The Egyptian collection, of which Nefertiti is the main attraction, is to be presented here until the Neues Museum has been completed.

Magnushaus
Magnus House
Georg Friedrich Boumann
1756
Am Kupfergraben 7

Magnus House is one of the few surviving stately residences dating from 18th-century Berlin. It was built by the Kupfergraben for Westphal, an official at the Prussian War Office, before becoming the home of physicist Gustav Magnus and, subsequently, of Max Reinhardt, the theatre director. It now accommodates the German Physics Society and the offices of former German President Richard von Weizsäcker.

Neues Museum
Neues Museum

Friedrich August Stüler;
David Chipperfield, London
1841–59;
1999–2005
Bodestrasse 4

The rapid growth of the Royal Prussian Collections and the growing interest in new branches of collecting during the 19th century inspired the construction of additional museum buildings on the Spree Island. In 1841, Friedrich August Stüler designed the Neues Museum, which was constructed parallel to the Kupfergraben. The slender side of this imposing building faces the Altes Museum, to which it was linked by a walkway resting on arches until 1966. On the east side, the main facade with the entrance was lined by tower-like projections adorned with caryatids on the top floor. The stairwell, designed as a festival hall with an open roof structure, was located in the upper part of the middle section. The interior design was inspired by the Egyptian collection, which will one day return to Neues Museum.
During the Second World War, the building was badly damaged and the north-west corner completely destroyed. Not until 1988 were steps taken to gradually secure the building. After the

Berlin Wall was opened up, a competition was held to restore the Museum Island. The first prize, which went to Girogio Grassi, was rejected following great controversy. In a second competition, Frank O. Gehry presented a design that envisaged radical alterations to the existing structure. An alternative was provided by the more cautious plan of English architect David Chipperfield, who began supervising the work in 1998 following some heated discussions. The existing structure is to be supplemented and the north-west wing completely restored. The new architectural designs foresee a square at the Kupfergraben, a central stairwell and a Greek and an Egyptian courtyard. There will again be two bridges linking Neues Museum with the Pergamon Museum and Altes Museum (s. p. 138).

13

Deutsches Historisches Museum

German Historical Museum

Arnold Nering,
Martin Grünberg,
Andreas Schlüter,
Jean de Bodt;
Friedrich Hitzig,
Ieoh Ming Pei, New York,
Eller + Eller Architekten,
Berlin/Düsseldorf
1695–1706;
1877;
1998–2001
Hinter dem Gießhaus/
Unter den Linden 2

The German Historical Museum, a limited company funded by the German state, is located in the Baroque Zeughaus (the old armoury). In 1695, work was started on the quadrangular building after plans by Arnold Nering and continued by Martin Grünberg and Andreas Schlüter. The building was finally completed by Jean de Bodt in 1706. In 1877, it was converted into a Prussian pantheon after plans by Friedrich Hitzig. Until the Berlin Wall was opened, it served as the Museum for German History in the GDR. In 1989, there were plans to have a new building – designed by Aldo Rossi – erected for the German Historical Museum at the Spreebogen opposite the Reichstag. Following German unification, the Spreebogen area was set aside for the government and parliament buildings, whereas the Zeughaus was available for use.

In 1996, the then German Chancellor, Helmut Kohl, commissioned the renowned architect Ieoh Ming Pei, without a prior competition, to design an extension to the building. On the irregular property to the north of the Zeughaus, Pei designed a homogeneous, triangular building for the exhibition rooms. A glass stair tower was erected in front of the convex front facing the chestnut trees by the Neue Wache. The foyer, also made of glass, is connected to the old building by a tunnel. A powder magazine, built in 1959, was

demolished to make way for the extension. The German Historical Museum's interior courtyard, named after the architect and sculptor Schlüter, will be covered by a filigree glass roof.

Neue Wache

New Guardhouse

Karl Friedrich Schinkel
1816–18
Unter den Linden 4
(s. ill. above)

One year after the end of the "German Wars of Liberation" against the armies of Napoleon, Schinkel was commissioned to design the new Royal Guardhouse close to the palace. The strict, rectangular ground plan and the corner towers recall a Roman citadel, whilst the portico of columns lends the building a solemn dignity. In 1930, the architect Heinrich Tessenow redesigned the interior as a memorial hall for the victims of the First World War. When the Nazis took power, they changed the building into a pantheon for the "heroic dead". During the Second World War, the building was damaged and gradually fell into decay. After it was reconstructed in 1958, the East German government established here the "Memorial to the Victims of Facism and Militarism". In 1993, following controversial discussion, the New Guardhouse was declared the official memorial of the Federal Republic of Germany to the "victims of war and tyranny". The building was restored to the condition it had been in 1930. Today however, an enlarged version of a Pietà the Christian figure by Käthe Kollwitz now stands in the centre of the room. This figure was the source of much discussion since it is four times the size of the original.

Schloßbrücke

Karl Friedrich Schinkel
1821–24

In the course of the planning for the Lustgarten, Schinkel replaced the old wooden "Hundebrücke" by the stone Schlossbrücke (Palace Bridge) in 1824.
The mechanism operning the central arch, through which ships passed, was removed around 1900 to accommodate the increase in road traffic between Unter den Linden and Alexanderplatz.
The Schlossbrücke clearly demonstrates the fact that, in Berlin, the historical routes cross the river, but do not run along its banks. For this reason, the city seems to turn its back on the river; it is also the reason why it now seems so difficult to integrate the River Spree into the city's public space.

Schinkel also designed the sculptural ornamentation of the bridge. The eight marble groups were created in 1842-57 (after Schinkel's death) by renowned Berlin sculptors. The figures idealise the life and death of a warrior, who is guided on his way by goddesses. They were removed during the Second World War and, after the Wall was erected, stored in a secure place in West Berlin. The East Berlin municipal authority exchanged them for the archives of the Royal Prussian Porcelain Manufacture in 1981, when they were restored to their former position as part of the reconstruction of Unter den Linden. Until 1991, the bridge was named after Karl Marx and Friedrich Engels.

14

Lustgarten

Karl Friedrich Schinkel;
Atelier Loidl
Landschaftsarchitekten,
Hans Loidl,
Berlin
1828–32;
1998–99
Am Lustgarten/
Karl-Liebknecht-Strasse

The Lustgarten, located between the Altes Museum and the site of the old Stadtschloss (demolished in 1950) is the only public square alongside the water and one of the most beautiful in Berlin. During the 16th century, it served the palace as a kitchen garden. However, in 1646, the Great Elector decided to have it redesigned to include an orangery and a teahouse. In 1713, Friedrich Wilhelm I had it levelled to create a parade ground. However, it was not until 1828-32 that it assumed its historical form after being redesigned by Karl Friedrich Schinkel. Schinkel conceived the ensemble of the Lustgarten and the Altes Museum as a civil forum – at the centre of the city – that could assert itself vis-à-vis the royal palace. Until 1889, the Lustgarten formed the end of Unter den Linden, thus serving as the counterpart to Pariser Platz at the other end. The increase in road traffic made it necessary to extend the street eastwards through and beyond the Lustgarten. Immediately after the First World War, in 1918, countless political demonstrations took place in the Lustgarten. In 1935 it was redesigned as an austere parade ground, a function it retained in the GDR after the Second World War. After the Stadtschloss was demolished in 1950, the Lustgarten was combined with the ensuing large empty space to form Marx-Engels-Platz. The parade ground was then used by the East German government to hold military-political parades displaying its own brand of state socialism.

After the Berlin Wall was opened, no immediate decision was made on the future appearance of the square. In 1994, a competition design by the artist Gerhard Merz planned to separate the Lustgarten from Karl-Liebknecht-Strasse by a long pavilion. His plans could not be implemented. In 1996, following yet another competition, garden architect Gustav Lange proposed placing a dense row of boxwood trees placed in terracotta pots on the granite grid dating from the '30s. This plan did not meet with any resonance either. Consequently, since 1998 plans have been implemented to restore the historical character of the Lustgarten by reverting to Schinkel's original design. To this end, the innermost rows of trees were cut down to provide a view of the colonnade of the Altes Museum behind them.
However, the urban environs of the Lustgarten and the Altes Museum will not receive a composed form until a final agreement has been reached on the plans for Schlossplatz.

Berliner Dom

Julius Raschdorff;
Günter Stahn,
Bernhard Leisering
1894–1905;
1975–93
Am Lustgarten

The monumental Berliner Dom (Berlin Cathedral) was designed to be the most important church of German Protestantism and the court church of the Hohenzollern Dynasty. The new structure replaced its predecessor, which had been erected in 1750 and was partially redesigned by Karl Friedrich Schinkel in 1816. The frontal view of the cathedral, with its entrance in the wide porch facing the Lustgarten, is dominated by the mighty dome and the towers at the sides. The family tomb of the Hohenzollern in the crypt, which contains tombs and sarcophagi from four centuries, is one of the most important collections of sepulchral sculpture.
In 1975-81 the domes were reconstructed after plans by Günter Stahn. A modern lantern was added. The church tower was renovated by Bernhard Leisering. Work was completed in 1993 and the cathedral solemnly inaugurated in 1996. Apart from serving as a place of religious worship, concerts and plays are also performed there, and private functions held.

12.4

12.4 *Ensemble*

Altes Museum

Old Museum

Karl Friedrich Schinkel
1822–30
Am Lustgarten/
Bodestrasse

The Altes Museum, designed by Schinkel, is the most important example of Berlin Classicism of the 19th century. It is a testimony to the emancipatory claims of the educated, rising middle classes, inspired by intellectual and cultural values, in a society dominated by monarchical ideals. It was not until the early 19th century that anyone thought of making the royal art collections accessible to the public. The calls became more persistent and concrete after the artworks that had been seized and taken to Paris by Napoleon's troops between 1806 and 1814 were brought back to Berlin. Berlin humanist, Wilhelm von Humboldt, advocated public museums as centres of universal education. From 1822 on, Schinkel presented King Friedrich Wilhelm III a number of designs for the museum. The plans envisaged the construction of a broad columned hall in front of a large square building. Schinkel also designed the stairwell behind the columns, with two staircases leading in divergent directions up to a balcony-like gallery. The anteroom and the stairwell used to be lavishly adorned with frescos. A rotunda, based on the Pantheon in Rome, is located in the centre of the building. The museum rooms are grouped around it. The sculptures used to be exhibited on the first floor and the paintings on the top floor. Until the Alte Nationalgalerie has been completely restored, selected masterpieces will be shown from its stocks alongside exhibits from the Antiquity collection.

12.5 *Ensemble*

Alte Nationalgalerie

Old National Gallery

Friedrich August Stüler;
Johann Heinrich Strack
1862–64;
1866–76
Bodestrasse 1-3

The execution of the Nationalgalerie was carried out by Strack after plans by Stüler. The collection was founded by consul Joachim Wagner, a Berlin businessman, who donated his collection of contemporary art in 1859 on the condition that a special building was erected for it. The temple-like building rests on a huge plinth, in front of which there is a perron with an equestrian statue of Friedrich Wilhelm IV. Although the building opened in 1876 was originally devoted to "German art", the collection had already come to include international contemporary art by 1900. As of 2001, 19th century art will be presented here together with works from the "Gallery of the Romantic Art" at Charlottenburg Palace.

Neuer Marstall
Ernst von Ihne
1896–1902
Schloßplatz 7/
Breite Strasse

The Neuer Marstall (new royal stables), used to stand next to the Stadtschloss. The building with the imposing facades is considered one of the most important works of Wilhelminian state architecture.
The gable crowning on the main front has been missing since the war. A memorial plaque recalls the November Revolution of 1918, when the building served as the headquarters of the revolutionary sailors' council.
The Alter Marstall (old royal stables) is located in Breite Strasse in the same complex. This building, dating from 1669, was badly hit during the war; it was reconstructed in 1960.

Schloßplatz, Palast der Republik

Berlin City Palace

15.1
Ensemble

Until 1950, the Berliner Stadtschloss, which dates from the 15th century and was repeatedly extended over the centuries, stood in the centre of Berlin. The culmination of these conversions and extensions was Andreas Schlüter's design for a new facade, which was realised from 1699 on. Until 1918, the palace was home to Brandenburg margraves and electors, and later to the Prussian kings and German emperors. It was demolished in 1950-51. Apart from the war damage, the main reason for tearing it down was ideological. The

15.1

middle of "Socialist" Berlin was not to have a work of architecture bearing testimony to the monarchy and feudalism, but a square for mass rallies. The Palast der Republik (Palace of the Republic), erected in 1973-76 by Heinz Graffunder and Karl-Ernst Swora, took up half of the ground plan of the old Stadtschloss. It is a prime example of urban development in the centre of the capital of the GDR. In 1958, work was started to rebuild the political and cultural centre of the GDR on the basis of the National Reconstruction Programme (of 1951) and as a response to the competition, launched by the West German Bundestag in 1957, entitled "Berlin – capital city" (which addressed Berlin as a whole). The East German plans initially focused on the area to the east of the River Spree. The Palast der Republik on the Spree Island was not constructed until the '70s. Apart from the tribune, which accommodated the state and party leadership during rallies, the People's Chamber of the GDR and other public institutions were housed in this glass building. In 1991, it was closed because of asbestos contamination. Since then its future has been the subject of controversial debate over whether to demolish, preserve or extend it. Despite the many proposals for a new building and the international competition in 1994 to find a new design for the Spree Island, it has not yet been possible to reach any consensus on how to adequately use this part of the city, which is of such significance politically, historically, symbolically and in terms of urban design. Ever since an impressive, imitation full-scale facade of the original Stadtschloss was erected provisionally a few years back, people have continued to discuss whether its facade, at least, should not be reconstructed. Instead of a reaching a hasty decision, many different camps now advocate a pause to think things over.

15.2 *Ensemble*

Ehemaliges Staatsratsgebäude der DDR

Former Council of State building of the GDR

Roland Korn,
Hans-Erich Bogatzky,
Klaus Pätzmann
1962–64
Schloßplatz 1

The former Council of State building was the seat of the highest constitutional organ of the GDR. It is one of the most important witnesses of the architectural history of the GDR, since it documents the departure from the "national

15.2

style" plans of the '50s and a turn to International Modernism. The building was erected across Brüderstrasse, thus closing it off from Schlossplatz to this very day. The "Strasse an der Schleuse" (which was blocked off until recently) alongside the building has now been made accessible to the public again as an embankment.
A number of historical buildings were sacrificed to make way for the Council of State building. The fourth portal of the old Stadtschloss has been asymmetrically inserted into the main facade. The new building also shares it's floor arrangement. The portal was of considerable political significance for the GDR, because it was from the portal balcony that Karl Liebknecht declared the "Free Socialist Republic" on 9 November 1918.
Until 1994, the building was due for demolition. In 1995-99, the Information Office on Capital City Planning presented a multi-media exhibition here on the building activities of the Federal Government in Berlin. The exhibition included the large model of the inner city, which can now be seen in the former Staatsbank at Bebelplatz. In the spacious rooms more than 800 competition entries for the government district at the Spreebogen were evaluated and exhibited. As of 1999, the provisional official residence of the German Chancellor will be located here until the new Federal Chancellery is completed at the Spreebogen.

Ehemaliges Kaiser-Wilhelm-Denkmal

15.3 Ensemble

Former Kaiser Wilhelm Memorial

Gustav Halmhuber, Reinhold Begas
1894–1897
Schloßfreiheit

Only the plinth remains of the former Kaiser Wilhelm Memorial, which was erected in 1897 in front of the western facade of the Stadtschloss in honour of the first German emperor, Wilhelm I, who died in 1888. An impressive building with colonnades, lavishly adorned with sculptures, extended on the plinth well into the Kupfergraben. It framed the equestrian statue of Kaiser Wilhelm, designed by Reinhold Begas. Of all the decorative figures only an eagle and the lions have survived; they have been placed in front of the enclosure for beasts of prey at the Tierpark (zoo) in the Berlin district of Friedrichsfelde. The

16

remains of the monument were torn down and melted when the palace was demolished in 1950. Now the plinth, a very costly masterpiece of engineering art with an impressive vault inside, is waiting for adequate use. It has been considered as the site for the "Memorial to the Murdered European Jews" and for the "Memorial to German Unity"; plans also include housing a café, cultural facilities or other activities in the vault.

16

Bundesministerium für Auswärtige Angelegenheiten

Federal Ministry of Foreign Affairs

Heinrich Wolff;
Kollhoff & Timmermann, Berlin,
Thomas Müller,
Ivan Reimann, Berlin
1934–39;
1997–99
Werderscher Markt/
Kurstrasse 36

In 1994, the Federal Ministry of Foreign Affairs was promised the old building of the Reichsbank at Werderscher Markt, after plans to move to the site of the destroyed Stadtschloss on the Spree Island were abandoned because of the site's unique quality. Both the exigencies of protocol and the lack of available space made an extension necessary. The Berlin architects Müller and Reimann were commissioned to design the extension after a competition in 1996. They erected a compact building with an entrance courtyard facing north and a library courtyard facing east. The building takes up the old road alignment and has another ceremonial courtyard opposite the old Reichsbank building.

The Reichsbank building (1934-40) occupied five street blocks, thus cutting off a number of cross connections in the city. It was one of the largest buildings (with a usable floor area of 60,000 square metres) and – due to its steel-skeleton structure – one of the most modern administration buildings of its day. It supplemented the Oberwallstrasse site of the Reichsbank (destroyed during the war), which is now a green area. In 1933, Reichsbank building director Wolff emerged as the winner of the first architectural competition held by the Nazis. The most famous architects of the Modern Movement, such as Walter Gropius, Ludwig Mies van der Rohe and Hans Poelzig also submitted proposals. However, a building with a traditional facade was chosen for the first prestigious building of the Nazi regime. In the GDR the large building served the Ministry of Finance (from 1949-58) and, subsequently, the Central Committee of the ruling SED (Socialist Unity Party)

until 1989. The interior of the historical building was modified considerably to suit these changes in function.
Since 1997, Berlin architect Hans Kollhoff has been responsible for refurbishing the building. He is taking recourse to the historical furnishings and design of the '30s, because the lighting as well as the woodwork and interior furnishings supplied by the Deutsche Werkstätten Hellerau/Dresden, an association so rich in tradition, were exemplary at the time. The central banking hall is being converted into a conference hall. A canteen and a garden are planned for the roof area. Cologne artist Gerhard Merz is responsible for designing the reception hall. The huge strongroom of the Reichsbank is still located in the cellar. This strongroom was used to store the banknotes for montary union in 1990.

Ehemalige Bauakademie

Former Bauakademie

Karl Friedrich Schinkel
1832–36
Werderscher Markt

The quadrangular lawn reflecting the ground plan, as well as the sculpture of Karl Friedrich Schinkel, which has been re-erected at its former site, call to mind the former Bauakademie (Academy of Architecture). It was not only one of Schinkel's most revolutionary buildings, but also housed two important institutions: the Bauakademie, from which the Royal Technical University – a forerunner of the present Technical University – emerged in 1879, and the Oberbaudeputation, an authority responsible for monitoring all state building projects.
To the Modernists, the skeleton structure of the cubic brick building was an exemplary piece of architecture. In 1962, the building, which had been reconstructed provisionally after being damaged during the war, had to make way for the new building for the GDR Ministry of Foreign Affairs.
Since its demolition in 1995, rebuilding of the Bauakademie at Werderscher Markt has been under discussion.

Friedrichswerdersche Kirche

Friedrichswerdersche Church

Schinkel used the church to impose order on the unstructured area of Friedrichswerder, which emerged from the first Baroque urban extension scheme and received the status of a town in 1662. Originally, the building was to serve both the German and the French communities in

17

Karl Friedrich Schinkel
1824–30
Werderscher Markt

Friedrichswerder. After a number of designs had been submitted, the architect was commissioned to design the church in Gothic style, which at the time was mistakenly seen as the original Germanic building style. The plan to divide the nave did not materialise, as the church solely served the German community living in the area. Restoration work was completed and a museum of sculpture established here in 1987, in time for the 750th anniversary of the city.

17 Hauptstadtrepräsentanz der Deutschen Telekom

Capital Headquarters of the Deutsche Telekom telephone company

Wilhelm Salzenberg,
Adolph Lohse;
Carl Schwatlo;
Henze + Vahjen,
Brunswick/Berlin
1864;
1877–78;
1902;
1998–2000
Oberwallstrasse 5/
Jägerstrasse 42-44

In 1999, the seat of Deutsche Telekom AG in Berlin will be moving into the restored building of the oldest telephone exchange in Germany and thus returning to the roots of German telecommunications. The building was erected in Französische Strasse in 1864 by Salzenberg and Lohse as a telegraph office for the first lines in Berlin. In 1878, Schwatlo, the architect of the General Post Office, added a wing with a splendid facade in Jägerstrasse. In this section of the building, the atrium and various rooms with craft ornamentation are in need of extensive restoration. The building is intended to serve representational purposes. The slab building (in Französische Strasse), which was only completed in 1989, will give way to a new, modern building with a main entrance and a visitors' centre. Its modern steel-and-glass facade is continued in the attic of the old building in Oberwallstrasse. The adjacent building with its simple brick facade – modelled on the facade dating from 1864 – is an extension completed in 1902.

18.1 Hausvogteiplatz

Ensemble

The characteristic triangular form of Hausvoigteiplatz goes back to the former "Jägerbastion" of the 17th century fortress, which was demolished in 1740. The "Hausvogtei", the Royal Court and Prison, was located in the neighbouring hunting lodge from 1750 on. Starting in 1850, a large number of textiles companies established themselves here. In the 19th century, Haus-

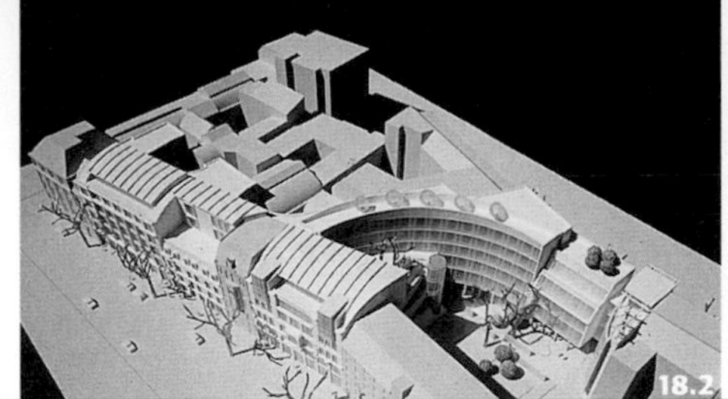

voigteiplatz became the centre of the Berlin fashion industry, which was largely in the hands of Jewish companies and designers – a tradition that disappeared with the expulsion and extermination of the Berlin Jews. Of the early production centres, the "Haus am Bullenwinkel" (Hausvogteiplatz 3-4) erected in 1893 by Alterthum & Zadek, and restored in 1997, remains an outstanding building. With the location of various television channels at Hausvogteiplatz, it is being revitalised as a centre of the media industry.

SAT 1 Sendezentrum

Ensemble 18.2

Dieter Hoffmann,
Frank Uellendahl, Berlin
1995–99
Oberwallstrasse 6-7/
Jägerstrasse 27-33/
Taubenstrasse 24-25

The private television company SAT 1 occupies a complex composed of a number of prestigious and, on the whole, listed old and new buildings, which are being converted and extended at great expense. The broadcasting company is thus concentrating its activities in Germany in one place. The main entrance is in a commercial property (dating from 1912) in Jägerstrasse; the former Kaufhaus Manheimer in Oberwallstraße, a department store that was completed in 1896, is being built higher. It will be give a glass barrel vaulted roof. In the courtyard a curved new section, housing the studios and technical equipment, extends to Taubenstrasse.

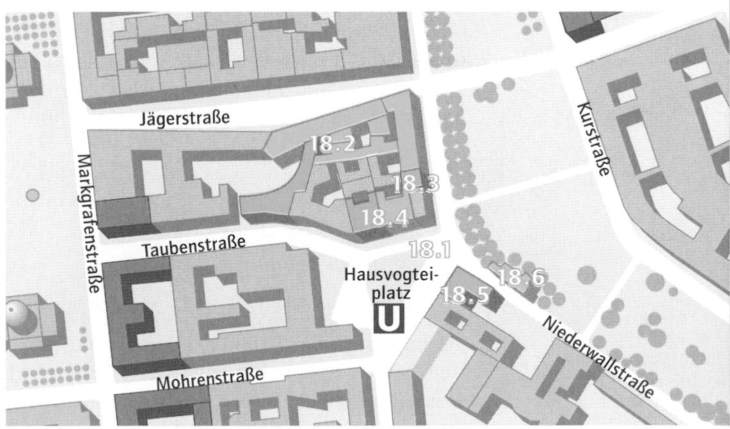

18.4

18.3 *Ensemble*

Hauptstadtrepräsentanz Pro7

Pro7 Capital Headquarters

Bothe, Richter, Teherani, Berlin
1997–98
Oberwallstrasse 8

The headquarters of the private television company Pro7 for Berlin and Brandenburg, was constructed on a narrow plot. The editorial and technical rooms are located in a new building surrounded by old buildings. A stairwell, preserved as being of historical interest, has been integrated into the new building.

18.4 *Ensemble*

Geschäftshaus, tv.Berlin

tv.Berlin building

Pysall, Stahrenberg & Partner, Berlin
1996–97
Hausvogteiplatz 2

The administration and management of the regional broadcasting company tv.Berlin are accommodated in a building with a red-sandstone grid facade. When conversion work has been completed on the building (1930, by Growald and Caspari) at Hausvogteiplatz 1, it will accommodate additional editorial rooms and studios.

18.5 *Ensemble*

Office Center am Auswärtigen Amt

Office Centre at the Ministry of Foreign Affairs

Christoph Czarniak, Wiesbaden
1998–99
Hausvogteiplatz 13/ Niederwallstrasse 1-2

The construction of a new building restores the original structure of the south side of the triangular Hausvogteiplatz. It has been added to an old building (1895, by Alterthum & Zadek) and follows the angles of a small inner courtyard. Shops are located on the ground floor. There are apartments in the roof parapet and the attic.

18.6 *Ensemble*

Botschaft des Königreichs Marokko

Embassy of the Kingdom of Morocco

GFB Gesellschaft für Bauplanung und Projektsteuerung mbH, Berlin
1998–99
Niederwallstrasse 39

The Moroccan Embassy is moving into a narrow old building which stood empty for quite some time and is now being completely renovated. This rather unobtrusive building is important in terms of both architectural and economic history. It was erected in 1770 and converted by Friedrich Waesemann, the architect of the Rotes Rathaus, in 1857. The building once belonged to the kurfürstlicher Jägerhof (Electoral Hunting Lodge), later used by the Reichsbank.

19

Bundesministerium für Justiz

Federal Ministry of Justice

Eller + Eller Architekten, Berlin/Düsseldorf
1896–1912;
1997–1999
Mohrenstrasse 36-37/
Jerusalemer Strasse/
Kronenstrasse 38-41

Since 1994, the Federal Ministry of Justice has been housed in a complex composed of buildings dating from different times. It occupies the eastern part of the block between Mohren-, Jerusalemer- and Kronenstrasse. The block lining Jerusalemer Strasse was begun before the Berlin Wall fell and completed in 1994. It was intended to be an extension of the GDR Patent Office. The courtyard contains a cubic raw building that now houses the library. The old buildings in Mohrenstrasse – the "Prausenhof" (1913, by Ludwig Otte), the "Haus Nagel" (1896, by Carl Bauer), the former "Graumann & Stern" textiles company (1901, by A. Wanckel) and a narrow commercial building (1914, by Hermann Muthesius) are protected buildings in the process of restoration. All of the buildings are linked to one another, even though their rooms are of varying height. The East German Press Office moved into the building of the Graumann & Stern textiles company in 1977. It was here, on 9 November 1989, that Günter Schabowski (a member of the party central committee) announced to the press – responding rather ambiguosly to the question of a journalist – that East German citizens were free to travel. His statement was understood to mean that the Berlin Wall was open.

Mohrenkolonnaden

Carl Gotthard Langhans
1787
Mohrenstrasse 37/40

The colonnades now installed in the house facades are an important architectural relic for the city of Berlin. The fortification ring and moat (realised after plans by Johann Gregor Memhardt) separated Friedrichswerder from what would later become Friedrichstadt. Only a few bridges crossed the moat. They were given an ornamental design at the end of the 18th century. Carl Gotthard Langhans designed the Mohren Colonnades erected on one of the bridges. The decoration was sculpted by Johann Gottfried Schadow and Bernhard Rode. When the moat was filled in, the bridge colonnades remained in the street area and were subsequently included in development.

20.1 *Ensemble*

Quartier 30

Claude Vasconi, Paris,
Joe Coenen, Maastricht,
Heinz Tesar, Vienna
1999–2001
Mohrenstrasse/
Markgrafenstrasse/
Kronenstrasse

The new building for Quartier 30 continues the block to the west of the Ministry of Justice. The complex consists of five office and residential buildings grouped around a common courtyard accessible to the public. Three architects were responsible for designing the buildings. The accentuated cornice marks the Berlin eaves' height on the fifth floor. The narrow-side of the office building (designed by Tesar) stretches from Mohrenstrasse to Kronenstrasse and forms the east facade. It is linked to the residential and administration buildings – with their three cubic roof extensions – designed by the architect Coenen. The head building in Markgrafenstrasse was designed by Vasconi. It consists of two horizontally articulated sections of unequal size.

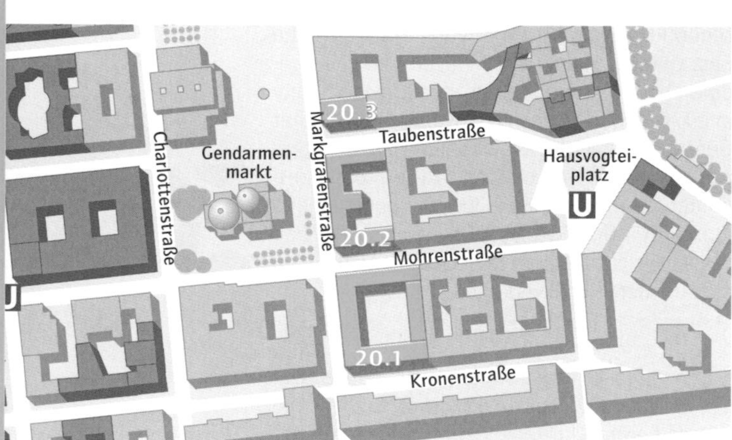

20.2 *Ensemble*

Markgrafenblock

Josef Paul Kleihues, Berlin,
Max Dudler, Zurich/Berlin,
Hilmer & Sattler
with Partner T. Albrecht,
Berlin/Munich
1994–96
Markgrafenstrasse 34/
Mohrenstrasse 45

Opposite the Deutscher Dom, three new buildings standing between Taubenstrasse and Mohrenstrasse border the eastern side of Gendarmenmarkt square. The southern office and residential building designed by Kleihues is characterised by its round tower, whose roof is crowned by the geometric figures of the barrel and the cube. Windows closely arranged side-by-side in the light-coloured sandstone facade form a horizontal band.

The symmetrical dark facade of the residential, office and commercial building in the middle of

20.3

the block was designed by Dudler. From 1885 on, the first public power station supplying the inner city with electricity was located here. It was constructed by the two electrical companies "Allgemeine Elektrizitätswerke, AEG" and the "Berliner Elektrizitäts Werke, BEW". The new building of the Bewag (the Berlin power-supply company) on this site takes up this tradition. The courtyard facade with its ochre facing serves as a reminder of the site's technological past. (The courtyard facades of industrial buildings in Berlin were traditionally light coloured)
Like the other buildings, the glimmering light pink corner house designed by Hilmer & Sattler has shops on the ground floor and offices on the upper floors. The unobtrusive facade is characterised by its sharp horizontal and rounded vertical edges.

Wissenschaftsforum Berlin

Berlin Science Forum

20.3 *Ensemble*

Wilhelm Holzbauer, Wien
1996–98
Markgrafenstrasse 37/
Taubenstrasse 30

The new building for the Wissenschaftsforum Berlin will be surrounded by the old building of the Berlin Brandenburg Academy of Sciences in Markgrafenstrasse and Taubenstrasse and completes the eastern side of Gendarmenmarkt square. The functional and institutional affinity between the two buildings is expressed in their uniform wall-pillar arrangement, their eaves' height and roof pitch. The steel construction of the roof is clad with slats revealing the set-back storeys behind them. A glass stairwell in Taubenstrasse marks the transition to the neighbouring building. Behind the main entrance there is a house-high atrium with an additional stairwell leading to passageways and galleries.
The Wissenschaftsforum, which was founded in 1991, brings together all of Germany's most important science organisations and locates their Berlin headquarters in the new building. The neighbouring Academy of Sciences dates back to the "Brandenburg Science Society" founded in 1700.
The institution arose in its present form in 1992, when the science academies in east and west Berlin were combined. After 1945 the academy in former East Berlin was housed in the complex designed by Paul Kieschke at Gendarmenmarkt. Before the Second World War, the complex

21.1

belonged to the Prussian State Bank (Preussische Seehandlung). With its new buildings and users, the Gendarmenmarkt, in contrast to the far-more-commercial Friedrichstrasse, once again represents the "tranquil" pendant of science and culture.

21.1 *Ensemble*

Deutscher und Französischer Dom

German and French Cathedral

Martin Grünberg,
Louis Cayart,
Abraham Quesnay;
Carl von Gontard;
Roland Steiger,
Ingeborg Konegen;
Jürgen Pleuser, Berlin
1701–08;
1781–85;
1983–89;
1992–96
Gendarmenmarkt 1-2, 5-6

Three blocks, where two small Protestant churches were erected in 1701-08, were kept free at the centre of the regular street network in Friedrichstadt. In 1701, Grünberg designed the Deutscher Dom and Cayart and Quesnay designed the Französischer Dom, which served the French Huguenot community. The Huguenots had been expelled from France and settled in Berlin following the Edict of Potsdam of 1685. The French Cathedral is since its restoration in 1984 the home of the Huguenot Museum. After 1781, architect Carl von Gontard had high tower structures erected in front of both churches. The towers, which were not really a part of the church buildings as such, served as landmarks with a purely prestigious function. Since the Deutscher Dom was rebuilt in 1983-89 and restored in 1996, it has housed the exhibition: "Questions on German History" which had previously been in the Reichstag. Pleuser, the architect responsible, has accentuated the new concrete installations inside the building to contrast them with the old, bare masonry, which still reveals the scars of war.

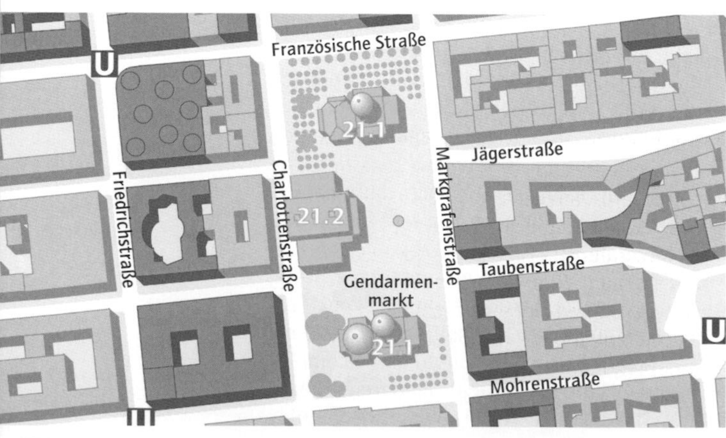

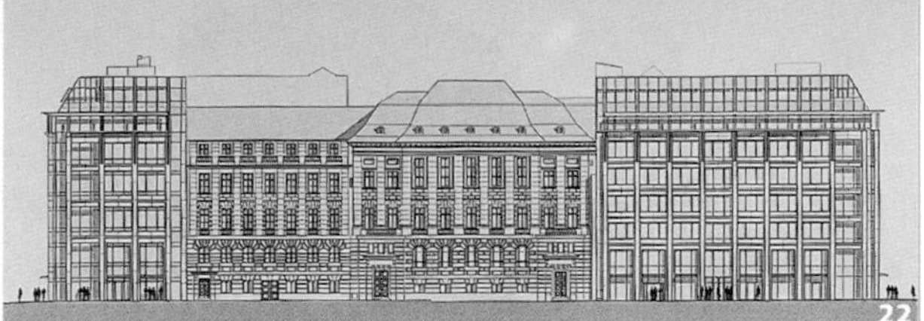

Konzerthaus

21.2 *Ensemble*

The Konzerthaus (concert hall), the Deutscher and Französischer Dom at the Gendarmenmarkt are the most beautiful ensemble of buildings in Berlin. The Konzerthaus was originally designed by Schinkel as theatre (1818-21) to replace the National Theatre, which had burned down. Inside, he created a completely new experience of space by constructing a lower and broader proscenium, instead of the higher Baroque stage. The building was badly damaged during World War II. It was reopened in 1984 following comprehensive restoration; the finished product did not remain faithful to the original building, but expressed its new function as a concert hall.

Karl Friedrich Schinkel;
K. Just, Manfred Prasser
1818–21;
1979–84
Gendarmenmarkt 3-4

Kreditanstalt für Wiederaufbau

22

Bank for Reconstruction

The Kreditanstalt für Wiederaufbau has established its administrative headquarters in the traditional Berlin banking district. It was founded as a bank under public law in Frankfurt am Main in 1948. With the aid of loans supplied under the Marshall Plan, the bank financed the reconstruction of Germany after the Second World War.
The extensive complex comprises a number of old buildings which have been supplemented by two new buildings. The prestigious buildings (dating from 1899) of the old Berliner Handelsgesellschaft in Behrenstrasse were designed by Alfred Messel. Those standing at the corner of Französische Strasse and Charlottenstrasse were completed in 1911 after designs by Heinrich Schweitzer. In 1949 the buildings were taken over by the State Bank of the GDR. The design of the new buildings in Behrenstrasse, at the corner of Charlottenstrasse and Markgrafenstrasse, was inspired by the surrounding buildings, which are under a preservation order. They are connected via courtyards and tunnels.
The plot at the corner of Französische Strasse and Markgrafenstrasse is being developed by the Colonia group. They are erecting a commercial building designed by Berlin architects Ehlers and Krop; the building will complete the block at the Gendarmenmarkt.

ABB,
Heinz Scheid,
Johannes Schmidt & Partner,
Frankfort on the Main
1999–2000
Markgrafenstrasse/
Behrenstrasse/
Charlottenstrasse

23.1 *Ensemble*

Bebelplatz

Forum Fridericianum

Plans were first drawn up for the prestigious royal "Forum Fridericianum" when Friedrich II came to power in 1740. The Forum includes what is now the developed square of Bebelplatz and Humboldt University (originally built as a palace). Georg Wenzeslaus von Knobelsdorff designed the Royal Opera House (now Deutsche Staatsoper – the German State Opera House), which was constructed in 1741-43 in the style of the Italian architect Andrea Palladio, on the eastern side of the square. The building was supposed to symbolise the freedom of artistic expression.

By having St. Hedwig's Cathedral constructed at the southern end of the Forum in 1747, Friedrich II set an example for the freedom of religious belief. Ever since the Reformation of 1539, Protestantism had been the dominant religion in Berlin and Brandenburg. Not until the 18th century was a small Catholic community able to establish itself. And it was for this community that this distinguished, central building, fronted by a columned hall, was erected.

On the western side, the Royal Library was constructed as a symbol of scientific freedom after plans by Georg Christian Unger. Inspired by the Michael Block of the Hofburg Palace (of 1726) in Vienna, the construction of the library was executed by Georg Friedrich Boumann (1774-80). The building now houses Humboldt University Library. The Baroque town square, once planted with bushes, has not been historically reconstructed but left as a paved area.

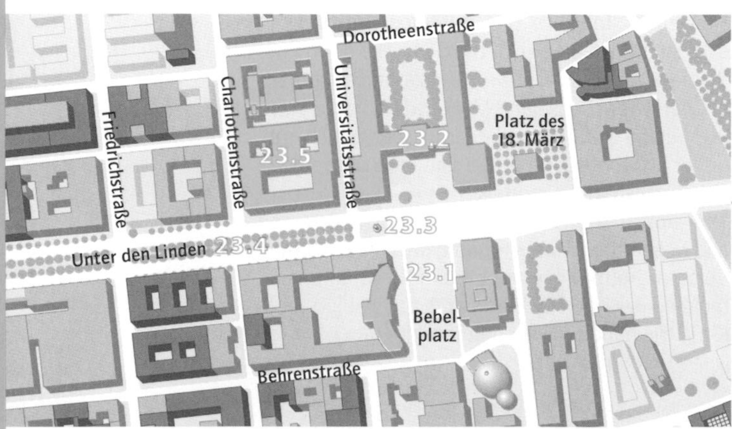

Since 1995, a memorial has stood in the centre to recall the "book-burning" organised by the Nazis. On 10 May 1933 a column of students led by Goebbels, the Minister for Propaganda, descended on the square and burned – in an act of barbarism – some 20,000 books of world literature written by Jewish, pacifist and anti-fascist authors on a fire in front of the library. The memorial was designed by Israeli artist Micha Ullman. Looking through a glass plate one can see a sunken, brightly-lit room with empty shelves symbolising the books that were burnt.

Humboldt-Universität

23.2 *Ensemble*

Georg Wenzeslaus von Knobelsdorff, Johann Boumann; Ludwig Hoffmann
1748–53;
1913–20
Unter den Linden 6

Humboldt University is the oldest university in Berlin, as well as being a testimony to the enlightened middle-classes emerging in the early 19th century. It was founded in 1810 at the instigation of Wilhelm von Humboldt, the humanist. In 1819 the Friedrich Wilhelm University moved into the former Stadtpalais of Prince Heinrich, which had been built in 1748-53 to complete the northern side of the Forum Fridericianum. In 1913, municipal building surveyor Ludwig Hoffmann had two wings added to the building, thus extending it on the northern side. After the GDR was founded in 1949, the university was named after Wilhelm von Humboldt, whose ideas had inspired its foundation. There were already signs in 1948 of the impending division of Berlin when the Freie Universität was founded with the support of the Western Allies in the Berlin district of Dahlem. After the opening of the Berlin Wall, it became necessary to reorganise the Berlin universities, which comprised the Freie Universität, the Technical University and the Humboldt University, as well as the Academy of Arts and Music.

Reiterstandbild Friedrichs II.

Equestrian statue of Friedrich II

23.3 *Ensemble*

Christian Daniel Rauch
1836–51;
1999
Unter den Linden

After Friedrich II died in 1786, a number of proposals were considered to find a site for an impressive monument in Unter den Linden. However, the equestrian statue by sculptor Christian Daniel Rauch was not completed and unveiled until 1851. It is his principal work, and one of the most important bronze sculptures of the 19th century. The King is presented as a dignified philosopher holding a cane and wearing a cocked hat. The three-step pedestal bears the portraits and inscriptions of names of important contemporaries as well as reliefs depicting scenes from the life of Friedrich II. For the very first time, a grand equestrian statue also honoured citizens, in this case Kant and Lessing, who were depicted sculpturally on the pedestal. The equestrian statue was removed for ideological reasons in 1950 and erected in Sanssouci Park in Potsdam in 1963. In 1981 it was returned to its original location in Unter den Linden. It remains to be seen whether the statue and its pedestal will be returned to their original location, about 12 metres to the west.

23.4 *Ensemble*

Unter den Linden

When Unter den Linden, Berlin's most splendid boulevard was constructed in 1647, it was still outside the city walls, linking the Stadtschloss with the royal hunting grounds in the Tiergarten. When the city was extended to include Dorotheenstadt and Friedrichstadt in the 18th century, Unter den Linden became the main urban axis of the two districts. It was only here that trees were planted to line the street. In principle, the boulevard now pointed far beyond the city to the royal summer residence in Charlottenburg. To the east, it was flanked by the royal, Prussian Adelspalais and, to the west, by the residential and commercial buildings of the emergent middle classes. The avenue between the Stadtschloss and Brandenburg Gate advanced in status from being a street that traditionally had few businesses but plenty of cafés and restaurants, to Berlin's principal boulevard. Great importance was attached to the design of the buildings, which found its expression in the "prescribed facades" of the 18th and the "Linden statute" of the 20th century. The gaps between buildings caused by the bombs of the Second World War were filled with block-length administration buildings by the GDR. This development spelled the end of the old commercial and residential structure of the area, which was based on small-scale units. After the Wall was opened, efforts have been increased to restore Unter den Linden to its former status of being a boulevard by erecting

new buildings and reconstructing existing buildings and roads. The western part between Brandenburg Gate and Friedrichstrasse is now dominated by buildings serving political, diplomatic and cultural purposes. Moving east – towards the Schlossbrücke – it is the cafés, businesses, hotels and the historical buildings of the New Guardhouse, the university, the State Opera House and the Zeughaus which predominate. In 1998, the promenade in the centre-strip of the boulevard was restored.

Staatsbibliothek Unter den Linden 23.5

Unter den Linden State Library

Ensemble

Ernst von Ihne
1903–14
Unter den Linden 8

In 1914, the imposing building of the Prussian State Library replaced the building complex in which the "Brandenburg Science Society" had held its first meeting in 1711. The society was founded by Gottfried Wilhelm Leibniz in 1700. Visitors entered the neo-Baroque sandstone building, through a picturesque ceremonial courtyard. They passed through a prestigiously designed stairwell on their way to the dome-covered reading room – then considered to be one of the finest in Europe. It was destroyed during the Second World War. In its place, the government of the GDR erected a soberly designed tower for storing books.

After the construction of the Berlin Wall in 1961, the New State Library was built at the Cultural Forum to make up for the loss. In 1990, the two establishments in the two halves of the city were united. The vast stock of the new library, with more than twelve million volumes, make it one of the largest in the world. Today, parts of the valuable collection are located in Poland and Russia, where they were taken during the Second World War.

Deutsche Bank AG, Deutsche Guggenheim 24

Benedict Tonon (design), Novotny & Mähner Assoziierte, Offenbach/Berlin
1994–97
Unter den Linden 13-15/ Charlottenstrasse

The head administration of the Deutsche Bank has had two listed buildings renovated and extended in co-operation with the Guggenheim Museum New York.

The building (1888-91, by Ende & Böckmann), which is adorned with a red sandstone facade is now a branch of the bank.

27.1

Two stories that were later added to the corner building (1922-25, by Bielenberg & Moser) were removed again.
The set-back section of the building in Charlottenstrasse was increased in height by two stories and given a glass facade. The section in Unter den Linden contains the German branch of the Guggenheim Museum, which also has branches in Venice and Bilbao.

25

Charlottenpalais

Patzschke, Klotz & Partner, Berlin
1997–98
Charlottenstrasse 35-36

Charlottenpalais is a new residential and commercial building replacing the one destroyed during the Second World War. The architects, Patzschke and Klotz, who also designed Hotel Adlon, have recreated the original building dating from the turn of the century.

26

Deutscher Sparkassen- und Giroverband

German Savings Bank and Giro Association

Wilhelm Martens;
Karl Heinz Schommer, Bonn/Berlin
1900–01;
1998–2000
Behrenstrasse 46/
Charlottenstrasse 47/
Rosmarinstrasse 10

The eastern side of block 209a, bounded by Behrenstrasse, Charlottenstrasse and Rosmarinstrasse is taken up by a bank built in 1901. New storeys were added in 1920. It was renovated and refurbished in simplified form in 1950. In 1998, work was started on totally converting the building for the Berlin headquarters of the Deutsche Sparkassen- and Giroverband. All that will remain of the original will be the listed facade and a stairwell in Behrenstrasse. The ground floor and first floor will be converted to include a foyer for functions and events. The top storey is being renovated to house prestigious conference rooms beneath a glass barrel roof.

27.1
Ensemble

Rosmarin Karree

Petra and Paul Kahlfeldt, Berlin,
Ingeborg Lindner-Böge, Jürgen Böge, Hamburg
1995–98
Rosmarinstrasse/
Behrenstrasse

The Rosmarin Karree arcade lies between Rosmarinstrasse, Friedrichstrasse and Behrenstrasse. The new buildings of a residential and a commercial building stand right next to a listed bank building. The nine-storey residential building set back in the complex was designed by Berlin architects Petra and Paul Kahlfeld. It is clad in shell limestone slabs, which distinctly set off the

characteristic steel structure of the winter gardens. Some of the 70 apartments have been designed as maisonettes.

The commercial building designed by Hamburg architects Böge and Lindener-Böge occupies the greater part of the block. It is constructed on a raised plinth with colonnades. The glass mezzanine makes the four main floors appear to float. The flush, smooth glass box extending over the entire facade is designed to create a hermetic air-conditioned space. The actual building can be identified by the wooden window frames behind the glass.

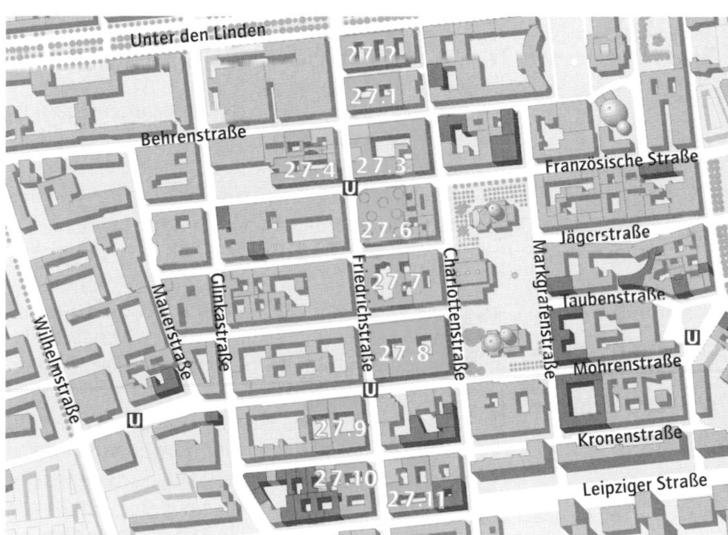

Lindencorso

27.2
Ensemble

Christoph Mäckler Architekten,
Frankfort on the Main/Berlin
1993–96
Unter den Linden/
Friedrichstrasse

The Lindencorso was one of the first new buildings to be completed in Friedrichstadt after the Berlin Wall was opened in 1989. This office and commercial building was one of the causes of the dispute among architects that raged in Berlin between 1991 and 1994 over whether to use glass or stone facades and open or closed, dense town plans (s. p. 159).

The stone character of this seven-storey building is accentuated by the workmanship of the limestone facing and the entablature resting on shoulders. Stone window frames protrude from the facades. The oval atrium, which extends over three floors, is accessible from Unter den Linden

27.3

and Friedrichstrasse. The previous building (1966) did not extend to this point, where a two-storey arcade now covers the walkway. Friedrichstrasse was then widened to 40 metres.
In 1993, the old building was torn down and a new one constructed with the aim of restoring the original dimensions of the Friedrichstrasse.

27.3 *Ensemble*

Hofgarten am Gendarmenmarkt

Hofgarten at Gendarmenmarkt

Josef Paul Kleihues, Berlin,
Max Dudler, Zurich/Berlin,
Jürgen Sawade, Berlin,
Kollhoff & Timmermann,
Berlin
1993–96
Französische Strasse/
Charlottenstrasse/
Behrenstrasse/
Friedrichstrasse

The Hofgarten Karree arcade is an attempt to combine the development of a large block with the individual qualities of different architectural styles in order to recreate the image of an urban scenario composed of small units. The overall plan of the block, with its subterranean garage, inner courtyard and house entrances, was designed by Kleihues. He also designed the Four Seasons Hotel on the eastern block edge towards the Gendarmenmarkt. Kleihues invited the architects Dudler, Kollhoff and Sawade to design the other houses in the block. Kollhoff designed the office and commercial building at the corner of Friedrichstrasse and Französische Strasse, providing it with a greyish-green granite facade with pilaster strips to create a vertical rhythm. Kollhoff's design encloses a Baroque building, which collapsed during construction work and had to be reconstructed as a copy. Sawade designed the highly polished, black office building in the style of Classical Modernism in Französische Strasse, and Dudler the austerely articulated apartment building in Behrenstrasse. The old building at the corner of Behrenstrasse and Friedrichstrasse was renovated, increased in height and integrated into the block development.

27.4 *Ensemble*

Forum des Deutschen Beamtenbundes

Forum of the Deutscher Beamtenbund

Karl Heinz Schommer,
Bonn/Berlin
1998–2001
Friedrichstrasse 165-170/
Behrenstrasse 23-26/
Französische Strasse 49-52

The Deutscher Beamtenbund (German Federation of Civil Servants) acquired the large complex, including listed buildings, between Friedrichstrasse, Behrenstrasse and Französische Strasse in 1997. A part of the complex, at Friedrichstrasse 165, was occupied in 1990 by various

popular movements and named the "House of Democracy" (1899, by Kayser & Grossheim.) For a number of years, questions of German unity were discussed here. The neighbouring commercial building (1899, by Wendelstadt and Welsch) and the "Automat" commercial building in Friedrichstrasse 167-168 (1905, by Bruno Schmitz) are also important works. A building in Behrenstrasse as well as the old Reichskreditgesellschaft building (1936, by Breuhaus de Groot), which was originally under a preservation order, are being demolished and replaced by new buildings.

Friedrichstraße

27.5 *Ensemble*

The intersection of Friedrichstrasse and Unter den Linden is considered to be the real civil centre of Berlin. Like Unter den Linden, Friedrichstrasse is also a product of the Baroque extension of the city in the late 17th century. It was the most important north-south link in Berlin and covers 3.3 kilometres from its starting point in the north (at Oranienburger Tor) to the present Mehringplatz in the south. It forms the backbone of the side streets branching off at right-angles in Friedrichstadt. It was only after 1850 that Friedrichstrasse, with its countless cafés, restaurants, department stores and businesses, became the busiest and most disreputable street it Berlin.
After the Second World War, the division of the city meant that Friedrichstrasse more or less ceased to be used by road traffic since it ran up against the Berlin Wall both in the north (where it continues as Chausseestrasse) and in the south, where it was interrupted by Checkpoint Charlie.
Since 1990, Friedrichstrasse, along with Potsdamer Platz, has become the most important scene of endeavours to revitalise the city. The architectural designs triggered a heated debate over contemporary "city architecture": should facades be clad in stone or glass? As a matter of principle, the development plans refused to fall back on the small-scale structures and units once so characteristic of Friedrichstrasse. Instead, a fundamental decision was made to adhere to the historical, narrow street profile and continue developing the large blocks that were begun in the GDR. In contrast to the past, Friedrichstrasse

has assumed a completely different character now that sophisticated retail businesses have located there. To the north of Unter den Linden and Friedrichstrasse railway station as well as to the south of Leipziger Strasse and Checkpoint Charlie, Friedrichstrasse is undergoing a radical change in character corresponding to the changes in clientele.

27.6 *Ensemble*

Galeries Lafayette (Quartier 207)

Jean Nouvel, Paris
1993–96
Friedrichstrasse 75

Although the FriedrichstadtPassagen, between Französische Strasse and Mohrenstrasse, appear in very different architectural guises above ground, they are linked by one subterranean passage. When the Wall was opened in 1989, the raw building of an East German department store covering three blocks stood here. It was demolished following an investors' competition (in 1990) in which the future developers undertook to involve a number of different architects in their planning. The aim was to create a diversified image of the city composed of different buildings. The structural form of Friedrichstrasse, which can be seen in exemplary fashion here, is the result of two divergent goals: on the one hand the stipulation that the Berlin eaves' height be observed, and, on the other hand, the desire to maximise land utilisation. As a consequence, developers have built downwards and added stepped-back storeys above the eaves' height.
The foundations of buildings here are on a brown-coal seam at a maximum depth of 40 metres. In contrast to Potsdamer Platz, groundwater management has not been necessary here. Given building ground conditions in Berlin, however, construction downwards increases costs to such an extent that it soon ceases to be commercially viable.
The Galeries Lafayette (designed by Nouvel), with its all-glass facade, cites the Berlin Modernists of the '20s, supplementing their style with contemporary effects of the '90s. The interior – a modern interpretation of the traditional department store atrium – is dominated by two spectacular cones that form an atrium extending over several storeys, giving the beholder a view of the entire department store at the core of the building. Office rooms are located above the Galeries Lafayette and on the street side.

Quartier 206

27.7 *Ensemble*

In his facade design, with its acute-angled oriels and folds, for Quartier 206, American architect Cobb follows the tradition of Expressionist architecture. Continuous row light fixtures and glass signs form a brightly shining "second skin" behind which the building almost seems to disappear at night. With a combination of escalators and perrons and colourful marble mosaic, the lens-shaped atrium inside the building provides scenic views of the lively courtyard facades. Luxury shops have been established on the lower floors; the upper floors are used as offices.

Pei, Cobb, Freed & Partners, New York
1992–96
Friedrichstrasse 71-74

Quartier 205

27.8 *Ensemble*

Quartier 205 (the numbers refer to blocks in the city) is by far the largest of the three buildings in the FriedrichstadtPassagen and fills the entire block as far as the Gendarmenmarkt. The eminent Cologne architect Oswald Mathias Ungers divided the huge solid structure into two layers. Six lower "houses" surround the eight-storey core building and structure the large complex. The facade colours change from bronze-brown to white. The windows are flush with the facade and only appear to have depth due to their colouring. The strictly geometrical quadrangular grid covers the building like a network, also dividing it internally into two atriums. Restaurants and shops are located in the lower floors. The storeys above them are used as offices. Without making any stylistic allusions, Ungers establishes a referential relationship to Schinkel's Konzerthaus building diagonally opposite.

Oswald Mathias Ungers & Partner GmbH, Berlin
1992–96
Friedrichstrasse 66-70

Bundesministerium für Familie, Senioren, Frauen und Jugend

28

Federal Ministry for Family Affairs, Pensioners, Women and Youth

Even after the German parliament and government have moved to Berlin, the Federal Ministry for Family Affairs will continue to have its second residence in Bonn. Its principal residence will be in a former bank building (1896, by Kayser & Grossheim) in Jägerstrasse and in a pre-fabrica-

Bultmann & Team, Berlin
1998–99
Taubenstrasse 42-43/
Jägerstrasse 8-9

29

ted building from GDR days. The ministry's rooms will be located in another building (1926, by Moritz Ernst Lesser).

29

KPMG-Verwaltungsgebäude

KPMG administration building

Christoph Mäckler Architekten, Frankfort on the Main/Berlin
1996–98
Taubenstrasse 45

The central administration of the KPMG auditing company is returning to the location where it had its domicile from 1927 to 1945. In 1990 it was able to purchase the property in an empty lot. The new building by Christoph Mäckler responds to the problematic location of a property surrounded by buildings on three sides by using the traditional Berlin structure of a double L-ground plan. The customary inner courtyard has been designed here as a glass, house-high atrium supplying the inner office rooms with light.

Pfarrhäuser der Dreifaltigkeitskirche

The vicarages of the Dreifaltigkeitskirche (Church of the Holy Trinity)
1739
Taubenstrasse 3/
Glinkastrasse

The two vicarages are the last surviving 18th century residential houses in Friedrichstadt. Originally there were three buildings, here in Taubenstrasse and Glinkastrasse. However, the residence of the eminent theologian and co-founder of the Humboldt University, Friedrich Schleiermacher, in Glinkastrasse, was destroyed during the Second World War.

30

n-tv

1895–1901;
1922–23
Glinkastrasse 13-15/
Taubenstrasse 1/
Mauerstrasse 18-21

In 1992, the n-tv news channel moved into a building constructed in 1895-1901 for the insurance company Allianz Versicherung. In 1922-23, the prestigious building was made higher. The facade, with its rustic plinth and pillar articulation, was left unchanged when it was renovated in 1991. The interior was redesigned for archives, editorial rooms and studios. Other broadcasting companies, such as the US news channel, CNN, have also moved into the building since 1992.

31

Bundesministerium für Arbeit

Federal Ministry of Labour

Karl Reichle;
Josef Paul Kleihues, Berlin
1935–40;
1998–99
Mauerstrasse 45-52/
Wilhelmstrasse 19

Like the Ministry of Finance (see p. 95), the Federal Ministry of Labour is also moving into a building constructed in Wilhelmstrasse during the Nazi period. Very few squares in Berlin have witnessed so many historical changes as Wilhelmplatz, which used to be the site of a palace converted by Schinkel in 1827 for Prince Karl. After 1933, it was used by the Ministry for Propaganda under Goebbels' leadership and extended as far as Mauerstrasse in 1935. The building was close to Hitler's Reich Chancellery. The old palace was destroyed during the war. Later, the intact buildings were used by the National Council as well as the Press and Information Office of the GDR.
The Ministry of Labour will extend to the adjacent "Kleisthaus". It was erected as the "Bankhaus Von der Heydt" by Bodo Ebhardt in 1912 and decorated with reliefs by Georg Kolbe. The entire complex was completed after plans by Berlin architect Josef Paul Kleihues, who chose to preserve the historical changes to the building in his design.

32

Landesvertretung Freistaat Thüringen

The Land representation of the Free State of Thuringia

Worschech & Partner,
Erfurt
1997–1999
Mauerstrasse 54-55/
Mohrenstrasse

The Free State of Thuringia is the only German Land that has been able to regain a property that it once owned. After the Berlin tax office demanded land tax with retroactive effect for a property of 750 square metres in the district of Mitte, the Thuringian government became aware of the existence of the plot where "Thuringia House" used to stand. Purchased in 1932, it was badly damaged during the war and was later pulled down. The site subsequently served as a car park.
The new building comprises two sections: a cubic stone office building on the outside and a glass structure inside with a view of the courtyard. Working and residential areas are planned in the stone building. There will be a restaurant in typical Thuringian style in the basement. The glass section is to contain a foyer, exhibition areas, conference rooms and a library.

27.10

27.9 *Ensemble*

Kontorhaus Friedrichstraße

Josef Paul Kleihues, Berlin,
Klaus Theo Brenner, Berlin,
Marlene Dörrie,
Vittorio Magnago Lampugnani, Milan/Zurich,
Walther Stepp, Berlin
1994–97
Friedrichstrasse 185-189/
Mohrenstrasse 13-16/
Kronenstrasse 60-65

The Kontorhaus Friedrichstrasse is based on the same organisational principle as the Hofgarten Karree. Here, too, Kleihues was responsible for the planning and included various architects in the design work. He designed the ground plan of the block – with its subterranean garage, an inner courtyard and entrances – using a modular construction system. Architects Klaus Theo Brenner, Marlene Dörrie in collaboration with Vittorio Magnago Lampugnani and Walther Stepp all participated in designing the individual houses. Kleihues also designed the glass-roofed atrium, the boarding house inside the complex and the commercial building – facing Friedrichstrasse – with its "ship-shaped"-entrance. Brenner's facade at the corner of Kronenstrasse is a remarkable piece of architecture. "Aluminium swords" placed between granite slabs accentuate the structural technique behind the stone curtain wall.

Zentralverband des Deutschen Handwerks

National Association of German Trades and Crafts

Georg Rathenau,
Friedrich August Hartmann;
Erich Kuhnert; Steinebach & Weber, Berlin
1908;
1950–57;
1997–99
Mohrenstrasse 20-21

The headquarters of the Zentralverband des Deutschen Handwerks is located in a building that uniquely documents the housing and construction policy of the early GDR. The commercial building, erected in 1908, was damaged during the Second World War. In 1950, the architect Erich Kuhnert was commissioned to reconstruct it. One year later, a decision was made at the highest political level to widen Friedrichstrasse and thus transform it into a 66-metre-wide boulevard. When the houses in Friedrichstrasse were demolished, the building in Mohrenstrasse became the corner building and a high tower was erected in front of the original compartment wall as a prestigious facade. These conversions were only carried out in 1957, however, after the GDR had already moved away from a "national style" of architecture (as in the buildings along the former Stalinallee, now Karl Marx Allee), and towards industrial construction design.

On completion, the building was occupied by the National Democratic Party of Germany (the NDPD). Apart from the offices a 45-metre frieze by Waldemar Grzimek has also survived. The Berlin office of Steinebach & Weber converted the building into an association headquarters.

Quartier 108

27.10 *Ensemble*

The imposing commercial building at block 108 rises above the intersection of Friedrichstrasse and Leipziger Strasse. The pavement and the shops are situated beneath two-storey-high colonnades. The shining granite facade exploits the interplay of silver and black. The facade is completed by an entablature projecting 2 metres. Looking above the entablature, one can see three attic storeys with a high-grade steel skin.

Thomas van den Valentyn
mit Matthias Dittmann, Cologne
1996–98
Friedrichstrasse 191

Atrium Friedrichstraße

27.11 *Ensemble*

The corner building designed by Marg, of the gmp team of architects in Hamburg, is crowned by a tower. It was only the reduction of Leipziger Strasse to its original width that made construction possible. Originally, the building was to be the prelude to a development extending along Leipziger Strasse as far as Charlottenstrasse, and was planned as a continuous passage parallel to Leipziger Strasse. However, the investor was not able to acquire the adjacent property. Consequently, nothing came of the magnificent gesture of creating a perron the width of an atrium in a space that had only itself as its reference point. The atrium is covered by a glass barrel roof and illuminates the inner office rooms above the mezzanine. It is enlivened by a sound-sculpture created by artist Bernhard Leitner.

gmp von Gerkan, Marg & Partner, Hamburg
1995–97
Friedrichstrasse 59-60/
Leipziger Strasse 101-102/
Kronenstrasse 16-17

U-Bahnhof Mohrenstraße

Mohrenstrasse underground station

Alfred Grenander
1906–08;
1950
Mohrenstrasse
(s. ill. above)

Mohrenstrasse underground station serves one of Berlin's oldest underground lines (now U 2). Work commenced on the line in 1902. In 1906-08, it was extended eastwards and westwards. Grenander designed most of the stations in a rationalist interpretation of Art Nouveau.

Until 1945 the station was named after the "Kaiserhof", a luxury hotel at Wilhelmplatz. Its location in the traditional government district made it very important. After the Second World War, the station interior was clad with wine-red marble (which still exists) taken from the nearby New Reich Chancellery, which was demolished in 1945.

Rund um die Spreeinsel

The surroundings of the Spree Island

Route 6 takes in the medieval and Baroque old city of Berlin and Luisenstadt, which dates from the 19th century. It passes the "Rotes Rathaus", today the seat of the government of Berlin and the Stadthaus, a prestigious building which was once the seat of the former Berlin City Parliament. The route passes the Nikolaiviertel district to come to the oldest parts of the city at Molkenmarkt and Spittelmarkt.

Route 6 begins at Alexanderplatz. It was once a cattle market outside the gates to the old town; from the 19th century on it developed into a traffic and business centre in the eastern part of Berlin. As Berlin became industrialised, it became the lower middle-class and working class counter-balance to the prestigious and elegant middle-class west of Friedrichstadt. At the beginning of the 20th century, it became the centre of gravity of the "cosmopolitan city" described by Alfred Döblin in his novel entitled "Berlin Alexanderplatz". As the first large square in Berlin, "Alex" was to be modernised and adapted to accommodate road traffic in 1930. Numerous public buildings were added by the GDR to make it the "social centre" of the German capital of socialism. After the Wall was opened, it once again came under the scrutiny of planners. With its large numbers of high-rises it is intended to be a counterpart to Potsdamer Platz in terms of urban vitality and dynamism.

Route 6 passes the Television Tower, the tallest structure in Berlin, and the remains of medieval and Baroque Berlin in Klosterstrasse, the location of the impressive Podewils Palace and the Parochial Church. After passing Molkenmarkt, the route comes to the building on Mühlendamm which houses the three leading associations representing German business and industry and can be seen as the beginnings of a new administrative centre of national significance. The foundations of the old city lie beneath the multiple-lane roads Gertraudenstrasse and Mühlendamm and in the undeveloped parts of Fisher Island. The Senate's "Masterplan for the inner city" envisages reconstructing this area in terms of its urban design. It is to be rebuilt as an intricate network of roads in accordance with historical plans and the area is to be structured by numerous residential buildings. The Berlin Senate has been pursuing this urban planning goal since 1995, which is ambitious from the cultural point of view and in terms of urban development history. In particular Spittelmarkt is to regain its significance as a square which has spatial dimensions and can be used by pedestrians.

The route once again encounters structures of the old city at Köllnischer Park and the city museum "Märkisches Museum". However, as the sites of the embassies of Australia, Brazil and the Netherlands as well as of the Senate Department of Urban Development and the Environment are located here, the appeal of the area is gradually growing. An impression which is confirmed in Alte Jakobstrasse and Wallstrasse by the exemplary redevelopment of industrial and residential buildings dating from the turn of the century.

Route 6 then proceeds to Luisenstadt, an extension of the city dating from the 19th century. Its development is heterogeneous and marked by the decades of the division of the city. On the one hand, the GDR housing developments of the '60s and '70s. They are now undergoing extensive renovation and new buildings are being added in the form of the Annen Courts and the Heinrich Heine Forum. On the other hand, wasteland where the Wall once separated East and West Berlin is to be replaced by a new belt of green. A striking feature is the former Luisenstädtischer Canal, which was built around 1850 to link the River Spree and the Landwehr Canal and filled in in the '20s.

The old Luisenstadt industrial estate, which now has modern functions, is in the immediate vicinity. The breathtaking architecture of the Trias office building on the north bank of the Spree is a new addition, a former machinery factory now houses architecture offices, artists' studios and the German Architecture Centre. The new Mitte combined heat and power plant, which lies next to it, provides many parts of the inner city – including Potsdamer Platz – with energy and is the most modern inner-city combined heat and power plant in Europe.

Route 6 ends at Jannowitzbrücke urban railway station, one of the oldest urban railway stations in Berlin. Its arches, which have been restored and now contain shops of different kinds, are a good example of the different and attractive uses to which technical structures can be put.

1

1 # Bahnhof Alexanderplatz

Bahnhof Alexanderplatz railway station

Johann Eduard Jacobsthal; Rebecca Chestnutt & Robert Niess, Berlin
1878–82;
1995–98

The station at Alexanderplatz is, after Ostkreuz, the second most frequently used S-Bahn station in Berlin, serving as many as 300,000 passengers a day. Converging here are three underground and four city railway (S-Bahn) lines, and several regional and long distance train lines. Since the end of 1998, a tram line connects Alexanderplatz with the station at Hackescher Markt, just as it did before the Second World War. The Alexanderplatz station was built 1878-82 by Jacobsthal. The majestic steel and glass shed was added in 1926. It was destroyed during the Second World War and rebuilt in 1965 (Hans Joachim May/Günter Andrich). From 1995-98, the American architects Chestnutt & Niess carried out the renovation and expansion of the station, during which the old viaducts were exposed. The architects also surrounded the restored arches with a new steel structure, acting as a second skin forming the actual facade. Inside, they refurbished the labyrinthine passageways with shops and light-filled arcades. The oval-shaped glass dispatch towers on the platforms received a design award.
To celebrate its 75th jubilee in 1999, during the summer months the Berlin S-Bahn (city railway) will operate a glass "panorama train" along the route between Charlottenburg and Ostkreuz.

2 # Alexanderplatz

This former military parade square was named Alexanderplatz in honour of the visit of Czar Alexander I of Russia in 1805. Though situated outside of the city wall at the time, it soon developed into an important centre for trade, commerce, and transportation, and became a legend during the '20s. The pulsing energy of the "world city" of Berlin was concentrated here, as described by Alfred Döblin in his 1929 novel "Berlin Alexanderplatz". 1929 also witnessed a high point of architectural urban design in the competition to redesign this area. However, the competition resulted only in the construction of the Alexanderhaus and the Berolinahaus, buildings designed by Peter Behrens.
The initial phase of post-war reconstruction

restored the square as an important transit node for the metropolis. The 1958 planning competition for the city centre envisaged Alexanderplatz simply as a connector between Stalinallee and the political centre at Marx-Engels-Platz. Not until 1964 did Alexanderplatz begin to develop into a large public space, in whose midst the "world clock", a popular meeting place, has stood since 1969.

The streets were dramatically widened around the square, which took on a new image with the addition of a modern 123-metre high hotel, a department store, the "House of the Teacher", the "House of Travel", and the "House of the Electronics Industry". The largest demonstration against the GDR government, a gathering of about one million people, was held here on 4 November 1989.

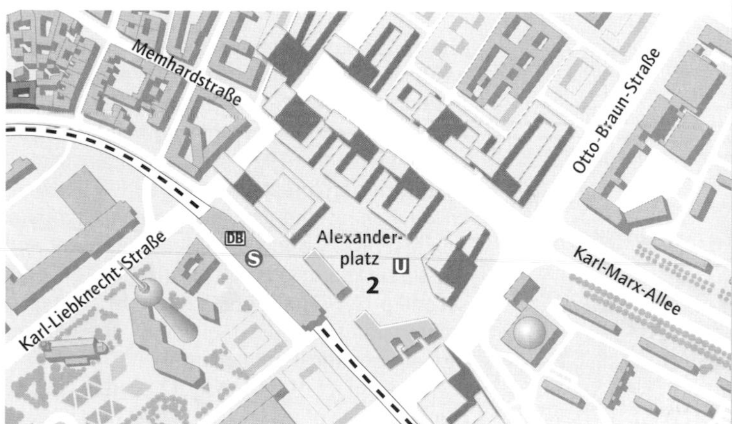

In 1993 Alexanderplatz again became the object of public debate, thanks to an urban design competition. It was won by Berlin architect Hans Kollhoff, who proposed to reduce the area of the square and encircle it with ten 150-metre high towers, each springing from a 36-metre high base building. A development scheme from 1998 envisaging new buildings up to Mollstrasse in the north proposes to demolish the entire spatially enclosed ensemble from the '60s, with the exception of the "House of the Teacher". Whether these controversial plans will be realised is not yet known.

„Haus des Lehrers" mit Kongreßhalle
"House of the Teacher" and the Congress Hall
Hermann Henselmann, Bernhard Geyer, Jörg Streitparth
1961–64
Alexanderplatz 3-4

The twelve-storey building, formerly serving as a cultural, educational and information centre for Berlin's teachers, forms the northeast boundary of Alexanderplatz. On the site of an earlier building for the teacher's union dating from 1908, Henselmann designed a new steel-frame structure with the GDR's first glass and aluminum "curtain wall" facade. Running along the facade at the height of the former book stacks is a 125-metre long continuous frieze made of glass, enamel and ceramics. Designed by Walter Womacka, it illuminates the building's function as the "House of the Teacher". Both it and the flat-domed Kongresshalle are the only buildings on the square which would not be torn down if the proposed development scheme is carried out.

3

Alexanderhaus, Berolinahaus

Peter Behrens; Pysall, Stahrenberg & Partner, Berlin
1930–32; 1993–95
Alexanderplatz 1, 2

The matching Alexanderhaus and Berolinahaus, designed by the German architect Peter Behrens, form a gateway from Alexanderplatz to the Rathausstrasse. They are the only buildings to be realised from the 1929 competition sponsored by the city architect, Martin Wagner. Six well-known Berlin architects were invited to compete. The first prize was given to Hans Luckhardt and Wassili Luckhardt with Alfons Anker, but only the second prizewinner, Peter Behrens, was given a commission to build two buildings, the Alexanderhaus and the Berolinahaus.
A novel aspect of the 1930-32 project was, at the insistence of its American investors, the use of rationalised building methods and technology and the involvement of the Berlin transit authorities in the design of the lower floors and tunnels. The rational reinforced concrete buildings are clad in limestone with steel window frames.
The European Building Preservation Award for 1998 was given to the architectural office of Pysall, Stahrenberg & Partner and the owners of the building, the Landesbank Berlin, for their excellent restoration work on the Alexanderhaus in 1993-95.

Fernsehturm
Television Tower

The 365-metre high Television Tower was built by the East German architects Fritz Dieter, Günter Franke and Werner Ahrendt according to a concept by Hermann Henselmann and Jörg

Streitparth. Marking the centre of the city, it is the highest structure in Berlin, and can be seen from great distances.
The facetted globe, which contains a rotating viewing platform and restaurant, seems to float atop the slender concrete shaft. Higher up, the broadcasting aerial restored in 1997 continues the vertical thrust of the tower, which embodies the notion of a crown for both the city and the state, meant to signify "socialist Berlin".

Fritz Dieter,
Günter Franke,
Werner Ahrendt
1965–69
Panoramastrasse

Marienkirche

Church of St. Mary

1270–80;
1380–1405;
1789–90
Karl-Liebknecht-Strasse 8

The Marienkirche is one of the oldest buildings in the city, originally emerging from a dense residential area. But after being damaged by both the war and ideologically-motivated urban renewal, it now stands completely isolated on a wide-open square. Built around 1270 as a parish church, it was restored and enlarged with a new western facade after a fire in 1380. In 1790 the tower was crowned with a neo-Gothic vaulted roof designed by Carl Gotthard Langhans. Inside, a frescoed frieze of the "dance of death" from 1485 and the marble chancel by Andreas Schlüter from 1703 are worth a visit.

Berliner Rathaus

Berlin City Hall

4.1 *Ensemble*

Hermann Friedrich
Waesemann;
Helge Pitz, Berlin
1861–69;
1991–99
Rathausstrasse 15-18

The Berliner Rathaus, richly decorated with terracotta ornamentation, was named "Rotes Rathaus" after the red brick used in its facade. It occupies the site of an older building that since 1716 had housed the magistrate of the Berlin Residence, organised seven years earlier to unite Berlin, Cölln, Friedrichswerder, Dorotheenstadt and Friedrichstadt. The monumental, nearly square building and 97-metre high tower, designed by Waesemann, documents the self-confidence of the urban citizenry in the face of the Prussian monarchy. In the parapets of the first floor balconies was built the "Chronicle in stone", 36 terracotta panels that tell the story of Berlin's history from the twelfth century to the founding of the German empire in 1871. In 1991, the Rathaus once again became the office of the mayor of Berlin. It was rebuilt in stages from 1991 to 1998 by Berlin architect Helge Pitz, who had already restored a number of landmarks.

4.2 *Ensemble*

Altes Stadthaus

Ludwig Hoffmann;
Gerhard Spangenberg, Berlin, with Martin Reichert
1902–11;
1996–2004
Jüdenstrasse/
Stralauer Strasse/
Klosterstrasse/
Parochialstrasse

The imposing Old Stadthaus, completed in 1911, was designed to provide space for ceremonial and formal functions for the neighbouring Rotes Rathaus. The high tower recalls the shape of the towers on the Gendarmenmarkt. The facade, with a heavy rusticated base and massive pillars and pilasters, is an example of the architecture of the reformist period after the turn of the century. As the city architect from 1896 to 1924, Hoffmann designed numerous architectural works that gave Berlin a distinctive image. The space in front of the building was created in 1935, when a densely built neighbourhood was cleared away. Following the Second World War, the city assembly, which reconvened from 1947 to 1948 with representatives from all of Berlin, held its sessions in the Stadthaus. During the '50s, it was used by the GDR council of ministers. The considerable alterations and additions then carried out were cleared away in 1996, returning the building more or less to its original condition. Gerhard Spangenberg, the architect in charge of the restoration and refurbishment, inserted a new atrium which provides natural climate control for the building.

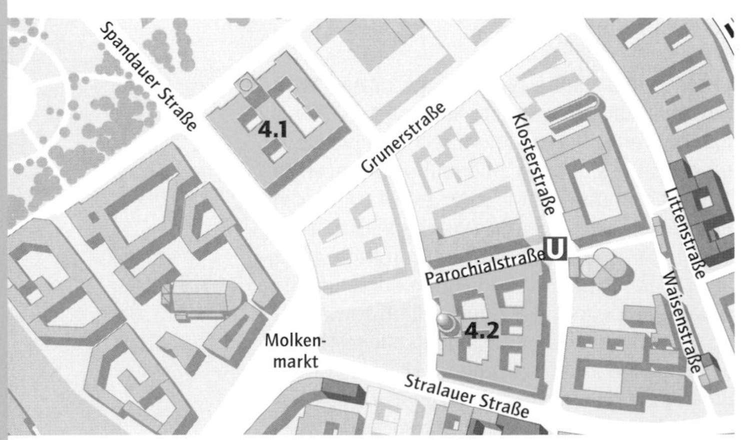

Ruine der Klosterkirche

Ruins of the Cloister Church
1260
Klosterstrasse 74

The church was part of the Franciscan cloister and until its destruction the most significant Gothic church in Berlin. After the Reformation, the first secondary school of the city, "Zum Grauen Kloster", was located here in 1574. Following the Second World War, the fragments of

the cloister complex were removed, while the ruins of the church became an open-air gallery, which still remains today.

Amtsgericht Mitte

Building of Mitte Local Court

Rudolf Mönnich,
Otto Schmalz,
Paul Thoemer
1896–1904
Littenstrasse 12-17

In 1904, the imposing building of the local and regional courts was counted as one of the city's greatest public buildings. The multi-winged complex expressed the ideals of the judicial branch of the empire. The outstanding architectural feature is the stair volume, with a double-run stairway designed in neo-Baroque style. The east wing was sacrificed to the widening of Grunerstrasse in 1969; the windows overlooking this street originally faced the inner courtyard.

„Haus der Verbände"

"House of the Associations"

Wolfgang Engel,
Klaus Zillich, Berlin
1998–2000
Littenstraße 7-11/
Voltairestrasse

The building complex of the "House of the Unions" lies directly adjacent to the old courthouse. It is made up of three separate office buildings on Littenstrasse and an building on Voltairestrasse. The balconies of the residential building differentiate it from the office block. The main entrance is located in the central and largest building, and leads to an atrium accessed from all of the buildings.
Located in the House of the Associations are the German Lawyers' Association, the Association of Tax Advisors, the German Institute of Lawyers, the Federal Chamber of Law and Justice, and other associations, as well as the local court, making Littenstrasse a national judicial and legal centre.

Waisenstraße mit ehemaliger Stadtmauer

Waisenstrasse and fragments of the old city wall

Fragments of the medieval city wall dating from the 14th century are preserved in the Waisenstrasse. Small houses from the late 17th century lean up against the four-metre high fortification, which is made of fieldstone and brick. In one of these buildings, whose core originated in the 16th century, is located an ancient pub called "Zur letzten Instanz".

6

Ehemaliges Palais Podewils
Former Podewils Palace
Jean de Bodt
1701–1704
Klosterstrasse 68-70

The elegant building dating from 1704, with a side wing facing Parochialstrasse, is the former residence of Prussian State Minister von Podewils and one of Berlin's few remaining Baroque-era residential blocks. The architect, Jean de Bodt, was the Prussian director of construction from 1698 to 1713. In 1880 a rear addition was built on the Waisenstrasse for the complex, which was then owned by the city. During the GDR era, it was restored as a youth centre and renamed "House of Young Talents". Today it is the home of the Podewil entertainment centre.

Parochialkirche
Parochial Church
Johann Arnold Nering, Martin Grünberg
1695–1703;
1713–14
Klosterstrasse 67

The Parochial Church was built in the middle of the historic old town according to a design by Johann Arnold Nering.
The square central volume with four semicircular niches was joined with an entrance hall and high bell tower in 1713. As part of the reconstruction work on the war-damaged church in 1999, a museum of sarcophagi of the 18th and 19th century was founded in the crypt. A number of mummified remains are preserved there, thanks to the particular climatic conditions in the vaults.

Haus Tietz
Georg Lewy
1904–06
Klosterstrasse 64

The 1906 building, whose portal bears the inscription "Gebr. Tietz" (Tietz Bros.), is the last of the remaining department stores owned by Hermann Tietz, presumably used as a headquarters. The company, founded in 1882 by Oskar Tietz and his uncle Hermann, began opening stores in Berlin after 1900. Its branches in the Leipziger Strasse, Alexanderplatz, and Frankfurter Allee were all destroyed during the Second World War.

6

Botschaft des Königreichs der Niederlande
Embassy of the Kingdom of the Netherlands

Rem Koolhaas, OMA, Rotterdam
1999–2001
Klosterstrasse/Rolandufer

The new embassy for the Netherlands was designed by the Dutch avant-garde architect Rem Koolhaas, of the Office for Metropolitan Architecture (OMA). The Netherlands deliberately chose a site for their embassy located outside of the diplomatic quarter. The waterside property along the River Spree they selected recalls their homeland.

The glass cube of the embassy is framed by a garden court opening on to the water, and by a forecourt, and the wall, activated with video and other media, is mirrored up to the top of the building. Koolhaas refrained from stacking the floors in the conventional manner, designing each with a different ceiling height. They are partly staggered, some projecting outwards or overlapping each other in places. One of the building's most prominent features is the stair winding up through the entire volume. It connects the floors from the entry at the ground level up to the roof terrace.
A second new building by Koolhaas is to be built on an open space north of the embassy. It will house a number of foundations and research institutes in a crystalline volume resembling a ruptured cube. Both buildings give new emphasis to the otherwise neglected embankment of the Spree.

Unternehmenszentrale Rolandufer

Rolandufer corporate centre

Joachim Ganz, Berlin
1997–99
Stralauer Strasse 42-45/
Rolandufer

A corporate office centre is being built along the Stralauer Strasse which consists of a new building and an enlarged landmark building. The older building was built from 1911-13 by Felix Lindhorst and comprises four volumes stepped parallel to Stralauer Strasse. They are linked together and enclosed into a perimeter block development by the new additions. There are two open courtyards and a roofed atrium in the interior. A small bridge crossing Jüdenstrasse – it leads from the Rotes Rathaus to the Stadthaus and will be extended to the Rolandufer – in order to connect to the new building, which is likewise used as commercial space. The main facade is turned towards the square in front of the Stadthaus. Apartments overlooking the river are located in both of the buildings.

Molkenmarkt

The Molkenmarkt, existing in name only today, was once the oldest marketplace in Berlin. After 1935, massive planning interventions were carried out in the historic structure and spatial fabric. With the goal of developing Berlin into a national-socialistic capital, the "small-grained" pattern of buildings, many with poor social and

hygienic conditions, was to be removed from the city centre. At the same time, only a few select buildings were preserved and rebuilt in the Nikolaiviertel and at Molkenmarkt as part of a recreated old town.
When the street was widened, the Palais Schwerin (a Baroque palace built 1704 by Jean de Bodt) was shifted to the south and extended with two new wings and a new roof. It was annexed to the Mint building, which was built by Fritz Keibel from 1936 to 1942. The building's historicising facade is embellished with a copy of the frieze designed by Friedrich Gilly and Johann Gottfried Schadow for the Old Mint. At the same time, elements typical of Nazi architecture can be found in the building's details; they are even more present in the factories along the Rolandufer.
The remaining fragments of the old town were destroyed in the '60s by the development of a 55 metre wide traffic artery.
In 1996, the Molkenmarkt became one of the central objects of "Planwerk Innenstadt Berlin", ("Masterplan for the inner city"), with which the Berlin Senate aims to regain historic urban spaces.

Nikolaiviertel und Nikolaikirche
Nikolaiviertel district and Nikolai Church
Poststrasse/ Nikolaikirchplatz

The Nikolaiviertel is part of the oldest quarter of the city of Berlin. In the centre, its namesake, the Nikolaikirche, was built beginning in 1220. The three-bay fieldstone and brick church hall still dominates the quarter today.
The original old town of Berlin has been lost. After heavy bomb damage in the Second World War, the church and the quarter were rebuilt as an replacement historic centre in time for Berlin's 750th anniversary in 1987. The few remaining genuinely old structures were taken away and reconstructed in the Nikolaiviertel, which was supplemented by new pre-fabricated buildings echoing the proportions and patterns of the old buildings. The newly created historic district was well-received by the public. From 1985-87, the sumptuous Ephraim Palace (a building from 1700 renovated in 1762-66 by Friedrich Wilhelm Diterichs) was reconstructed, albeit displaced twelve metres away from its original site. Once owned by Veitel Heine Ephraim, Frederick the Great's court jeweller, it had been taken apart and stored while urban

8

renewal was carried out in the Mühlendamm area. Today it is used to house a branch of the city museum.

Mühlendammbrücke mit Schleuse

Mühlendamm Bridge with canal lock

Wasserbaudirektion Kurmark
1936–42
Mühlendamm/
Rolandufer

The Mühlendamm Bridge is actually an eight-lane concrete roadway laid over the most important historic trading centre of Berlin. Archaeological excavations have exposed the traces of the first Berlin settlements dating from the last quarter of the 12th century. Historic documents first mention the existence of Cölln on the Spreeinsel in 1237, and the town of Berlin on the opposite riverbank in 1244. Around the same time, the Mühlendamm was built as the first bridge crossing the river Spree to join the towns of Berlin-Cölln. It regulated the water level of the river and was used by a number of mills, part of a mainly manufacturing area up to the 19th century.
From 1889-94 the complex was expanded by a river lock and a number of bridge structures dividing the Spree into an upper and lower river. The bridges and the lock were physically separated in 1935. The new east-lying Mühlendammschleuse had become necessary after the completion of the Mittelland Canal (shipping canal), which joined the industrial areas of Silesia with the Hamburg harbour. In 1969 the wide road bridge was laid out as part of a new traffic axis between Leipziger Strasse and Alexanderplatz. In its 1996 "Masterplan for the inner city", the city planning administration has earmarked this area for the formation of a "recognisable street space".

Deutscher Industrie- und Handelstag (DIHT), Bundesverband der Deutschen Industrie (BDI), Bundesvereinigung der Deutschen Arbeitgeberverbände (BDA)

8

Architekten
Schweger + Partner,
Hamburg/Berlin
1997–99
Breite Strasse 20-21/
Gertraudenstrasse

A number of leading German business associations will occupy a new central location in a building on the historic Spree Island. The first planning schemes and the invited competition of 1994 envisaged an administrative building here for the German League of Industry and Commerce (DIHT). In 1995, the Federal Union of German Industry (BDI) and the Federal Union of German Employer Associations (BDA) also decided to move from Cologne into the new Berlin building. United, the building complex takes up the historic pattern of perimeter block development and is divided into three volumes, each with a different colour and window arrangement. They are grouped around a central courtyard, which is spanned by a glass skylight. The BDI occupies the portion of the building on Breite Strasse north of the main entrance, which is designated by a recessed opening in the facade. The DIHT faces Mühlendamm and also occupies the lightly elevated conference tower on the Spree embankment, while the BDA borders the old Marstall to the north of the site.

Fischerinsel
Fisher Island
1965–73

The south bank of the area formerly called the Fisher Island also belongs to the oldest settlement of Berlin. The town of Cölln was located here during the Middle Ages. Its dense development was destroyed during the Second World War, and six residential towers were built there from 1965 to 1973. The "Ahornblatt" (maple leaf) restaurant with its pointed concrete shell structure is a special sight on Fisher Island. Designed as a cafeteria for ministry and government staff in 1970 by the engineer Ulrich Müther, the building testifies to the influence of international modernism on the socialist architecture of the '60s.

Ehemaliges Bauministerium
Former Building Ministry
Rolf Göpfert
1967–68
Scharrenstrasse 2-3

In 1994, before work began on the new facilities for the government and the parliament, the Berlin office of the Federal Building Ministry moved into the former headquarters of the GDR Building Ministry. The facade of the building is embellished with a ceramic frieze designed by Walter Womacka in 1968. After the national elections of 1998, the Federal Building Ministry, which also maintains offices in the former Staatsratsgebäude on Schlossplatz, was consolidated with the Ministry of Transport, whose building in the Invalidenstrasse is to be extended with a new wing (see p. 32).

Brüderstraße

Brüderstrasse once linked Schlossplatz with the parish church of St. Petri, neither of which exist today. Today the former Council of State building blocks off the space.
Only a few historic buildings now stand on Brüderstrasse. The corner building at Scharrenstrasse is the only remaining part of the Rudolph Hertzog department store (1909 by Gustav Hochgürtel), which originally took up most of the block. The building at number 10, dating from 1688, was redesigned in 1805 as a simple classical building for the use of the rectory of the Petrikirche. After 1825 the author and publisher Friedrich Nicolai lived at number 13, an 18th century building where he established a centre of intellectual life in Berlin.

Landesvertretung Freistaat Sachsen

The Land representation of Saxony

Reimer & Körte;
Dietrich Dörschner, Berlin
1905;
1998–99
Brüderstrasse 11-12

Saxony is one of the few federal German Laender that decided not to locate its offices in the former Ministerial Gardens, choosing instead a site in a listed building on the Spree Island. The neo-Baroque building, once an insurance headquarters (1905 by Reimer & Körte), contains ground floor spaces for exhibitions, conferences, and receptions, which are also sometimes held in the covered courtyard.

Geschäftshaus

Commercial building

Max Jacob, Georg Roensch
1894–98
Gertraudenstrasse 10-12/
Kleine Gertraudenstrasse/
Friedrichsgracht

The commercial building, which was originally sited on a prominent shopping street, now stands fairly isolated after the removal of surrounding buildings.
The original neo-Gothic stone facade is decorated in ornate detail. The building's elevation corresponds to a type frequently used at the turn of the century, but is preserved in only a few facades today.

Gertraudenbrücke

Gertrauden Bridge

Otto Stahn
1894–95;
1969
Gertraudenstrasse

Archaeologists have established that there was a bridge at this spot crossing the southern arm of the Spree as early as the 13th century. Today the old Gertrauden Bridge from 1895 serves only pedestrians, as it has ever since the Gertraudenstrasse was widened and a new bridge was erected for the street, which was relocated to the

10

southeast. The new bridge disrupted the earlier spatial network of the city; the old bridge had linked the commercial shopping street of Leipziger Strasse with the Fisher Island via nearby Spittelmarkt, which is no longer distinguishable. In 1896, in memory of the defunct Gertraudenhospital once located nearby, the sculptor Rudolf Siemering executed a bronze of St. Gertrude, patron saint of travellers. The figure was spared the fate of many sculptures during the Second World War – namely melting down for weapons and ammunition.

10

Bürokomplex am Spittelmarkt

Commercial centre at Spittelmarkt

HPP Hentrich-Petschnigg & Partner KG, Berlin
1995–98
Spittelmarkt/
Beuthstrasse/
Seydelstrasse

This commercial and residential complex was built following an urban design scheme by the London-based Iranian architect Zaha Hadid. Spittelmarkt, named after the hospital church of St. Gertrude, existed since 1660 and was a popular shopping and business centre up to the Second World War.
The architects Hentrich, Petschnigg & Partner (HPP) built a building at the head of the complex, continuing the row of high-rise slabs along Leipziger Strasse from 1969, and creating a transition to the angled Gertraudenstrasse. At the same time it makes a first step toward bringing back the nearly imperceptible Spittelmarkt.
The elevations are hung with a steel and glass curtain wall facade. A lower wing leads along Seydelstrasse, reopened on the east side. A low-rise building west of the high-rise (Ebbinghaus) is to be taken down in order to connect Axel-Springer-Strasse to Leipziger Strasse and the Spittelmarkt.

11.1
Ensemble

Wohn- und Geschäftshäuser

Residential and commercial buildings

Hans D. Strauch HDS & Gallagher Inc., Boston,
Dieter W. Schneider & Partner, Berlin
1995–97
Seydelstrasse 2-7

Connecting to the main building by HPP on Spittelmarkt, between Beuth- and Seydelstrasse, are ten residential and commercial buildings. Their floor plans take up the pre-war pattern of small-scale building lots. The buildings enclose three courtyards. The older building at Seydelstrasse 5 was integrated into the complex.

Luisenhof

11.2 Ensemble

Luisenhof, located between Seydelstrasse and Neue Grünstrasse, was designed by the architect P. Coenen of Cologne, who used balconies to compose the facade. Cylindrical and octagonal towers emphasise the corners. The building is purely residential, in order to restore a district destroyed in the Second World War, which could not be rebuilt because it bordered the Berlin Wall near Kommandantenstrasse.

RCA, P. Coenen, Cologne
1997–99
Neue Grünstrasse 9-11 /
Seydelstrasse 20

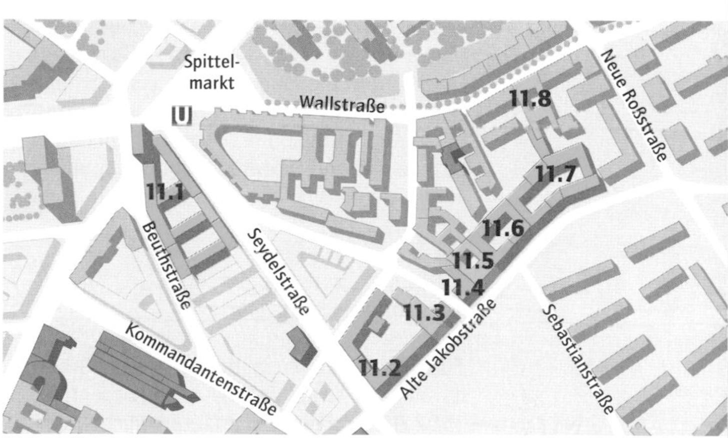

Umspannwerk Spittelmarkt

Transformer station at Spittelmarkt

11.3 Ensemble

The original Spittelmarkt transformer station was built in 1905 by Franz Schwechten, the architect of the Kaiser Wilhelm Memorial Church. The electric company Bewag's chief architect, Hans Heinrich Müller, redesigned the brick building in the courtyard in 1925, and built a rear wing in 1928. Schmalz and Galow added the new transformer to the old structure on Alte Jakobstrasse, which took over the function of the old building. The light brick facade changes into a glass wall enclosing office spaces. The old line of the Berlin Wall on Alte Jakobstrasse is now marked by a double row of paving stones along the street.

Franz Schwechten;
Hans Heinrich Müller;
Schmalz & Galow, Berlin
1905; 1928;
1996–98
Alte Jakobstrasse 90-91

11.4 *Ensemble*

Kontorhaus und Wohnhaus Alte Jakobstraße

Warehouse and residential building on Alte Jakobstrasse

Jakob Lehrecke, Berlin
1997–2000
Alte Jakobstrasse 87-88

The complex designed by the Berlin architect Lehrecke is actually two buildings joined together. Each has a subdued brick facade, which harmonises with the older structure, the brick of the transformer station, and the white glazed bricks of the neighbouring commercial building. The connecting building with a side wing was conceived as an apartment building with French windows. Banded windows on the western half give a hint at its function as an office building. Integrating the underground district heating pipes coming from the power plant in Mitte presented a challenge to the architect and the builder that necessitated elaborate foundation work.

11.5 *Ensemble*

Kontorhaus am Spittelmarkt

Warehouse at Spittelmarkt

Michael König, Berlin
1900;
1992–94
Neue Grünstrasse 17-18/
Alte Jakobstrasse 85-86

The listed commercial building from 1900 with its elegant street facades was modernised in 1992-94 by the Berlin architect Michael König. The office complex, with a total of four courtyards, takes up the block between Alte Jakobstrasse and Neue Grünstrasse.

11.6 *Ensemble*

Verwaltungsgebäude

Administration building

Walter Krüger, Berlin
1995–97
Alte Jakobstrasse 81-82

The new headquarters of the Techniker Krankenkasse insurance company was built in the centre of the perimeter block development on Alte Jakobstrasse, which was built during the last few years. The gridded side wings flank the glazed centre section which is roofed by an overhanging stepped gable structure. A double-height drive-through leads to the inner courtyard. A residential building abuts the building to the rear.

Büro-, Geschäfts- und Wohnhäuser „Alte Jakobstraße"

11.7 Ensemble

Office, commercial and residential buildings on Alte Jakobstrasse

The northern part of Alte Jakobstrasse was heavily damaged in the Second World War. Various office, commercial and residential houses were built since 1995, enclosing two courtyards of different sizes. The most prominent building is a narrow, green residential tower with a half-barrel vaulted roof perpendicular to the street. The old "Wallhöfe" building on Wallstrasse is connected via a passageway from Alte Jakobstrasse number 77.

Planungs AG für Bauwesen (Neufert, Mittmann, Graf), Cologne
1995–97
Alte Jakobstrasse 76-80, 83-84

Wallhöfe

11.8 Ensemble

The Wallhöfe built in 1907 are a monumental office complex with retail spaces around the two inner courtyards. The brick pier-lined facade and wide windows are typical of commercial architecture design from around the turn of the century. In 1994-95 the Wallhöfe were restored and expanded by the Hamburg architecture firm Giffey & Thüs. The half-oval glass pavilion in the courtyard is used by the district of Berlin-Mitte for civil wedding ceremonies.

Giffey & Thüs, Hamburg
1907;
1994–95
Wallstrasse 23-24

Miethaus und Gewerbebau

Apartment house and commercial building

1872
Wallstrasse 84, 85

These two apartment buildings dating from 1872 are good examples of urban apartment dwellings of the "Gründerzeit", or "founding era" around 1871. On the elaborately designed facades, the formal, upscale dwellings on the belle etage are clearly demarcated on the first and/or second storeys. Both buildings have side wings enclosing a small courtyard. They were carefully restored several years ago.

Geschäftshaus

Commercial building

Johann Hoeniger & Sedelmaier;
Pysall, Stahrenberg & Partner, Berlin
1913;
1997–98
Wallstrasse 27/ Neue Rosstrasse

The representative corner building was designed as a commercial structure by the architects of the Jewish Community in Berlin, Hoeniger and Sedelmaier. With its restrained ornament and modern-looking composition, the building documents the departure from Art Nouveau and the arrival of a rational design approach. In 1997-98, it was modernised by the Berlin firm Pysall, Stahrenberg & Partner.

13

12 Australische Botschaft
Australian Embassy

Fritz Crzellitzer;
Bates Smart, Melbourne,
Braun, Schlockermann and Köhler, Berlin
1912;
1999–2001
Wallstrasse 76-79/
Märkisches Ufer 6-8

The Australian Embassy will occupy a modernised building complex on the Spree. The two older buildings on the Märkisches Ufer and the office building, with an elaborate majolica facade on Wallstrasse, surround an inner courtyard. After winning a competition open only to Australian architects, the Melbourne architect Bates Smart founded a collaborative firm with German architects. The living quarters of the ambassador are located facing the river promenade, while the administrative offices are arranged in the more formal building along Wallstrasse.

13 Art'otel

Nalbach + Nalbach, Berlin
1994–97
Wallstrasse 70-73/
Märkisches Ufer 12

In keeping with the concept of the Art'otel hotel chain, the individual buildings are designed by well-known artists. The lobby and rooms are decorated with works by the German painter Georg Baselitz. The new building is an addition to the historic Ermelerhaus, a residential building from 1770 that originally stood on Breite Strasse and made way for the construction of the East German Ministry of Building. The Ermelerhaus was rebuilt on the Märkisches Ufer in 1969. The old side wings in the inner courtyard are connected to the new building, whose clearly organised facade expresses the functions of the hotel. The entry, which leads to a small two-level exhibition space, is set off by a coloured frame. The hotel room windows, horizontally divided into three sections, are grouped in the middle section of the facade, while the windows of the last three bays, where the services are located, are lightly recessed.

Gewerkschaftshaus
Union building

Max Taut, Franz Hoffmann;
Walter Würzbach
1922–23;
1930–32
Wallstrasse 61-65

The building designed by the architect Max Taut for the Amalgamated German Unions (ADGB), caused a great sensation because the design of the modern gridded facade was mainly derived from the reinforced concrete frame. The areas between the structural columns were filled in with masonry and simple windows. Certain expressionistic features are also present, such as the gently angled columns and windows and the crystalline facets along the roofs.

Botschaft der Föderativen Republik Brasilien

Embassy of the Federal Republic of Brazil

The Brazilian Embassy will occupy a portion of a brand-new building in an ideal central location on the southern bank of the Spree, very close to the Märkisches Museum. The guest house formerly occupying the site, built in 1969 for the use of the central committee of the East German Communist Party, was torn down in 1989. The main facade is oriented to the small park.

Pysall, Stahrenberg & Partner, Berlin
1998–2000
Wallstrasse 59

Märkisches Museum

Ludwig Hoffmann
1899–1908
Am Köllnischen Park 5

Before the Märkisches Museum could move into its new home in 1908, it had to wait twelve long years. In the meantime, the museum association, founded 1874, occupied temporary spaces in the Podewils Palace. The expressive ensemble was created by Ludwig Hoffmann, the city architect who designed all of Berlin's public buildings erected between 1896 and 1924. The freestanding museum building was designed with several different facades that recall various landmarks from Mark Brandenburg. The complex and its tower were spatially oriented to the defunct Waisen Bridge, once an important link in the old city ring from Littenstrasse to Waisenstrasse, Wallstrasse and Oberwallstrasse.
The triangular form of the adjacent Köllnischer Park comes from a bastion of city fortifications whose construction began in 1658, planned by Johann Gregor Memhardt. In the centre is a bear cage holding living specimens of Berlin's official mascot.

Senatsverwaltung für Stadtentwicklung, Umweltschutz und Technologie

Senate Administration for Urban Development, Environmental Protection and Technology

Alfred Messel
1903–04
Am Köllnischen Park 2a-3

The eastern edge of the Köllnischer Park is formed by the building of the old State Insurance Company, which the Berlin Senate Administration for Urban Development, Environmental Protection, and Technology has occupied since 1996. Messel, who built it in 1904, used a light red brick on the facade. The street elevation is composed with columns running the height of the building. Messel first developed this column system for his famous Wertheim department store on Leipziger Platz. It signified modern architecture because it departed from the customary horizontally stacked, hierarchical arrangement of base, centre floors, and attic storeys.

16.1 16.1

Zentralverwaltung der Allgemeinen Ortskrankenkasse (AOK)

Central Administration of the AOK

Albert Gottheiner
1931–32
Rungestrasse 3-6

The formal administration building used by the insurance company AOK forms the southern wall of the Köllnischer Park. A steel frame structure clad with brick, slanted columns and the interplay of stone on the facade make it a powerful example of expressionist architecture. On the rear elevation, between the two wings, is a customer service hall with a glass roof. Until 1989, the Karl Marx College, run by the communist party, was located in the building.

15

Heinrich-Heine-Viertel

Heinrich-Heine-Viertel residential complex

Werner Dutschke
1959;
1968;
1998
Heinrich-Heine-Strasse/
Schmidstrasse

The Heinrich-Heine residential complex, lying to the east of the street of the same name and very close to a former border crossing point, is a typical example of inner city socialist housing. The buildings were constructed in two phases, using large-scale pre-fabricated slabs. In the first phase, dating from 1959, four-storey buildings and a few shops and services were completed. The second phase begun in 1968 included a ten-storey perimeter block complex enclosing courtyards and kindergartens within. Renovation work, being carried out step by step, began in 1998.

The task of upgrading such slab buildings involves the addition of insulation and other energy-saving methods as well as aesthetic changes. The work exemplifies the revitalisation of entire districts elsewhere, as in Marzahn, Hellersdorf, and Hohenschönhausen, where further planning measures, like the design of new greenspaces, are giving new life to run-down housing projects.

Annenkirche

Church of St. Ann

Hermann Blankenstein
1855–57
Annenstrasse 52-53

The Annenkirche, erected in 1855, was the first church built by Hermann Blankenstein, a city architect who had much influence on the city's architecture. The church, which he designed while still a student, owes much to the tradition of Karl Friedrich Schinkel. Additions were made in 1865 and 1889. All his life, Blankenstein favoured the use of brick, a frequently used material here, since the supply of stone was limited in Berlin and Brandenburg.

Heinrich-Heine-Forum

16.1 Ensemble

Until recently, the war-damaged ruins of the old Exerzierhaus once belonging to the Kaiser Franz Grenadier Regiment (1829 by Carl Hampel), stood on Heinrich-Heine-Platz, the square opening onto Annenstrasse. The building was retrofitted as a department store and now stands in the midst of new residential and commercial buildings, revitalising a war-damaged neighbourhood that had not been rebuilt until now.

Karl-Heinz Cammann, Berlin
1995–98
Annenstrasse/
Heinrich-Heine-Platz

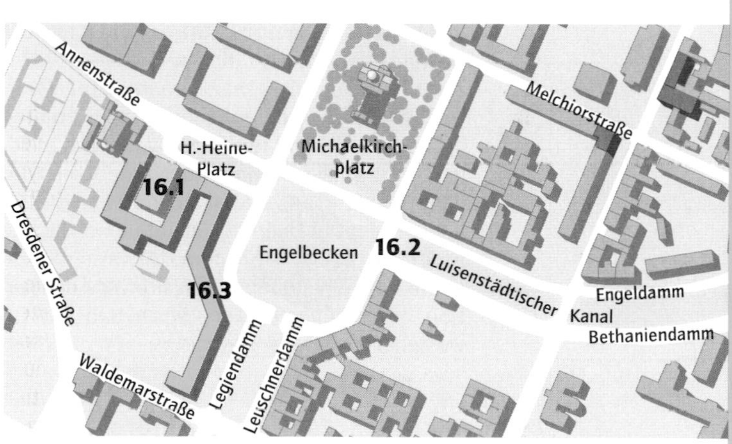

Luisenstädtischer Kanal

Luisenstadt Canal

16.2 Ensemble

The Luisenstadt quarter, designed in 1800, was named after the popular Prussian queen Luise. It spans between Spree to the north and the former excise wall running from Schlesisches Tor to Mehringplatz in the south. A prosperous manufacturing and trading suburb during the 19th century, Luisenstadt later became part of the section of Kreuzberg called "SO 36". From 1848 to 1852, the landscape architect Peter Joseph Lenné laid out the Luisenstadt Canal, used for drainage and shipping, between the Spree and the Landwehrkanal. The Engelbecken was a large open area of the Luisenstadt Canal, which reflected the facade of the Michaelkirche. The rectilinear plan of streets, squares and residential blocks typifies early 19th-century planning. In 1926, the canal, which had been drying out, was filled in and was then redesigned as a public park by the director of gardens, Erwin Barth. The Ber-

Peter Joseph Lenné
1848–52
Erkelenzdamm/
Leuschnerdamm/
Engeldamm

16.3

lin Wall, which cut across Engeldamm between Engelbecken and Schillingbrücke bridge, blocked any further development. Since 1992, the area has been slowly transforming back into a city park.

16.3 *Ensemble*

Wohnbauten am Engelbecken

Residential buildings on Engelbecken

Klaus Lattermann, Berlin,
Schmitz and Partner, Düsseldorf,
NPS & Partner, Berlin
1995–98
Legiendamm 2-20

The eastern edge of the Engelbecken and the Luisenstadt Canal is made up of residential buildings from the turn of the century, while the western edge is lined with new buildings.
The reason for this is the old route of the Berlin Wall: the existing older buildings were situated in West Berlin, and renovated, while the buildings in the East Berlin border zone were torn down. Since 1994, several architects have built new residential buildings maintaining the historic street plan. They restored the western edge of the square, restoring the architectural delineation of the Engelbecken, which had been a wasteland for nearly 50 years.

St.-Michael-Kirche

Church of St. Michael

August Soller
1850–61
Michaelkirchplatz

The Church of St. Michael, located on the north side of the Luisenstadt Canal and the Engelbecken, was the second Catholic church built in Berlin, after the St. Hedwig's Cathedral. It is unusual that it is a free-standing building; most Catholic churches were embedded within the block structure. This was because land for Catholic churches normally had to be purchased from the community, while Protestant churches, belonging to the official state religion, could be built on publicly-owned property.
This basilica-shaped church was designed by August Soller, an architect influenced by Karl Friedrich Schinkel. Its tripartite facade is embellished with medieval and classical iconography. The main entrance of the church was oriented toward the reflecting pool of the Engelbecken. Heavily damaged in the last war, it was not fully restored because of its proximity to the Berlin Wall. The south portal, the crossing, and the apse of the brick structure are intact, while only the outer walls of the nave remain. Lack of funds have prevented the completion of reconstruction work.

Gewerkschaftshaus, ehemals Haus des Deutschen Gesamtverbandes
Union building, former House of the German Public Service Workers' Union
Max Taut
1929–30;
1997
Engeldamm 70/
Michaelkirchplatz 1-2

The 1930 building formerly used by the public service workers' union was designed by Max Taut, who built a number of union buildings. In this building, he was inspired by an idea used in a competition entry designed by his brother, Bruno Taut. The then progressive organisational idea of a single large labour union incorporating a number of smaller unions is also expressed here, using strictly modern architecture. The facade design is dictated by the building's concrete frame structure, with horizontal bands wrapping around the corners to create a dynamic expression. After 1935, the building became the headquarters of the Nazi "German Labour Front", an organisation that united and politically neutralised all labour unions. During the GDR-era, the leadership of the united unions (FDGB) was based here. After the opening of the wall, it was returned to the ÖTV, the public sector workers' union, which has used the building since it was renovated in 1997.

Wohn- und Geschäftshaus „Am Engelufer"
"Am Engelufer" residential and commercial building
Reimer & Körte;
Ingenieurbüro KBA GmbH
PPB, Berlin
1897–1900;
1999
Engeldamm 62-64

The brick structure opened in 1900 as the first union building in Germany. It was the initiative of Leo Aron, a physicist and social democrat who assembled a total of 92 small labour unions on the site.

In 1933, this building also came under the control of the Nazi German Labour Front ("Deutsche Arbeitsfront").

After the Second World War, it became in turn a Soviet emergency clinic, a part of the city hospital in Berlin Mitte, and finally a facility for the Institute of Tropical Medicine.

In 1999, the listed building will be modernised and a new building will be added to its courtyard.

St.-Thomas-Kirche
Church of St. Thomas
Friedrich Adler
1864–69
Mariannenplatz

The Church of St. Thomas is located on Mariannenplatz, which was created as part of the Luisenstadt Canal development, the street pattern and formal square on axis with Michaelkirchplatz dating from around 1850. Along the western edge is located the Krankenhaus Bethanien, a hospital built by Theodor Stein in 1847. In 1862, a competition was held for a new church building in order to give the long square a visual terminus and endpoint to the north.

The main features of the Church of St. Thomas are its double tower and portal, its circular cen-

tral space, and the brick cupola. Like many other churches today, it is too large for current use and will therefore be rebuilt to accommodate commercial and cultural functions that would generate revenue to help maintain the church building.

Viktoriahof
Kurt Berndt
1909–10
Köpenicker Strasse 126

The Viktoriahof, built in 1910, is among Luisenstadt's few remaining commercial buildings from the turn of the century. The architect Kurt Berndt built a number of such courtyard manufacturing complexes in Berlin; here he created one with a powerful facade design.

Bürohaus
Office building
1866;
1995
Köpenicker Strasse 125

Now an office building, this structure once housed the fire station of Luisenstadt, which was in service till 1945. The waggons emerged through gateways right to the street, but their horses had to be first led from the courtyard, which took time. The process became much faster after motorised fire engines came into use. The brick building was converted into an office.

17 Deutsches Architektur Zentrum

German Architecture Centre (DAZ)

Claus Anderhalten, Berlin,
Assmann, Salomon & Scheidt, Berlin
1994–96
Köpenicker Strasse 48-49

The DAZ was founded in 1995 and took up quarters in the old Stock factory dating from 1903. It is a typical example of the industrial structures in historic Luisenstadt. An East German textile cooperative moved into the shored-up ruins of the bombed-out building in 1962. The property was taken over by 97 artists, architects and small manufacturing companies after reunification. In 1993, the National Association of German Architects (BDA) bought the building and rebuilt it for the use of 38 architects, planners, artists, and other tenants. They retained the original white glazed-brick facades in the courtyard. The main entrance is marked by a steel and glass structure that also supports new penthouse studios. In addition to the national BDA administration, a number of architecture-related associations, offices, and producers rent space here. Through exhibitions and conferences, the DAZ facilitates direct contact between architects and the building industry.

Heizkraftwerk Mitte 18

District Heating Plant for Mitte

D. Zimbal;
Jochem Jourdan,
Frankfort on the Main
1961–64;
1994–96
Köpenicker Strasse 59-73

On the site of the old heating plant for the district of Mitte built in 1961-64, Bewag constructed the most modern inner city generator in Europe. The gas and steam powered plant has an electricity output of 380 megawatt and provides 620 megawatt of heat for the entire demand of the parts of Berlin between Ostbahnhof station and the Charité Hospital. The electricity generated is fed into the Bewag power grid.

The building, whose separate functions are clearly articulated, was designed by the architect Jochem Jourdan. From the banks of the Spree, where natural gas and heating oil are delivered by barges, the complex steps up along the two turbine buildings to the sections where heat and electricity are generated.

By applying the principle of co-generation, the plant is able to achieve a fuel efficiency level of nearly 90 per cent, an improvement over earlier methods achieving only 45 per cent efficiency. Because of its location within a residential area, the power plant was designed with extensive noise and emissions protections. It is linked to the power station on Stresemannstrasse (see p. 75), which delivers district heating as well as cooling/air conditioning for buildings at Potsdamer Platz.

Architecturally, the power plant belongs to the tradition of the large Bewag buildings in Berlin from the early 20th century. Sculpture by the Danish artist Per Kirkeby ("Wall and Tower") and benches warmed with waste heat from the transformer designed by the Turkish artist Ayse Erkmen have been placed in the open spaces and along the Spree riverbank – works of art whose content relates to both the power plant and to urban space. Still to come is a water basin with a pavilion open to the public, which was designed by the American artist Dan Graham.

Büro- und Geschäftshaus „Trias" 19

"Trias" commercial and office building

The distinctive bow-shaped towers of the Trias office complex built in 1996 take up a narrow strip of land between Holzmarktstrasse and S-

Lucia Beringer,
Gunther Wawrik, Munich
1993–96
Holzmarktstrasse 15-18

Bahn (city rail). The complex is organised with a horizontal bar along the street and the three unusual office towers. On their narrow site, they are connected to the bar and their shape in plan becomes more oval facing towards the Spree. They enclose two inner courtyards which are raised up just about reaching the level of the rail tracks. The complex cleverly mediates between the high exhaust stacks of the power station across the Spree and the uniform residential development north of Holzmarktstrasse. The Treuhand-Liegenschaftsgesellschaft (TLG), the successor to the Treuhand Agency, which was in charge of privatising East German property and buildings, and the management of the Deutsche Bahn AG are the two main tenants of the building.

20

Jannowitz-Center

HPP Hentrich-Petschnigg
& Partner KG, Düsseldorf
1993–97
Brückenstrasse

The new Jannowitz Centre building stretches along Brückenstrasse up to the River Spree where it forms a small forecourt planned to eventually lead to the water. While along the narrowed Brückenstrasse the character of the facade is restrained, towards the Spree side it becomes more colourful and lively with recesses and protrusions. The building is crowned with a clock on a pointed mast. The main tenant is the Senate Administration for Urban Development, Environmental Protection, and Technology.

21

S-Bahnhof Jannowitzbrücke

S-Bahnhof Jannowitzbrücke city railway station

Ernst Dircksen;
Hugo Röttcher;
Wehner · Gaisser · Schulz, Berlin
1881–82;
1927–32;
1994–98

The special feature of the Jannowitzbrücke city rail station is its direct placement on the water. During restoration and reconstruction of the landmark structure, the pillars were exposed, and the previously walled-in great arches were opened up to create large windows. Double-height retail spaces are being designed here that can be seen and reached from walkways bridging the water, as well as from the passage leading underneath the tracks. As early as 1895, the tracks were enlarged with a steel structure cantilevering over the arches. The current rational glass shed dates from 1927, as does the underground station, which was built by Alfred Grenander.

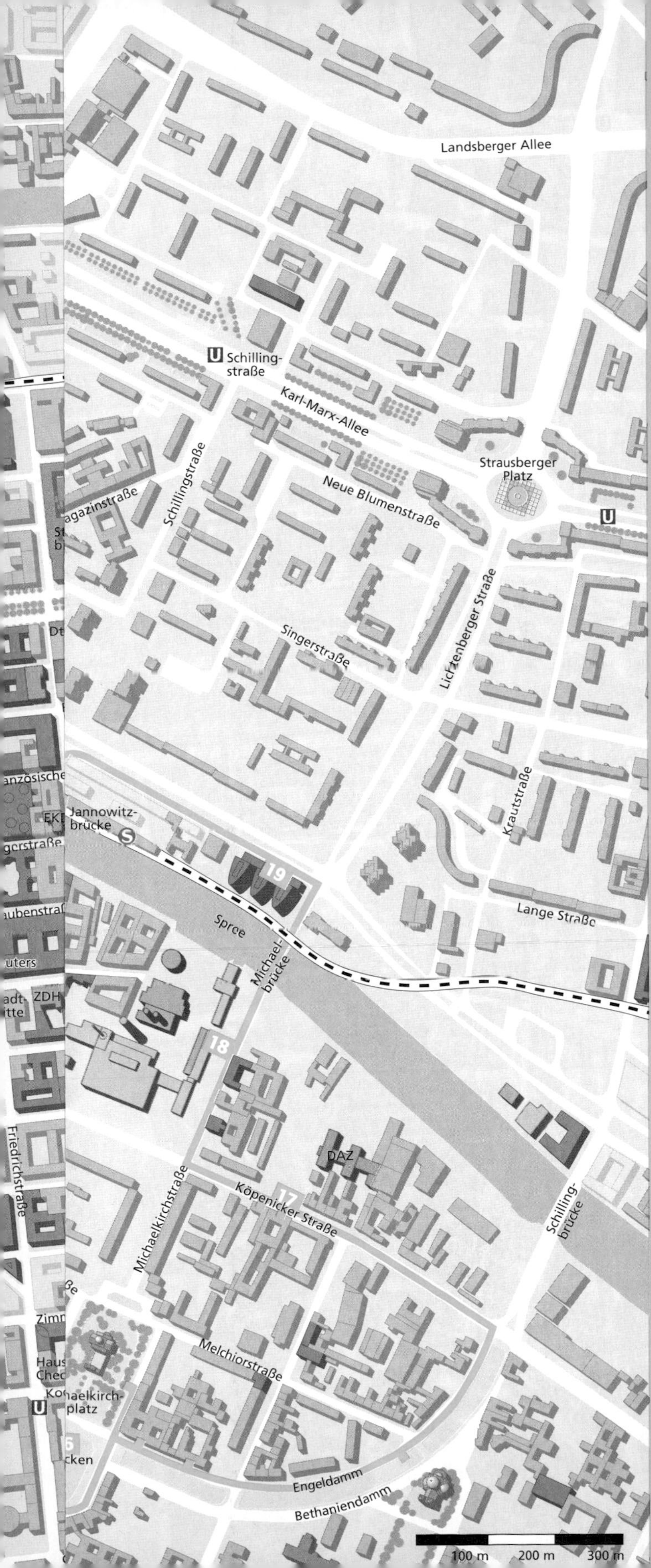

Landsberger Allee
Schilling-
straße
Karl-Marx-Allee
Strausberger
Platz
Neue Blumenstraße
Schillingstraße
agazinstraße
St
bi
Dt
Singerstraße
Lichtenberger Straße
anzösische
EKI
Jannowitz-
brücke
gerstraße
Krautstraße
19
Lange Straße
aubenstra
Spree
Michael-
brücke
uters
adt-
itte
ZDH
18
Friedrichstraße
DAZ
Köpenicker Straße
17
Schilling-
brücke
Michaelkirchstraße
ße
Zimn
Melchiorstraße
Haus
Chec
Ko
haelkirch-
platz
6
cken
Engeldamm
Bethaniendamm
100 m
200 m
300 m

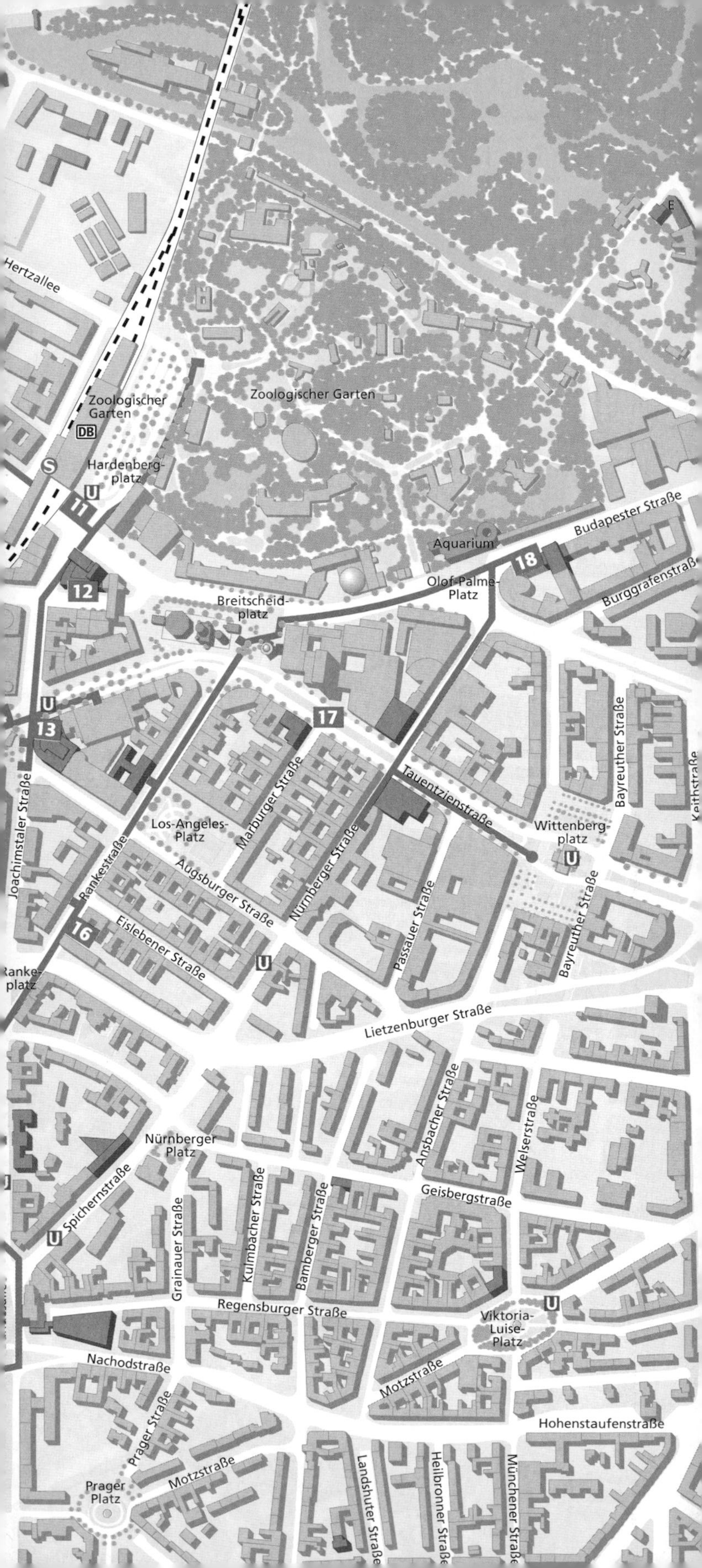

Hertzallee
Zoologischer Garten
DB
S
Hardenbergplatz
U
11
12
13
16
17
18
Zoologischer Garten
Aquarium
Budapester Straße
Burggrafenstraße
Olof-Palme-Platz
Breitscheidplatz
Joachimstaler Straße
Rankestraße
Los-Angeles-Platz
Marburger Straße
Nürnberger Straße
Tauentzienstraße
Wittenbergplatz
Bayreuther Straße
Keithstraße
Augsburger Straße
Eislebener Straße
Passauer Straße
Rankeplatz
Lietzenburger Straße
Ansbacher Straße
Welserstraße
Nürnberger Platz
Spichernstraße
Geisbergstraße
Grainauer Straße
Kulmbacher Straße
Bamberger Straße
Regensburger Straße
Viktoria-Luise-Platz
Nachodstraße
Motzstraße
Prager Straße
Hohenstaufenstraße
Prager Platz
Landshuter Straße
Heilbronner Straße
Münchener Straße

City West

Route 7 passes through what is today known as the City West, the centre of what was once West Berlin. At the time of the division between East and West it symbolised freedom, liberalness, affluence and the cultural diversity of the political system of the West. The "Ku'damm" boulevard stretching from Halensee to the Kaiser Wilhelm Memorial Church and the Europa-Center soon became an international symbol of a self-assured city.

The focus of route 7 is on the urban development of the beginning of the century. The most impressive feature of the City West is the rich heritage of the bourgeois city. With its broad, tree lined streets, attractive squares and block development it is in contrast with the "stone appearance" of the inner city. It still provides a "healthy" mix of residential property, shops and businesses, cultural and entertainment facilities.

Route 7 begins at Adenauer Platz. The intersection and the layout of the square reflect the town planning of the '60s which was designed to cater for the needs of road traffic. An unusual consequence of such demolition planning exists today in the form of Berlin's narrowest office building at Adenauer Platz. Olivaer Platz also owes its present form to a plan to bypass the centre of the City West. The Lietzenburger Strasse was intended to be a feeder for an urban motorway. Town planners did not abandon these plans and return to development which reflected urban needs until the '80s, a fine example of which can be seen in the "Leibniz Colonnades" in the Leibnizstrasse.

The Kurfürstendamm was laid out in the 1880s and soon developed into a fashionable residential and business district. Later on, the addition of theatres, variety theatres, restaurants and numerous "cinema palaces" made it the centre of Berlin's night life and it is still today considered to be synonymous with the roaring twenties. Today the Kurfürstendamm is once again a city boulevard with offices, fashionable stores and exclusive shops.

The area between Kurfürstendamm, Kantstrasse, Savignyplatz and Fasanenstrasse was discovered by intellectuals, gallery owners, filmmakers and the in-crowd. Savignyplatz with its bookshops, restaurants and cafés became the centre of

West-Berlin's cultural scene, but in sharp contrast to the centres of the "alternative scene" in Kreuzberg and Schöneberg. Since the opening of the Wall in 1989, the area, which until then had had an undisputed status, found itself facing increasing competition from parts of the districts of Mitte and Prenzlauer Berg.
Route 7 follows Fasanenstrasse along its entire length: from the Technical University at its northern end, past the spectacular new buildings of the Chamber of Commerce and Industry (IHK) and the triangular "Kant-Dreieck" building to the modern sewage pumping station at its southern end. In the late '60s plans to radically alter the street sparked off a row over the concept of a car-orientated city which had been propagated until then and was diametrically opposed to the alternative of preserving a charming and attractive old middle-class district. Fasanenstrasse became a symbol of a new way of thinking in urban development: it was preserved in the face of great resistance put up by those in favour of razing it to the ground to make way for a motorway approach road. The ensemble consisting of the "House of Literature", the Kollwitz Museum and the Villa Grisebach, which at the time were threatened by demolition and have since then been restored, are excellent examples of the benefits gained from this change in approach to urban development.
As the route comes to an end, it passes along Rankestrasse to reach Breitscheidplatz and the Europa-Center – once the pride of West Berlin. A high-rise development around Breitscheidplatz is planned in order to counter the competition which it is feared will be posed by businesses in the municipal district of Mitte and by plans to build high-rises at Alexanderplatz. "Neue Kranzler-Eck" and the "Zoofenster" high-rise are the first steps to realise such plans. However, they face fierce opposition from the municipal authority concerned, residents and experts as they fear that the balanced mixture of residential, business and entertainment uses could give way to a monoculture in the form of a centre consisting virtually entirely of offices.
Route 7 ends at Wittenbergplatz and at KaDeWe, "Kaufhaus des Westens". It is one of the oldest department stores in the world and with its extraordinary range is today one of the world's leading department stores.

U-Bahnhof Adenauerplatz 1

Underground station at Adenauerplatz

1976–78

One of the consequences of the construction of the Berlin Wall was that the underground system in West Berlin became much more important. Among the reasons for this was the fact that many people boycotted the S-Bahn (city railway), which was operated by the East German Reichsbahn railroad authority. The U 7 underground line with its station Adenauerplatz was among the new lines that were constructed by the west during the '60s and '70s. The longest route in the underground system, the U 7 connects the district of Rudow in the southeast with Spandau in the northwest.

Bürogebäude Adenauerplatz 2

Office building at Adenauerplatz

Murphy/Jahn Architects, Helmut Jahn, Chicago
1992–94
Kurfürstendamm 70

The most slender office building in Berlin occupies a lot that is only 2.5 metres wide. The parcel was left over after a building was demolished when the street was widened to build the express traffic tunnel crossing underneath the Kurfürstendamm. The new "sliver building" was designed by Helmut Jahn, a German architect based in the United States. The building is cantilevered out above ground level along five metres, virtually doubling the floor area and enabling it to function as an office building. Various elements in the steel and glass facade quote the architecture of the '20s.
The generous width of the streets here, similar to those around "an der Urania", stems from the pro-automobile traffic planning of West Berlin in the '60s and '70s.

Bayer-Haus

Geber & Risse
1951–52
Kurfürstendamm 178-179

This commercial building was one of the first new buildings to be completed as part of the postwar reconstruction projects carried out in West Berlin during the '50s. Its simple modular grid structure and restrained facade details created a look which soon became common among commercial buildings here, and immediately earned it the title of "the most beautiful building in Berlin" when it was opened. In 1988, Bayer AG received an award for its careful restoration work on the structure.

3

3 Leibnizkolonnaden

Kollhoff & Timmermann, Berlin
1997–99
Leibnizstrasse 49-53/ Wielandstrasse 19-22

The design of the Leibnizkolonnaden project comprises two parallel bar buildings bracketing a rectangular open plaza, which is embellished with trees and a fountain. The two building volumes are divided into units of different sizes with individual facades. The building complex will consist of an office building for firms and associations, three residential houses, and a hotel. In the two upper floors of the south wing, space is also set aside for a kindergarten, which is joined by a special stairway to small pavilions at the roof level. The flattened U-shape connecting the bars to adjacent buildings creates small inner courtyards.
Before this project was carried out, the property had remained unbuilt since the turn of the century, despite a frenzy of development in the surrounding area. Because the architects Kollhoff & Timmermann proposed a more public urban architecture, rather than an introverted courtyard residential block, the design elicited a good deal of controversy, resulting in the project's delay of over ten years.

Wohnanlage
Residential complex
Paul Weingärtner
1919
Niebuhrstrasse 14-19b

Immediately after the First World War, this "emergency housing project" was constructed for veterans and families with many children. It originally consisted of five two-storey rows with small private gardens. Only two wings survived the demolitions carried out during the urban renewal programmes of the '50s and '70s. The project, which was added to the list of protected buildings in 1994, documents municipal efforts to relieve the severe housing crisis following the war.

4 Ehemaliges Abspannwerk

Former Bewag transformer equipment building

Hans Heinrich Müller; Petra and Paul Kahlfeldt, Berlin
1927–28;
1999–2000
Leibnizstrasse 65-68

The heavy brick building for the old transformer station of 1928 provided domestic electricity for Charlottenburg's residential buildings. It was designed by the director of the Bewag construction department, Hans Müller. The modern steel frame structure, hung with sparingly decorated brick cladding, was the trademark of the many Bewag buildings built in Berlin during the '20s.

Bewag produced high-current electricity for the city in outlying power plants, which was then stepped down to lower voltages for residential use, using decentralised transformers.
Later technological advances rendered the transformer stations superfluous. After the equipment was shut down in 1984, the listed building was converted into a design centre. The Berlin architects Kahlfeldt planned the total retrofit, managing nevertheless to preserve the wall consoles in the circuit switching hall in the top floor, which is now used as a meeting hall.

Kant-Garagenpalast
Kant parking garage
Louis Serlin, Hermann Zweigenthal, Richard Paulick
1929–30
Kantstrasse 126-127

The first parking structure in Germany, built in 1930, testifies to the rapid spread of the private automobile at the time. With its reinforced concrete structure containing 300 parking spaces, the building belongs to the "rational" style. The idea of building two separate ramps for entering and exiting to ease circulation was first introduced in Germany. The Kant parking garage, which is still used today, has changed very little over the years and is now a listed building.

Wohn- und Geschäftshaus

Residential and commercial building

Schmölling Bode & Partner, Dinklage
1998–99
Kantstrasse 137/
Schlüterstrasse 62

The design of this residential and commercial building closes up one of the few open corners remaining in Charlottenburg since the war. It replaces a one-storey, temporary shed building along Kantstrasse. Kantstrasse is one of the most important commercial streets and traffic arteries of "City West" and joins the commercial centre around Breitscheidplatz with the convention centre and Theodor-Heuss-Platz in New-Westend. Its selection of shops and services is more modest than that of the Kurfürstendamm.

Savignyplatz
Erwin Barth
1926–27
Kantstrasse/
Savignyplatz

Reformist ideas about health and hygiene called for the incorporation, in the new extension plans for Charlottenburg and Wilmersdorf, of public squares to provide ventilation and open space, which were badly lacking in the dense historic centre. Bisected by the Kantstrasse, Savignyplatz is a typical decorative (but functional) square from the Hobrecht plan of 1862. Laid out at the end of the 19th century, its garden design be-

6

longs to the 20th century. The current landscaping of the square is true to the 1926 scheme designed by city garden director Erwin Barth. When Berlin was divided, Savignyplatz became a popular meeting place for artists and intellectuals, offering many restaurants, cafés, bookstores, and art galleries. Today, however, it faces strong competition for this urban clientele from the newly gentrified area around Hackesche Höfe in Mitte.

Wohnhaus, ehemals „Tattersall des Westens"

Residential building former "Tattersall des Westens"

A. Ziechmann,
Heinrich Mittag
1900
Grolmanstrasse 47

The words "Reitschule" and "Tattersall des Westens" on the front and rear of the brick building from 1900 in Grolmanstrasse tell of the well-loved riding and training school once located here.

The name stems from the English stable master Richard Tattersall, who became a horse auctioneer in 1766. The "Tattersall" company quickly became widely known and is still represented in many countries.

The stables were located on Uhlandstrasse and were torn down after the Second World War.

6

stilwerk Design Center

Novotny, Mähner
& Assoziierte,
Offenbach/Berlin,
Studio + Partners, Milan
1998–99
Kantstrasse 17-20/
Uhlandstrasse 9-11

A number of different shops for interior decoration and home furnishings will be located in this centre now in construction on the northern side of Kantstrasse, designed by the Berlin architects Novotny & Mähner, together with Studio + Partners, Milan. The project became feasible after the Dresdner Bank, whose Berlin headquarters occupied a '50s building on the site, moved eastwards. The bank's offices are no longer in Charlottenburg, but are divided between two locations, one at Pariser Platz and the other at the Ostbahnhof station. Almost all of the monumental but modern postwar building was removed, leaving only one section along Uhlandstrasse. The old safes in the basement level at the corner of the block will also remain, to be hidden underneath a new curving glass lobby and three glass-walled floors supported on piloti (slender round columns). The various portions of the complex are differentiated by projections and set-backs, all enclosing a narrow atrium, from where elevators lead to the upper level retail spaces.

7

The arching viaducts of the city railways, completed in 1882, were originally open but some were later enclosed and used for storage spaces, stables, and workshops. They became an object of renewed interest in West Berlin when their potential as spaces for shops and restaurants was discovered during the '80s. As a result the Stadtbahn viaduct no longer has the effect of a barricaded enclosure cutting off the neighbouring blocks, and its new storefronts help it become a part of the public space.

S-Bahn-Viadukt
S-Bahn viaduct of the city railways
Ernst Dircksen
1878–82
Uhlandstrasse
(in the direction of Grolmanstrasse)

„Kempinski Plaza"

7

The Kempinski Plaza, a commercial building, creates a through-block arcade linking Uhlandstrasse with its parallel neighbour, Fasanenstrasse, and the Kempinski Hotel. The building symbolises the effort to increase public access to the inner courtyards of the commercial blocks in the City West, typically making use of atriums, continuous galleries, and passages.

Rolf Rave, Jan Rave, Roosje Rave, Dieter Meisl, Berlin
1990–93
Uhlandstrasse 181-183

The idea for creating the Kurfürstendamm stems from the town-builder J.A.W. von Carstenn-Lichterfelde, who proposed around 1870 that the riding path leading westwards from the city to the royal hunting lodge in the Grunewald forest become a 30 metre wide grand boulevard. With the Champs-Élysées in Paris in mind, Otto von Bismarck insisted on increasing the width to an even grander 54 metres. The street branched off from Tiergartenstrasse and established a route beginning south of the Zoological Gardens (today Budapester Strasse) at Auguste-Viktoria-Platz (today Breitscheidplatz) where the Kaiser Wilhelm Memorial Church was later built. Nicknamed the "Ku'damm", the tree-lined avenue leads further westwards to the lake at Halensee. Along the southwest, it borders the villa colony of Grunewald (near Bismarckplatz today), developed with palatial homes during the 1880s and '90s. The 19th-century city expansion plans drawn up by Peter Joseph Lenné and James Hobrecht included many similarly tree-lined streets, a contrast to the 18th-century Baroque-era development of Friedrichstadt.

Kurfürstendamm

The Kurfürstendamm soon developed into an important shopping boulevard with many artists' cafés, theatres, variety theatres, and cinemas; its attractions epitomised the exuberant cultural life of the roaring twenties.
After the Second World War, the area took on the function of a downtown for the western half of the divided city, resuming its role as an entertainment and commercial centre, thus bearing testimony to the German economic miracle of the '50s. Public life centred on the area between Adenauerplatz and Breitscheidplatz, while the western portion of the street, lined with fashionable apartment houses, was more residential. During the '70s, the street's splendour declined somewhat with the addition of fast-food restaurants and inexpensive shops. But the city administration and landlords joined forces in the '80s to upgrade its appearance. Part of this effort was the new fountain built at Breitscheidplatz.
After reunification, the rivalry between the west and east downtown city centres (Kurfürstendamm, Friedrichstrasse, Alexanderplatz) further motivated improvements made in the Kurfürstendamm area. Today it is once again a prime location for luxury boutiques and fashionable shops. The lasting attraction of the Kurfürstendamm, which passes through the districts of Charlottenburg and Wilmersdorf, owes much to the character of the sidestreets, where a good balance of shopping, office, and residential spaces is still maintained.

Ehemaliges Salamander-Haus

Former Salamander Building

Ferdinand Döbler;
Johann Emil Schaudt
1891;
1927–28
Kurfürstendamm 28

This residential and commercial building dating from 1891 was given a modern facade in the '20s when its long-time tenant, Salamander Shoes, hired the architect Emil Schaudt to redesign its store. The eclectic architectural ornamentation was replaced with streamlined curving balconies and dark green ceramic tile. In 1994, the ground floor and first floor above ground were completely reconfigured for the Deutsche Bank in a more contemporary architecture, adding a third layer to the reading of the building.

Hotel Kempinski

Paul Schwebes
1951–52
Kurfürstendamm 27/
Fasanenstrasse

The Kempinski was the first new hotel to be built in West Berlin after the Second World War. The curved corner of the building recalls the architecture of the '20s, yet its ground plan respects the historic block pattern of the area. The projections and setbacks along Fasanenstrasse were added in 1957 and 1965. The well-known building is named after its first owners, a Jewish family who opened an elegant restaurant there in 1926. Despite the Nazi expropriation of the property in 1935, the name was not changed. Finally in 1994 a memorial plaque was mounted on the building exterior.

Bankhaus Löbbecke

8

Wolf-Rüdiger Borchardt,
Berlin
1992–96
Fasanenstrasse 76-77

The main offices of the Löbbecke bank occupy a listed building and two new buildings in this ensemble. Villa Ilse, built 1872-74 by H. Sobotta and named after its first owner, Leopold Ilse, was converted into a customer service centre for the bank by the Berlin architect Wolf-Rüdiger Borchardt. He also designed the two new buildings, known as the glass house and stone house, which enclose a small plaza. The Berlin artist Mona Fux designed the bridge linking the glass house with Villa Ilse.

Jüdisches Gemeindehaus

Jewish Community Centre
Dieter Knoblauch,
Heinz Heise
1957–59
Fasanenstrasse 79-80

The Jewish Community Centre was built on the site of a synagogue that was heavily damaged during the pogrom of November 1938 and then taken down in 1957. The original synagogue was designed by Ehrenfried Hessel in 1912. With stylistic references to the architecture of Romanesque churches, an elaborate interior, and its placement directly on the streetfront, it was an important public expression of the cultural identity of German Jewry. During the Nazi era, the great majority of the 160,000 Jewish citizens living in Berlin were either forced to leave or killed in concentration camps. Only very few were able to survive the war carefully hidden within the city.
Fragments of the old portal and facade of the old synagogue were integrated into the main entrance of the new building. Today the Berlin Jewish community is growing once again, especially with the addition of emigrants from East Europe.

9

Künstlerhaus St. Lukas
St. Lukas Artists' Residence
Bernhard Sehring
1889–90
Fasanenstrasse 13

The St. Lukas artists' studios and residential building in Fasanenstrasse is an outstanding example of the historic revival of the turn of the century architecture.
The architect-builder Bernhard Sehring brought paintings and art objects from Italy to decorate the interior.
The current owner, a relative of the architect Bernhard Sehring, was awarded the Ferdinand von Quast prize for the well-done restoration of the building in 1987.

9

Kant-Dreieck

Kant-Dreieck office building

Josef Paul Kleihues, Berlin
1992–95
Fasanenstrasse 81/
Kantstrasse 155

This office building situated on a triangular lot, by the Berlin architect Josef Paul Kleihues, was originally designed to be a third higher than it is. The Charlottenburg city planning authorities forced the change in the original plans, in order to prevent an unwanted "jump in scale" in the City West area. The large metal "sail", which marks the dimensions of the planned building, has since become a focal point in the cityscape. The eleven-storey truncated tower is one of the first office buildings of the '90s in the City West. It intersects with a five-storey wing whose facade of dark slate and glass follows the curve of the S-Bahn tracks. A waterfall flows down from street level along Fasanenstrasse, and the forecourt on Kantstrasse extends the open space in front of the Delphi-Kino, making a gesture to the historic spatial configuration. In 1994 the building won the BDA (Bund Deutscher Architekten) design award. Recently there have been calls to have the missing floors added on. In the meantime, the barrack-like building on the front plaza has until now defied all plans for its demolition.

Theater des Westens, Delphi-Kino, Gartenanlagen
Bernhard Sehring
1895–96,
1927–28
Kantstrasse 12/
Fasanenstrasse 11

This historic monumental building for the privately operated "Theater des Westens" was restored step-by-step during the last few years. The complex can be categorised as "built stylistic history", incorporating a number of periods, from medieval Romanesque, with half-timber walls, battlements, and pointed arches, up to the most exaggerated neo-Renaissance style on the main facade. Originally the building could be entered via the "Emperor's stairs" leading from the

theatre garden to the ornate lobby. The Delphi-Palast cinema was designed as a dance club during the '20s, and the garden was redesigned at a later date. After its refurbishment in 1997-98, the "Emperor's stairs" and the original facade of the Delphi Kino will be also restored.

Ludwig-Erhard-Haus

Ludwig Erhard Haus stock exchange

Nicholas Grimshaw & Partners, London/Berlin
1994–98
Fasanenstrasse 83-84

The British high-tech architect Nicholas Grimshaw designed this unusual building on Fasanenstrasse for the Chamber of Commerce (IHK) and the Berlin Stock Exchange, which is located right next door to the IHK's old office building (1954-55 by Franz Heinrich Sobotka and Gustav Müller). For the irregularly-shaped building lot, Grimshaw designed a structure of 15 great arches that form a ribbed volume easily accommodating the slight curve in the shape of the property. The individual office levels of the building are supported by steel cables hanging from the giant arches. A passage from the public lobby through the building offers access to the two atria. At the behest of the city, the arch structure had to be closed off with a "customary" fire-rated party wall, so that the elegance of the building is a bit obscured, and can be perceived only on the interior or from above.

Hochschule der Künste

Kayser & Großheim
1898–1902
Hardenbergstrasse 32/ Fasanenstrasse

The Hochschule der Künste ("College of the Arts") put down roots at the western edge of the Tiergarten around the turn of the century, very close to the Technical University, which was established in 1879. Of the then extensive complex, comprising dozens of pavilions and studios, only a few structures survived the war intact. Among them are the neo-Baroque main building facing Hardenbergstrasse. In 1953-55 Paul Baumgarten designed the addition of the neighbouring concert hall for the Hochschule der Musik, which he later expanded with the rehearsal stage located to the north along Fasanenstrasse. Herbert von Karajan directed the Berlin Philharmonic Orchestra in the concert hall until the completion of the Philharmonie at the Kulturforum on Potsdamer Strasse in 1963.

11

11

Bahnhof Zoologischer Garten

Bahnhof Zoologischer Garten railway station

Ernst Dircksen;
Fritz Hane;
ArchitektenSocietät
Figallo, Rottwinkel,
Rottwinkel-Tuncel,
Birkel,
Berlin
1878–82;
1934–41;
1994–96/99
Hardenbergplatz

This station building was designed in 1882 by Ernst Dircksen to serve both the city railway and the long distance railway systems. The strikingly modern glass sheds were added in 1934. After the construction of the Berlin Wall in 1961, it became the main railway station in West Berlin. It was also the central local transit station, with links to two underground lines and a large bus station.

During the initial renovation work begun in 1994 up to 1996, the interior was considerably altered. The second phase, begun in 1998, will concentrate on the exterior: the facades will be restored and the most of the original arches on Hardenbergplatz will be exposed; the upper level restaurant, designed in the '50s, will also be redone. Since service was resumed at the Ostbahnhof station, Bahnhof Zoo is no longer the end station for trains arriving from the west.

Zoologischer Garten

Hardenbergplatz

The Berlin Zoo, is a rare example of an urban zoo. It was founded in 1841 by Martin Lichtenstein, who selected the southwestern portion of the Tiergarten for its location, along with Peter Joseph Lenné. The site was previously occupied by the Pheasantry that was founded in 1742 to enrich the cuisine of the royal court. After its founding, a number of prominent architects designed the various animal habitats of the Zoo, each adopting a special architectural theme; only a few remained after the end of the war. Today the oldest zoo in Germany is entered through the reconstructed Lion Gate on Hardenbergplatz, or via the Elephant Gate on Olof-Palme-Platz, next to the aquarium, which was built in 1913. The Zoo, home to a total of 13,826 animals, also boasts the largest number of species in world.

12

Zoofenster

The shapers of Berlin's city planning policy after 1990 decided that the eastern part of Berlin should be developed as its major downtown area, because of its greater number of existing cultural and academic amenities. The commercial district of West Berlin around Breitscheid-

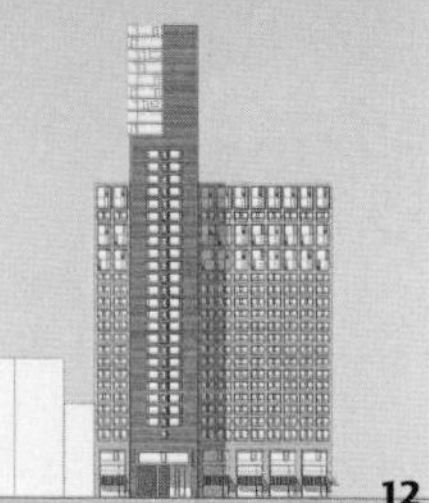

platz was to be strengthened, nevertheless, in order to compete with the redeveloped historic center of Berlin in the east.

In 1991, the British architect Richard Rogers designed a 91-metre high "Zoofenster" tower on the corner site at Hardenberg-, Kant-, and Joachimstaler Strasse.

The architect Helmut Jahn designed a new building on property belonging to the Victoria Insurance Company, near the Cafe Kranzler. Overriding strong protests from both the Zoologischer Garten, which saw itself threatened by shadows of tall buildings, and the district of Charlottenburg, the two projects were approved by the Senator of Building in 1993. In 1998, Rogers' design was rejected, and an alternative design by the Frankfort architect Christoph Mäckler was chosen for construction which emphasises a gateway configuration towards Breitscheidplatz. However, Mäckler's project increased the building's height to 120 metres, changing the original 32 floors of office and hotel space into 37 floors of residential apartments. As a result, the entire '60s development of Breitscheidplatz as commercial center will be revised. Included is a listed building, Schimmelpfeng-Haus, built from 1957-60 by Franz Heinrich Sobotka and Gustav Müller, part of which is suspended across Kantstrasse. Because it takes up part of the site in question, there are plans for its demolition in order to unblock the vertical space above the street.

These plans are extremely controversial, however: some think that a new building would harm the existing mixed-use character of the area,

Christoph Mäckler Architekten,
Frankfort on the Main/Berlin
1999–2001
Hardenbergstrasse/
Joachimstaler Strasse/
Kantstrasse

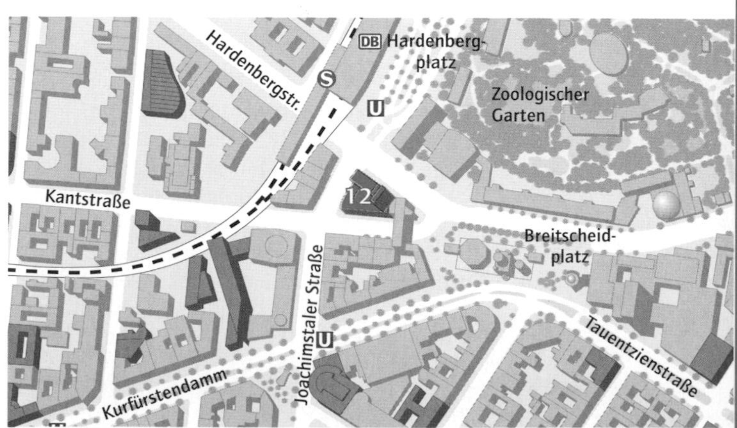

13

while others hope that intensive commercial use would reinforce the area's identity as a downtown urban centre.

13

Ku'damm-Eck

gmp von Gerkan, Marg & Partner, Hamburg
1998–2000
Kurfürstendamm 227-228/ Joachimstaler Strasse

The new Ku'damm Eck (corner) will contain a hotel, department store, and gallery, all anchored at the centre of "City West". The wavy facade and horizontal layering of the ten-storey corner building at the intersection of three streets recall the commercial buildings of the '20s. The dynamic curves of its predecessor, the Grünfeld-Haus, were dramatically displayed at night with specially designed lighting. After the war, the Grünfeld-Haus was replaced by the 1968-72 building complex with a white metal skin and large advertising wall, designed by Werner Düttmann. Düttmann's building was torn down in 1999 to make way for the commercial, aesthetic, and spatial improvements of the new project.

Kaufhaus Wertheim
Wertheim Department Store
Werner Düttmann, Hans Soll; Haus Rucker & Co.; Bassenge, Puhan-Schulz, Heinrich and Schreiber, Berlin
1971; 1983;
1991
Kurfürstendamm 230-233

Nearly all branches of the once famous Wertheim department store chain in Berlin were destroyed in the last war. In 1971, the company had a new building put up on the Kurfürstendamm designed by the former Senate Building Director Werner Düttmann. Its architectural expression was a strong contrast to its surroundings. In 1983, the Austrian architectural firm Haus Rucker & Co. updated the street facade by adding on a giant projecting window, arching five-stories high. In 1991, Bassenge, Puhan-Schulz, Heinrich and Schreiber added on the penthouse level.

Verkehrskanzel Joachimstaler Platz
Traffic control tower at Joachimstaler Platz
Werner Klenke, Werner Düttmann, Bruno Grimmek
1953–55
Joachimstaler Platz

The traffic control tower on Joachimstaler Platz is a typical relict of the '50s. It was meant to continue a tradition begun at Potsdamer Platz in 1924, to regulate the turbulent traffic of the big city. It became a symbol for car-oriented city planning of the day. But soon afterwards, it was overwhelmed by the amount of street traffic and could no longer function. Integrated with telephone boxes, kiosks, and an entrance to the underground, the listed complex represents the ideal of modern urban design of the '50s.

The former headquarters of the Allianz Insurance Company originated in an urban design competition called "Rund um den Zoo" ("Around the Zoo") sponsored in 1948 by a business group, whose goal was to redevelop the City West commercial district. Breitscheidplatz stood at the centre of the competition site, while Joachimstaler Platz formed its southern edge. The idea was to build high-rise buildings, but set them back behind the traditional 19th century lot lines. The 14-storey stone tower forms a high wall for the square, while the six-storey wing encloses the space arching towards the Kurfürstendamm. The Café Kranzler complex north of the boulevard was intended to become part of the ensemble with the monumental Allianz building that will be renovated for a new tenant, since the insurance company has relocated its offices eastwards to the Treptowers complex at Treptower Park (s. p. 258, 259).

Allianz-Versicherung
Allianz Insurance Tower
Alfred Gunzenhauser,
Paul Schwebes
1953–55
Joachimstaler Strasse 10-12

Neues Kranzler-Eck
New Kranzler-Eck

The new Kranzler-Eck will embellish the existing ensemble around the world-famous Cafe Kranzler, built by Hanns Dustmann in 1955-63. Included are the adjoining two-storey commercial building and the Karstadt Sports store (formerly the "bilka" retail store) at the corner of Kantstrasse. Designed by the American-based Helmut Jahn, the main feature of the new project is a 16-storey high oblong tower perpendicular to the Kurfürstendamm. Its structure is extruded out from the glass enclosure at the corners, with beams meeting at sharp angles supporting east-viewing observation decks on every other storey. A nine-storey volume frames the remainder of the site. The new buildings contain shops and offices, and the courtyards provide a through-block pedestrian link from the Ku'damm to Kantstrasse. These public spaces will be animated with stands for food, crafts, and other items, as well as a specially designed 17-metre high habitat for several species of birds.

Murphy/Jahn,
Helmut Jahn, Chicago
1998–2000
Kurfürstendamm/
Kantstrasse/
Joachimstaler Strasse

Hotel am Zoo
Alfred Messel;
Paul Baumgarten
1891–92;
1956–57
Kurfürstendamm 25

In 1910, this building designed by Alfred Messel in 1892 was converted into a hotel. Baumgarten added the new entry and reception hall with glass elements in 1950, and six years later the building was enlarged with two upper stories. The sober design deliberately contrasts with the surviving original decoration. The setbacks create small terraces for the hotel rooms. The design of the lobby as it now stands is from a more recent date.

Kino Filmbühne Wien
Filmbühne Wien cinema
Nentwich & Simon
1912–13
Kurfürstendamm 26

The current Filmbühne Wien on the Kurfürstendamm, built in 1913, was one of the first buildings ever designed specifically to function as a cinema. From then on, the area attracted large cinema buildings of all kinds and shapes, making the Ku'damm a popular place for entertainment and amusements long before the '20s. Since 1981, the Wilhelmine edifice has been divided into a total of eight smaller cinemas, while the original formal lobby space is occupied by shops.

Literaturhaus, Kollwitz-Museum, Auktionshaus Villa Grisebach
Literaturhaus, Kollwitz Museum, Villa Grisebach Auction House
Wilhelm Martens;
Becker & Schlüter,
Hans Grisebach
1871;
1889–90
Fasanenstrasse 23-27
(s. ill. above)

A special ensemble of buildings, consisting of several villas and rowhouses dating from the late 19th century, is grouped along Fasanenstrasse. During the '60s, they were nearly torn down to make way for a new city highway off-ramp. A focal point of the ensemble is the neoclassical brick villa (1889-90 by Becker & Schlüter), set back from the street, which is the home of the Literaturhaus Berlin (and restaurant). Directly next door is the oldest villa of the group (1871 by Wilhelm Martens), which contains a museum dedicated to the work of the socially-engaged artist Käthe Kollwitz. Around 1890, two other free-standing houses were built closer to the street; a well-known art dealer is located in the one named after its architect, Hans Grisebach.

Wohnhaus am Fasanenplatz
Residential building on Fasanenplatz
Gottfried Böhm
1980
Fasanenstrasse 62

The tall cylindrical forms of the bays of this residential building on Fasanenplatz, designed by the Cologne architect Gottfried Böhm, give it an expression resembling a medieval castle. The octagonal inner courtyard is roofed over and surrounded by open walkways leading to the flats.

Fasanenplatz

Johann Anton Wilhelm von Carstenn-Lichterfelde
1870

Fasanenplatz is part of a north-south oriented, simple geometric pattern of streets laid out during the Gründerzeit by von Carstenn-Lichterfelde, a town-builder who founded the Berlin suburb of Lichterfelde in 1865. The street configuration, roughly oval-shaped in plan, is formed by Schaperstrasse to the north, Fasanenstrasse and Nikolsburger Platz to the west, and Nürnberger and Prager Platz in the east. The squares were laid out with gardens that were embellished over the years; by 1895 residential buildings lined the streets. The postwar redevelopment of the centre axis of Bundesallee created a wide traffic artery that disrupted the area's spatial coherence. The urban design concept represented by Fasanenplatz and Fasanenstrasse is a radical contrast to the car oriented modernist planning of the '60s and '70s.

Ehemalige „Freie Volksbühne"

Former "Freie Volksbühne" theatre

Fritz Bornemann
1961–63
Schaperstrasse 24

A socially-minded cultural organisation founded in 1890, the "Freie Volksbühne Verein", set out to make literature and theatre accessible to less advantaged segments of the population. By means of donations and membership fees, the Verein was able to finance the construction of the Volksbühne, located on what is now Rosa-Luxemburg-Platz in Mitte, which then became the group's permanent venue. After the Wall divided the city in 1961, the group relocated to the district of Wilmersdorf in the west, building a new theatre designed by Fritz Bornemann. This rather modern concrete and glass theatre possesses an elegance that was rare among the architecture of the '60s. In 1992, the Freie Volksbühne theatre was closed down. The imposing building on Rosa-Luxemburg-Platz in the east had become available once again.

Kirche am Hohenzollerndamm

Church on Hohenzollerndamm

Fritz Höger
1931–32
Hohenzollernplatz

The powerful expressionistic architecture of this church, designed by the Hamburg architect Fritz Höger in 1932, makes use of a modern concrete structure. The blue-red firebrick cladding produces an impressive effect on the facade. The vertical emphasis suggested by its closely spaced narrow brick pilasters is echoed by the tall bell tower. The entrance and nave of the church were designed using Gothic-influenced pointed arches, creating a mystical atmosphere in the space.

15

15

Hauptpumpwerk Wilmersdorf

Wilmersdorf central pumping station

Hermann Müller;
Kurt Ackermann & Partner, Munich
1906;
1993–97
Hohenzollerndamm 208

The old pumping station built in 1906 was a mainstay of the city's canalisation system originating during the time of Hobrecht (see p. 81/82). The station pumped away the waste water, carrying it to outlying sewage fields. The facility, which was housed in an elaborate work of architecture, is typical of the progressive hygiene reforms of the time. Its function has been overtaken since 1997 by a new building housing machines and pumping facilities on three levels sunken below grade. Passers-by can get a glimpse of the underground infrastructure through a lightweight glass curtain wall structure.

Investitionsbank Berlin

Horst Haseloff,
Klaus Hendel,
Wolfgang Hotzel;
Stankovic + Bonnen Architekten, Berlin
1971–75;
1996–98
Bundesallee 208-210

In 1975, this twelve-storey office building was completed for the Wohnungsbau-Kreditanstalt, an agency which financed most of the social housing in Berlin. During the '60s and '70s, disruptions of the older, conventional spatial relationships between street and building were common in architectural and urban development: The relatively high building is situated parallel to the Bundesallee and blocks off the space above Regensburger Strasse. The Berlin architects Stankovic and Bonnen replaced the building's original dark-brown aluminium panels with green granite cladding. Prior to this, the Wohnungsbau-Kreditanstalt became part of the Investitionsbank in 1995.

Ehemaliges Bundeshaus Berlin

Former Bundeshaus Berlin

Bernhardt & Wieczorek
1893–95
Bundesallee 216-218
(s. ill. above right)

For nearly 40 years, the former Bundeshaus provided the government in Bonn with office spaces in Berlin. In accordance with the four-power agreement controlling Berlin, which lasted until 1990, the city was administered as an independent political entity with its own constitution. Under the terms of the Allied agreement, the west German government was not permitted to maintain an official presence in Berlin. In 1950, this neoclassical building, put up in 1895 for the Royal Prussian Artillery Testing Commission, was rechristened the "Bundeshaus" by the then Chancellor Konrad Adenauer. Its offices represented the highest levels of the federal government in Berlin. At the same time, the old Kaiser-Allee was renamed Bundesallee.

This elongated edifice originally served as the Joachimsthalsche Gymnasium (secondary school), founded in 1607. After many different tenants, it now houses the music department of the Hochschule der Künste. The ornate 1880 building was designed in the style of the Italian high Renaissance. The central high pedimented volume emphasised the centre axis; figures of Plato and Aristotle peer out from its niches. Along the axis on the courtyard side was the school's auditorium, which has since become a concert hall for the Hochschule der Künste's musicians. The architectural office of Nalbach + Nalbach designed the renovation of the concert hall in 1995.

Hochschule der Künste

Johann Heinrich Strack,
Ludwig Giersberg,
Johann Eduard Jacobsthal;
Nalbach + Nalbach, Berlin
1875–80;
1995
Bundesallee 1-12

Geschäftshaus

Commercial building

This commercial building is actually the result of the conversion of a three-storey parking structure, in which it received a new laminated metal panel cladding. An addition of the same height was also built on the south side.

Georg Heinrichs & Partner, Berlin
1992
Rankestrasse 21/
Eislebener Strasse

A simple brick structure was originally built for the fire station on Rankestrasse by Paul Bratring, then the city architect for Charlottenburg. The station was enlarged with a functional new building in 1970-72 and still serves the City West fire department.

Feuerwache Ranke

Ranke Fire Station

Paul Bratring, Theodor Peters; Günther Hönow, Winnetou Kampmann
1896–97; 1970–72
Rankestrasse 10-12

The two side wings and courtyard portion of this office building, designed by Schwebes in 1955 for the Agrippina company, were rebuilt and reorganised to enclose a small space in 1993-97. The front and rear portions of the building are joined together by bridges on the second and third storeys.

Agrippina-Haus

Paul Schwebes;
Ulrich Findeisen & Sedlacek, Cologne
1955–56;
1993–97
Rankestrasse 5-6

In memory of Kaiser Wilhelm I, the first German emperor, after his death in 1888, Schwechten's neo-Romanesque church was built at the heart of western Berlin. In 1956 a design competition was held to determine the future of the heavily damaged church and its surroundings. After considerable public debate, Eiermann's reworked winning scheme, which called for the removal of

Kaiser-Wilhelm-Gedächtnis-Kirche

Kaiser Wilhelm Memorial Church

Franz Schwechten;
Egon Eiermann
1891–95;
1957–63
Breitscheidplatz

the nave while retaining the west façade and tower, was carried out. Eiermann placed an octagonal new church towards the west, flanking the fragment containing the old bell tower and sacristy with a new pentagonal bell tower on the east. The outer walls of the new structures are faced with honeycomb-like pre-cast concrete panels with bright blue windows. The jewel-like geometric volumes share a common plinth. The postwar complex at Breitscheidplatz soon became one of the foremost symbols of the divided western half of Berlin. After 1980, some of the streets at the perimeter of the complex were closed to create a new square with a "world fountain" designed by Joachim Schmettau. Facing the northern side of the square is the Bikini Haus, so named because the building was originally horizontally separated into upper and lower enclosures, the two pieces leaving a narrow strip of space between them (like a two-piece swimsuit). The American-financed building was a part of the "Zentrum am Zoo" project. After reunification there were plans to demolish the ensemble, although the high-rise slab on Hardenbergplatz, the Zoo Palast cinema, and the eight-storey Bikini Haus on Budapester Strasse are all listed buildings. The ten-year long debate was finally settled by a 1998 court ruling in favour of keeping the buildings. During the same period, the Europa Center inevitably wound up in the sights of city planners, who envisaged an upper storey addition and an uninterrupted street surface surrounding the building: as a result, the underpass dug out along Budapester Strasse in 1960 will be filled back in, restoring a grade level connection that would better unite the Bikini Haus with Europa Center and Breitscheidplatz.

17.1 *Ensemble*

Tauentzienstraße

Tauentzienstrasse is the westernmost part of the "Generalzug", a sequence of new streets laid out by Peter Joseph Lenné around 1860 to link the area now known as Kreuzberg with Charlottenburg. The streets were named after the Prussian generals who had fought in the wars of liberation against Napoleon from 1811-14: Kleist, Bülow, Yorck, Tauentzien and Gneisenau. After the last war, Tauentzienstrasse developed into a central commercial street for the western half of

Berlin, a kind of continuation of the Kurfürstendamm.
Now in competition with the historic centre of Berlin, the countless renovations and new additions made along the street since 1990 attest to a strong desire to maintain the area as a commercial centre.

Salamander-Haus

17.2 *Ensemble*

The Salamander-Haus, designed by the Hamburg architects gmp, was built immediately after the Berlin Wall was removed. The six-storey rational glass and steel structure replaced a two-storey '50s building. In 1997, the same firm designed a nearly identical version of this building for Friedrichstrasse 106-108.

gmp von Gerkan, Marg & Partner, Hamburg
1990–92
Tauentzienstrasse 15/
Marburger Strasse

Europa-Center

17.3 *Ensemble*

The construction of the Europa Center in 1965 aided the post-war development of a downtown for West Berlin around Breitscheidplatz. The 22-storey glass and steel monolith was the first genuinely tall building in the city and the first of many enclosed shopping arcades to be built afterwards. With large offices located on the upper floors – the Senator for Culture occupied space here until 1991 – the surrounding lower volume was designed as a place for consumers to encounter a special "shopping experience". Until the 1980s, the Europa Center also featured a popular ice-skating rink.

Helmut Hentrich,
Hubert Petschnigg
1963–65
Tauentzienstrasse 9

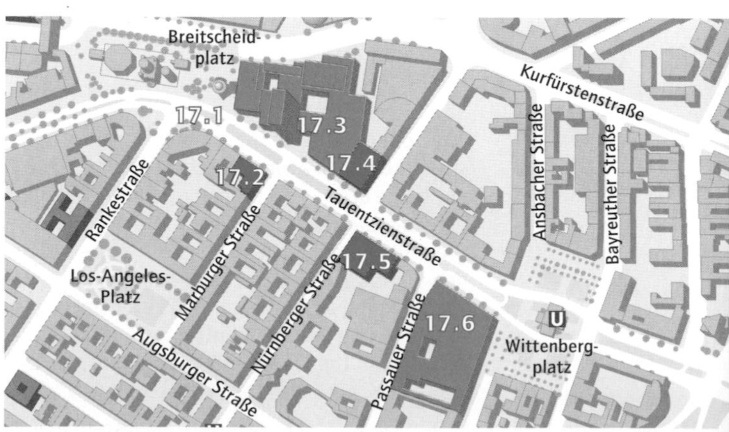

18

Deutsches Institut für Normung
German Institute for Standardization (DIN)

Johannes Heinrich,
Architektengemeinschaft
Bassenge, Puhan-Schulz,
Heinrich, Schreiber, Berlin
1997–99
Burggrafenstrasse 6/
Budapester Strasse 41

The main office of the German Institute for Standardization (DIN) is located in this '80s building on Burggrafenstrasse. In the new addition, the massing of the high volume penetrating the street facade is continued by a new addition suspended above the courtyard by architect Johannes Heinrich; it extends further back into the site until it projects out over the older rear facade on Budapester Strasse, where it is supported by five-storey high columns and bisected by an angled vertical slab. Side wings are connected on either side towards the street line. There is a garden in the courtyard designed by Berlin landscape architects Müller/Knippschild/Wehberg in 1993-95.

17.4
Ensemble

Wohn- und Geschäftshaus
Residential and commercial building

Eller + Eller Architekten,
Berlin/Düsseldorf
1994–99
Tauentzienstrasse 7b-c/
Nürnberger Strasse

The store facades of the building, built in 1994-99, are articulated with vertical stripes in black granite. Spaced between them are three-storey bays whose solid parapets alternate with strips of windows wrapping the sides and corners. The united base and first upper floor have a great deal of window area, clearing indicated the building's commercial function. The cubic effect seen from the street is contrasted by a more animated facade overlooking the courtyard. Rounded walkways run from the third level roof garden up to the ninth storey.

17.5
Ensemble

Peek & Cloppenburg-Haus
Peek & Cloppenburg Building

Gottfried Böhm, Cologne
1994–95
Tauentzienstrasse 19

The upper portion of the exposed concrete frame structure pulled away from this building's glazed enclosure echoes the hipped-roof form of Berlin's older department stores (like KaDeWe). Between the tall piers, long curved glass panels slope down and tilt out over the street, forming clear shop awnings. The design strikes a compromise between the requirements of a closed stone facade and the transparency of a glass curtain wall.

17.5

This 150-metre long modern office building for the government agency controlling all alcohol distilling was designed in 1931 using the "rational" style of the "Neue Sachlichkeit". Horizontal ribbon windows run along the travertine exterior, which is interrupted by projecting bays and the stairwell volume. The ground floor shops take on a more formal public expression thanks to the brass trim used to frame the doors and windows.

Tauentzienpalast, ehemals Femina Palast

Tauentzienpalast, the former Femina Palast

Richard Bielenberg,
Josef Moser
1928–31
Nürnberger Strasse 50-55

Kaufhaus des Westens

17.6
Ensemble

The Kaufhaus des Westens ("Department Store of the West") became an important member of the legendary department store culture of the turn of the century. Following in the footsteps of the grand emporiums at Alexanderplatz and Leipziger Platz, the KaDeWe launched a third retail centre in the west on Wittenbergplatz. Schaudt designed the building and later directed its renovation in 1929-30. Founded by Adolf Jandorf in 1907, KaDeWe was sold in 1926 to Hermann Tietz. The Tietz chain of department stores was expropriated and placed under the control of an Aryan company in 1935. KaDeWe was the only one of the inner city department stores to survive the Second World War intact. Ever since its reconstruction in 1950, it has been the most well-known department store in the city. Frequently renovated and added on to, its original main entrance with gold mosaics was modernised in 1997. Since then, it ranks as the largest department store on the continent and is a guarantee that City West will continue to be in demand among shoppers in the years to come.

Johann Emil Schaudt;
H. Ströming,
Ernsting & Partner, Münster
1906–07,
1929–30;
1993
Tauentzienstrasse 21-24

The Wittenbergplatz underground station, first opened in 1902 as part of the trunk line between what is today Ernst-Reuter-Platz and Warschauer Strasse, became an important transit node in the up-and-coming commercial district. In 1911, when the lines from Wilmersdorf and Charlottenburg were brought through, Grenander designed a classically-inspired station building on a cruciform plan. In 1980 the listed building was restored. Since 1995 the underground line originating in Charlottenburg at Ruhleben and making a stop here was reunited with the original terminus at Vinetastrasse in the east.

U-Bahnhof Wittenbergplatz

Underground station at Wittenbergplatz

Alfred Grenander
1900–02,
1911–13
Tauentzienstrasse

Neue Botschaften

New Embassies

Route 8 passes through the new embassy district of Berlin and across the Tiergarten Park. It takes in the area which Berlin has made available to foreign embassies and the representations of a number of German Laender. Route 8 ends at the Hansaviertel district, the ambitious attempt undertaken in the '50s to seek architectural alternatives to the established block structures of the traditional European city.

The route begins at the underground station at Nollendorfplatz. From there it leads north through the former Kielgan Viertel district. Only a few houses of the once elegant colony of villas dating from the end of the 19th century still remain. Large numbers of buildings were destroyed during the Second World War and in many cases replaced by large-scale housing complexes and the buildings of furniture department stores. House Fromberg, which has been restored in keeping with original plans, is an excellent example of the respect which has been paid to the old city in the last few years. The same holds true of a number of modern buildings dating from the '80s, which were designed in keeping with historical proportions.

The former Geheimratsviertel ("privy councillor's estate") lies to the north of the Landwehr Canal. It stretched from Potsdamer Platz in a westerly direction along Tiergartenstrasse. Its mansions and villas made it one of the most exclusive addresses in Berlin and a part of the legendary "Old West" district of the city: bankers, affluent businessmen and intellectuals resided here. The former Imperial Navy Office was built by the Landwehr Canal in 1914, one of the last major building projects of the German Empire. The headquarters of the Wehrmacht (the name of the German armed forces between 1935 and 1945) was here. Today it is the site of the Memorial to the German Resistance in memory of the resistance led by Graf Stauffenberg, who planned the assassination of Hitler in 1944 and were shot by firing squad in the courtyard of the building. Since 1993 the building has served as the Berlin offices of the German Ministry of Defence.

The embassy district developed in the "privy councillor's estate" between the Landwehr Canal

and Tiergarten Park after 1900. The district was given the official name "Diplomatic Quarter" in 1937 when Albert Speer had the site cleared to provide accommodation for the diplomats of the allies of Nazi Germany. Large numbers of residents were relocated, the Jews were expelled just as was the case in the Alsenviertel district. The old villas were demolished and replaced by imposing embassy buildings. Some of the old embassies which had survived the war bombing served as consulates during the period of the division of Germany.
Following the opening of the Berlin Wall, the area was once again planned as an embassy district. A number of countries were able to make new use of their old properties, further embassies and the representations of the German Laender as well as the offices of confederations and political parties will also be located here. The embassy district between Potsdamer Platz and the Tiergarten triangle, where the Nordic countries share embassy facilities, is now once again one of the most prestigious addresses in Berlin.
At Lützowplatz the tour reaches a central area of the International Building Exhibition (IBA 87). The historical structures served as the basis for the redesign of the square. The symmetrically arranged urban villas on Rauchstrasse illustrate how the modern architecture of the IBA 87 still reflects the urban design of the former Geheimratsviertel district.
The route enters the Tiergarten Park at the point where it passes the monumental Spanish embassy building. Today's layout of the former royal hunting area dates back to the design of Peter Joseph Lenné from 1850. Work to gradually restore the park, which was severely damaged during the Second World War, to its historical condition began in the '50s. The only changes to be retained were those made by Albert Speer at the Grosser Stern. In 1937 he had had the Column of Victory moved here from its historical location on Königsplatz in front of the Reichstag to create a landmark on the avenue which was then known as the "East-West Axis".
Finally, route 8 passes through the Hansaviertel district and ends at Tiergarten city railway station. The Hansa district was the response of West Berlin to the socialist urban development on what was then "Stalinallee" in East Berlin.

2

1

U-Bahnhof Nollendorfplatz

Nollendorfplatz underground station

Cremer & Wolffenstein;
Alfred Grenander
1900–01;
1925–26

The Nollendorfplatz underground station by Cremer & Wolffenstein is part of the first line constructed in the elevated and underground inner city rapid transit network in Berlin. Today designated U 2, the line was laid out by Siemens & Halske between 1896 and 1902, and covered the east-west route between Warschauer Strasse and what is today Ernst-Reuter-Platz. Whereas in the richer west it was built just a few centimetres below grade, the section to the east of Nollendorfplatz, which led to the poorer districts, was built as an elevated railway in order to save money. From 1908 to 1910, a second line, the U 4, was begun here which led south to Rathaus Schöneberg. Also stopping here and running parallel for part of the way is the U 1, many of whose stations were designed by Alfred Grenander, the architect for the greater majority of the system's station and service buildings. Nollendorfplatz was the first time in the history of the U-Bahn system that two transit lines and stations were stacked vertically. In 1926 Grenander a small memorial added to the new entry building, honoring the transit workers who died during the First World War. The elevated portion of the station was taken out of service in 1971 and was used as a flea market until 1994, when line U2 to Pankow was re-established.

2

Verbandshaus der Deutschen Bauindustrie

German Construction Industry Federation

Architekten
Schweger + Partner,
Hamburg/Berlin
1996–98
Kurfürstenstrasse 129

The German Construction Industry Federation built a new building for itself in 1998 which it will begin to occupy once the government transfer from Bonn to Berlin takes place. A generously proportioned lobby at the ground level serves public functions and leads to the courtyard garden to the rear. Offices are arranged around a narrow atrium, while the uppermost level is reserved for the union leadership. The subdued, closed facade is clad with green-toned concrete panels, a high-quality pre-fabricated material which serves as a demonstration of the prowess of the German building industry.

Umspannwerk Lützow

Max Dudler
1987
Einemstrasse 20-20c

This transformer station, built as part of the International Building Exhibition programme (IBA), provides the southern part of the Tiergarten district with electric power. The sober, solid facade of metal cladding characterises the building as a technical structure, while the use of fire bricks recalls the Bewag buildings of the '20s.

Hotel Berlin

Paul Schwebes,
Hans Schoszberger;
Michael König,
Betz and Partner, Berlin
1958;
1986–87;
1990–91;
1995–96
Einemstrasse/
Lützowplatz

Designed by Schwebes and Schoszberger, the Hotel Berlin was completed in 1958 as one of the first new hotels built in West Berlin after the war.
In 1996 a new eight-storey wing was added on Schillstrasse. A glass penthouse floor with a cantilevered glass roof is pulled back above the smooth stone facade supported by a colonnade. The deep recessed windows and metal awnings animate the facade. The building mass helps bring back the clearly defined contour of the formerly densely built street. As part of the IBA held in 1987, the southern edge of Lützowplatz was redefined by an extension and a further wing was added on the east side.

Wohnhaus

Apartment house
Hilmer & Sattler,
Munich/Berlin
1988–89
Kurfürstenstrasse 59

Adopting a contemporary architectural expression, this free-standing apartment house by Hilmer & Sattler continues the tradition of the urban villa that characterised this quarter in the latter half of the 19th century. It corresponds in volume and height to the ornate villa next door, which is the home of the Café Einstein. The cubic building, made up of three residential floors and a penthouse level, has four social housing dwellings per floor, which are accessed by an oval stairwell. The building received an award from the Bund Deutscher Architekten in 1992.

Haus Fromberg

Cremer & Wolffenstein;
Reinhard Müller, Berlin
1895–96;
1993–95
Kurfürstenstrasse 132

This house commissioned by Georg Fromberg in 1895 is one of the last remaining structures originally built as part of the district known as the Kielgan Viertel that was developed here. Executed in the country house style, it represents an "urban villa", a type which is somewhat unusual for the inner city. After he restored the building, the architect and developer uses it for his offices.

4

Zwölf-Apostel-Kirche

Church of the Twelve Apostles

Hermann Blankenstein
1871–74
An der Apostelkirche/
Kurfürstenstrasse

This Protestant church from 1874 is yet another example of the extensive collection of works built by Blankenstein, then the city architect. The brick building stands at a right-angle to Kurfürstenstrasse and its high tower receives the visual axis. Although brick was widely used for a variety of Berlin's public buildings around 1850, after the German empire was founded in 1871, public buildings were more frequently designed in sandstone. Only everyday structures, like schools, hospitals, barracks and factories, were still built using the local brick of the region. Brick also remained the material used to build many churches.

Wohnhausgruppe „Begaswinkel"

"Begaswinkel" apartment complex

Ernst Klingenberg
1872–73
Genthiner Strasse 30

Genthiner Strasse is dominated by the furniture stores that opened here in the '70s. Behind the furniture stores is one of the narrow streets that used to penetrate the deep blocks. The homogeneous group of late 19th-century residential buildings still conveys a spatial impression of the typical building fabric of the time.

4

Bundesministerium für Verteidigung

Federal Ministry of Defence

Reinhardt & Süßenguth;
Krupp & Druckemüller;
Burckhardt, Emch & Berger, Berlin/Bern
1911–14;
1938;
1997–2000
Reichpietschufer 74-76/
Stauffenbergstrasse 11-14

The Berlin offices of the Defence Ministry, which will not entirely move from Bonn, have been located since 1993 in the former Imperial Navy building situated between the Landwehrkanal and Tiergarten. The imposing building was one of the last administrative buildings to be completed during the imperial era (1911-14), and was used by the military until 1945. With the return of general conscription in 1935 and the concommitant weapons build-up, the high command of the military, army and navy all shared the same complex.

An addition was made to the building along the former Bendlerstrasse (today Stauffenbergstrasse), using materials and massing that help it fit in with the formal architecture of the older main building. In the courtyard of the "Bendlerblock" a memorial was erected in honour of the group of anti-Nazis led by Count von Stauffenberg, who were executed here following their failed attempt to assassinate Hitler on July 20, 1944.

Shell-Haus

5

Emil Fahrenkamp;
Atelier Christoph Fischer Architekt, Berlin
1930–31;
1998–99
Reichpietschufer 60-62/
Stauffenbergstrasse

Overlooking the banks of the Landwehrkanal, the Shell building from 1931 is an outstanding example of the architecture of the Weimar Republic. The rippling facade rises in height from five to ten storeys. The modern steel frame structure made it possible for the ribbon windows to be wrapped around the zig-zagging corners of the building.

Provisional repairs were made after the last war, and in the '80s the landmark was supposed to be completely renovated. But preservationists argued that the plans for reconstruction would have significantly altered the original architectural effect of the building. They were able to block an effort to hang an aluminum facade and a second plan to add insulation to the travertine facade, which would have resulted in a deeper window profile.

Instead, a new renovation concept was developed that preserved the look of the building's exterior as well as the original interior. Work has now been underway on the building since 1997. The two free-standing towers on the north side were added by Paul Baumgarten in 1965-68.

Diplomatenviertel

Diplomatic Quarter

6.1

Ensemble

Tiergartenstrasse

The area south of the Tiergarten between Tiergartenstrasse and the Landwehrkanal became the most elegant district in the 18th and 19th century just outside the city gates of Berlin. Spreading outwards from Potsdamer Platz, it was a collection of luxurious villas and manor-like homes, many of whose owners were high-ranking state officials, hence the name Geheimratsviertel, or "Privy Councillor Estate". After the First World War a series of embassies were built along the southern edge of the Tiergarten, so that a diplomatic district developed here. The monumental schemes launched by Albert Speer in 1937 in order to redesign Berlin as the "world capital Germania", which focused on a north-south axis beginning in the Alsenviertel near the Reichstag, resulted in the removal of many of the embassies. It was decided to relocate them in this diplomatic quarter in Tiergarten. In 1938,

37 embassies and 28 consulates settled here, and by 1943 nine new embassy buildings had been added. During the Second World War, the area was nearly wiped out, and many embassies were eventually abandoned because the delegations had to be divided between the two German capitals, Bonn and East Berlin. The Cultural Forum, situated at the east end of Tiergartenstrasse, and the IBA buildings on the western

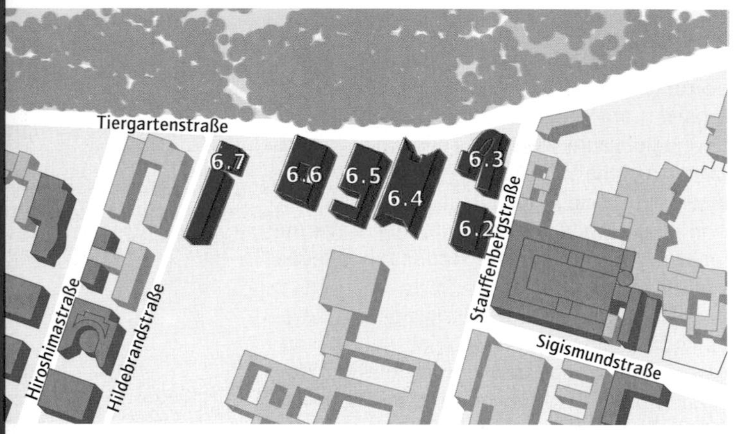

end remained the only large construction projects in this area until the Wall was dismantled in 1989. After that, many countries decided to resume using their former embassy sites, some moving into the old buildings. The city administration of Berlin then redesignated this area as an official quarter for embassies and national headquarters of the German Laender. A number of countries, as well as some German Laender, instead moved their delegations in the immediate vicinity of the Federal Government. Tiergartenstrasse, which forms an important spatial connection between the central part of Berlin at Potsdamer Platz and the younger area in City West, is primarily a traffic axis and sharply divides the Tiergarten park from the embassy quarter. The reconstruction of the historical lanes, walkways, and visual axes of the Tiergarten could help frame it, but this is not currently being considered.

There are more embassies scattered in other parts of the city. One of the most important outer areas is Pankow, where many were located during the GDR era.

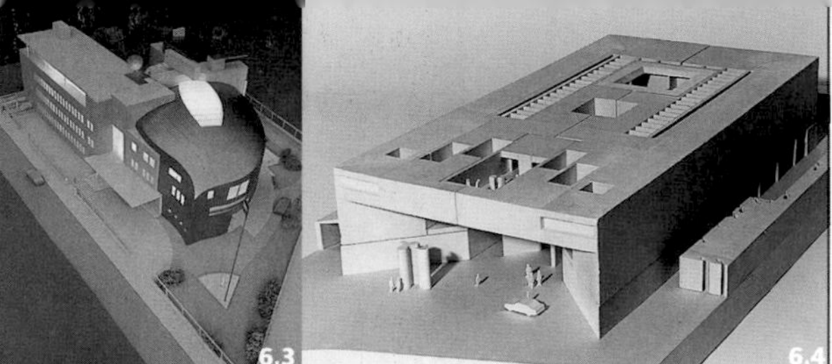
6.3
6.4

Botschaft der Arabischen Republik Ägypten

Embassy of the Arab Republic of Egypt

6.2 *Ensemble*

Stauffenbergstrasse 6-7

Egypt will build its new embassy opposite the Picture Gallery. The country had an embassy in the diplomatic quarter before the Second World War. The architect is currently being selected through an invited competition.

Botschaft der Republik Österreich

Embassy of the Republic of Austria

6.3 *Ensemble*

Hans Hollein, Vienna
1999–2000
Tiergartenstrasse 12-14/
Stauffenbergstrasse 1-3

The site of the Austrian Embassy marks an important gateway to the diplomatic quarter. It lies just a few parcels north of its pre-war location, and directly borders the Cultural Forum. The Austrian architect Hans Hollein, who had also submitted unsuccessful proposals for the Cultural Forum in 1983, won first prize in a design competition for the new Austrian embassy in 1996 that was open to all architects in the European Union. The three overlapping and intersecting building volumes display the various functions of the embassy, using different architectural languages: at Stauffenbergstrasse is the four-storey consulate. It takes on the regularised building type of the development across the street. The entrance to the embassy is demarcated with a deep awning which leads into a high foyer space. The curving copper-clad volume at the corner of Tiergartenstrasse is given a formal hall for receptions and events. The oval plan of the hall is designed to accommodate the requirements of diplomatic protocol and makes a transition to the residence of the ambassador which is ensconced within the site. A loggia glazed to the top of the building, containing a banquet hall and conference rooms, faces the garden.

Landesvertretung Baden-Württemberg

Land representation of Baden-Württemberg

6.4 *Ensemble*

Dietrich Bangert, Berlin
1998–2000
Tiergartenstrasse 15

Baden-Württemberg is moving its representation into a new building on Tiergartenstrasse which was designed by the Berlin architect Dietrich Bangert, the winner of the final phase of a 1997 EU-wide design competition. The building takes

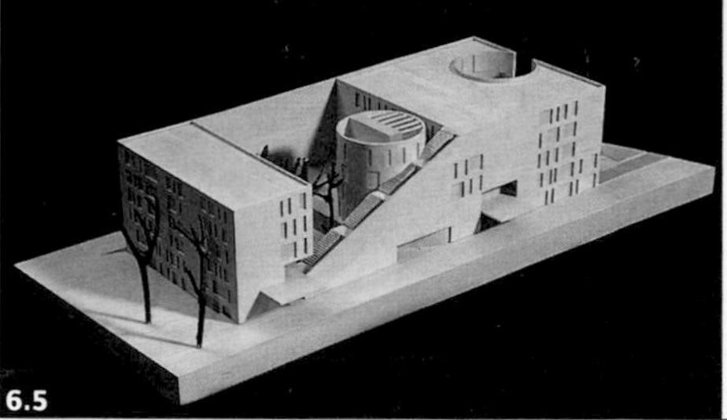
6.5

up most of the rectangular site and will be only 16 metres high, in keeping with the special height restrictions applying in the quarter. The main entrance is situated on the narrow end; movement is guided by two walls angled toward the interior, creating a roofed courtyard of honour. The embassy portion of the building lies on Tiergartenstrasse, while all work and administrative areas are oriented to the narrow garden on the side. The covered inner courtyard in the rear portion of the building opens onto the garden, also flanked by angled walls.

6.5 *Ensemble*

Botschaft der Republik Indien

Embassy of the Republic of India

Hilde Léon,
Konrad Wohlhage,
Siegfried Wernik, Berlin
1998–2000
Tiergartenstrasse 16-17

The Indian Embassy stretches across a very narrow piece of property. The long, rectangular building mass is clearly organised, strongly articulating its programmatic functions. In the main building to the north are the consulate and administrative offices as well as exhibition spaces. Several paths and access routes converge at a cylindrical pavilion. The ambassador's residence lies to the rear of the garden, which is flanked by a long exterior stairway leading to the top of the building. The German architects sought to give the building an "Indian character" by means of fragments of reddish sandstone from India and integrated into the concrete on the facade.

6.6 *Ensemble*

Botschaft der Republik Südafrika

Embassy of the Republic of South Africa

Tiergartenstrasse 17a-18

This property belonged to South Africa as early as 1934. The country acquired the adjacent parcel, in 1938. A neoclassical residence built there in 1923, damaged in the war, was demolished in 1951. A national competition was carried out in 1998 for the new embassy project, but a decision had not been reached by the time of this printing.

6.7 *Ensemble*

Botschaft der Republik Türkei

Embassy of the Republic of Turkey

1999–2002
Tiergartenstrasse 19-21/
Hildebrandstrasse

Turkey's new embassy will be located on this site along Tiergartenstrasse, designed by the winner of a national design competition.

Botschaft der Italienischen Republik

Embassy of the Republic of Italy

Friedrich Hetzelt;
Vittorio de Feo, Rome
1939–42;
1999–2000
Tiergartenstrasse 21a-23/
Hiroshimastrasse

The embassy built from 1939-42 for Italy, at the time a close political ally of Germany, remains the largest building within the new diplomatic quarter. From 1937 to 1945, all new architectural plans had to be approved by Albert Speer, the general building director. It was his job to guarantee that a uniform level of design would be followed, which would manifest Nazi ideology and claim to superiority. For this reason he commissioned only German architects to design the embassy buildings. The architect Friedrich Hetzelt designed the monumental three-wing complex, whose porch with massive columns and reddish-pink stucco were meant to evoke Italian architecture, particularly Roman palaces. After the Second World War, the only still usable wing of the building was used as a consulate, while the remaining two-thirds lay in ruins for decades. A national design competition was held in 1995 for the reconstruction and expansion of the building. The first prize was awarded to Roman architect Vittorio de Feo, whose concept was a faithful reconstruction of the embassy, keeping close to its earlier design and outfitting. Formal areas will be in the main building, while the residence and a cultural institute will occupy the heavily damaged east wing.

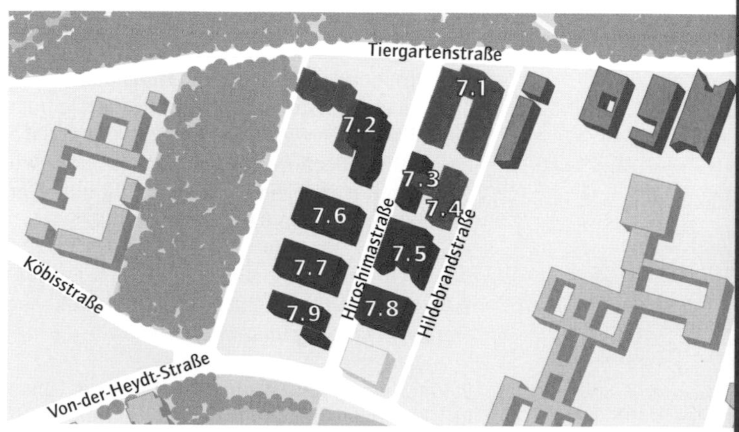

7.2

7.2 *Ensemble*

Botschaft von Japan
Embassy of Japan

Ludwig Moshamer;
Kisho Kurokawa,
Tajii Yamaguchi;
Ryohel Amemiya, Tokyo
1938–42;
1987–88;
1998–2000
Tiergartenstrasse 24-27/
Hiroshimastrasse

It became necessary to construct a new embassy building for Japan in 1938, because in the same year, the building at the eastern end of Tiergartenstrasse that had housed the legation since 1919 was demolished to make way for buildings to be constructed on the north-south axis. The German architect Ludwig Moshamer designed a severe, stripped-down building with two wings. The small golden sun on the roof symbolises imperial Japan. The building was heavily damaged in the war and fell into disuse for 40 years. In 1987, as part of the International Building Exhibition programme (IBA), the Japanese architects Kisho Kurokawa and Tajii Yamaguchi oversaw a faithful reconstruction of the building. Afterwards it became a Japanese-German centre for cultural and intellectual exchange. At the time, however, there was much controversy over whether the listed building should be reconstructed at all, given its association with the Nazi era.
After 2000, the embassy's facilities will be enlarged with a new chancellery located on Hiroshimastrasse, designed by the Japanese architect Ryohel Amemiya.

7.3 *Ensemble*

Botschaft der Griechischen Republik
Embassy of the Republic of Greece

G. C. Krause;
Constantin Kouvelis, Berlin
1911;
1999–2000
Hiroshimastrasse 13-15

This property, located between Hiroshimastrasse and Hildebrandtstrasse, and the villa dating from 1911, have been owned by Greece ever since the early 1920s. Because the building was not used after the war, it declined considerably, but after repairs it will be again used as an embassy.

7.4 *Ensemble*

Botschaft der Republik Estland
Embassy of the Republic of Estonia

Kayser & Groszheim;
Olavi Nömmik, Tallinn
1870;
1999–2000
Hildebrandstrasse 5

Estonia, which was occupied by the Soviet Union in 1940 and regained its independence in 1991, is now able to make use of the property in the diplomatic quarter that it has owned since 1923. The residence on the site bordering the Greek Embassy, built in 1870, has been preserved

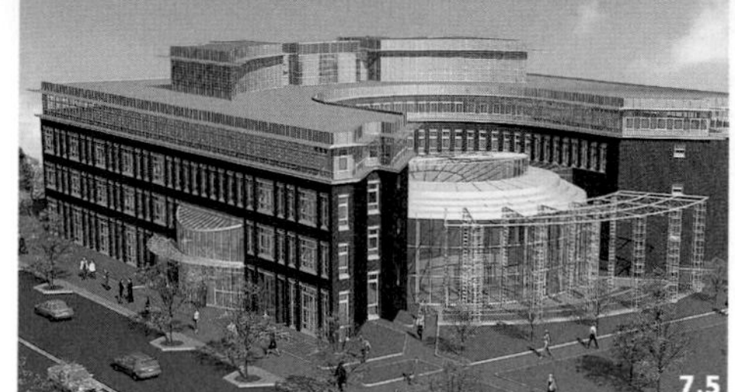
7.5

largely intact. After the war, it was used as a dwelling, which saved it from falling into disrepair. Olavi Nömmik was selected in a national competition to be the architect for the renovation of the embassy. The top floor of the three-storey portion of the building will be expanded to accommodate the residence.

Seminarzentrum der Friedrich-Ebert-Stiftung

Conference Centre of the Friedrich Ebert Foundation

Ensemble 7.5

The Friedrich Ebert Stiftung, a foundation associated with the Social Democratic party, is located in a new building in the midst of the diplomatic quarter between Hiroshimastrasse and Hildebrandstrasse. The main part of the building contains the administrative and seminar rooms. At the core of the complex is a circular glass conference and exhibition area open to the south side. Designed to seat 250, it can be expanded to accommodate up to 500.

Fritz Novotny,
Arthur Mähner,
Volkhard Weber
with Novotny Mähner &
Assoziierte, Berlin
1997–99
Hiroshimastrasse 17-25

Landesvertretung Nordrhein-Westfalen

Land representation of Nordrhein Westfalen

Ensemble 7.6

Along with Baden-Württemberg and the city-state of Bremen, Nordrhein-Westfalen will locate its national headquarters in the diplomatic quarter. A design competition, open to architects from all EU countries and Switzerland, was held to select 25 architects for the second round who will compete along with 15 invited architects.

2000–2001
Hiroshimastrasse

Botschaft der Vereinigten Arabischen Emirate

Embassy of the United Arab Emirates

Ensemble 7.7

For the embassy of the United Arab Emirates, to be housed in a new building in the diplomatic quarter, an architect is being selected through an invited competition. The final decision is still pending.

Hiroshimastrasse 16-20

7.9

7.8 *Ensemble*

Botschaft der Portugiesischen Republik
Embassy of the Republic of Portugal

Inés Varela Maia Lobo,
Lisbon
Hiroshimastrasse 23-25

The office of Varela Maia Lobo won an EU-wide architectural competition for the new Portugese Embassy.

7.9 *Ensemble*

Landesvertretung Freie Hansestadt Bremen
Land representation of Bremen

Hilde Léon,
Konrad Wohlhage,
Siegfried Wernik,
Berlin
1998–99
Hiroshimastrasse/
Reichpietschufer

The headquarters representing the city-state of Bremen in the German capital will be built according to plans drawn up by Léon, Wohlhage and Wernik. The design was selected during a 1996 competition for invited architects. The tower on the southern edge of the property, which contains guest apartments, creates a spatial transition from solid masses to open volumes. Slightly further away it is the volume containing the actual headquarters, a compact building comprising administrative and legal offices as well as spaces for official receptions and ceremonies.

Villa von der Heydt

Hermann Ende
1860–61
Von-der-Heydt-Strasse 18

August von der Heydt, who commissioned building of this neoclassical villa dating from 1860, was a Prussian Minister of Trade, Commerce, and Public Works who played a central role in promoting the nation's industrialisation during the 19th century. The villa remained in family ownership until 1919 and was a private sports club until it was acquired by the German Reich in 1938. Today the Villa von der Heydt is the only survivor from this once exclusive area. It is now the main offices of Stiftung Preussischer Kulturbesitz, the foundation managing many of Berlin's museums and cultural institutes.

Hiroshima-Steg

Hiroshima footbridge

Benedict Tonon,
Klaus Theo Brenner
1986–87
Reichpietschufer/
Lützowufer

The old bridge that once linked the residential area south of the Landwehrkanal with Tiergarten was destroyed in the Second World War. The reconstruction of Lützowbrücke was organised as part of the International Building Exhibition (IBA) in 1987. Brenner and Tonon were commissioned to build their single-arch curving steel structure to again provide a way for pedestrians to cross the canal.

Grand Hotel Esplanade

Jürgen Sawade
1986–88
Lützowufer 15/
Lützowstrasse

One of Berlin's first-class hotels, the Grand Hotel Esplanade was originally planned as a mixed-use office and residential building in the IBA project of 1987, whose goal was to repair the war-damaged area around Lützowplatz. The solidly massed building has a clear gridded facade opening above ground level toward the canal and the park; concealed behind a protective wall below is its street entrance, which leads to a generous lobby, restaurants, and conference spaces.

Lützowplatz

Lützowplatz redevelopment

Lützowplatz was once the centre of the elegant residential district called the Kielgan-Viertel, named after the property developer Georg Friedrich Kielgan. In 1868 he began to transform the area into a homogeneous collection of mainly two-storey high villas that became the home of many artists and literary figures. The pattern of development changed radically after the war and again with the later urban renewal carried out in the area.
Not until an IBA project in 1987, designating Lützowplatz as part of the building exhibition, could the streets and open space of the square be redeveloped.

Bauhaus Archiv

Bauhaus Archive

Walter Gropius;
Alec Cvijanovic
1971–78
Klingelhöferstrasse 14

The Bauhaus school, founded in 1919 as a state-run school in the city of Weimar, gained international acclaim for its modern educational philosophy. It set new aesthetic standards in art, the fine arts, photography, industrial design, and architecture. In response to pressure from right-wing factions in the provincial government of Thuringia, its founder and strategist, Walter Gropius, moved the institution to Dessau. There he built the architecturally ground-breaking Bauhaus building in 1925. In 1932, renewed pressure from the Nazis caused the school to move again, this time to Berlin, but it had to shut down only a year later.
After the Second World War, the by then internationally adopted teachings and aesthetic ideas of the Bauhaus, especially in architecture and urban design, found renewed interest in West Germany. The building containing the documentation and exhibition spaces now known as the Bauhaus Archive, was actually originally designed by Walter Gropius in 1964 for a site in Darm-

8.1

stadt. Alec Cvijanovic, a long-time associate of Gropius, eventually executed the building in Berlin from 1971 to 1978. Slight alterations were made necessary by the change in location; the orientation of the building was changed and it was bisected by a long entry ramp from Klingelhöferstrasse.

8.1 *Ensemble*

1998–2000
Klingelhöferstrasse/
Corneliusstrasse/
Stülerstrasse/
Rauchstrasse

Tiergarten-Dreieck

Tiergarten-Dreieck Development

This triangular parcel known as the Tiergarten-Dreieck – earlier called the Klingelhöfer-Dreieck – lies between City West and the diplomatic quarter. Following lengthy planning, it is only now being developed, albeit not with office space alone but with a mixture of housing and "political" buildings. The 1995 urban design competition resulted in a winning commission for Machleidt & Stepp, whose concept involves perimeter block development of buildings designed by eleven architects and placed around a central greenspace. This "vestpocket park" will be designed by the Berlin landscape architects Müller and Wehberg. The uniform 18-metre building height is only exceeded by the lens-shaped pavilion of the CDU party headquarters. Along Klingelhöferstrasse are buildings for various organisations and firms; lining the north side of Rauchstrasse are new embassies, while luxury apartments face Stülerstrasse and Corneliusstrasse, a quiet street along the Landwehrkanal. The only remaining older building in the area is an urban villa on Rauchstrasse built in 1912 by

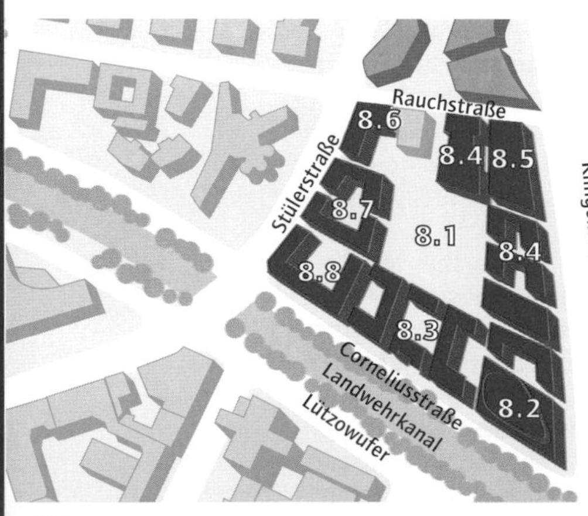

Georg Rathenau and Friedrich August Hartmann. It is used by the German Foundation for International Development.

CDU-Bundesgeschäftsstelle Berlin

CDU national party headquarters

8.2 *Ensemble*

The national party headquarters of the German Christian Democratic Union (CDU) is being built on the most prominent part of the Tiergarten-Dreieck, a sharply angled corner site. Above the base storey is a glass hall in which is inserted a second lens-shaped structure, forming a winter-garden encasing four floors. Two upper levels, in which the offices of the party executive will be housed, are contained in the form resembling an inverted keel emerging from the glass enclosure. The building will make use of energy-saving methods, including photovoltaic equipment and natural air-conditioning and ventilation technologies.

Petzinka, Pink and Partner, Düsseldorf
1998–2000
Klingelhöferstrasse/Corneliusstrasse

Wohnhäuser

Residential Buildings

8.3 *Ensemble*

This symmetric arrangement of four residential buildings on the quiet Corneliusstrasse along the Landwehrkanal encloses a small, cloister-like garden. The easternmost building is a U-shaped volume designed by the Munich architects Hilmer & Sattler, who also designed the neighbouring building facing the canal.
The western portion is by the American firm of Moore Ruble Yudell; Gesine Weinmiller designed the building which has elevations facing both the inner courtyard and the "vestpocket park".

Moore Ruble Yudell, Santa Monica,
Gesine Weinmiller, Berlin,
Hilmer and Sattler with Partner T. Albrecht, Berlin/Munich
1998–99
Corneliusstrasse

Geschäftshäuser

Commercial office buildings

8.4 *Ensemble*

Along the busy street of Klingelhöferstrasse four architects are building four office buildings for use by a number of organisations. They will be situated between the CDU party headquarters to the south and the Mexican Embassy to the north. Placed on roughly equal-sized parcels, the four buildings each have a main section with a street

8.5

S. M. Oreyzi, Cologne,
Petzinka, Pink and Partner, Düsseldorf,
Gesine Weinmiller, Berlin,
Moore Ruble Yudell, Santa Monica,
Büttner-Neumann-Braun, Berlin
1998–2000
Klingelhöferstrasse/ Rauchstrasse 26

facade towards Klingelhöferstrasse and a parallel rear portion towards the inner garden. The intervening space will either be built with a connecting wing or an enclosed atrium.
The facade designs will vary. The main facade of the building designed by Cologne architect Oreyzi consists of a glass surface and asymmetrical stone frame intended to provide a stylistic transition between the glass corner building of the CDU and the gridded stone facades of the neighbouring office buildings. The building by the Düsseldorf architects Petzinka, Pink & Partners and the Berlin architect Weinmiller are characterised by a tightly gridded facade, similar to the building for the Federation of Private Building and Loan Institutions, designed by the Californian firm of Moore Ruble Yudell.
The building housing the Association of accounts will be on Rauchstrasse next to the Mexican embassy, currently being designed by the Berlin architectural office of Büttner-Neumann-Braun.

8.5 *Ensemble*

Botschaft von Mexiko

Embassy of the United States of Mexico

Teodoro Gonzales de Léon,
Francisco Serrano,
Mexiko City
1998–2000
Klingelhöferstrasse 3/ Rauchstrasse 27

The new embassy building for Mexico, located on the northwest corner of the Tiergarten-Dreieck complex, was integrated into the urban design concept of the whole area. The unusual design, by the Mexican architect Gonzales de Léon and Serrano, was selected during an invited national building competition in 1997. The rather abstract facade is formed by a large rectangular frame that is draped with two "curtains" of slanting vertical panels of marble and concrete, forming the main entrance which leads to a circular lobby. The consulate and ambassador's residence are both located within the building.

Botschaft der Republik Jemen

8.6 *Ensemble*

Embassy of the Republic of Yemen

The new building will be on the property recently acquired at the corner of Stülerstrasse and Rauchstrasse. An architectural design competition is planned for 1999.

Stülerstraße/
Rauchstrasse

Wohnhäuser

8.7 *Ensemble*

Apartment houses

The two U-shaped buildings enclosing a small courtyard contain apartments and a children's day-care centre. The boarding house to the north was designed by the office of Faskel & Becker, while the south-facing building, containing apartments for single people, is by Walther Stepp.

Faskel & Becker, Berlin,
Walther Stepp, Berlin
1999–2000
Stülerstrasse

Büro- und Geschäftshaus

8.8 *Ensemble*

Commercial office building

The two L-shaped buildings along the Landwehrkanal are joined by a glass volume, forming a U-shaped complex. The courtyard is covered by a glass roof. Parts of the roof will be used as a garden. Originally planned as a residential building, on its completion the structure will serve as the administrative offices of a bank.

Pysall, Stahrenberg
& Partner, Berlin
1999–2000
Stülerstrasse 13-15/
Corneliusstrasse 8-9

Konrad-Adenauer-Stiftung

9

Konrad Adenauer Foundation

The Konrad Adenauer Stiftung, a foundation associated with the Christian Democratic Union, commissioned the construction of a new building for conferences and special events. Its architectural expression is to fit in well with the atmosphere of the embassy district. It is to be expanded in a second phase by an office wing placed parallel to Klingelhöferstrasse. This building will become its headquarters, should the Konrad Adenauer Stiftung decide to move from St. Augustin to Berlin. The solid cubic form clad in natural stone houses the larger public spaces, and above them the office spaces are indicated by the windows wrapping around all four sides. The two-storey high rotunda at the core of the building is used as a lecture hall.

Thomas van den Valentyn
with Anja Zeisner, Cologne
1996–98
Tiergartenstrasse 35

10 *Ensemble*

Nordische Botschaften:

Embassy complex for the Nordic countries:

Kingdom of Denmark
Republic of Finland
Republic of Iceland
Kingdom of Norway
Kingdom of Sweden

Alfred Berger,
Tiina Parkkinen, Vienna,
with Pysall · Ruge
Architekten,
Berlin
1997–99
Rauchstrasse 1

With their decision to house their embassies within a single building complex, the five Nordic nations of Denmark, Finland, Iceland, Norway and Sweden adopted a new and unusual strategy in which the otherwise closely guarded territorial rights of sovereign states have been transferred into a single compound.

The Austrian-Finnish architects Berger & Parkkinen based in Vienna won first prize in an EU-wide urban design competition. In their scheme, the individual embassy buildings are drawn together by a high copper-band wrapping around most of the complex to imbue a sense of belonging (s. ill. above). Exhibition spaces, a hall for receptions and lectures, a restaurant, and a sauna for use of all diplomatic staff and their guests are housed in a common building called the "Felleshus", designed by Berger & Parkkinen (s. ill. p. 235). The driveway into the underground garage separates the courtyard area from the high-security zone protecting the embassies. Each of the architects of the embassies, which represent the political sovereignty of the individual states, was selected through a national design competition. The Danish embassy was designed by Nielsen, Nielsen &

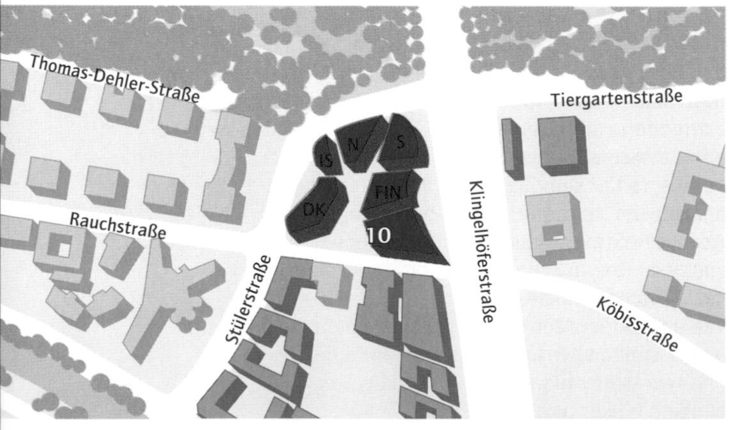

Nielsen, Århus; the Icelandic embassy by Pälmar Kristmundsson, Reykjavik; the Norwegian embassy by Snøhetta A. S., Oslo; the Swedish embassy by Wingårdh Arkitektkontor, Göteborg; and the Finnish embassy will be built by VIIVA Arkkitehtuuri Oy (Rauno Lehtinen, Pekka Mäki, Toni Peltola), Helsinki. Each of the buildings will feature fine materials specially imported from its respective homeland. Most notable is the 15-metre high, 120-ton granite slab which was shipped with great effort from Norway to Berlin. The 900-million year old stone will be used for the narrower facade of the embassy.

„IBA-Piccola"

Rob Krier
1983–84
Rauchstrasse 4-10

Rauchstrasse was one of the key planning projects of the IBA '87 programme, whose goal was the "urban repair" of the southern part of the Tiergarten district. As a reminder of the earlier villa colony in the area, several "urban villas" were built here along Rauchstrasse. The colourful free-standing multiple dwelling structures are arranged around a common garden within the block in an interpretation of the former spatial pattern of this former villa district between Tiergarten and City West. The apartment units they contain are social housing. The overall planning concept stems from Rob Krier, the winner of an international design competition in 1980, who designed a symmetrical composition for the 240 units. He also designed the gateway building, whose curving centre section is flanked by two cubic volumes. The six free-standing apartment blocks arrayed behind them are the work of different architects, who were free to design floor plans and facades as they liked, provided they respected the given area and building height.

Ehemalige Norwegische Botschaft

Former Norwegian Embassy building

Otto von Estorff, Gerhard Winkler
1940–41
Rauchstrasse 11

This stately building, completed in 1941, was designed by von Estorff and Winkler as part of Albert Speer's scheme for a new diplomatic quarter. As part of the IBA 87, it was converted into offices and apartments by the Freie Planungsgruppe Berlin. The aim was to preserve the building and incorporate it into design concept of the new town villa district. The Italian architect Aldo Rossi responded to the L-shaped plan of the old embassy in his adjacent housing project.

Ehemalige Jugoslawische Botschaft

Former Yugoslavian Embassy

Werner March
1938–40
Rauchstrasse 17-18

The embassy building once serving Yugoslavia's ambassador was conceived as a villa with two wings. It was designed by Werner March, the architect of the Olympic Stadium. The facade ornamentation was added by the sculptor Arno Breker, whose art followed the dictates of Nazi ideology. The main wing projecting outwards and clad in limestone contains the pubic spaces.

Akademie der Deutschen Telekom, ehemalige Dänische Botschaft

Deutsche Telekom Academy, formerly the Danish Embassy building

Johann Emil Schaudt
1938–40
Drakestrasse 1/
Thomas-Dehler-Strasse 48

Originally built to accommodate the Danish Embassy after its older quarters in the Alsenviertel were demolished to make way for the axis planned by Albert Speer, the building's limestone cladding and curving facade emulate Danish neoclassicism. The projecting bays at either end continue into side wings facing the courtyard; the entrance is marked by a porch lined with columns.

The building was purchased from Denmark in 1987, a time when West Berlin had no need of embassy buildings. Since 1988 it has been used as a training academy for executives of Deutsche Telekom.

11

Botschaft des Königreichs Spanien

Embassy of the Kingdom of Spain

Johannes and Walter Krüger;
TYPSA,
Jesus Velasco Ruiz, Madrid
1938–43;
1998–99
Lichtensteinallee 1/
Thomas-Dehler-Strasse

The Spanish Embassy is returning to its historic location in this heavy two-winged building at the southwestern edge of Tiergarten. It was built from 1938 to 1943, a time when Spain, an ally of Nazi Germany, was ruled by General Franco. The Krüger brothers collaborated with the Spanish architect Muguruza Otano on the design of the building, whose west wing, the only portion to survive the war intact, was subsequently used as a consulate. In Velasco Ruiz's scheme for a radical intervention on the listed building, the columns, entrance, stairwells and the eastern facade of the main wing of the original building will be preserved; behind the facade a new structure will be built. The Spanish architect has also completely replaced the west wing. The materials he has chosen match the older portions of the building.

Tiergarten
Tiergarten park
Fasanerieallee

Originally a hunting ground situated to the west of the historical centre, Tiergarten functions today as the "Central Park" of Berlin. It is framed by a number of new political and cultural buildings. Among the buildings encircling Tiergarten are the official seat of the Federal President, the Chancellery, the Bundestag, and other parliamentary institutions, all comprising the "Band des Bundes", or ribbon of Federal buildings. Lining the southern edge of the park will be new buildings housing the representations from the various German Laender and the embassies of the diplomatic quarter, while to the northwest and southeast lie the Hansaviertel and the Cultural Forum, realised in the '50s and '60s according to the concept of a "city landscape".
At the heart of the park is the "Great Star" with the Column of Victory monument. The diagonal avenue called the Fasanerieallee originally led from here to the royal pheasant reserve referred to in its name that was later incorporated into the Zoo.
Lined with trees, the avenue opens up a visual axis to the "Grosser Stern" (Great Star), now occupied by the Column of Victory, which originally stood in front of the Reichstag.
The park suffered heavily during the Second World War. In the unusually cold winter of 1945/46 were cut down nearly all of its old trees for firewood. Afterwards only 700 trees remained of the original 200,000. In 1949 a reforestation programme, directed by the garden designer Wilhelm Alverdes, begun. From 1985 on, restoration work has been underway to shape the park much the way it looked in the 19th century.

Siegessäule
Column of Victory
Johann Heinrich Strack
1864–73
Straße des 17. Juni/
Großer Stern

On September 2, 1873, Emperor Wilhelm I presided over the unveiling of the Column of Victory, which became the first national monument of the newly-formed second German empire. At the time it stood on Königsplatz, now called Platz der Republik. It was erected to commemorate the "wars of unification" successfully fought against Denmark (1864), Austria (1866), and France (1870-71), which led to the founding of a new German state. The column, whose shaft is decorated with canons seized from the enemy, is crowned with a gilt sculpture representing both the goddess of victory, Victoria, and Borussia, the allegorical figure of Prussia. The entire monument was taken down in 1938 in connection with the Speer plan for transforming Berlin into the "world capital Germania". In order to embellish the "East-West-Axis" through the Tiergarten, it was reassembled at "Grosser Stern" in 1939 and heightened by addition of a further drum-shaped section. Though there was talk of dismantling the monument after 1945, the then victorious French simply removed the bronze relief panels from the pedestal and took them to Paris. But they were returned to Berlin in time for the 750th anniversary of Berlin's founding in 1987, and re-attached to the pedestal, deliberately leaving them in their fragmented condition. Today visitors can climb 265 steps to the observation deck.

Hansaviertel: Interbau 1957

1954–58
Altonaer Strasse/
Bartningallee/
Klopstockstrasse

The Hansaviertel is an outstanding artifact of the urban design and architecture of the '50s. It represents the modernist notions of low-density urban development made popular during the postwar era. In the context of the political status of divided Berlin, the Hansaviertel was also assigned the role of representing the modernism of the west against the "national style" of the German Democratic Republic, as expressed in the monumental Stalinallee project built a few years earlier between Strausberger Platz and Frankfurter Tor along what is now Karl-Marx-Allee (s. p. 243).

But before its engagement in what has been called "the Cold War of architectures", the Hansaviertel was a densely built residential neighbourhood of richly ornamented upper-class courtyard apartment houses dating from the "Gründerzeit" following German unification. Heavily damaged during the war, the neighbourhood was evacuated and levelled to become the site of the International Building Exhibition of 1957, called "Interbau". The purpose of the programme was to demonstrate the economic and political strength of the western sectors by expressing their will to build a new vision of the "City of Tomorrow". The Berlin architect Otto Bartning was given the job of directing the project. According to the planning scheme by Jobst, Kreuer and Schliesser, buildings were placed in a park-like setting southeast of the S-Bahn city railway line between the stations at Tiergarten and Bellevue. Architectural contributions were made

by leading architects from 14 countries, using a range building types, including high-rises, rows of houses accommodating several families buildings, and clusters of single-family units. A new community was created with the addition of two churches, a shopping centre at the Hansaplatz underground station, and the new Academy of the Arts. Also among the array of projects built elsewhere as part of Interbau 1957 were the Kongresshalle in the Tiergarten, today called the Haus der Kulturen der Welt, and the Unité d'habitation near the Olympic stadium, a work by the Swiss-French architect Le Corbusier.

Wohnhaus
Apartment house
Hermann Ende
& Wilhelm Böckmann
1886–87
Joseph-Haydn-Strasse 1

One of the few remaining buildings of the Hansaviertel quarter dating from the "Gründerzeit", this apartment house gives an idea of the original pattern, scale, and architectural grandeur that existed here before the destruction which took place during Second World War. Standing directly adjacent to the train tracks of the S-Bahn line completed in 1882, it was built in 1887 by the well-known prolific office of Ende & Böckmann.

Berlin-Pavillon
Berlin Pavilion
Hermann Fehling,
Daniel Gogel,
Peter Pfankuch
1956–57
Strasse des 17. Juni
(s. ill. above)

The diminutive but expressive Berlin Pavilion was designed to serve as an information centre for the Interbau 1957 building exhibition. It bears the architectural signature of its designers in its composition of geometric elements, central diagonal emphasis and use of unconventional building materials.
In 1991 this significant work was restored and renovated by Daniel Gogel, and has been used since then by the city planning administration as a venue for public discussions and exhibitions on architecture and urban planning.

Königliche Porzellan Manufaktur
Royal Porcelain Factory
Gustav Möller;
Bruno Grimmek
1868–72;
1955–62
Wegelystrasse 1

The Royal Porcelain Factory (Königliche Porzellan Manufaktur, KPM) is an old establishment belonging to the region of Berlin and Brandenburg. It was founded in 1763 to create a Prussian rival to the factory in Meissen that had been producing fine porcelain since 1710. The first Berlin production facility was located on Leipziger Strasse. In the middle of the 19th century it was relocated to the Spreeufer to the west, where

there was more space and better access to shipping. The KPM's archives were initially kept in East Berlin after the Second World War, but in 1981 they were exchanged for the sculptures from the Schlossbrücke which had been stored for safety in the west. Since 1998, the KPM building has been renovated and enlarged. In 1994 Josef Paul Kleihues was awarded first prize in a competition for a scheme for a new complex on the site, including buildings for the use of the College of the Arts, the Senate Library, the KPM, and various residential and commercial buildings, but the project has yet to be realised.

12 S-Bahnhof Tiergarten

Tiergarten city railway station

Ernst Dircksen;
Dörr, Ludolf, Wimmer, Berlin
1878–82;
1995–97
Bachstrasse/
Strasse des 17. Juni

Tiergarten city railway station was built in 1882 at the western edge of the Tiergarten. Its severely styled entry volume was designed in 1937 to accommodate Nazi taste, since it is located directly on the "east-west axis", which was used for military parades at the time. Further traces of the period are the streetlamps designed by Albert Speer for the axis, now called the Strasse des 17. Juni. After the last war, all S-Bahn lines in Berlin came under the control of East Germany, and the large station concourse with an open-roofed structure. A merger between the west-controlled BVG (Berlin transportation company) and the S-Bahn did not become possible until the '80s. After the 1989 opening of the Berlin Wall an extensive programme was launched to repair and renovate the urban railway stations and integrate the system into the larger regional rail network. From 1995 to 1997, the roof of the Tiergarten station as well as its dispatcher booths and passenger benches were refurbished with steel and light-coloured wood. Glass partitions shielding the benches from wind permit a view of the entire platform.

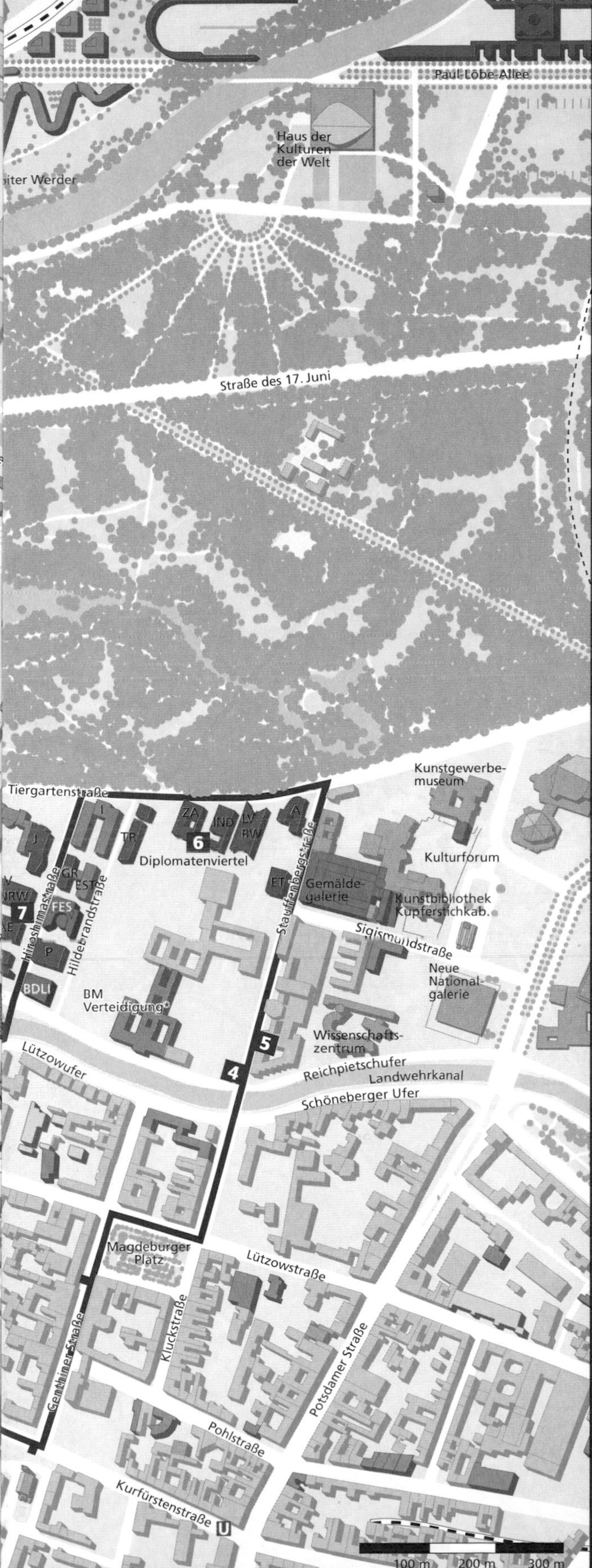
Paul-Löbe-Allee
Haus der Kulturen der Welt
Straße des 17. Juni
Tiergartenstraße
Diplomatenviertel
ZA
IND
LV BW
A
TR
J
GR
EST
NRW
FES
P
BDLI
Hiroshimastraße
Hildebrandstraße
Stauffenbergstraße
ET
Gemäldegalerie
Kunstgewerbemuseum
Kulturforum
Kunstbibliothek Kupferstichkab.
Sigismundstraße
Neue Nationalgalerie
BM Verteidigung*
Wissenschaftszentrum
Reichpietschufer
Landwehrkanal
Schöneberger Ufer
Lützowufer
Magdeburger Platz
Lützowstraße
Kluckstraße
Genthiner Straße
Potsdamer Straße
Pohlstraße
Kurfürstenstraße
U
100 m
200 m
300 m
4
5
6
7

Frankfurter Allee
Samariterstraße
Frankfurter Allee
Mainzer Straße
Boxhagener Straße
Colbestraße
Kinzigstraße
Jungstraße
Finowstraße
Weichselstraße
Scharnweberstraße
Jessnerstraße
Dossestraße
Straße
Boxhagener Platz
Wismarplatz
Traveplatz
Krossener Straße
Weserstraße
Müggelstraße
Gürtelstraße
Gärtnerstraße
Seumestraße
Knorrpromenade
Boxhagener Straße
Wühlischstraße
Simplonstraße
Sonntagstraße
Neue Bahnhofstraße
Wiesenweg
Hirschberger Straße
Schreiberhauer Straße
Marktstraße
Ostkreuz
14
Laskerstraße
Persiusstraße
Bödikerstraße
Corinthstraße
Markgrafendamm
Kynaststraße
Rummelsburger See
Elsenbrücke
Kratchtstraße
13
Alt-Stralau
Bahrfeldtstraße
Treptower Park

Im Osten viel Neues

Things are happening in the east

Route 9 passes through the eastern inner city districts of Friedrichshain and Kreuzberg and Treptow in the south-east of the city. It takes in traditional industrial areas of Berlin and in many places reveals the dramatic changes which the city is undergoing at the end of the industrial age. At the same time, the enormous development potential in Berlin is also apparent.

Route 9 starts at the Weberwiese high-rise, which was built in 1951, marking the beginning of the National Reconstruction Programme in East Berlin. Stalinallee, now Karl-Marx-Allee, between Frankfurter Tor and Strausberger Platz was in sharp contrast to the Western modernist architecture of the Hansaviertel. The luxuriously fitted "residential palaces for workers" were in Soviet architectural style with ornaments and reliefs. The building site on Stalinallee was the starting point of the uprising on 17 June 1953. Today, the buildings, which recently underwent extensive restoration, are again considered to be model examples of urban residential architecture.

Route 9 initially turns south to the Ostbahnhof railway station. The station, which was built in 1842 and known as Frankfurter Bahnhof, has been rebuilt and renamed a number of times since then. In the plans for the railway system in New Berlin it is to be the eastern terminus of the ICEs and a mainline station for routes to the east. The surrounding areas to the north and south of the railway lines are being restructured. The banks of the River Spree, which so far have been cut off from public access by industrial sites are to be opened up for public use in a number of planning stages. Riverbank paths and green areas as well as passages leading between public buildings are to provide a link between the river and the residential and business areas.

Route 9 then passes by the East Side Gallery, which was once a section of the Berlin Wall and separated Friedrichshain from Kreuzberg until 1989. Paintings done by international artists in 1990 have made it the longest open-air gallery in the world. The paintings are comments on the division and reunification of Berlin and Germany. The adjacent Oberbaumbrücke bridge has been restored and since 1995 has again provided a link between the municipal districts on either side of the river.

The Oberbaum-City serves as an example of the conversion of former industrial sites into service centres. Light bulbs were manufactured here from 1908 to 1992. The interiors of some of the old buildings, which have been classified as protected buildings on account of their interesting historical architecture, had to be entirely removed before they could be converted. The tower which once bore the NARVA logo and to which five stories have been added remains as a landmark. Similar measures have been planned for the old warehouse building and the egg cold-storage depot at the east docks.

On the other side of Oberbaumbrücke bridge route 9 enters Kreuzberg, the most important exhibition area of the "socially committed" part of the 1987 International Building Exhibition in Berlin (IBA-Alt). Its aim was a model development of the legendary "SO 36" district of the squatters' movement. The IBA worked together with citizens action groups to preserve existing building structures which provided cheap residential accommodation; new buildings were built on a number of empty lots.

Route 9 takes in the Treptower, the highest office building in Berlin, and an example of the new strategy of developing service industry centres along the circular urban railway line Stadtbahn. Further office tower buildings and the Twin Towers are located on the site of the former electrical appliances company EAW in the vicinity of Treptower Park. The River Spree and the circular urban railway line provide easy access to the city centre. Investors on the Stralau peninsular on the north side of the Spree and the Rummelsburg bay also plan to take advantage of this newly discovered locational advantage. This will be the site of an exhibition which, as part of EXPO 2000, will show cutting-edge technologies and projects which have water as their theme. Model "waterside residential developments" are to be built here as an alternative to residential areas located on the city outskirts.

Route 9 ends at Ostkreuz railway station. This is where two lines of the urban railway system intersect at one of the busiest rail interchanges in Berlin. The area surrounding Ostkreuz is being developed into a major new office location in the city.

U-Bahnhof Weberwiese
Weberwiese underground station

Alfred Grenander
1927–30
Weberwiese

The Weberwiese underground station serves line U 5, which was extended from Alexanderplatz to Friedrichsfelde in the eastern part of Berlin in 1930. Construction on the line was possible without tunneling as the line followed the course of Karl-Marx-Allee and Frankfurter Allee. Between 1983 and 1989 the line was extended to Hönow in the district of Hellersdorf. In the future it will be extended westwards from Alexanderplatz to Brandenburg Gate, the Reichstag, and Lehrter Bahnhof rail station. By integrating the parliament and government district as well as the distance rail station into the subway network, these northern sectors of the city will be directly linked to the periphery. The Weberwiese underground station is named after the meadow located south of Frankfurter Allee where weavers used to bleach their fabric. The design of the station makes use of a frequently used type that was developed by Grenander. The colours of the wall tiles are systematically changed in each station to differentiate them from one another.

Karl-Marx-Allee, Hochhaus an der Weberwiese
Karl-Marx-Allee and apartment tower at Weberwiese

Ensemble 2.1

This apartment tower overlooking the Weberwiese was the first of the model projects built in the National Reconstruction Programme launch-

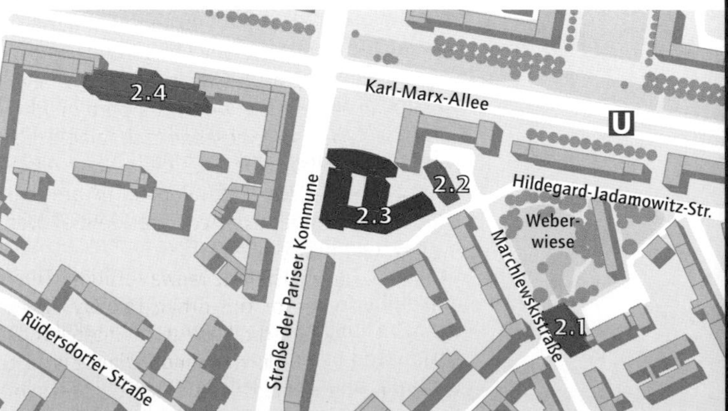

Hermann Henselmann
1951–52
Marchlewskistrasse/
Weberwiese

ed by the GDR in 1951. It replaced plans to follow the principles of low-density and functionally zoned development. Implementation of principles, put forward by Hans Scharoun in 1949 for the "Friedrichshain living cell" (neighbourhood), had already started with two gallery-entry apartment blocks on the south side of Karl-Marx-Allee designed by Ludmilla Herzenstein and Richard Paulick.

The National Reconstruction Programme – propagated as the boundaries dividing the east and west sectors became increasingly hardened – was heavily influenced by Soviet planning models. Ideologically the programme was compatible with the systematic introduction of socialism across the country. In 1949 Frankfurter Allee was renamed Stalinallee, and, on the stretch between Strausberger Platz and Frankfurter Tor, it was transformed into a monumentally scaled boulevard leading eastwards, magnifying its significance both politically and urbanistically. The construction of Stalinallee provoked West Berlin into quickening reconstruction efforts. This resulted in the International Building Exhibition, "Interbau 1957", in the Hansaviertel.

Henselmann's high-rise set the standard for the Stalinallee buildings and gave expression to the GDR's intention to allow workers to live in palatial buildings. It resembles the architecture of the conservative modernists of the '20s, but also unites functionalist elements with the national architectural traditions of Schinkelesque neoclassicism. Unlike the later buildings on Karl-Marx-Allee, the ornament on the Weberwiese building is rather reserved. The words inscribed above the main entrance, "Peace in our land/ Peace in our city/that it may well house/those who built it" were written by Bertolt Brecht.

The worker demonstrations that led to the failed uprising of June 17, 1953, began in and around Stalinallee. In 1961, Stalinallee was split into Frankfurter Allee and Karl-Marx-Allee, and a large statue of Stalin erected at no. 70 was removed. At the same time, there was an official retreat from the labor-intensive formalistic, classical style of architecture in favor of industrialised methods of pre-fabrication and standardisation. The buildings of the former Stalinallee were designated as protected landmarks during the GDR-era, and since 1990 renovation work has been conducted in stages. The high cost of the

2.3

work is being financed in part by a special programme for modernising social housing that is supported by the Berlin Senate with the aim of making Karl-Marx-Allee an attractive boulevard.

Kulturamt und Heimatmuseum Friedrichshain

2.2 Ensemble

Friedrichshain cultural office and local history museum

The cultural office and museum of local history for the district of Friedrichshain moved into the old "Memel", as this reconstructed fire station building is called, in 1998. The building was designed in 1884 by city architect Hermann Blankenstein. This fire station remained in service until 1965, in spite of war damage. Now enclosed by the development of the '50s but separated from Karl-Marx-Allee, the building's site still reveals the original route of the street and the historic urban fabric in Friedrichshain.

Hermann Blankenstein;
Wörle & Partner,
Munich
1884;
1997–98
Marchlewskistrasse 6

Bürohaus Karl-Marx-Allee

2.3 Ensemble

Karl-Marx-Allee office building

This new office and commercial high-rise stems from 1991 for developing the central section of the wide, long Karl-Marx-Allee/Frankfurter Allee corridor leading out of the city. The competition proposal intended a 120-metre high tower to be joined by a second tower at Frankfurter Allee. This was also to be the site of a city square, planned during the GDR National Reconstruction Programme of 1951, oriented toward the cemeteries in the north. The high-rise tower built parallel to the street is set back to create a square marking the approach to the Ostbahnhof distance rail station to the south.

Wörle & Partner, Munich
1995–97
Karl-Marx-Allee 90/
Strasse der Pariser Kommune

Architektenkammer Berlin

2.4 Ensemble

Business offices of the Architektenkammer Berlin (architecture association)

The Architektenkammer Berlin, a professional association representing architects, interior designers, urban planners, and landscape architects

3

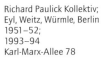

Richard Paulick Kollektiv; Eyl, Weitz, Würmle, Berlin
1951–52;
1993–94
Karl-Marx-Allee 78

working independently or in firms was one of the first public institutions to move from west to east, where it took up quarters in this building on the Karl-Marx-Allee. The imposing structure was designed in 1951 by Richard Paulick, a former Bauhaus student, Bauakademie professor, and leading GDR architect. Aside from carefully preserving the building, the Architektenkammer also restored the interior of the old Karl Marx bookstore to its original condition, for which it received the Ferdinand von Quast award in 1994.

Grundschule

Primary school

Anton Gerber
1954
Rüdersdorfer Strasse 20-27

Set apart from the Stalinallee, this primary school was built in 1954 in the midst of the typical block pattern of the historic city plan. The colonnaded porch and arcaded hallways of its monumental, expansive three wings typify the stylistic requirements of the National Construction Programme.

3

City-Carré

Fischer & Fischer, Cologne
1993–96
Koppenstrasse 93

The City-Carré is located in the immediate vicinity of the Ostbahnhof rail station. It takes up a large city block directly adjacent to the railroad tracks. A total of five skylit courts and a cylindrical atrium organize the interior of the administrative building. A listed school building (1871-73 by Hermann Blankenstein), which has been converted into a hotel, is integrated into the complex. The main tenant of the City-Carré is the Dresdner Bank. Formerly located on Kantstrasse in Charlottenburg, the bank's executive offices are located in a new stately building on Pariser Platz.

4.1 *Ensemble*

Ostbahnhof

Ostbahnhof distance rail station

Becker Gewers Kühn & Kühn, Berlin
1998–2000
Am Ostbahnhof

Repeatedly renovated and renamed over the years, the Ostbahnhof rail station is again undergoing alterations, in which the Berlin architects Becker Gewers Kühn & Kühn refer back to the original Frankfurter Bahnhof that began service here in 1842. It was expanded and renamed Schlesischer Bahnhof in 1869, and in 1882 was linked to the Stadtbahn local rail system; this also established a continuous route from Paris all

the way to Moscow. In 1925 the Stadtbahn portion was covered with a large steel and glass shed; the same was done for the distance rail tracks in 1937; the two, slightly offset, are interconnected. After the war, the south side became the main entrance of what was then called Ostbahnhof. On the occasion of the 750th city founding anniversary in 1987, it was given a new facade and re-christened "Hauptbahnhof". But the name Ostbahnhof was restored to the regional and distance rail station at the 1998 reopening of the Stadtbahn following extensive repairs and modernisation, which helped the station meet its new function as the terminus of the ICE lines. The western tracks were enlarged, and

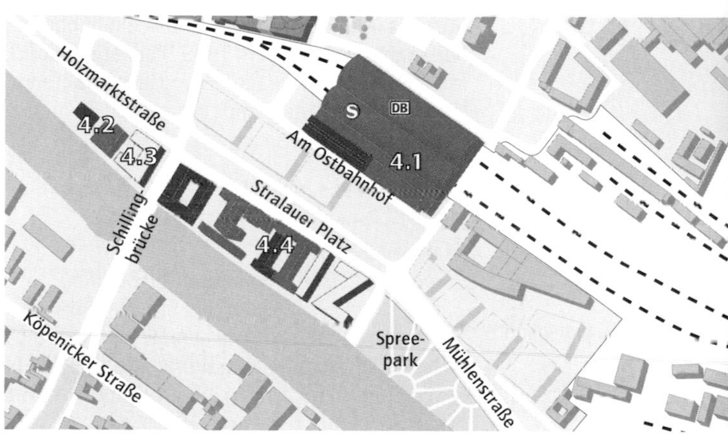

the layers were removed that concealed the original south wall that is lined with round-arched windows. Adjoining the station are a new hotel and glass-enclosed reception hall which open towards Stralauer Platz and contain several floors of shops and services. In the new "mushroom concept" of the German rail system (s. p. 38), the Ostbahnhof relinquishes its former role, since it is no longer a transfer point in the system.

4.2 *Ensemble*

Richard Tettenborn;
Bauabteilung der Berliner Wasser Betriebe, Berlin
1879–80;
1904–05;
1998–99
Holzmarktstrasse 31-33a

Abwasserpumpwerk V

Wastewater pumping station V

This pumping station was established in 1881 after the completion of the canalisation of the district of Friedrichshain. Richard Tettenborn, who designed a number of technical structures, designed a formal building here whose main facade overlooks the Spree River. The waste water was brought in using a gravity feed and then pumped out to sewage fields in Falkenberg, south of the city. The complex was the fifth of its kind built for the sewer system laid out in 1873 by James Hobrecht (s. p. 81). In 1905 the dwelling and machine house as well as the boiler house and stack were added. The pumping station was used until a new pump in a neighboring building took its place in 1999. The rational brick facade of the new machine house is oriented to the old building; its pumps are sunken 15 metres below grade.

4.3 *Ensemble*

Nalbach + Nalbach, Berlin
1999–2000
Holzmarktstrasse 34/
An der Schillingbrücke

Geschäfts-, Hotel- und Wohngebäude

Commercial, hotel, and residential building

The three portions of the complex designed by Nalbach + Nalbach are assigned the function of office, hotel, and apartments respectively. The office wing faces towards Holzmarktstrasse, a busy street; the hotel rises toward the Spree on the Schillingbrücke, and the housing directly faces the riverbank. The various functions are differentiated by window arrangements. The courtyard garden opens toward the neighboring pumping station.

Schillingbrücke

Schilling Bridge

Seeck;
Lasker & Kolleck
1871–73;
1912
Stralauer Platz

Built in 1873, the Schilling Bridge is the oldest bridge on the Spree River done in traditional heavy masonry construction. It replaced a wooden bridge crossing the canal in Luisenstadt that was commissioned by Schilling for the collection of tolls. Water and gas supply lines leading to the gasworks on Stralauer Platz were built into the bridge. In 1912 it was widened with a new steel structure concealed by sandstone friezes depicting river allegories by the sculptor Emil Hundrieser. The Schilling Brigde managed to survive bombing and Hitler's orders to dynamite all bridges during the final days of the last war. Since the Wall was opened, it has become one of the most important links between the Stralauer Viertel and southern Luisenstadt. In the reorganisation of the city planned for the year 2001, the district of Friedrichshain and Kreuzberg will be united, which will lend the bridge a symbolic meaning.

Ostbahnhof – Umfeld

Ostbahnhof rail station area

Ensemble 4.4

Stralauer Platz

The area around the Ostbahnhof rail station is being developed as a business and shopping centre. The goal is to integrate the rail station into its environment, design new uses for dormant track spaces, and open the entire area up to the river. At the core of the planning project are Holzmarktstrasse, Mühlenstrasse, and Stralauer Platz.
In the 18th and 19th centuries, the many industrial and manufacturing facilities located here completely cut off the nearby residential zone from the water. A reminder of this past is the old central warehouse complex in the gasworks (1906-08 by Reimer & Körte), which was used as a repair workshop after first Berlin gas system of 1847 was dismantled.
In 1993 the Berlin architects Hemprich and Tophof drew up a scheme for four buildings between the Schilling Brigde and a new bridge extending the Strasse der Pariser Kommune. The new buildings will not obstruct the view of the Spree (hence the name "Spree Windows"), and a riverside promenade will be included. An international solar centre integrated with the old gaswork buildings is also planned here. Among the buildings is also a glass tower with a Z-shaped plan after a design by Helmut Jahn, which will house the main offices of the gas company Gasag.

Ostgüterbahnhof

Ostgüterbahnhof freight rail station

Lying east of the Ostbahnhof, this freight rail station dating from 1880 was formerly called the Schlesischer Güterbahnhof and is now used by the German post office. The water tower, boiler house, and turntable from the 19th century have been preserved. A service road, numerous track connections and storage yards made the freight

Müller;
Richard Brademann
1880–1907
Strasse der
Pariser Kommune 3-8/
Mühlenstrasse 33

rail station an important transit point for east-west trade. The buildings were oriented to a bridge (Brommybrücke) which was eventually destroyed in the war. Towards the west side of the site on Strasse der Pariser Kommune is the gently curved parcel sorting facility built for the post office from 1904-07 by Wilhelm Tuckermann. From April to October in the year 2000, an exhibition called "Forum-Stadt" will be held in this spaces by the Senate Department of Urban Development, Environmental Protection, and Technology. The subject of the show will be the transformation and modernisation of Berlin.
Most of the property is to be converted for large-scale residential and commercial use.

5

East Side Gallery

1961;
1990
Mühlenstrasse 47-80

The East Side Gallery is a 1.3 km long completely preserved section of the 1961 Berlin Wall running in Mühlenstrasse between Schilling Brigde and Oberbaum Brigde. In January 1990, 118 artists from 21 countries painted images on the concrete panels celebrating the end of the division of Berlin. An open-air gallery and a relict of the border, it became a listed monument in 1992.
Behind it, bare strips of space along the water are being turned into a public park. The long-term planning goal is to develop the Spree embankment into an attractive urban space.

Ehemalige Roggen- und Weizenmühle
Old flour mill
Frohneike, Blumenberg & Schreiber
1886–87;
1910
Mühlenstrasse 8, 78-80

The buildings of this old flour mill, like the name of the street, are a reminder of the many mills, some dating from as early as the 17th century, that were gathered along the banks of the River Spree.
After 1842 the area gained new interest due to its proximity to Frankfurter Bahnhof station (Ostbahnhof). The mill, the silo, and the machine works (built by Blumenberg & Schreiber from 1886-87) are connected directly to the tracks. Towards the street lies the more formal warehouse containing the owner's dwelling (1887 by Frohneike). The large granary, which can be accessed from the water, was added in 1907. Its facade was originally meant to be richly ornamented, but the more functional, stripped-down

6.1

6.2

design by Schreiber was eventually chosen instead. The mill complex is a protected industrial building.

Bahnhof Warschauer Straße

6.1 *Ensemble*

Underground and cityrail station at Warschauer Strasse

Paul Wittig, Otto Stahn
1896–1902; 1993–95
Warschauer Strasse

The city rail station from 1884 and the terminus of the oldest subway line in Berlin (built in 1902 by Wittig and Stahn, today the U 1) make up the transit station at Warschauer Strasse. The different levels of the stations are interconnected by a stair pavilion. The main station building of the U 1 has a street-level entrance lobby leading over the viaduct to the platform shed. There is also an elegant lightweight iron and infill masonry switching station along with large service sheds to the south. The old two-storey workshop servicing the elevated train and streetcars that was built parallel to the Stadtbahn (1907 by Alfred Grenander) is no longer in use. When the city was divided in 1961, the station was shut but it was re-opened after repairs on its structures and Oberbaum Brigde were completed in 1995.

Fachhochschule für Technik und Wirtschaft

Business and Technology School

Ludwig Hoffmann
1909–14
Warschauer Platz 6-8

Today this school teaches technology and business, but it originally trained young weavers. It was one of the over 60 schools built by Ludwig Hoffmann during his tenure as city architect for Berlin.
A neo-Gothic building with a vertically composed facade in terra cotta, it bears a strong resemblance to the Wertheim department store designed by Alfred Messel in 1904 that once stood on Leipziger Platz.

Oberbaum-City

6.2 *Ensemble*

Wilhelm Walther, Theodor Kampffmeyer, Hermann Dernburg; WEP Effinger & Partner, Munich, Architekten Schweger + Partner, Hamburg/Berlin, Reichel & Stauth, Brunswick,

Located near Oberbaum Brigde, the Oberbaum-City is one of the most important inner city redevelopment sites, where a former light bulb factory will be transformed into a modern commercial and service centre.
The first industrial building near the Warschauer Strasse underground station was built of brick in 1906 by Walther, Kampffmeyer and Dernburg for the Deutsche Glühlicht AG. Along with later

Schuh & Hurmer,
Munich
1906–14;
1993–2001
Warschauer Platz/
Rudolfstrasse/
Lehmbruckstrasse/
Rotherstrasse

buildings, it was designed to fit into the surrounding residential fabric, keeping all the streets open to the public. In 1919 the company merged with AEG and Siemens, taking the name "Osram" combining the chemical elements osmium and radium.
After the Second World War, it became an East German cooperative, the "VEB Glühlampenwerk"; after 1969 it was called "Narva" – nitrogen, argon and vacuum.
After the operation was shut down in 1992 the old buildings were upgraded; some were totally gutted because their masonry was saturated with mercury.

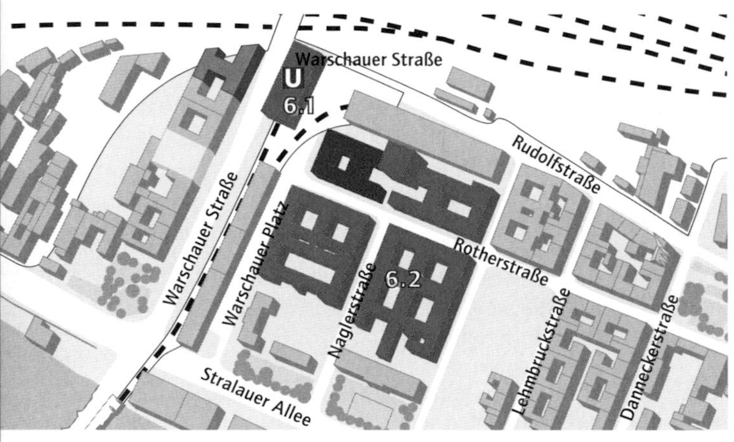

Five stories of steel and glass will be added to the already prominent old tower, and a new annex was built on the west side. The numerous courtyards are open to the public, where they can find a restaurant and the International Design Centre, the IDZ.
In the future some of the gaps in the street frontage along Stralauer Allee will be closed by new buildings.

7 *Ensemble*

Abwasserpumpwerk XII

Wastewater pumping station XII

Richard Tettenborn,
Karl Meier
1889–90;
1998
Rudolfstrasse 15

The construction of the sewage and drainage system initiated by James Hobrecht in 1873 was completed with this pumping station. It was built in 1893 to collect wastewater from the Stralauer Viertel, as well as from Lichtenberg and Rummelsburg to the north, using an elaborate tunnel

network. Portions of the technical equipment installed in 1916 have been preserved. The site is still used by the Berlin's water company. A new building was added in 1995 to provide waste removal for most of the district of Friedrichshain.

Zwinglikirche mit Gemeindehaus

Zwingli Church and Parish House

Jürgen Kröger;
Fritz Buch
1905–08;
1927
Rudolfstrasse 14/
Danneckerstrasse 2-4

The Protestant Zwingli Church was built on the western edge of Rudolfplatz in 1905-08. It was financed by donations by members of the parish and by the industries gradually collecting in the area.
The church structure is inserted into the existing perimeter block fabric. The corner is marked by a tower. A life-size bronze statue next to the main portal recalls the patron and reformer Ulrich Zwingli.
In 1927-28, the German architect Fritz Buch built the expressionistic brick parish hall in Rudolfstrasse.
Rudolfplatz originally included both sides of Rudolfstrasse and is now recognizable only on the southern part of the "ornamental square"; on the northern side is a daycare centre.
Most of the homogeneous apartment houses from the turn of the century were built by Sigismund Koch, the brother of the project's developer, Maximilian Koch.

Osthafen, Spree-Speicher

Friedrich Krause;
Schuwirth Erman & Partner, Hanover
1907–13;
1999–2000
Stralauer Allee 1-16

Opened in 1913 on the north fork of the Spree, the Osthafen (east docks) served as a shipping facility for the materials needed by neighbouring industries.
The granaries, warehouses, depots, yards, and administrative buildings on the naturally formed 1.3 km long river harbour were directly connected to the Ringbahn rail.
All of the buildings, except for the smallest petroleum tanks, were preserved and will continue to be used.
The power plant on the eastern edge was cut off from the actual dock area by the Elsen Brigde built after the war. The two large buildings on Oberbaum Brigde will be converted into a modern office centre ("Spree-Speicher").
The nearly solid facade of the cold storage building, which can accommodate up to 75 million eggs, is to be taken down and replaced with a

9

glass exterior designed in a diamond pattern, a reference to the old brick facade. A transparent volume projecting over the water creates the link to the large warehouse.
According to the current land use plan, the Osthafen will no longer be used as a dock; instead shipping will be shifted to facilities further south-east. This creates an opportunity to transform the warehouse district into an attractive riverside centre.
A new function is being sought for the rest of the extended industrial zone that will increase public access to the area.

9

Oberbaumbrücke

Oberbaum Bridge

Otto Stahn;
Santiago Calatrava, Zurich,
König, Stief & Partner GmbH, Berlin
1894–96;
1992–95
Stralauer Allee/
Oberbaumstrasse

Oberbaum Brigde spans the 150-metre width of the Spree and connects up the ring of streets along Danziger-, Petersburger-, and Warschauer Strasse to Skalitzer- and Gitschiner Strasse. The bridge was opened on the occasion of the industrial exhibition held at Treptower Park in 1896, in conjunction with the elevated rail for the underground line between the Zoologischer Garten and Warschauer Brigde. The elaborate brick structure, the most important part of Berlin's bridge construction programme carried out during the last century, was begun in 1876, when all wooden bridges were reglaced by solid masonry. The "Oberbaum" toll station was located on the site of the Oberbaum Brigde from 1724 on; it is analogous to the Unterbaum Brigde near the Reichstag (today Kronprinzen Brigde). Oberbaum Brigde's function as a customs control point greatly influenced the design resembling a city gate with arcades, heavy piers, and fortified towers done in the brick neo-Gothic style of the region.
The dynamiting of Oberbaum Brigde at Hitler's command in March of 1945 caused severe damage. The construction of the Berlin Wall in 1961 separated Friedrichshain and Kreuzberg from one another. In 1972 the bridge became a pedestrian control point open only to West Berliners. After the Wall was taken down, the bridge again joins the two halves of the city. While the elevated rail system underwent modernisation and repairs, the centre portion of the bridge was redesigned by Santiago Calatrava,

using an elegant steel structure for the elevated line crossing the bridge to Warschauer Strasse, put back into use in 1995. Tracks were carefully laid in 1994 for a planned extension of the tram lines.

Wohngebäude IBA

IBA residential building

Alvaro Siza Vieira
1982–83
Schlesische Strasse 7-8/
Falckensteinstrasse

This residential building by Alvaro Siza, a Portugese architect, was executed early on in the IBA programme. It belongs to a densely built part of Kreuzberg, "SO 36", dating from the "Gründerzeit", cut off by the Wall it became a central focus of both the urban repair section of the IBA programme, called "IBA-Alt", and the "IBA-Neu" section for new buildings. IBA-Alt was a response to problems encountered during earlier urban renewal projects that restructured various parts of West Berlin during the '60s and '70s. Its goal was to support the combination of living and working which existed in the older neighbourhoods.

The programme became widely known outside of Berlin for its model of the "Kreuzberg mix". Many action groups took part in helping IBA-Alt and its successor, S.T.E.R.N., repair and revive about 50 per cent of the run-down buildings in the area.

The intention behind this corner building by Siza, who earned a reputation for his involvement in residential construction, was to demonstrate how a new building could be incorporated into the existing urban fabric. The regular window pattern inspired an unknown graffiti artist to christen the building "Bonjour Tristesse" by spraying these works on its gable.

Lohmühleninsel

Lohmühleninsel industrial island

Vor dem Schlesischen Tor

This island was created at the fork of the Spree when the Landwehr Canal was dredged. The Schlesische Brigde (1900) and the Obere Freiarchen Brigde (Otto Stahn, 1894) join it with Kreuzberg and Treptow.

The old brick control house from 1859 indicates the old city limits bounded by Schlesisches Tor. Nearby is the oldest gas station in Berlin, built from 1928-29 by Paul Schröder and Max Pohl. Originally used commercially, the island was abandoned after the Wall went up in 1961.

Because the SO 36 district of Kreuzberg was cut off from its traditional recreation spaces in Trep-

10 11

tower Park, part of IBA 87 was devoted to the transformation of the old manufacturing sites to create a substitute. The multiple use Flatow sports complex (1986-88 by Stephan and Thomas Dietrich), was a first step towards revitalisation.
Particularly important was the redesign of the old Görlitzer Bahnhof railyard as a public park, for which a competition was held in the year 1984. Work did not begin on the site until the '90s, however.
In 1998, a terraced fountain named after the Turkish city of Pamukkale was opened here and quickly became a popular attraction.

10

Ehemaliger Wachturm, Museum der verbotenen Kunst

Old border control tower, Museum of Forbidden Art

1963
Puschkinallee

East German border guards once manned this monolithic control tower in the no-man's-land between Kreuzberg and Treptow. Today it contains the "Museum of Forbidden Art", which shows works by artists persecuted by the GDR and documents the history of the Wall.

11

Bewag-Hauptverwaltung

Bewag head offices

Liepe & Steigelmann, Berlin
1993–95
Puschkinallee 52

The Bewag electricity utility company has maintained its main office on the Schlesischer Busch, a park in the district of Treptow since 1995. The municipal electricity company was founded in 1884, taking the name Bewag in 1923. The Soviet authorities ordered the division of Bewag in 1948 into two entities, and their organisations were completely separated by 1952, so that West Berlin became a totally self-sufficient "electricity island". After the wall was opened Bewag (in the west) and the energy supply collectives in the east merged. Bewag has provided the entire city with energy and heat since 1966, making it largest energy supplier in Germany.
The administrative building designed by Liepe and Steigelmann is comprised of two buildings with linked U-shaped ground plans. To the south they are connected to a long bar with four blunt

wings oriented to the west. Programmatically, the building complex is equally well-equipped for district heating, natural cooling, and solar energy. The glass pyramid in the entry court is clad with solar panels for energy gain.

„Arena"
Arena concert hall
Bruno Buch;
Franz Ahrens,
Alfred Warthmüller
1915–17;
1927–28
Eichenstrasse 4

In 1995, this old garage building belonging to a bus depot was given a new life when it became the Arena concert hall. It is located in a 19th-century riverside industrial site whose older brick buildings were built by Bruno Buch during World War I were taken over by the Berlin municipal bus company (ABOAG) in 1925. Ahrens and Warthmüller added the 7,000 square metre garage in 1927-28. The entrance portal decorated with brick sculptures by Arminius Hasemann dates from the same time. During the GDR era, the complex was used as a service yard by the transit authorities. Thanks to a long-term lease signed in 1998, this industrial landmark could be preserved. The large hall is used for performances. The retrofit project will add a new stage and modernise the roof with an automatic darkening mechanism and solar cells to provide energy.

Twin-Towers und Karrees

12.1
Ensemble

Kieferle & Partner,
Georg Kieferle,
Eberhard Bender,
Cornelia Kieferle-Nicklas,
Stuttgart
1995–98
Hoffmannstrasse/
Eichenstrasse/
Fanny-Zobel-Strasse

This office complex derives its name from the matching pair of 60-metre high towers overlooking the river that share a three-storey base. The slender buildings, on a square footprint, are crowned with projecting roofs and a rounded penthouse. The project includes two additional office buildings, each of which encloses a square courtyard.

12.2 *Ensemble*

Wohnhäuser

Residential buildings

Wörle & Partner,
Munich,
J·S·K Architekten,
Berlin
1997–98
Hoffmannstrasse 1-27/
Eichenstrasse

Three apartment blocks featuring square floor plans are joined in a common spatial composition with the Twin-Tower complex. The five-storey buildings, closed on one side by low two-storey rowhouses, frame a central courtyard. The buildings are oriented to a public park. On the Spree banks, two further buildings resembling the Twin-Towers are planned.

12.3 *Ensemble*

Treptowers

Treptowers office centre

Gerhard Spangenberg
with Brigitte Steinkilberg,
Berlin,
Reichel & Stauth,
Brunswick,
Architekten Schweger
+ Partner,
Hamburg/Berlin
1995–98
Hoffmannstrasse/
An den Treptowers

The focus of this new commercial centre "Treptower" located directly on the Spree River in Treptow is one of the tallest buildings in Berlin, a 125-metre high tower designed by the Berlin architect Gerhard Spangenberg.

Three ten-storey slabs perpendicular to the river were designed by the Hamburg firm of Schweger + Partner to complete the complex, which also integrates older utilitarian brick structures designed by Ernst Ziesel from 1928 to 1938. The latter belonged to the Elektro Apparate Werke EAW.

After the facilities were renovated and enlarged by Reichel & Stauth, they became the Berlin office of the Allianz insurance company. This area, which must compete with alternative sites in Schönefeld and Wilmersdorf, is making a strong contribution towards achieving the role

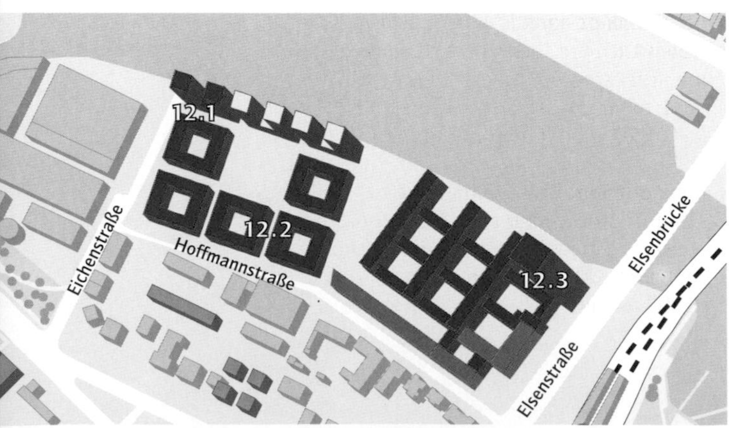

intended for the whole area around the Ostkreuz station.
Part of the Elsenstrasse between the Spree and Hoffmannstrasse was renamed "An den Treptowers". In return the Allianz company promised to finance two child daycare centres and create a riverside promenade. This will be embellished by two artworks: a "water curtain" by the landscape architect Gustav Lange, and a composition by the American artist Jonathan Borofsky comprising three 30-metre high figures anchored in the river, symbolising the neighboring districts of Kreuzberg, Friedrichshain and Treptow.

Treptower Park

Gustav Meyer
Hermann Mächtig
1876–88
Am Treptower Park/
Alt-Treptow/
Puschkinallee

Treptow Park was laid out in 1876 by Gustav Meyer, who was director of city gardens at the time. Unlike the public parks of Friedrichshain (1846) and Humboldthain (1869), which are located in densely populated working class districts and provide local public recreation space, Treptow Park and the nearby Plänterwald forest were actually parts of a forest strip closely bordering the city.
They became a destination for excursions that was especially popular among the residents of the Luisenstadt as far back as the early 19th century.
After Meyer's death, his successor Hermann Mächtig oversaw the work on the park until 1888. In the centre of the greensward lay a large playing field designed as a hippodrome, an oval space surrounded by fields, ponds, and rows of plane trees. In 1896, the Prussian trade fair took place here.
On display was the world's longest telescope at the time, designed by Friedrich Archenhold, which is still here. Richly ornamented with sculptures, the spacious garden also includes the Island of Youth and the Zenner guesthouse (built 1820, rebuilt by Hermann Henselmann in 1955).
An experimental tunnel underneath the Spree joining Treptow with the Stralau peninsula, making use of a new "shield driving method", was built here by AEG and Siemens in 1896; portions of it still remain.

13 13

From 1947 to 1949, the vast Soviet Soldiers' Memorial was built in Treptow Park. The symmetric composition takes up the older shape of the hippodrome. The central axis, which is lined with commemorative stone tablets, leads to the bronze statue of a Soviet soldier crushing a Nazi swastika. Altogether, the conical base and the fields to either side, where war dead were already buried in 1945 – the main reason for siting the monument in Treptow – contain the remains of a total of 5,000 Soviet soldiers.

13 *Ensemble*

Wasserstadt in der Rummelsburger Bucht

Wasserstadt Stralau/
Rummelsburger Bucht waterside development

1996–2015
Alt-Stralau,
Hauptstrasse

The bay formed by the Stralau peninsula and the Rummelsburger Ufer form one of Berlin's main development sites: Rummelsburger Bucht. It was conceived as a model residential development featuring waterside living as an alternative to the settlements at the edge of the city. Stralau has well-maintained greenspaces, is close to Treptower Park, and is well connected to the transport network.
The peninsula was originally primarily used for fishing. In spite of the increased industrialisation after 1880 on the western side of Stralau, the tip of the peninsula remained a favorite destination for outings. The 1881 palm-oil silo by Albert Diebendt and the 1929-30 bottling tower of the brewery by Bruno Buch are among the buildings which are under a preservation order, along with an old orphanage and workhouse that were last used as a barracks and a prison, as well as old machine houses.
During the GDR years Rummelsburger Bucht was mainly used by industries that were harmful to the environment. The ground and the water were polluted by over a hundred years of contamination with industrial waste of various kinds. The land was cleaned up after all industrial production was closed down in the year 1990, and new paths were laid out along part of the waterfront.
The area around the Rummelsburger See was envisaged as an Olympic village in Berlin's unsuccessful bid to stage the Olympic Games in the year 2000. German architect Klaus Theo Brenner

worked with the landscape architects Duquesnoy and Thomanek to develop a scheme for the peninsula adopting the motif of an "urban landscape". In 1997 the city of Berlin founded a company to develop the site, called "Wasserstadt GmbH".

By 2015 over 5,900 dwellings, 425,000 square metres of office and commercial space, two schools and six children's daycare centres are to be completed here.

The first dwellings, with gardens overlooking the bay, were completed by Pudritz + Paul in 1997. In the late fall of 1998 the Wasserstadt GmbH began work on a daycare centre designed by Alsop and Störmer. In the Wohnpark Stralau, a group of long slabs and a large semicircular building by Dutch architect Hermann Hertzberger were constructed. His first proposal to place each of the buildings directly on the water with small canals proved unfeasible.

The old palm oil silo located directly on the water is flanked by a small open square. This quarter was also provided with a daycare centre.

South of Alt-Stralau Strasse and in Stralau-Dorf (village) free-standing villas will be built. The expansive park space to come includes a river-

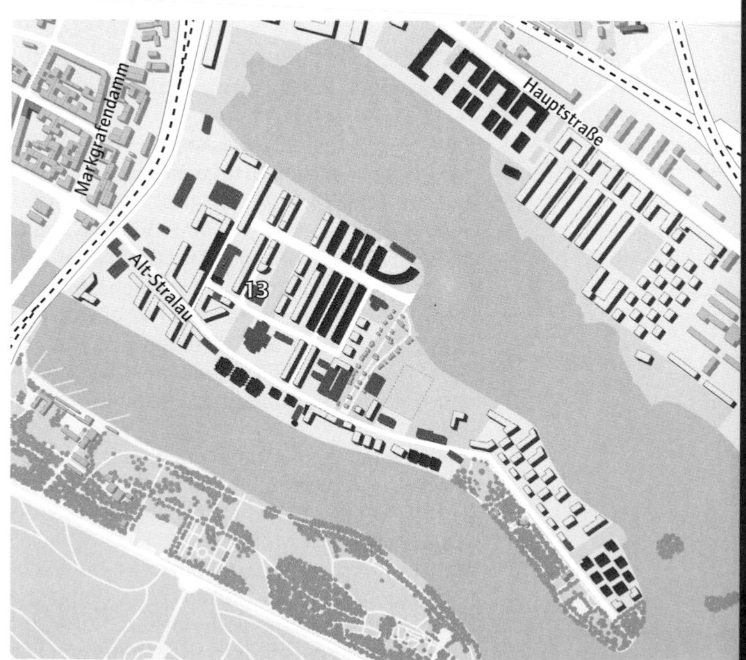

14.1

side promenade and large open areas adjacent to an old school building (1891-94) with an expressionistic gymnasium (1928 by Meurer) and a fieldstone church from the 15th century.
The Rummelsburger Bucht will be planned and developed by Wasserstadt GmbH together with investors in accordance with the same principles of sustainable urban development followed by Wasserstadt GmbH in the project "Wasserstadt am Spandauer See". Its objective is to achieve rerubanisation of the water front of the city.
The project "Rummelsburger Bucht" as a model of sustainable urban development is the largest of the projects Berlin is contributing to EXPO 2000. They focus on themes of life on the water, dwelling in the urban landscape, mobility, water research and technology. There will be six separate EXPO projects in a joint presentation on the site of the old Stralau glass factory. These projects are as follows: "sustainable water management", a commercial vehicle washing centre operated according to ecological principles", "environmentally compatible water traffic in the Greater Berlin area", "car sharing", "a model school for the year 2000" and "a model bread factory for the region".

14.1 *Ensemble*

Bahnhof Ostkreuz

Bahnhof Ostkreuz city railway station

Ernst Dircksen;
J · S · K Architekten, Berlin
1881;
from 2000
Markgrafendamm/
Sonntagstrasse

Bahnhof Ostkreuz, like Westkreuz in Charlottenburg, is an important junction in the Stadtbahn and the Ringbahn city rail lines. The Ringbahn originally encircled the inner city and is today the boundary of the inner city. The old rail station at Stralau-Rummelsburg was renamed Ostkreuz in 1933. The cluster of tracks next to and above one another are still existing, if in a bad state. The J · S · K architecture firm is designing a project for the restoration and expansion of the station.
Once the gap in the Ringbahn system is closed with the work at Gesundbrunnen, the number of daily passengers travelling through Ostkreuz is expected to reach a total of 240,000.
The most important development in the Bahnhof Ostkreuz project is the reorganisation of the tracks, so that each track is devoted to trains moving in one direction rather than two. The

north-south oriented Ringbahn station building serves as a distributor for the east-west tracks at the lower levels. Ostkreuz will also be joined to the inner city highway ring with a new north-bound segment extended from the intersection at Neukölln along the cityrail tracks to Ostkreuz, with some stretches submerged in a tunnel. It will eventually be continued further north to Frankfurter Allee.

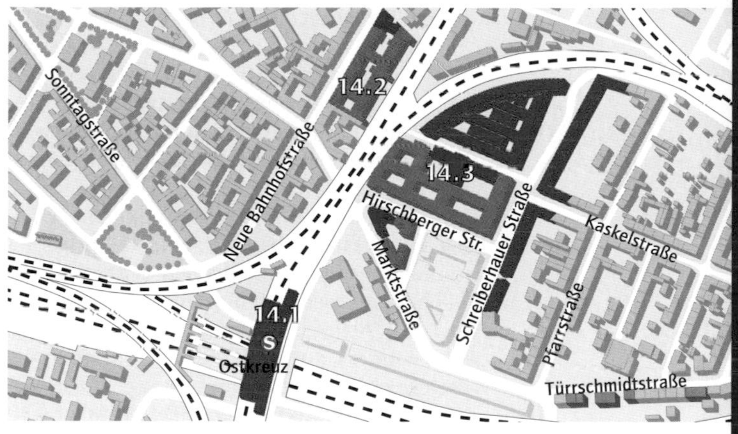

Ehemalige Knorr-Bremse

Knorr Bremse old railroad brake factory

Ensemble 14.2

Alfred Grenander,
Friedrich Lange,
Alfred Fehse;
J · S · K Architekten, Berlin
1913–16, 1922–27;
1993–95
Neue Bahnhofstrasse 9-17/
Hirschberger Strasse 4

The manufacturing plant of the Knorr Bremse company was situated northwest of Bahnhof Ostkreuz since the end of the 19th century. The company was named after Georg Knorr, the inventor of a high-speed brake mechanism with which all trains and trams were equipped. In 1913-16, a new building was constructed to house the factory and administrative offices on Neue Bahnhofstrasse. Interior and exterior were designed by Alfred Grenander. The furnishings, ceiling and wall decoration that have been preserved are clearly ordered and very well-made. They are on view in the museum of the history of the Knorr Bremse company. Today the Berufsakademie Berlin, a trade school, occupies the old building as well as a new structure on the northern side, which closed up a gap left after the war. In 1922-27 Grenander added a second phase of construction, expanding the complex along Hirschberger Strasse. The new section was con-

nected by a tunnel to the older building. The high towers are a characteristic feature of the masonry brick structure. After remodelling and expansion work was completed in 1995, the German social security agency (BfA) moved out of its former location in Wilmersdorf into the building. Both complexes are among Berlin's most significant industrial architecture.

14.3 *Ensemble*

Dienstleistungszentrum Ostkreuz

Ostkreuz commercial/retail centre

J · S · K Architekten, Berlin
1991–2000
Hirschberger Strasse/
Schreiberhauer Strasse/
Marktstrasse

To the east of the Ostkreuz rail station a new "Ringcenter" has been established which provides commercial tenants with direct access to the rail lines departing from the city via the Ringbahn junction.
Named after Britain's Queen Victoria, the "Colonie Viktoriastadt" of 1872, still stands like an island in the midst of a number of rail tracks. It will be revitalised with a new complex, designed by J · S · K Architekten. Situated along the curve in the tracks north of the modernised Knorr Bremse plant, the complex will be completed in the year 2000 and will include a total of 330 apartments on Schreiberhauer Strasse. Shopping and services will be provided by the Victoria centre, which will create 10,000 new jobs, about the same number as the Daimler Benz complex at Potsdamer Platz.

Zwischen Kiez und Schickimicki

Between local neighbourhood and trend setters

Route 10 passes through the former working-class districts in the north-east of Berlin: Wedding and Prenzlauer Berg. Before the Second World War these two municipal districts were working-class residential areas. Route 10 takes in the cradle of industrialisation, the AEG site in Brunnenstrasse, and then proceeds to what today is the chic district around Käthe-Kollwitz-Platz. In terms of its urban design history route 10 traces the sharp contrast between affluence-based modernisation in West-Berlin in the '70s and "urban conservation" in East Berlin due to lack of financial resources.
Route 10 starts at Gesundbrunnen railway station. The name originates from a spa and swimming baths for the working classes which existed there in the early 19th century. The railway system which is planned for the New Berlin will once again make it an important junction in the north of the city, a status which it had in the pre-war era. To the south beyond the Humboldt hain Park lies the AEG site and hence the area which was once the most important industrial area in Berlin. This is the place from which AEG Berlin and Emil and Walther Rathenau provided Germany and large parts of Europe with electrification at the turn of the century. Since the '70s media companies, innovative technology companies and scientific service-sector businesses have located here in the disused sheds, which are impressive examples of industrial architecture designed by Peter Behrens.
From here route 10 goes on to trace the contrasting urban development in West and East Berlin at the time of the Wall. The Brunnenstrasse redevelopment area was the first programme of its kind in West Berlin in the '60s. New development today is more moderate as can be seen from the buildings at the corner of Brunnenstrasse and Voltastrasse. On the other side of the railway embankment, which is reached via the Gleim tunnel, Prenzlauer Berg, the socially and historically related municipal district in what was once East Berlin, is an example of the homogeneously dense development typical of the late 19th century. It remained in existence during the GDR era partly for a genuine lack of money and partly for ideological reasons. In Husemannstrasse route

10 encounters one of only a few exemplary redevelopment programmes, which was begun in the last few years of the GDR; the main purpose of this programme was to trace the social culture of daily life of the time around 1900.
As it passes through Prenzlauer Berg, route 10 touches on the new "Mauerpark" (Wall Park) located on the former division between East and West Berlin. Together with the sports facilities of the Jahn Stadium and the new Max Schmeling Hall it is the counterpart to the Humboldthain Volkspark. The tour then proceeds to the former Schultheiß brewery and the Pfefferberg brewery, examples of conversion of former production centres into cultural and restaurant facilities and business premises.
At Käthe-Kollwitz-Platz route 10 reaches the cultural heart of the Prenzlauer Berg district. During GDR times is was the meeting place of those opposed to the East German regime. Writers, artists and intellectuals of the "Prenzlberg Bohemia" had established themselves in the dilapidated and cheap apartments in the district. Large sections of the "Kreuzberg scene" moved to Prenzlauer Berg in the early '90s. The intention was to demonstrate opposition to what was seen as a process of gentrification in Kreuzberg, i.e. modernisation and conversion of property into luxury residential accommodation. The area was declared a redevelopment area in the mid-'90s. Steps were taken to ensure preservation of the old building fabric and existing social structures. Today Käthe-Kollwitz-Platz is a favourite haunt of followers of alternative culture. Countless cafés, restaurants an pubs provide plenty of opportunities to enjoy the authentic charm of the "old, honest Berlin".
The route passes the Jewish Cemetery on Schönhauser Allee, a place of tranquillity in the densely built-up district, as it proceeds to Schönhauser Tor, one of the gateways to the old city of Berlin. This is where a tollgate and wall once marked the beginning of the inner city area. The tour ends at Rosa-Luxemburg-Platz; the art-nouveau building of the Volksbühne theatre has made it a popular meeting place for young people. The square lies at the centre of the Scheunenviertel district, which was demolished around 1900 and rebuilt in the '20s. It is the site of the building which was once the headquarters of the German Communist Party.

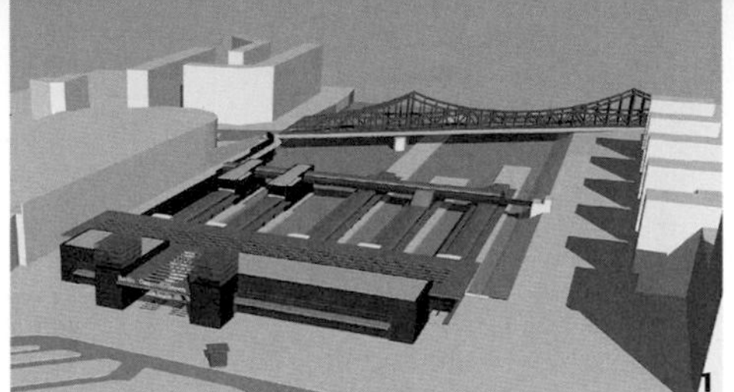

U-, S- und Fernbahnhof Gesundbrunnen

Gesundbrunnen underground, city railway and Regional railway station

Axel Oestreich,
Ingrid Hentschel, Berlin
since 1996
Badstrasse/
Behmstrasse/
Bellermannstrasse

The rail station at Gesundbrunnen, connecting the urban rail system to the northbound distance rail lines, was opened on the Ringbahn circle rail line in 1877. In 1930, Alfred Grenander designed the new underground station. But Gesundbrunnen lost its function as the city's northern junction when the distance rail station was closed down in 1952; this was followed by the breakup of the Ringbahn itself after the Wall went up in 1961.

Today the Gesundbrunnen station is being gradually refurbished as an S-Bahn (city rail), regional rail, and distance rail station once again. Competition winners Oestreich and Hentschel began modernizing the tracks and station facilities in 1996. In 1998 the S-Bahn platforms were restored and linked to the U-Bahn. The connection to the eastern portion of the Ringbahn, which also completes the entire ring system, will be opened for service in 2002. The most extensive construction tasks are related to the redevelopment of the station as a regional and distance rail station. As part of the new "mushroom concept" for the reorganization of the Deutsche Bahn rail system (s. p. 38), the station at Gesundbrunnen will bundle the northbound, eastbound, and westbound routes, merging them into the north-south line to Lehrter Bahnhof. To prevent them from having to cross over each other, the tracks are stacked on three levels. On the east side of

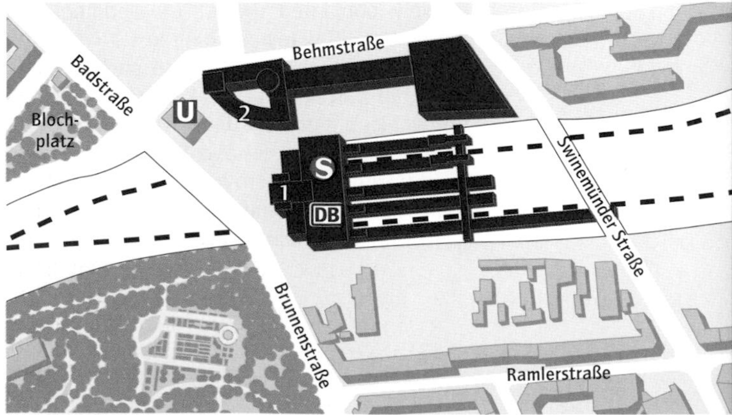

the station, a footbridge linking all the tracks will be built. The structure of the bridge on the western Badstrasse will be substantially widened and a broad square built at its base. The design of the low formal station building is oriented to the rational brick facade of the older underground station entrance. From its glazed rear portion, the imposing Swinemünder Brücke, a sturdy bridge built of steel, can be glimpsed.

2 Gesundbrunnen Center

Jost Hering,
Manfred Stanek,
Hamburg
1995–97
Badstrasse/
Behmstrasse

The Gesundbrunnen Centre was planned as part of the restructuring of the area around the rail station.
Following the 1992 urban design guidelines drawn up by Hentschel and Oestreich, the Hamburg firm of Hering and Stanek built an oblong building parallel to the Ringbahn. Its foyer opens out on what will become a station square built over the tracks. The space will be enclosed by the curving facade and glass tower of the centre, the underground station, which is listed as a protected building, and the reception hall of the rail station.

Volkspark Humboldthain

Gustav Meyer;
Günther Rieck
1869–72;
1948–51
Brunnenstrasse/
Gustav-Meyer-Allee

The Humboldthain public gardens were laid out in honour of the 100th birthday of Alexander von Humboldt in 1869. The landscape architect Gustav Meyer, who also planned the Volkspark Friedrichshain and Treptow Park, designed the park on the site of an old cattleyard. The park became an important recreation centfe for the densely populated district of Wedding. The World War II flak towers (built in 1941 for anti-aircraft artillery) destroyed the park grounds. After the war, Günther Rieck oversaw the creation of hills out of the leftover rubble. One of the flak towers now serves as a lookout point, and overlooking the eastern half of the city from its top is a sculpture named "Reunification" designed in 1967 by Arnold Schatz.

Himmelfahrtskirche

Otto Bartning
1954–56
Gustav-Meyer-Allee 2

Aside from having an important role in the urban planning projects of the '50s, Otto Bartning had a strong influence on modern church design in Berlin. His reconstruction of the Protestant Himmelsfahrtkirche made use of the salvageable fragments of its war-damaged predecessor.
The exposed structure on the interior relates to the clear outer composition of the building massing.

Ehemaliges AEG-Werkgelände

Former AEG Factory Complex

3.1 *Ensemble*

Franz Schwechten,
Peter Behrens
1895–1941
Gustav-Meyer-Allee 1/
Brunnenstrasse/
Voltastrasse/
Hussitenstrasse

In 1892, the AEG (Allgemeine Elektrizitäts-Gesellschaft) moved to a large site located between Gustav-Meyer-Allee, Hussitenstrasse, Voltastrasse, and Brunnenstrasse, creating one of the most important industrial facilities in Berlin. Machines were produced up to the 1980s in the buildings designed by Schnebel, Lauter and Schwechten, as well as those added after 1907 by the AEG's "chief designer" Peter Behrens.
The large motor assembly halls on Hussiten- and Voltastrasse which were designed by Behrens in 1912 are especially significant works of architecture. Mies van der Rohe, who worked for Behrens at the time, was able to implement his architectural ideas for the first time here. Since production ceased in 1986, a few of the buildings have been taken down, but in the northwestern part of the complex the Technical University has opened an "innovation centre".

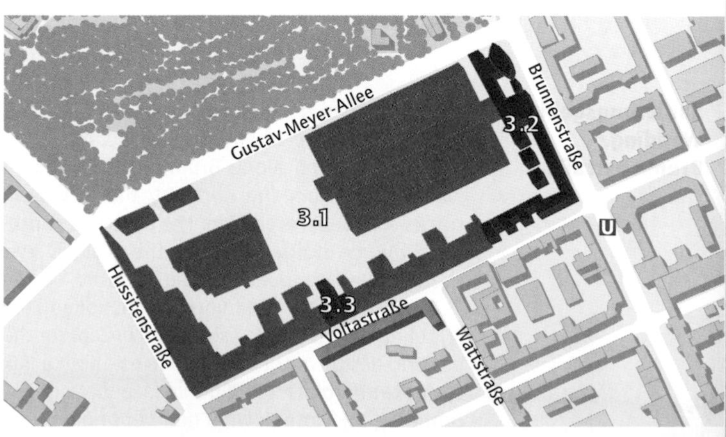

3.2
Ensemble

Josef Paul Kleihues, Berlin
1995–98
Brunnenstrasse 111

Wohn- und Geschäftshäuser

Office and residential buildings

These mixed-use buildings by the Berlin architect Josef Paul Kleihues were meant to revive the northeastern block edge of the historically significant AEG industrial site on Brunnenstrasse. The 13-storey freestanding tower demarcates the corner parcel, forming a vertical counterweight to the long perimeter block development along Brunnenstrasse. The tower overlooks a small piazza and the old AEG factory gate, built in 1897 by Franz Schwechten. A high lobby of a bank building now stands here. The new long slab buildings cover a large factory shed built in 1984, which is now used as a computer centre. The brick-clad buildings harmonise with the industrial architecture, adding to the contrast with the residential construction of the '70s along Brunnenstrasse.

3.3
Ensemble

Josef Paul Kleihues, Berlin
1994–96
Voltastrasse 6

Media Port

The Media Port, which was by the Deutsche Welle radio and TV station, was designed by the Berlin architect Josef Paul Kleihues. In the narrow gap between the western facade of the factory (1907 by Johannes Kraaz, facade by Peter Behrens in 1911) and the renowned small motor factory (1912, Peter Behrens), Kleihues inserted a building on a T-shaped ground plan that emulates the innovative design of its architectural neighbors, connecting to them by short wings. At the centre is a 45-metre high tower mounted with transmitters and aerials.

Sanierungsgebiet Wedding/ Brunnenstraße

Wedding/Brunnenstrasse urban renewal projects

1966–89

The first urban renewal programme in West Berlin was launched after the construction of the Wall in this area along Brunnenstrasse, which was cut off from the north by the Ringbahn tracks and separated from the east and southwest by the border. Despite the Wall, it was thought Berlin would soon be reunited, so the Federal Ministry of Building commissioned Fritz Eggeling in 1963 to devise a new concept for the use and design of the area and to establish a link to Alexanderplatz. Land Berlin later bought the property, and tore down a number of old build-

4.1

ings to build new structures. The old streets were maintained, as was the typical building height, while the blocks were partly developed with closed perimeter blocks, partly with looser, less dense development.
It was here that many of today's established architects got their first chance to build, including Kleihues, Sawade, Düttmann, Pysall & Stahrenberg, Oefelein, and Jan and Rolf Rave. The project was finally completed 27 years later in 1990 – just after the Wall was opened. A less than positive public response to such radical, total-clearance urban renewal projects of the '60s and '70s eventually led to a different approach, such as that of IBA's "careful urban regeneration/repair" programme in Kreuzberg.

Gleimtunnel
Zabinski
1904
Gleimstrasse

The "Gleimtunnel" provided an important link between the districts of Wedding and Prenzlauer Berg under the wide railyards of the old Nordbahn freight station.
Today it again helps to close up this ringroad system. Built wide enough to accommodate several lanes of traffic and a protected pedestrian path, the tunnel was cut off after the Wall was erected. With slender cast-iron supports, the tunnel is one of the most important technical artifacts of its time.

Max-Schmeling-Halle

4.1 *Ensemble*

Joppien Dietz Architekten,
Berlin/Frankfort on the Main
1993–97
Am Falkplatz

Named after a Berlin boxing idol, Max Schmeling, this large sports centre was initially planned as part of Berlin's bid for the 2000 Olympic Games. Well in advance of the final decision, many facilities were renovated and expanded and new ones were planned in order to meet Olympic standards. These facilities included a new bicycle track and swimming pool complex on Landsberger Allee (1993-98, Dominique Perrault, Paris), and the Sportforum Hohenschönhausen (1994-95 by Jentsch, Bush, Khomiakow, Metz, Jensen, Geppert, Berlin). After the bid to host the Games failed, plans were dropped for a new stadium complex designed on the site of the former Walter Ulbricht Stadium on Chausseestrasse, which had already been torn down.
The Frankfort architects Joppien and Dietz were awarded first prize for their 1992 competition

4.2

entry for the Max-Schmeling-Halle. It is now the largest sports and multiple-use complex in the city, with main arena seating over 10,000, and three smaller pavilions accommodating up to 1500 people.
Situated mostly below-grade, the vast building has partly been incorporated into the sunken volume of the adjacent Jahn Stadium. The large volume is thus barely noticeable from the street and is subordinated into the landscape with the Wall park. The only prominent facade is the north-facing glass enclosure on Falkplatz, which is topped by the flattened oval of the steel truss roof.

4.2 *Ensemble*

Mauerpark
Wall Park

Architekten
Schweger + Partner, Hamburg/Berlin,
Gustav Lange, Hamburg/Berlin
1993–2000
Schwedter Strasse/
Eberswalder Strasse/
Gleimstrasse

The Wall Park is located on the site of the old north freight station, which was bisected by the line of the Berlin Wall in 1961. After 1989, plans were drawn up for a park. The first prize in the planning competition went to the Hamburg office of Schweger + Partners and Gustav Lange, landscape architect. They treated the Schwedter Strasse as the main north-south axis, arranging various landscape elements from Gleimstrasse up to Eberswalder Strasse. The scheme incorporates a variety of plantings and materials, including seating clusters, open spaces, and a wall for

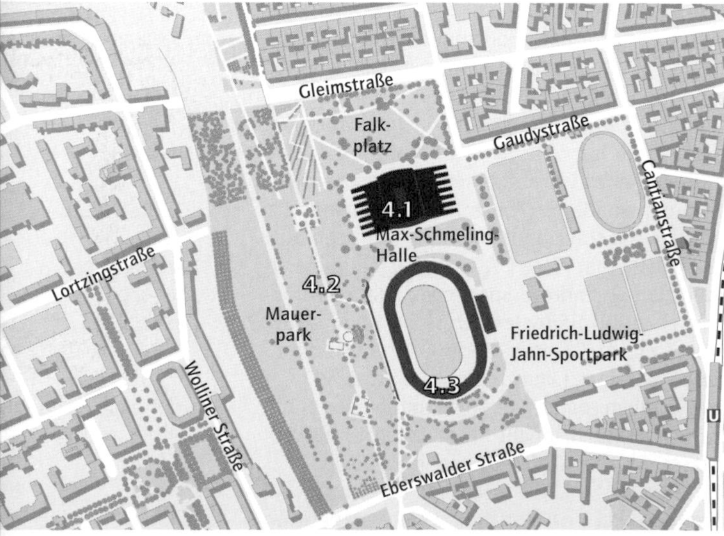

4.2

graffiti facing the Jahn- Stadion to make the park interesting for young people. The planning concept also called for the spatial integration of the old railroad tracks, Falkplatz and the sports facilities.
The individual sections were commissioned to different landscape architects. The northernmost section is designed by Thomas Guba with a children's play farmyard by Angelika Dohnert, Near Max-Schmeling-Halle, an ecological garden was laid out where visitors can learn about the many uses of rainwater. The Wall park is financed by the Allianz-Stiftung and the Land Berlin government.

Friedrich-Ludwig-Jahn-Stadion

4.3
Ensemble

Rudolf Ortner
1951
Eberswalder Strasse

The Friedrich Ludwig Jahn Stadium was built by the GDR for the "Third Annual World Youth Games" in 1951. In that year, the East German government had launched a special construction programme for new sports facilities for the young, with a central competition and training centre. Competitive sports were seen as a crucial means of conveying political ideas both nationally and internationally.
The Jahn Stadium, the "Stadion der Weltjugend" (Walter-Ulbricht-Stadium) in Berlin Mitte, which was demolished in 1992, and the Sportforum Hohenschönhausen were among the most important complexes built at the time. Replacing an older sports park built in 1926, the complex was mainly used by the Sportsclub Dynamo, whose members worked for the dreaded GDR state security agency. In anticipation of the 2000 Olympic Games, the complex was modernised and conceived as part of a new "Friedrich Ludwig Jahn Sportpark" incorporating the Max-Schmeling-Halle and the Wall Park.

St.-Elisabeth-Stift

St. Elizabeth Home

Friedrich August Wilhelm Strauch;
Kurt Berndt
1875; 1892
Eberswalder Strasse 17-18

Now a protected building, the St. Elizabeth Home was built in 1875 by Strauch and enlarged in 1892 by Kurt Berndt. The elegant building, with its high central bay, is a fine example of Berlin's late neoclassical architecture. It was originally opened as a hospice for women invalids, and still functions today as a nursing home.

Hochbahnviadukt
Viaduct of the elevated railway
Alfred Grenander, Johannes Bousset
1911–13
Schönhauser Allee

Originally called Danziger Strasse, this station was named Dimitroffstrasse after 1950 and changed to Eberswalder Strasse in 1992. It is part of the underground line built in 1911-13 by Alfred Grenander, extending services from Gleisdreieck to Schönhauser Allee, where it intersects with the Ringbahn. North of Senefelderplatz, the line was designed as an elevated rail, following the model of New York and Paris. The tracks are supported by thin steel arches set in the middle of the street. Most of the original station structures remain; restoration work was begun in 1993.

5

Kulturbrauerei

Ensemble
Franz Schwechten; Weiß & Faust, Berlin
1871–1926; 1998–2000
Knaackstrasse 75-97/ Schönhauser Allee 36-39/ Sredzkistrasse 1-17

The extensive facilities of the old Schultheiss brewery have been carefully preserved and adapted for a number of different uses. Founded around 1850, the Berlin brewery hired Franz Schwechten to design its new headquarters here, which he executed in the vernacular style of yellow brick with red trim. The complex was continually expanded until 1926. In 1990 it was taken over by the Treuhand privatisation agency, and the spaces were made available to various cultural groups and a special collection of GDR industrial design. The entire site is currently being retrofitted as a centre for culture and commerce, with galleries, artists' studios, theatres, a multiplex cinema, a food market and office spaces.

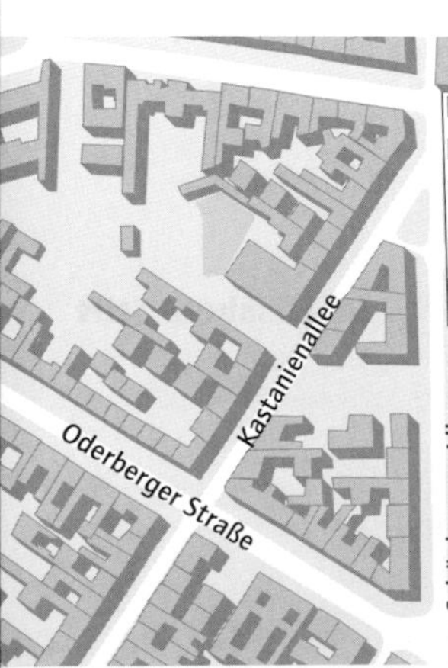

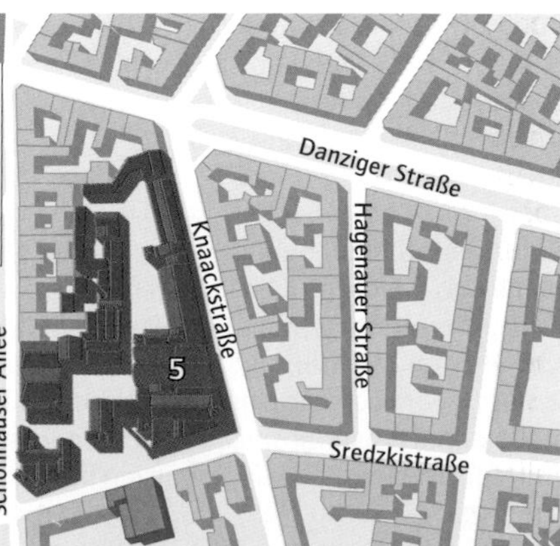

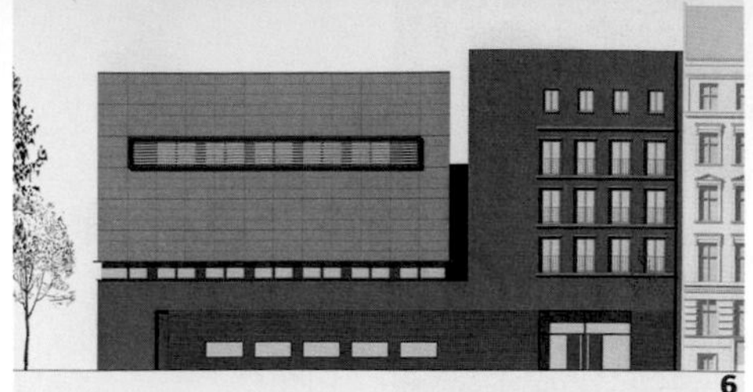
6

Sporthalle

School gymnasium

Axel Oestreich,
Ingrid Hentschel,
Berlin
1999–2000
Sredzkistrasse 8-10

Axel Oestreich and Ingrid Hentschel were selected in a 1994 competition to design a gymnasium as an extension of a primary school.
A thin, brick-clad building adjoins the neighbouring apartment building and contains three dwellings for local goverment employees. The residential portion is separated from the gymnasium by a gap made in the building massing. The concrete cube is lifted up on a brick base; inside are two large multi-purpose halls arranged on top of one another. An internal pathway leads to the schoolyard.

Husemannstraße

1880–90 ;
1983–87

The densely built, nearly identical blocks dating from the 1870s that form the development pattern of so much of Prenzlauer Berg stem from plans drawn up by James Hobrecht. For the 750th anniversary of the city's founding in 1987, Husemannstrasse was selected by East Berlin to become a showcase of the historic architecture and everyday life of the turn of the century. During the '50s and '60s, over '90 per cent of the war-damaged facades of old buildings were removed or stripped-down in West Berlin's extensive reconstruction programme, but in East Berlin, hardly any work of this kind was done, mainly due to lack of funding. As a result, the ornate old facades remained intact. From 1983-1987, the elaborate, plaster-ornamented street elevations of the apartment buildings on Husemannstrasse were restored, and shops and restaurants were added on the ground floors.

Kollwitzplatz

This square was named after the social-minded artist Käthe Kollwitz and her husband Karl, a "poor people's doctor".
Their apartment and medical practice were located in a now defunct building at the corner of Kollwitzstrasse and Knaackstrasse. In 1996/7, the Berlin architects Stankovic and Bonnen built a somber new building here. It stands opposite a reproduction of a 1932 sculpture by Kollwitz called "Mother love". In 1958, a seated portrait of the artist by Gustav Seitz was also erected on the square. The rusty portal at Knaackstrasse 41

7

originally led to a narrow path between the apartment blocks to a side entrance to the Jewish Cemetery.
On the southeast corner stands one of the many completely automatic street toilets that since 1995 were installed to replace the old public facilities, dubbed "Cafe Octagon", which are now more than a century old.

Synagoge Rykestraße
Johann Hoeniger
1903–04
Rykestrasse 53

Located in a courtyard, this synagogue was designed in a neo-Romanesque brick style by the community's architect, Johann Hoeniger. The community facilities are located in the section facing the street. The temple, which followed conservative religious practice, was badly damaged but not destroyed in the "crystal night" pogrom of 1938. After it was repaired in 1953, it was the only synagogue left in the eastern half of the city.

Wassertürme Prenzlauer Berg
Prenzlauer Berg Water Towers
Henry Gill
1852–75
Knaackstrasse/
Belforter Strasse

In 1852, the kingdom of Prussia and an English waterworks company signed a contract for the construction of an enclosed water supply system for Berlin.
In 1854 the country's first elevated water tank was erected by architect Henry Gill in the midst of the then undeveloped property on the Mühlenberg. It provided "running water" for the first time in Germany.
The open water containers were covered in 1873 and a broad water tower was added to the slender standpipe tower.
Surrounding the core of the tower there are five levels of apartments. In 1915 the facility had to be shut down, and the site was subsquently transformed into a park. Today concerts and theatre performances are held in the former subterranean water tank.

7

Spielhaus, Bauspielplatz
Play house

Felicitas Mossmann, Berlin
1998–99
Kollwitzstrasse 37

A special permanent play house for older children was put up on Kollwitzstrasse on a "play" construction site begun in 1990. Simple materials were deliberately chosen, like recycled tiles, wood, and clay; a roof garden, rainwater collector, and solar panels were added to make

the imaginative structure into a model ecological project. The Network for Play and Culture built and operates the play house; the project was financed by Land Berlin and the European Union.

Jüdischer Friedhof Schönhauser Allee
Jewish Cemetery on Schönhauser Allee
Friedrich Wilhelm Langerhans
1825–27
Schönhauser Allee 23-25

After 1794, when a Prussian state law was passed banning all graves within the city limits in order to protect public health, the Jewish community began to look for cemetery space beyond the city walls.
When this cemetery was opened in 1827, the old Jewish cemetery on Grosse Hamburger Strasse was closed.
In 1885 an even larger cemetery was founded in Weissensee, after which few new graves were dug in Prenzlauer Berg. The old cemetery is now surrounded by apartment buildings except for the main entrance on Schönhauser Allee. The cemetery could also be entered via the so-called "Jew paths", narrow walks between the apartment blocks. Among those laid to rest here are the banker Gerson von Bleichröder, painter Max Liebermann, the entrepreneur Ludwig Loewe, composer Giacomo Meyerbeer, and publisher Leopold Ullstein.

Senefelderplatz

Hermann Mächtig
1885; 1995

Senefelderplatz, a triangular site, is located just beyond the historical city gate at Schönhauser Tor on Schönhauser Allee, an arterial road leading north. It bears the name of the inventor of lithography, Alois Senefelder. A monument to Senefelder, designed by Rudolf Pohle and financed by printers and lithographers in Berlin, was unveiled here in 1892. It was the first monument in Berlin to be dedicated to an artisan. Below the seated figure of Senefelder, a cherub writes his name in reverse script, which a second cherub decodes using a mirror. Both the monument and Senefelderplatz were restored in 1995.

Brauerei Pfefferberg
Pfefferberg Brewery

The old Pfefferberg Brewery was founded in 1841 by the master brewer Karl Pfeffer, and it was gradually enlarged up to 1914. It consists of the production facilities in the centre of the block, cellars with vaulted ceilings nearly eight metres high, and the raised terrace of the beer

9

Carl Koeppen, A. Rohmer, G. Dittrich
1842–1914
Christinenstrasse 18-19/
Schönhauser Allee 176

garden on Schönhauser Allee. Four of the eleven breweries originally located in Prenzlauer Berg are now being converted into office, shopping and cultural centres. The Pfefferberg was declared a protected building in 1990 and is to be adapted for commercial, artistic and socio-cultural functions, in close cooperation with the Pfefferwerk cooperative, the local residents, and the S.T.E.R.N. corporation for urban regeneration.

Sanierungsgebiet Teutoburger Platz
Teutoburger Platz redevelopment
Fehrbelliner Strasse/
Templiner Strasse/
Zionskirchstrasse/
Christinenstrasse

In 1994 the area around Teutoburger Platz, an ornamental square laid out in 1862, officially became one of five sites in Prenzlauer Berg where redevelopment was planned. The square is surrounded by buildings erected between 1870 and 1900. In 1910, the square was redesigned as a playground, and Bewag built a transformer station here in 1928, which was connected to a "milk bar".
From 1993 to 1996, residents, students, the parks department, and private sponsors joined together to upgrade the square. The work reflected the experience gained during the IBA 87 ("Alt") programme for "careful urban repair" (s. p. 81), and was geared to reflect the interests and needs of those living in the neighbourhood. Environmentally sustainable heating systems, traffic control, and the use of planting are planned for the repair and modernisation measures underway.

9

Königstadt-Terrassen
Königstadt Terraces

Thomas Müller,
Ivan Reimann, Berlin
1995–96
Schönhauser Allee 10-11/
Saarbrücker Strasse 18-24

The Königstadt Terraces were built at the centre of the restored buildings of the old Königstadt Brewery. The Terraces are a beer garden on a raised platform, open on several sides, above the lower level which is used for a variety of commercial uses. The terraces are shielded from street noise and offer a good view of the surrounding area, as do the office spaces above.
The older brewery structures were built along the sloping Schönhauser Allee by Rohmer and Alterthum between 1885 and 1906. Like many other run-down breweries in Berlin, the administrative and production buildings, which are listed

as protected buildings, were adapted for use as commercial space.
In 1998 the building on Saarbücker Strasse was converted into a youth centre by the architect Anne Lampen.

„Schönhauser Tor"

"Schönhauser Tor" centre

FFNS und Giese-Bohne Planungsgesellschaft mbH, Karlsruhe/Düsseldorf/Berlin
1994–95
Torstrasse 49/ Schönhauser Allee

This building on the eastern corner of the intersection was originally built in 1928. It was stripped down to its original steel frame and its facade clad with new granite panels, in the '90s. Together with the building across the street it helps frame the "New Schönhauser Tor" gateway. Torstrasse follows the route of the old customs wall which ringed the historic city centre of Berlin.
Today the street, previously called Wilhelm-Pieck-Strasse, forms the boundary between the district of Mitte from Prenzlauer Berg. The historic name of Torstrasse was chosen when the street was renamed in 1994, but this name originally applied to only a part of it.
The sections beyond were named Elsasser Strasse and Lothringer Strasse, after Alsace and Lorraine, French provinces annexed by Germany in 1871.
Naming the whole street Torstrasse avoided a return to the original symbolic references.

Volksbühne

Volksbühne Theatre

Oskar Kaufmann
1913–14
Rosa-Luxemburg-Platz
(s. ill. p. 280)

The "Freie Volksbühne", a "people's" theatre group founded in 1890, was dedicated to bringing modern poetry and drama to the poorer sections of the population. In 1913 it joined together with the "Neue Freie Volksbühne", founded in 1892, in order to build a new theatre. Financed by membership fees and contributions, the modern theatre was designed by Oskar Kaufmann, who lined its curving facade with thick columns. The theatre boasted many great directors, including Max Reinhardt, Heinz Hilpert, and Erwin Piscator, as well as famous actors Heinrich George, Heinz Albers, Helene Weigel, and Tilla Durieux. Post-war repair work simplified the building's appearance, and the inscription on the gable "Art for the people" was removed. During the GDR era, the theatre was operated by the FDGB Free Confederation of German Trade Uni-

ons, whose mandate was to resume the original purpose of a "people's" theatre.
After the Wall was removed, highly acclaimed contemporary plays and provocative modern interpretations of the classics were staged here. Today, moderately-priced tickets help draw a wide public, especially the young, to the highly esteemed theatre.

Karl-Liebknecht-Haus

Keibel
1912
Kleine Alexanderstrasse 28/
Weydingerstrasse

The Party of Democratic Socialism (PDS) was founded in 1990 as the successor to the East German communist party, or SED. Its national headquarters were based in the Karl-Liebknecht-Haus opposite the Volksbühne. The 1912 structure was originally designed as an office/retail building by Keibel. It functioned from 1926 as the office of the central committee of the Communist Party of Germany (KPD), until the party was disbanded in 1933.

Rosa-Luxemburg-Platz

Rosa-Luxemburg-Platz was named after the socialist Rosa Luxemburg, who, together with her friend and comrade Karl Liebknecht, was murdered by troops from a volunteer corps on the Landwehrkanal (in Tiergarten) in 1919. This triangular space was originally named Bülowplatz. Laid out in 1906, it is part of the old "Scheunenviertel", named after the barns and sheds that populated the area around 1700. The working class quarter was a centre of a predominantly east European Jewish community in Berlin, but it was also heavily ridden with crime and prostitution. After 1933, the Nazis used the name Scheunenviertel to refer, with some derision, to the entire Spandauer Vorstadt district.
The residential development around the square was built from 1928-29 by the Berlin architect Hans Poelzig. The focus of restoration of the historical buildings is on the Babylon Cinema. Although large portions of the interior were destroyed during the heavy-handed renovation work carried out in 1948, the Babylon is the only remaining large cinema in Berlin that dates back to the silent film era. The original theatre organ, which mechanically produced all sound effects as well as musical accompaniment for the films, is still preserved intact, a now priceless object.

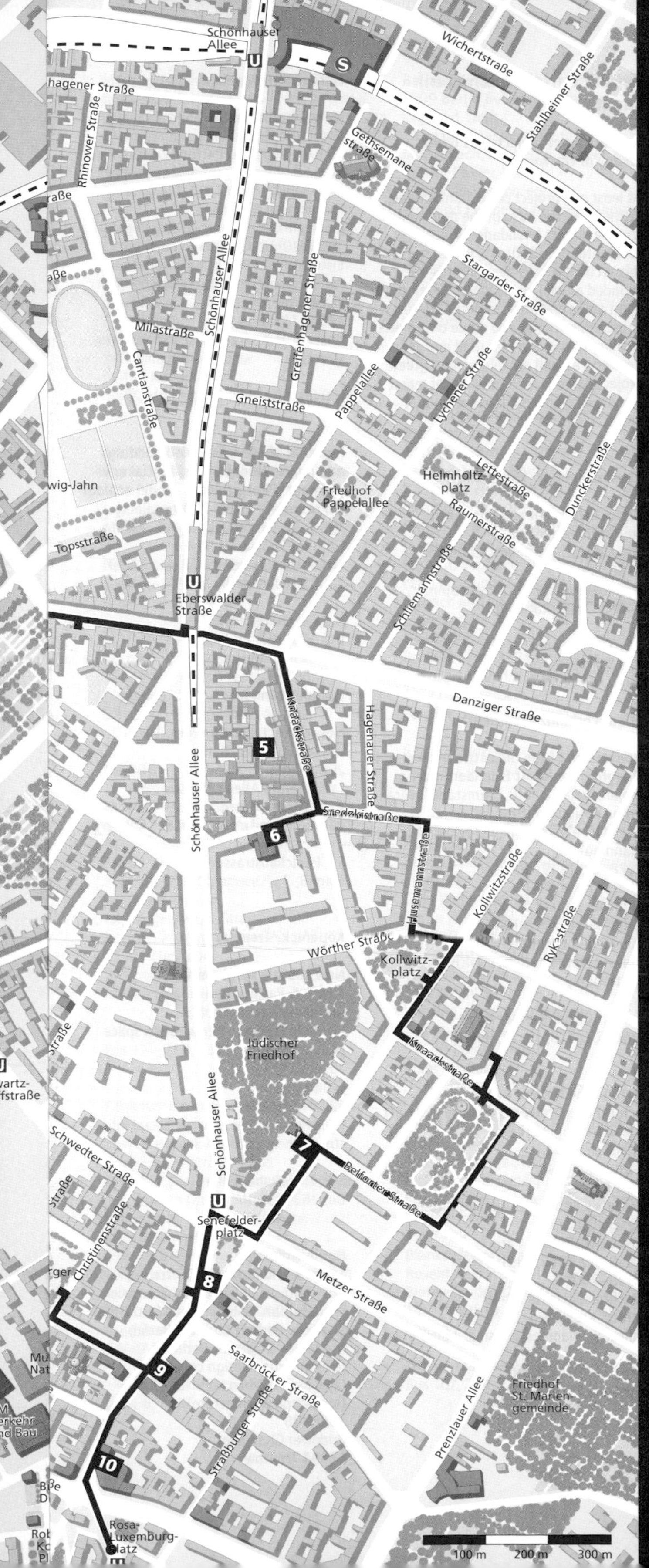
Schönhauser Allee
Wichertstraße
Stahlheimer Straße
Gethsemanestraße
Rhinower Straße
Schönhauser Allee
Greifenhagener Straße
Stargarder Straße
Milastraße
Cantianstraße
Gneiststraße
Pappelallee
Lychener Straße
Helmholtzplatz
Letteestraße
Dunckerstraße
Friedhof Pappelallee
Raumerstraße
Topsstraße
Schliemannstraße
Eberswalder Straße
Danziger Straße
Knaackstraße
Hagenauer Straße
Sredzkistraße
Husemannstraße
Kollwitzstraße
Rykestraße
Wörther Straße
Kollwitzplatz
Jüdischer Friedhof
Knaackstraße
Schwedter Straße
Belforter Straße
Senefelderplatz
Christinenstraße
Metzer Straße
Saarbrücker Straße
Straßburger Straße
Prenzlauer Allee
Friedhof St. Mariengemeinde
Rosa-Luxemburg-Platz
100 m
200 m
300 m

1999 Berlin Building Exhibition: Karower Damm
Gesellschaft für Planung, Berlin
(land-use plan)/
Birgit Hammer, Berlin
(landscape planning)
1998–99
Lindenberger Strasse/
Strasse 56/Ahornallee
13129 Weissensee
housing

S 8, 10 Blankenburg
Bus 150, 158

New suburb: Karow-Nord
Moore, Ruble & Yudell, Santa Monica
(masterplan)/
Müller, Knippschild, Wehberg, Berlin
(open space planning)
1994–96
Bucher Chaussee
13125 Weissensee
housing, industry, services, social infrastructure

S 8 Karow
Bus 150, 158, 350

Reinickendorf

Borsigturm residential and industrial district
Claude Vasconi, Paris
(urban design concept)
1995–99
Berliner Strasse 19-37/Veitstrasse
13507 Reinickendorf
industrial estate, business centre for new companies, Multiplex cinema, retail outlets, hotel, offices, housing, gastronomy

U 6 Borsigwerke, S 25 Tegel
Bus 133

Schöneberg/Tempelhof

Papestrasse station (southern railway station)
J · S · K Architekten, Berlin
date of commencement: 1999/2000
General-Pape-Strasse/Sachsendamm
12101 Tempelhof
main line railway station

S 2, 4, 45, 46 Papestrasse
Bus 146, 204

Südgelände nature park (EXPO 2000 project)
ÖkoCon/Planland, Berlin
(planning concept),
Odius, Berlin
(artistic building elements)
1996–99
main entrance:
S-Bahnhof Priesterweg
10829 Schöneberg

S 2, 25 Priesterweg
Bus X 76, 170, 174, 176

Spandau

Spandau main line and city railway station
gmp von Gerkan, Marg & Partner, Hamburg
1996–98
Klosterstrasse/Seegefelder Strasse
13581 Spandau

U 7 Rathaus Spandau

New residential development for government employees at the former Gatow Airfield
Linie 5 – Architekten
(M. Gerke, W. v. Horlacher, G. Ruoff), Berlin
(urban planning report)/
Büro A. Röntz, Berlin
(landscape planning)
date of commencement: 1999
Ritterfelddamm
14089 Spandau
housing, social infrastructure

Bus 135, 234

Spandau waterfront development
Hans Kollhoff, Berlin/
Christoph Langhof, Berlin/
Klaus Zillich, Berlin (planning directors)/
Heike Langenbach (landscape planning)
date of commencement: 1995
housing, retail shops, offices

Pulvermühle quarter
1995–2000
Daumstrasse/Pulvermühlenweg
13599 Spandau
U 7 Haselhorst
Bus 133, 204

Parkstrasse Süd "Schultheiss" quarter
1998–2000
Neuendorfer Strasse/
Triftstrasse/Parkstrasse
13585 Spandau
U 7 Altstadt Spandau
Bus 131, 231, 331

Havelspitze quarter
1996–2004
Maselakeweg/An der Havelspitze
13587 Spandau
U 7 Rathaus Spandau
Bus 131, 231, 331

Maselake Nord quarter
1996–98
Rauchstrasse/Goltzstrasse/Mertensstrasse
13587 Spandau
U 7 Rathaus Spandau
Bus 131, 231

Steglitz/Zehlendorf

Allies Museum
opened in 1998
Clayallee 135
14195 Zehlendorf
permanent exhibition: "The Allies in Germany and Berlin between 1945 and 1994"

U 1 Oskar-Helene-Heim
Bus 115, 183

Index of architects

Index of places

Photographic acknowledgement

Photographs by Erik-Jan Ouwerkerk, Berlin, unless otherwise indicated.

13: Meyerfoto, Berlin; 16: A. Schultes Architekten, Berlin; 17: Diener & Diener Architekten, Basel; 18 r.: G. Peichl & Partner, Wien (Schwingenschlögl, Wien); 19: S. Braunfels, München/Berlin (B. Lehn, München); 22: H. Leiska, Hamburg; 25 l.: S. Braunfels, München/Berlin (J. Weber, Berlin); 25 r.: Nalbach + Nalbach, Berlin; 26 r.: gmp, Hamburg (P. Wels, Hamburg); 29: H. Deubzer, J. König, Berlin; 32 r.: M. Dudler, Zürich/Berlin (S. Müller, Berlin); 37: O. M. Ungers, Köln/ Berlin (S. Müller, Berlin); 38: gmp, Hamburg (©Archimation®); 42: S. Lehmann Architekten, Berlin; 49: C. Dierkes, Berlin; 50: C. G. Schulz in Linie 5, Berlin; 52: Höger Hare Architekten, Berlin; 54: reitermann/sassenroth architekten, Berlin; 59, 60: Modersohn & Freiesleben, Berlin; 61: Bischoff & Compagnons Property Networks GmbH (A. Weiße); 62: SONY Berlin; 67: debis GmbH, Berlin (V. Mosch); 74: Hypo-Real GmbH, Berlin; 78: P. Zumthor, Haldenstein (R. Führer, Felsberg); 81: SL, Leinfelden-Oberaichen with F. Otto, München; 82: J. Ganz, Berlin; 83: U. Wolff, H. Pitz, Berlin (artec GmbH); 89, 99: Frank Thiel, "Die Alliierten", 1994/1998, 3,0 x 2,4 m; 92: Büro 213, Berlin; 93 l.: Rave Architekten, Berlin; 95: Architekten Schweger + Partner, Hamburg/Berlin; 104: M. Sauerbruch, L. Hutton Architekten, Berlin/London (U. Rau, Berlin); 116 l.: M. Christl, J. Bruchhäuser, Frankfurt a. M.; 116 r.: gmp, Hamburg, (H. Leiska, Hamburg); 117 l.: Alt & Britz, Saarbrücken (IMAGING/ Heisler, Saarbrücken); 117 r.: Heinle, Wischer and Partner, Stuttgart; 118 l.: Cornelsen & Seelinger, Darmstadt (Eiken Fotografie, Mühltal); 122: Ambassade de France – Bureau de Berlin; 124: Moore, Ruble & Yudell, Santa Monica (Del Zoppo 8/95); 125: M. Wilford, London (R. Davies); 126 l.: G. Peichl & Partner, Wien; 128: T. Baumann, Berlin; 133: D. Chipperfield, London (T. Miller, London); 143: T. Müller, I. Reimann, Berlin (Studio Ivan Nemec, Frankfurt a. M.); 144: Henze + Vahjen, Braunschweig/Berlin (©Archimation®); 145: SAT 1. Berlin (Tölle, Berlin); 151: ABB, H. Scheid, J. Schmidt & Partner, Frankfurt a. M.; 159: K.-H.-Schommer. Bauten and Projekte, hrsg. von I. Flagge, Hamburg 1998, S. 179; 163 r.: Dr. Worschech & Partner, Erfurt; 173: W. Engel, K. Zillich, Berlin; 174: OMA/R. Koolhaas. Die Niederländische Botschaft in Berlin. Aedes, Berlin 1998; 177: Architekten Schweger + Partner, Hamburg/Berlin (J. A. Gonzales, M. Ley): 179: D. Dörschner, Berlin; 185: Pysall, Stahrenberg & Partner, Berlin; 196: Kollhoff & Timmermann, Berlin; 198: stilwerk Berlin; 205: C. Mäckler, Frankfurt/Berlin; 206: gmp, Hamburg; 207: Murphy/Jahn, Chicago; 214: J. Heinrich, AG Bassenge, Puhan-Schulz, Heinrich, Schreiber, Berlin; 221: Landesdenkmalamt Berlin (Foto: W. Reuss); 223 l.: Atelier H. Hollein, Wien; 223 r.: D. Bangert, Berlin; 224: H. Léon, K. Wohlhage, Berlin: 224 (R. Hochstetter, Berlin); 226: HPP GmbH, Berlin; 227: Novotny Mähner & Assoziierte, Berlin (©Archimation®); 228: H. Léon, K. Wohlhage, Berlin; 230, 231: VISTA GmbH, Berlin (M. Ley/F. C. Hofmann); 232: Botschaft von Mexiko – Aussenstelle Berlin; 235: A. Berger, T. Parkkinen, Wien; 247: Becker Gewers Kühn & Kühn, Berlin (J. Willebrand, Köln); 252: Architekten Schweger + Partner, Hamburg/ Berlin (B. Kroll); 253: HI-COM, Berlin; 260 l.: Wasserstadt GmbH, Berlin; 262, 264: J·S·K Architekten, Berlin; 267, 275: A. Oestreich, I. Hentschel, Berlin